Revisiting Silent Reading

New Directions for Teachers and Researchers

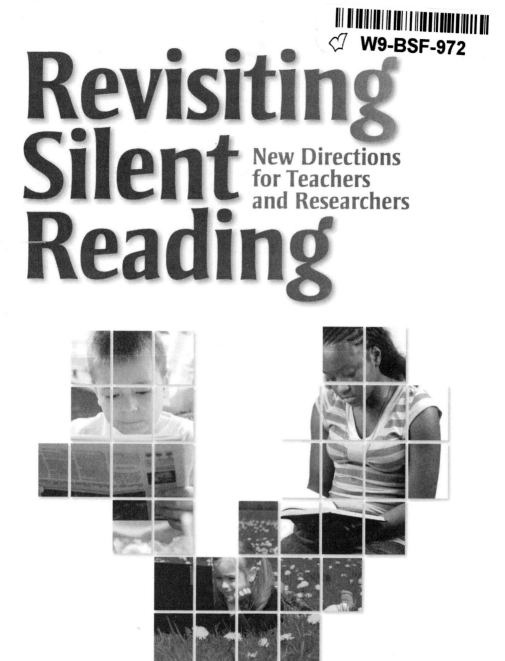

Elfrieda H. Hiebert & D. Ray Reutzel
Editors

INTERNATIONAL
Reading Association
800 BARKSDALE ROAD, PO BOX 8139
NEWARK, DE 19714-8139, USA
www.reading.org

The International Reading Association attempts, through its publications, to provide a forum
for a wide spectrum of opinions on reading. This policy permits divergent viewpoints without
implying the endorsement of the Association.

Executive Editor, Books   Corinne M. Mooney
Developmental Editor   Charlene M. Nichols
Developmental Editor   Tori Mello Bachman
Developmental Editor   Stacey L. Reid
Editorial Production Manager   Shannon T. Fortner
Design and Composition Manager   Anette Schuetz

Project Editors   Charlene M. Nichols and Christina Terranova

Cover   Design, Linda Steere; Photographs (clockwise from left): © iStockphoto.com/
ForsterForest, © iStockphoto.com/hartcreations, © iStockphoto.com/Trout55

The publisher would appreciate notification where errors occur so that they may be corrected
in subsequent printings and/or editions.

Library of Congress Cataloging-in-Publication Data
Revisiting silent reading : new directions for teachers and researchers / edited by Elfrieda H.
Hiebert and D. Ray Reutzel.
       p. cm.
Includes bibliographical references and index.
ISBN 978-0-87207-833-8
1. Silent reading. I. Hiebert, Elfrieda H. II. Reutzel, D. Ray (Douglas Ray), 1953-
LB1050.55.R48 2010
372.41'6--dc22
                                    2010027125

Suggested APA Reference
Hiebert, E.H., & Reutzel, D.R. (Eds.). (2010). *Revisiting silent reading: New directions for
teachers and researchers*. Newark, DE: International Reading Association.

CONTENTS

SECTION 1
Silent Reading: Perspectives and Frameworks

SECTION 2
Silent Reading: Instruction and Opportunity

SECTION 3
Silent Reading: Different Contexts, Different Readers

Elfrieda H. Hiebert, PhD, is Adjunct Professor in the Graduate School of Education at the University of California, Berkeley, California, USA. She is also a principal investigator at the National Center for Research on the Educational Achievement and Teaching of English Language Learners. Dr. Hiebert has worked in the field of early reading acquisition for 40 years as a classroom teacher, teacher educator, and researcher. Her research addresses methods for supporting students who depend on schools to become literate and for fostering students' reading fluency, vocabulary, and knowledge through appropriate texts. Dr. Hiebert's model of accessible texts for beginning and struggling readers—Text Elements by Task, or TExT—has been used to develop several reading programs that are widely used in schools.

Dr. Hiebert is a recipient of the William S. Gray Citation of Merit, awarded by the International Reading Association (IRA), and a member of the Reading Hall of Fame. She has made a commitment to making research accessible to educators through her work on *Becoming a Nation of Readers: The Report of the Commission on Reading* and the *Every Child a Reader* monograph series. She is the author or editor of 10 books and numerous journal articles.

D. Ray Reutzel is the Emma Eccles Jones Distinguished Professor and Endowed Chair of Early Childhood Education at Utah State University, Logan, Utah, USA. He has served as technical assistant to the Reading Excellence Act and the Reading First federal reading reform projects in the state of Utah. Years ago, he took a leave from his university faculty position to return to full-time, first-grade classroom teaching. Dr. Reutzel has taught in kindergarten, first grade, third grade, and sixth grade.

He is the author of more than 185 refereed research reports, articles, books, book chapters, and monographs published in a variety of professional and research journals in literacy and education. He has received more than $8 million in research/professional development funding from private, state, and federal funding agencies, including the Institute of Education Sciences and the U.S. Department of Education.

Dr. Reutzel is the past editor of *Literacy Research and Instruction*, the journal of the Association of Literacy Educators and Researchers, formerly known as the College Reading Association (CRA). He was the coeditor of the IRA journal *The Reading Teacher* from 2002 to 2007.

He received the A.B. Herr Award from the CRA in 1999 for Outstanding Research and Published Contributions to Reading Education. Dr. Reutzel was given the John Chorlton Manning Public School Service Award from IRA in May 2007. He served as a member of IRA's Board of Directors from 2007 to 2010.

CONTRIBUTORS

Richard L. Allington
Professor of Education
University of Tennessee, Knoxville
Knoxville, Tennessee, USA

Gwynne Ellen Ash
Professor
Texas State University–San Marcos
San Marcos, Texas, USA

Devon Brenner
Associate Professor of Reading and
Language Arts
Mississippi State University
Mississippi State, Mississippi, USA

Jill M. Castek
Postdoctoral Associate
University of California, Berkeley
Berkeley, California, USA

Nicki Clausen-Grace
Fourth-Grade Teacher
Carillon Elementary School
Oviedo, Florida, USA

Cassandra S. Coddington
Postdoctoral Associate
Georgia State University
Atlanta, Georgia, USA

Meaghan Edmonds
Social Science/Humanities Research
Associate
The Meadows Center for Preventing
Educational Risk
The University of Texas at Austin
Austin, Texas, USA

Susie Goodin
PhD Candidate
Graduate School of Education
University of California, Berkeley
Berkeley, California, USA

John T. Guthrie
Professor Emeritus
College of Education
University of Maryland
College Park, Maryland, USA

Angela Hairrell
Postdoctoral Fellow for The Meadows
Center for Preventing Educational
Risk
The University of Texas at Austin
Austin, Texas, USA

Elfrieda H. Hiebert
Adjunct Professor
Graduate School of Education
University of California, Berkeley
Berkeley, California, USA

Cindy D. Jones
Assistant Professor of Literacy
Education
Utah State University
Logan, Utah, USA

Timothy B. Jones
Associate Professor of Educational
Leadership
Sam Houston State University
Huntsville, Texas, USA

Michelle J. Kelley
Assistant Professor of Reading
Education
University of Central Florida
Orlando, Florida, USA

James S. Kim
Assistant Professor
Graduate School of Education
Harvard University
Cambridge, Massachusetts, USA

Melanie R. Kuhn
Associate Professor
Boston University
Boston, Massachusetts, USA

Donald J. Leu
John and Maria Neag Endowed Chair
  in Literacy and Technology
Professor of Education
Director, New Literacies Research Lab
University of Connecticut
Storrs, Connecticut, USA

Marsha Lewis
Second-Grade Teacher
Kenansville Elementary School
Kenansville, North Carolina, USA

Marta Lewis
Research Analyst
Nexus Treatment Facilities
Golden Valley, Minnesota, USA

Jacquelynn A. Malloy
Assistant Professor
George Mason University
Fairfax, Virginia, USA

Maryann Manning
Professor
University of Alabama at
  Birmingham
Birmingham, Alabama, USA

Anne McGill-Franzen
Professor
University of Tennessee, Knoxville
Knoxville, Tennessee, USA

Terry H. Newman
Fifth-Grade Teacher
Fairfield Area School District
Fairfield, Pennsylvania, USA

Gary J. Ockey
Director of Assessment
English Language Institute
Kanda University of International
  Studies
Chiba, Japan

P. David Pearson
Dean
Graduate School of Education
University of California, Berkeley
Berkeley, California, USA

Timothy V. Rasinski
Professor, Curriculum and
  Instruction
Kent State University
Kent, Ohio, USA

D. Ray Reutzel
Emma Eccles Jones Endowed Chair
  Professor of Early Childhood
  Education
Utah State University
Logan, Utah, USA

Nancy Roser
Professor
The University of Texas at Austin
Austin, Texas, USA

S. Jay Samuels
Professor
University of Minnesota Twin Cities
Minneapolis, Minnesota, USA

Paula J. Schwanenflugel
Professor
The University of Georgia
Athens, Georgia, USA

Ross Sherman
Professor
The University of Texas at Tyler
Tyler, Texas, USA

Deborah Simmons
Professor
Texas A&M University
College Station, Texas, USA

Emily A. Swan
Associate Clinical Professor
University of Utah
Salt Lake City, Utah, USA

Guy Trainin
Associate Professor
University of Nebraska–Lincoln
Lincoln, Nebraska, USA

Sharon Vaughn
H.E. Hartfelder/Southland Corp
    Regents Chair
Executive Director, Meadows Center
    for Preventing Educational Risk
The University of Texas at Austin
Austin, Texas, USA

Thomas G. White
Senior Scientist, Center for Advanced
    Study of Teaching and Learning
University of Virginia
Charlottesville, Virginia, USA

Kathleen M. Wilson
Associate Professor
University of Nebraska–Lincoln
Lincoln, Nebraska, USA

Jo Worthy
Professor
The University of Texas at Austin
Austin, Texas, USA

Gary Wright
Professor
The University of Texas at Tyler
Tyler, Texas, USA

PREFACE

*R*evisiting Silent Reading: New Directions for Teachers and Researchers brings together in a single volume current research and theory on silent reading practice, instruction, and assessment. Although correlational evidence demonstrates a robust relationship between volume of reading and students' reading achievement, the empirical evidence showing a causal relationship between volume of reading and students' reading achievement at the turn of the millennium was unconvincing and fragile. Building on and updating the conclusions and findings of the National Reading Panel (NRP; National Institute of Child Health and Human Development [NICHD], 2000) that questioned the effectiveness of independent, silent reading to promote students' reading fluency, achievement, and motivation, this new volume brings together scholars who for the past decade have focused their research and development of theory on understanding silent reading practice, instruction, and assessment to provide new directions for teachers and researchers.

One of the unintended consequences of the NRP's (NICHD, 2000) report, in which the members of the panel indicated a lack of converging and convincing evidence for what was then the prevalent use of independent, silent reading in school classrooms, is what many have come to characterize as a knee-jerk suppression of silent reading practice in school classrooms across the United States. Although independent, silent reading had been gently criticized prior to the NRP's report, sharp critiques of the typical conditions for practicing reading independently and silently increased significantly after the NRP's report was published. When precious classroom time was allocated for reading practice after the publication of the NRP report, and in an era of high-stakes accountability, many students from first grade to high school were no longer allowed to read silently. Rather, students were expected to real orally, often repeatedly, with someone who could hear them read and give them feedback on their reading to be compliant with the "evidence base" for providing effective reading practice. As a result, independent, silent reading, which had previously reigned supreme in classrooms across the United States, was deposed by evidence-based guided, repeated oral reading with feedback as the dominant process for providing students with regular reading practice.

As a new emphasis on repeated oral reading with feedback began to take hold in classrooms, it became apparent that this singular mode of providing school reading practice was at odds with the principal way in which most accomplished adolescent and adult readers read—independently and silently. Although repeated oral reading seemed to make sense in the earliest stages of reading acquisition, when it continued into later years of schooling and the length of books increased, questions of practicality and utility around repeated oral reading began to surface among researchers and practitioners. Other questions about when and how

Revisiting Silent Reading: New Directions for Teachers and Researchers, edited by Elfrieda H. Hiebert and D. Ray Reutzel. © 2010 by the International Reading Association.

accomplished oral readers could or should make the transition to beneficial forms of silent reading practice also began to take shape.

The contributors to this volume show that, for many students, silent reading proficiency does not automatically develop but, rather, depends on their participation in appropriate instructional experiences. The contributors to this volume are leading experts in the field of reading education and, through their contributions, this volume brings together evidence and issues related to the silent reading proficiency that underlies proficient comprehension of text—the foundation of full participation in the global–digital community of the 21st century.

Revisiting Silent Reading is divided into three sections beginning with updated and fresh theoretical perspectives on silent reading processes. The first section addresses a new model of silent reading that includes perspectives on the work of the eye in silent reading. This section also focuses on theoretical issues related to the motivation to read silently, developmental considerations in transferring oral reading skills to silent reading, and how students develop silent reading habits over time.

The second section of this new volume focuses on how silent reading instruction and the conditions surrounding silent reading practice can be revised, modified, or transformed to increase students' reading fluency, achievement, and motivation. Scholars update research findings on one of the most prevalent past practices associated with independent, silent reading—sustained silent reading—and its derivatives.

Other chapters in this section examine how to use oral and silent reading as complementary processes for developing proficient readers, report research documenting what students do when they are reading silently, and offer insights into how to motivate students to engage in silent reading and stay engaged. In addition, chapters in this section report research on reforming independent, silent reading practice to increase students' silent reading in a core reading program; scaffolded silent reading, a complement to guided oral repeated reading with feedback; R⁵ a silent reading makeover; and new findings on the effects of wide reading compared with repeated reading.

The third and final section addresses differing needs of silent readers, including English learners and struggling readers, and new contexts in which silent reading can take place. Chapters focus on silent reading in an online context, in bilingual classrooms, assessing silent reading for English learners, and silent reading pitfalls experienced by struggling readers. One feature that is sure to be popular in this volume is the "Questions for Professional Development" found at the conclusion of each of the chapters. Finally, the conclusion provides a coherent discussion of new directions in silent reading for researchers and teachers in classrooms.

The time is ripe for *Revisiting Silent Reading* if students are to be provided efficacious opportunities that develop silent reading proficiencies and habits. Such opportunities that make effective use of allocated academic reading instructional time depend on clear and thoughtful recommendations for teachers. Not since the publication of Anderson, Wilson, and Fielding's (1988) article entitled "Growth in Reading and How Children Spend Their Time Outside of School" has silent reading been the singular focus of a major publication in literacy education. There is a need and desire among educators to increase students' opportunities to engage with books and reading not only for the love of reading but also for the expectation that time spent in silent reading practice will lead to increased student achievement, fluency, and motivation to read. More research is needed to understand the processes of silent reading and how to optimize its power in classroom reading practice. *Revisiting Silent Reading: New Directions for Teachers and Researchers* will entice interested researchers across disciplinary boundaries to once again set their sights on solving the many unanswered questions related to silent reading processes and how to improve silent reading instruction in classrooms across the United States and the world.

EHH

DRR

REFERENCES

Anderson, R.C., Wilson, P.T., & Fielding, L.G. (1988). Growth in reading and how children spend their time outside of school. *Reading Research Quarterly, 23*(3), 285–303.

National Institute of Child Health and Human Development. (2000). *Report of the National Reading Panel. Teaching children to read: An evidence-based assessment of the scientific research literature on reading and its implications for reading instruction* (NIH Publication No. 00-4769). Washington, DC: U.S. Government Printing Office.

Silent Reading:
Perspectives and Frameworks

CHAPTER 1

Silent Reading Pedagogy: A Historical Perspective

P. David Pearson

University of California, Berkeley

Susie Goodin

University of California, Berkeley

The story of how silent reading instruction developed is not simple. When we set out on this journey to unearth the story, we anticipated a pathway of continuous progress toward ever more fluent and efficient silent reading processes prompted by advances in reading research over time. Instead, we found a meandering pathway of fits and starts, progress and regress, dead ends and cul du sacs. Moreover, the practices in any given period were shaped as much, perhaps more, by forces outside education as inside education; these were social norms, political events, economic factors, and literacy technologies that played out in the larger cultural ecology. We describe the changes in the roles that silent reading has played in instruction by mapping them onto norms and events in the larger society and culture, arguing that silent reading as a social practice existed for some readers, the avid and advantaged, long before it became a regular part of reading pedagogy. In short, silent reading has almost always been a tough pedagogical sell—and by some standards (e.g., the 2000 National Reading Panel report), it still is.

Silent reading as a cultural practice developed over a long period of time, lurching ahead in intermittent surges, propelled by the advances in the technologies of written language: punctuation, word spacing and capitalization, the printing press, popular books for the masses (including children), and mass media. Inside the walls of schools, reading pedagogy and assessment migrated from a dominance of oral reading (through the 19th century) to silent reading (emerging in the first third of the 20th century), as reading for meaning burst onto the scene as an explicit theoretical and pedagogical goal around the time of World War I (Pearson, 2000; Smith, 2002).

To tell the story of silent reading development, we examined documents that traced either or both educational and cultural histories of reading and literacy, looking for references that revealed something about silent reading practices. After gathering a rich body of evidence, we had to sort and winnow it to a manageable

Revisiting Silent Reading: New Directions for Teachers and Researchers, edited by Elfrieda H. Hiebert and D. Ray Reutzel. © 2010 by the International Reading Association.

size so we could accomplish our goal: to describe both the cultural and pedagogical practices of silent reading in each historical era of literacy development, juxtaposing the cultural and the pedagogical to analyze continuities and discontinuities between the two within and across periods. What follows is the story that emerged from our efforts.

An Abbreviated Examination of Ancient and Medieval Reading

Oral Reading as a Social Practice, Historically Derived

Oral reading predominated in the early history of reading. It was *the* way of doing all tasks under the rubric of reading—copying, performing, *and* interpreting a text—in the early days of Christianity. An oft-cited incident (Allington, 1984; Kern, 2006; Manguel, 1996; Mathews, 1966) describing St. Augustine's surprise at seeing St. Ambrose reading silently in 383 AD signals that silent reading practiced by individuals was an anomaly. Within ecclesiastic circles, silent reading was suspect because it was not subject to official public monitoring, no doubt to make sure there was no slippage in interpreting the sacred word. This concern for interpretive accountability was one of the reasons that silent reading was slow to enter common practice (Manguel, 1996; Mathews, 1966; Smith, 1966/2002). A secular rationale for the persistence of oral reading, according to Manguel (1996), was the expectation that written words would be rehearsed and spoken as the means of bringing to life the thoughts of the absent writer; only then was the text completed as a part of the writer-intended conversation with the reader. Even with oral reading dominant, silent reading lived a clandestine life; reports from as far back as the seventh century about the delights of silent reading indicate that some avid readers valued the benefits of voiceless reading and reflections on text (Manguel, 1996).

Religious Influences. Reading aloud was also the practice of scribes in early scriptoria before writing conventions emerged. Before standards of punctuation, word spacing, and capitalization existed, reading aloud was the only mnemonic device available to help scribes remember passages to be copied. Typically, narrow columns of text, of 15 to 25 letters strung contiguously, were copied on the available manuscript material. The difficulty of remembering and copying such strings of text was thought to be reduced by oral recitation; thus, even monks who had taken a vow of silence were granted special dispensations to read aloud for copying text (the only resource available prior to the printing press for making multiple copies of a single text). Oral reading in the scriptoria persisted until the 10th century, when silence was reintroduced to the copying rooms in response to advances in orthographic representation (e.g., spacing). These advances had an immediate and serendipitous side effect in the hinterlands of the Roman Empire. Word spacing and punctuation were especially important at the edges of the Empire in places like Ireland, which was populated by Saxon and Celtic priests who had such a shaky mastery of Latin that they had to rely on word spacing to access otherwise unavailable religious texts (Manguel, 1996; Pang, 2003; Saenger, 1982).

One can imagine ancient scriptoria and medieval libraries as "a rumbling din" (Manguel, 1996, p. 43), as many heads bent over desks reproducing or studying texts in mumbling tones. Later medieval libraries were also noisy, with limited and valuable reference books chained to lecterns as individuals shared and disputed texts. There is consensus among historians that word spacing and punctuation promoted the practice of silent reading long before the invention of the printing press. Some have claimed that these conventions even influenced critical thinking and the drive toward the idea of individual interpretation that was a fundamental premise of Reformation theologians (Pang, 2003; Saenger, 1982). What is undisputed is that technologies of writing affected oral and silent reading practices and that some individuals, monks among them, practiced silent reading even when the norm in society and schools was oral reading.

Access. The social norm of oral reading allowed for sharing of scarce textual resources in ancient and medieval times (Allington, 1984; Smith, 2002) and required practice, or rehearsal similar to practicing a musical score, to correctly re-create the author's meaning. The invention of the codex made of parchment (what we would call the modern bound book form) replaced the scroll and had gained popular acceptance by 400 AD. It had the two key virtues: portability and security. It could be hidden away more easily than could a scroll (Manguel, 1996). With the codex, silent reading became a more regular practice, libraries evolved to serve scholarship, and the individual reader was free to explore and challenge intellectual ideas (Pang, 2003; Saenger, 1982).

The demand for books increased, waiting to be satisfied, at least for wealthier clients, by Gutenberg's invention of the printing press between 1450 AD and 1455 AD. The production response was swift. According to Manguel (1996), by 1500 AD more than 30,000 books had been printed in Europe. Some have argued that the rise of access to texts for individual silent reading and reflection contributed to the independent thinking that characterized the rise of new beliefs, such as Martin Luther's "The 95 Theses" (Manguel, 1996; Mathews, 1966; Olson, 1994; Pang, 2003; Saenger, 1982). Certainly, the availability of a permanent text for continuous revisiting (unlike the ephemeral rendering in oral reading), analysis, and even critique is consistent with the fundamental questioning of authority that marked the Reformation. Some scholars argue that the Reformation ideal is a reflection of the broader modernist view emerging in natural science (see Olson, 1994) that close observation and description of the natural world would reveal its secrets. Thus, when it comes to scripture, it is within the power of the individual, with enough close reading, to reach its meaning. The individual who has the persistence to read and reread scripture will discover its truths (and this is the key point of the Reformation) without the interpretive guidance of a cleric. This sort of close, individual, independent, silent reading of texts was possible only when societies could avail themselves of all of the technological advances that had accrued over the ages (e.g., spacing, punctuation, the codex format, and transparently reproducible fonts); thus by the early modern period marked by the beginning of the Reformation, the stage for new cultural practices for reading had been set. It took centuries, however, for the pedagogy to catch up to the cultural opportunities available.

Early Reading Pedagogy

Although we will not closely examine early reading pedagogy (i.e., the time before reading English came to the Americas), we can sum up the progress from ancient to modern times by noting that the Greeks and Romans were known to use the highly synthetic alphabetic form of instruction typified by a reliable sound–symbol relationship and rigorous repetition and recitation of single letter sounds and names (Mathews, 1966). Syllable instruction came next, with the emphasis always on oral production of "the river of speech" (Mathews, 1966, p. 3) practiced in metered lines or choral songs. We know also that oral reading instruction was tightly connected to religiosity and morality as reflected in early texts copied by monks. These Christian texts, required by a decree in 813 AD in the 44th Canon of the Council of Mainz stating that children should be taught religious instruction, became the early primers (Smith, 2002).

These ancient and medieval perspectives and cultural practices are important to us because they establish the background for practices of oral and silent reading in the United States and point to recurrent relationships among historical norms, religious cultures, and reading practices.

Colonial America: Silent Reading Practices and Pedagogy

Early in the colonial history of the United States, the main purpose of reading, oral or silent, was to gain religious insight. Beyond religion, reading for the common man was considered important to community involvement and commerce, but the founding fathers of New England also "saw themselves as part of an international world of men of letters" (Monaghan, 2005, p. 12). Reading was regarded mainly as oral reading, books were scarce, and those available were read intensively and repeatedly. Even then, "At the most accomplished end of the scale, men and women read as we do today, copiously, intently, and presumably often silently. How they read depended on what they were reading" (Monaghan, 2005, p. 13). In one notable example of silent reading from the late 1600s, Monaghan (2005) reports Cotton Mather's prodigious ability to skim dense texts for key ideas. Beneath this very elite minority of accomplished readers, however, one finds a great unevenness in the literacy practices, access to books, and opportunities to learn to read. Those with money to buy books had increasing access to a range of texts, including fiction for adults and children.

Access to Books

In 1638, the first printing press was established in Cambridge, Massachusetts; previously all books were imported from Europe, mostly from London. Books other than the Bible and the basic primer for children were out of reach for the lower classes. Books in general were primarily produced for the adult male reader until John Newbery started printing "pretty books" (Monaghan, 2005, p. 321) for children in 1744 in London. It is interesting to note that Newbery deliberately included girls in his audience by subtitling *Little Pretty Pocket-Book* with *Intended for the Instruction and Amusement of Little Master Tommy and Pretty Miss Polly* (Monaghan, 2005). Newbery's intent to publish books to influence education could also be seen within his texts. In *The Valentine's Gift*, published in 1765, a young scholar denounces the dull lesson books of school and asserts that he could learn anything in such pretty books as offered by a benefactor (Monaghan, 2005, p. 323).

Telling evidence of the paucity of books comes from the history of the Library of Congress. Initiated by legislation in 1800, the Library of Congress started with a collection of 740 books and three maps, all ordered from London as the primary congressional resource (Cole, 1993). Even by 1814, when the British burned the Capitol building in Washington, DC, the library had grown to only 3,000 volumes; they were replaced after the fire through the purchase of Thomas Jefferson's personal library of 6,487 volumes (Cole, 1993). Jefferson's individual library was known to be extraordinary for the times not only for its size, but for the breadth of topics in its holdings.

Learning to Read

According to Smith (1966/2002), the method of teaching reading was incidental to the religious content of the texts. Early colonial reading instruction applied the alphabetic approach to a small set of religious texts, using recitation tasks to evaluate progress; this was the approach imported from 13th and 14th century "petty schools" in England (Mathews, 1966; Monaghan, 2005). A progression of five texts universally supported the teaching of the names of letters first along with first syllables on the hornbook, then came a primer for practice of short passages (to be read orally), then further scriptural texts meant for religious instruction. "They composed what the English philosopher John Locke would call, in 1693, the "ordinary Road" of the reading instruction sequence: "the Horn-Book, Primer, Psalter, Testament, and Bible" (Monaghan, 2005, p. 13). The missionary nature of reading instruction—to save the soul—is evidenced in the Code of 1656 from England requiring that children learned to read well enough to read the scriptures and other good books in English.

Monaghan's (2005) history reveals that reading instruction in the New England colonies was provided in free town schools to male children who might also advance to Latin study. Before the end of the 1600s, girls were regularly taught domestic skills and reading in dame (i.e., home) schools to read religious texts, but by the end of the century many northern town schools were including girls in their education programs. This became a crucial issue at the end of the 1600s and early 1700s, as the need for more female reading teachers to provide the first step in young students' reading education was perceived. The pedagogy for both boys and girls in the various schools was oral, and the alphabetic method of instruction was uniform.

In the first example of a methods text used for early reading instruction, devised in the mid-1700s, the practice of taking turns to read aloud (i.e., the round robin routine) to demonstrate accuracy was noted in records from a young teacher, a German immigrant in Pennsylvania (Monaghan, 2005). Though this teacher's other methods may have been unusual for the time, turn-taking in reading aloud was the norm. The rise in popularity of the spelling book, first imported from England, then printed in the colonies in 1644, indicated a new instructional focus on teaching standard pronunciation of the letters. The new spelling books, beginning with the 1644 book published by Stephen Daye (no known title), became an essential text in ordinary instruction (Monaghan, 2005). Early spelling books attended to sound–symbol relationships, perhaps without clarifying the confusion between letters and sounds, the alphabet and phonemes, but it was the beginning of instruction that accounted for the difference (Monaghan, 2005).

Spelling books were used to teach orally without any writing and progressed from individual letters to monosyllables and then to multisyllabic words. Rules introduced in the spelling books included the long and short nature of vowels, though not called by those names (Monaghan, 2005). The spelling books included short passages of prose as well. By 1787, Noah Webster's *Elementary Spelling Book*— what we have come to call the *Blue Back Speller*—improved on other spelling books with a clear, uniform pronunciation key. This book was favored even into the 1800s when other instructional texts such as William Holmes McGuffey's *Eclectic Reader* gained followers (Monaghan, 2005). Webster's spelling book remained the primary reading text for the populations of slaves and freedmen learning to read, long after it was replaced in most schools by other instructional books.

Several changes in colonial American times laid the groundwork for a shift in reading instruction in the century after the American Revolution, according to Monaghan (2005). First, changes in instruction were driven by the advent of Locke's notion of the "innocent child," born innocent and hence not in need of salvation through spiritually based instruction. Second, the increase in popularity of pretty books and other pleasure-reading texts indicated changing attitudes about children and their interests, and an acceptance of secular topics for students. Spelling books reflected the same turn toward secular topics. Third, the number of texts produced for adults and children, both boys and girls, increased the likelihood of individual reading for pleasurable purposes. So while oral reading was still the accepted practice in reading education, especially for younger students, improving access to books and changing understandings about the purposes for reading were expanding in ways that would ultimately support silent reading practices in school.

U.S. Expansion: 1800s Through Early 1900s

Literacy as a Social Force

In characterizing his construct of "literacy expansion" (Venezky, 1991, p. 48) as it applies to the growth of literacy over the last millennium, Venezky (1991) describes literacy as both a "national aspiration and a set of human practices anchored in space and time" (p. 46). Using these explanatory tools, he contextualized a wide range of influences on literacy development that tie social forces and individual experiences to literacy development. In describing the modern era, he suggests that three large historical factors—a market economy, the ideals of the Reformation, the intertwined development of printing and schooling—intersected to provide individuals with an expanded personal (mental and physical) space in which to communicate with an ever-expanding world. His theory "predicts that social changes which enlarge individual space offer the greatest opportunity for the spread of print culture and that where print culture expands, literacy expands" (Venezky, 1991, p. 48). As we have suggested, expansion had consequences at every level—personal, cultural, and pedagogical. At no time were these forces more powerful than during the late 19th century.

As the United States expanded in the 1800s through early 1900s, stretching across the continent, broadening its industrial and commercial base, and greatly increasing the access to all kinds of publications, expansive reading for most people became possible. Even though the First Amendment to the U.S. Constitution protected people's right to publish, the social standard for publishable text remained narrow. The early 19th century dominance of religious texts gave way to secular texts with high moral content, but works of fiction were slow to be accepted until late in the century.

The development of public libraries in the late 1800s and early 1900s provides a compelling example of the tension between controlling text access and the expansion of literacy as a cultural practice. Garrison (1979) examined public library leaders' social ideals and their dual (if contradictory) missions to elevate the masses while maintaining the status quo for a cultured United States. Often the library mission was couched in religious terms: librarian as literary pastor "must be able to become familiar with his flock...to select their reading, and gradually to elevate their taste" (Garrison, 1979, p. 37). Firmly fixed in the mores of their time, these leaders demonstrated a certain cultural arrogance based on the notion of "material and moral advancement through education" (Garrison, 1979, p. xiv) expressed as a missionary impulse to improve the lives of others, especially the masses.

This mission shaped librarians' concerns for the quality of literature enjoyed by library patrons. With a decidedly paternalistic air, librarians meant to improve the lot of the laboring masses through education accomplished in the selection and reading of morally uplifting texts. In what became known as the "fiction problem," library users, mainly women, defied the librarians by preferring lowbrow fiction: adventure, romance, and counterculture representations of female lives. The escapist stories of independent women defying social mores became a vexing problem addressed repeatedly in library literature (Hall, 1908) and American Library Association conferences for decades between the 1870s and early 1900s (Garrison, 1979).

Throughout the decades of power struggle over the social norms of reading selections, the records show that most librarians stocked the "immoral" literature they denounced publicly to maintain their circulation. Popular fiction was slowly and reluctantly embraced by public librarians as they balanced circulation statistics showing the power of popular culture against their goals of promoting high culture. For instance, in 1878 the Mercantile Public Library in San Francisco recorded fiction circulation at 71.4% versus 0.6% for religious texts (Garrison, 1979). Reading practices shifted from the intensive reading of a narrow range of texts to the extensive reading of a wide range of texts. The idea of a reading public that demanded entertaining books was clearly established in the first quarter of the 20th century. Of course, the wide reading of an extensive array of texts or pleasure reading is consistent with an ethic of silent, not oral, reading.

Libraries and schools were not always on the same side during this period. Teachers resisted allowing public library texts into the schools (Smith, 2002). This resistance was slowly undermined by persistent crusades on the part of public librarians, but it was not until the 1890s that they made headway in providing supplementary texts within schools. Despite librarians' attempts to control reading materials for children, they eventually gave in to the demands for popular children books. Noting that "the urchins had better be reading these than doing nothing downtown" (Garrison, 1979, p. 213), public librarians by 1915 had relented and included these entertaining texts in the collections. This tension continues today in the disputes about approved texts versus self-selected reading and free-reader response.

Thus, throughout the late 19th and early 20th centuries, secular reading became the rule rather than the exception. As more reading materials became available, extensive silent reading of many secular texts, rather than intensive public oral reading of a few texts such as the Bible and religious tracts, was increasingly practiced (Birkerts, 1996; Smith, 2002). By 1870, high regard for reading in silence was exemplified by Ralph Waldo Emerson, an avid, respected silent reader (Manguel, 1996), but oral reading instruction in school was still the norm, especially for younger students (Monaghan, 2005).

The Pedagogy of the Period

Concerned about the lifeless rote learning they witnessed in the pedagogy of the early 19th century (i.e., the alphabetic approach to early reading acquisition combined with the norm of fluent oral reading), many U.S. educators became disciples of the Prussian education techniques for teaching reading (Mathews, 1966; Smith, 2002) that had evolved in the 18th century. In 1843, Horace Mann observed and acclaimed the whole-word (i.e., words-to-letters) approach of Prussians and introduced it to the Massachusetts Board of Education. One early European innovator was Friedrich Gedike, a German educator who believed children should learn through holistic study of the cultural and natural worlds—and whole words. U.S. reformers translated this prevailing Prussian notion of "whole to part" to instruction of whole words instead of whole texts, and many primers, such as John Russell Webb's 1846 version, were developed with lists of words spelled in the "normal manner." A beginning analytic approach was born. It was not until nearly a century later that the whole-word approach became dominant, and throughout the 19th and early 20th century, there was continual tension between the established alphabet approaches and the "reform" word-based approach.

In the early 20th century, professional books, including an influential one by Buswell in 1922 and the first U.S. reading research book by Huey, contributed to the scientific constructs of pedagogy (Smith, 2002). By the early 1900s, silent reading instruction began to be widely supported over oral reading, as were supplemental materials that included a diversity of reading selections, many of them both secular and moralistic. Early reading research began before 1910 with a concern for visual aspects of reading and oral fluency, but Huey (1898) and Thorndike (1917) also foreshadowed the concern for comprehension. As research and experimentation in the field developed, an instructional methods debate about silent versus oral reading instruction gained momentum.

The broad debate over oral reading pedagogy that had begun in the mid-1800s was initiated by figures like Horace Mann, who became the champion for a shift from rote to meaningful learning (which included shifts away from the synthetic approach to learning phonics to a whole-word/meaning-based pedagogy), and sustained at the end of that century by leaders like Francis Parker, who criticized the dominance of oral reading and questioned its efficacy, emphasizing instead the need for students to learn to read for meaning, a goal that typically involves more reliance on silent reading (Smith, 2002).

Parker was joined in this quest for a clear focus on reading for meaning by Huey, whose landmark 1908 book *Psychology and Pedagogy of Reading* (a genuine treat in substance and rhetorical elegance—preferably read silently) became a standard part of the discourse on reading research and pedagogy in the early 1900s. Huey argued that expression (i.e., fluent oral reading with all the right prosodic features) helps thought and thought is necessary for expression, but that silent reading was a matter of "thought getting and thought manipulating" (Smith, 2002, p. 151) more than expression.

Research from that time confirmed the superiority of silent reading over oral reading in speed and comprehension, initiating the call for silent reading in schools (Mathews, 1966). Studies by Mead (1915, 1917) and Printner and Gilliland (1916) compare the effectiveness of oral and silent reading in students' ability to retain "points" (i.e., main ideas) while reading, finding silent reading results to be superior. The advantage of silent reading was conveyed in the influential yearbooks of the National Society for the Study of Education between 1916 and 1920. In 1921, a whole section of the yearbook was devoted to the issue of silent reading—

lamenting the lack of effective pedagogy for it and concluding that reading instruction should aim at effective *silent* reading.

Alas, practice lagged behind research. There were a few strongholds where silent reading prevailed, and the instructional materials began to include genuine literature selections, but pedagogy had a hard time ridding itself of the hold on oral reading. This is evidence that despite the early calls for silent reading instruction, oral skills were still paramount in the schools—even as the United States moved toward the Great Depression.

The United States at War

Social Forces at Work

World War I jolted the education community and U.S. society at large in regard to the reading comprehension ability of troops, or the lack of it, as young men demonstrated poor reading skills assessed on enlistment. The "shocking rediscovery" (Smith, 2002, p. 251) in World War II of the same inadequacy in reading was ascertained by changes in troop assessments that required soldiers to read test items silently to construct or choose correct answers. Newly developed scientific measurement scales led to the discovery that many soldiers could not read well enough to follow written instructions and prompted public calls for better reading research and reading instruction (Pearson & Hamm, 2005).

In the meantime, children's reading practice outside of school was being supported in reading programs designed by public librarians. In the progressive era from the turn of the 20th century through the 1920s, librarians engaged in a new enthusiasm for social reform manifested in library social centers, library extension work, and a new focus on children in libraries. The first children's room in a public library was established in 1890 in Massachusetts; before that, children under 12 years of age were routinely excluded from the public library. Soon, children's service was expanded to separate rooms with special functions involving storytelling and book clubs meant to engage wayward youth. The growth was fast paced: "In 1913 the ALA [American Library Association] estimated that children's books comprised about one-fifth of the nation's library collections and about one-third of the total circulation" (Garrison, 1979, p. 210). The expectation was that children in the public library would read silently and develop a taste for good literature. Gray (1924) espouses silent reading—for pleasure, and development of imagination and information—and supported school libraries on behalf of these pursuits.

The Emergence of Reading Research

Understanding about the new social conditions for silent reading—abundant materials, universal reading expectations, rapid communication, and pervasive written communication as the chief way of communicating—elicited, perhaps demanded, broad support for silent reading in the schools (Smith, 2002). Attention to the reading habits of adults as a guide for instructional goals in "intelligent silent reading" (Gray, 1924, p. 348) aligned with Huey's (1908/1968) earlier insightful statement positioning "reading as the art of thought getting" (p. 359). Some of the reading research conducted during this period probed the effects on comprehension in response to oral versus silent reading; however, the research spawned contradictory findings that did little to quell pedagogical debates and differences on the question of oral versus silent superiority (Allington, 1984; Holmes, 1985; Juel & Holmes, 1981).

The Pedagogy of the Period

From its initial successes early in the 1900s, the words-first approach gradually evolved into the highly popular look–say approach associated with the work of William Elson and William S. Gray. Working with Scott-Foresman, Elson, then Elson and Gray, and then Gray and others developed this approach involving Dick and Jane and their family and neighborhood until, by the 1940s, it became the dominant Curriculum Foundation Series (Gray, Artley, & Arbuthnot, 1952). Children were expected to learn whole words first, then focus on understanding the story. They built sight-word recognition before moving on to analytic phonics. Most important, silent reading always preceded oral reading for expression and fluency (Chall, 1967; Pearson, 2002), even in first grade. Publishers increased teacher resources, printed multiple texts for each grade level, and paid attention to supplemental materials of interest to children that would also reflect future reading demands as adults (Pearson, 2002; Smith, 2002).

The method of expecting students to read silently first, then orally, was supported by many in the field (Buswell, 1947; Gray, 1924; Karp, 1943). In an extreme example of silent reading instruction, McDade initiated an approach in the Chicago public schools that allowed no oral work during reading class, the principle being to avoid vocalization at all costs so as not to interfere with comprehension. McDade's (1937, 1944) research did not have a strong following and was later discredited, and a call for a balanced approach to oral and silent reading emerged by the early 1950s (Allington, 1984). Oral reading practices outside of school had diminished greatly during this time, and reading research counseled a balanced approach to oral instruction. Even so, the professional literature of the period reveals constant complaints of round robin oral reading, implying that it was still a widespread practice in the late 1950s and early 1960s, especially at the lower grades (Allington, 1984; Hoffman, 1987).

Immediately before and after World War II, the individualized reading approach—with roots dating back to the 1920s (Hunt, 1967)—gathered momentum, mainly through the efforts of champions such as Lyman Hunt, Willard Olson, and Jeanette Veatch. Guided by the motto of seeking, self-selection, and pacing (Olson, 1952), it operated on the premise that no classroom or even small-group approach could ever meet the needs and interests of individuals, so every child deserved an individualized reading program (IRP)—a substantial portion of each reading period for individually paced reading, when each student could read whatever he or she desired. A few schools devoted the entire school day to these IRPs, but more often than not they reserved only 20–60 minutes for independent reading.

Often, IRPs entailed individual book conferences between the teacher and each child on a weekly, bimonthly, or monthly basis—a time when the teacher would engage the big ideas in the book, query the child's comprehension, and check up on oral reading—to see if the book was truly at the child's instructional level and whether word-attack skills were sharp and improving. According to McCracken (1971), the movement reached its apex in the 1960s when Hunt coined the acronym USSR (Uninterrupted Sustained Silent Reading) to identify the practice of devoting a daily period (typically 15–30 minutes) for everyone, including the teacher, to engage in self-selected silent reading. Popular through the 1960s, IRPs faded in the wake of the return to basics and phonics first prompted by Chall's 1967 book, *Learning to Read: The Great Debate*, but it resurfaced in full flower in the constructivist reforms (i.e., whole language and literature-based reading) of the mid-1980s and early 1990s.

Contemporary U.S. Reading Instruction

Print Access in Contemporary United States

Over the last half century, access to print, especially the sorts of print media that would support silent reading, has been something of a rollercoaster ride. As suggested in our analysis for the period between World War I and World War II, public libraries supported silent reading with greatly expanded service to children. In the period since World War II, much has happened to change student access to books and other texts, and these changes have a direct impact on the effectiveness of silent reading practices in schools. First, the launch of the Sputnik I satellite by the Soviet Union in 1957 prompted U.S. legislation promoting science and math education, followed by the first direct federal funding of school library materials in the Elementary and Secondary Education Act of 1967 (Michie & Holton, 2005). Federal funding, though erratic over contemporary decades, helped to increase school library book collections from 3 books per student nationally in 1953–1954 to 18 per student in 1993–1994. Unfortunately, the ratio decreased to 17 per student in 1999–2000 (Michie & Holton, 2005). Though financial support for materials earmarked for school libraries has not been maintained, it helped establish school libraries as a valued part of public education, in part for their contribution to independent reading programs (Gray, 1924).

Second, a burgeoning interest in children's literature led to an explosion of juvenile book publication, supported and promoted by an awards system tied to the commercial interests of publishers. One indication of enormous growth in publishing is that in the United States the number of literary prizes has risen from 21 in 1929 to 232 in 1959 and to 367 in 1976—and as of the end of the 1990s the number was at least 1,100 (English, 2005). Many of these are for children's literature, starting with the Newbery Award established in 1922, but are joined by awards for picture books, nonfiction categories, lifetime contribution awards for authors, subject domain awards, and, more recently, by regional and state awards based on children's choices.

Unfortunately, the access attributable to the expanding selection of children's literature is not evenly distributed in the general population. While some school-age children have bountiful access to texts for independent reading, other children have substantially less access to reading materials (Neuman & Celano, 2001; Smith, Constantino, & Krashen, 1997) and text types (Duke, 2000; Wade & Moje, 2000). This creates a problem for advocates of independent, silent reading programs, because access to a wide range of books at varied reading levels is seen as an element crucial to success (Allington, 2001; Krashen, 1993). It may be that schools need to take responsibility for providing time not only for silent reading (rather than considering it solely a homework assignment) but also for physical and intellectual access to books within the school program.

Third, print media and books for youth in new formats with new perspectives and enlarged topic boundaries (Dresang, 1999) increased in this same period as multimedia texts in all formats and new technologies populated students' lives (Kearney, 2000). The rise of the Internet and mobile devices, along with existing visual media such as television, engage youth for an enormous amount of time each day, perhaps limiting the time that might otherwise be spent in silent reading of books. According to a recent survey, people between the ages of 8 and 18 spend an average of 7 hours and 38 minutes a day using entertainment media, including the Internet (Rideout, Foehr, & Roberts, 2010). Access to new media may challenge silent reading practices as we have known them.

Although space constraints prevent us from delving into the literature on new technologies and their impact on independent silent reading, we can speculate with our fellow authors (see Chapter 9 and Chapter 13 in this volume; also Kern, 2006) that new computer technologies affect reading and writing in ways we do not yet fully understand. We can imagine that traditional pathways through texts (Kern, 2006) and the sense of authority in composition (Fabos, 2004) along with collaborative digital literacy practices (Lankes, Silverstein, & Nicholson, 2006; Weinberger, 2007) are affected by new media and composing arenas. We can show that these new literacy practices are shaping the design of academic and school libraries in ways that promote collaborative, digital knowledge construction in a new learning commons idea (Asselin & Doiron; 2008; Bennett, 2003; Roberts, 2007). There is, however, a fundamental tension in praising the possibilities of collaborative reading and sense-making in digital environments because collaboration requires, or at least gives privilege to, oral modes of reading over silent—a paradox to be resolved by those who champion these new literacies.

Scholarly Context

In the last third of the 20th century, understanding about reading instruction in the primary grades was affected by *Learning to Read: The Great Debate* (Chall,

1967) and studies of first-grade reading pedagogy (Bond & Dykstra, 1967). Chall describes the look–say approach to reading instruction that was popular at the time and recommends a change to a strong, synthetic phonics approach for first graders that dovetailed nicely with findings from the first-grade studies. Though no one pedagogical approach was found to be significantly superior for all children (Bond & Dykstra, 1967), the consensus was that a phonics-first approach had been neglected. Accompanying these pivotal studies, and following them into the 21st century, was a large and expanding set of reading research studies from multiple disciples: scholars in linguistics, psycholinguistics, cognitive psychology, sociolinguistics, and literary theory added to understanding of the reading process (Pearson, 2000, 2002). A host of perspectives and models of reading developed, affecting reading instruction practices, including the practice of silent reading in school. New cognitive models of reading, attention in the 1990s to student motivation and engagement as an important factor in learning to read effectively (see Guthrie & Wigfield, 2000), and studies in regard to access to texts of all types influenced reading instruction.

In the 1980s, Stanovich pioneered work showing what he called a strong Matthew effect (Stanovich, 1986) that explained the ever-increasing gap between good and poor readers: Using the Biblical proverb of "the rich get richer and the poor get poorer," he argues that those who can read, read more, learn more, and improve more and that those who struggle with reading, read less, learn less, and fall even further behind their peers. In a classic article about struggling readers from the same decade, Allington (1977) puts forward the same argument: "If they don't read much, how they ever gonna get good?" Anderson and his colleagues contribute to the theory and research base for the value of silent reading in a series of studies that demonstrated how "just plain reading" serves as a rich source, indeed the primary source, for vocabulary acquisition (Nagy, Herman, & Anderson, 1985) and contributes to growth in measured reading achievement (Anderson, Wilson, & Fielding, 1988). Another particularly strong empirical claim for the efficacy of silent reading can be made on the basis of a study from Taylor and colleagues (Taylor, Frye, & Maruyama, 1990), who found that allowing the students in the experimental group to read independently (compared with a control group that spent an equal amount of time practicing skill sheets) promoted greater achievement on a standardized test.

Other research studies followed up on earlier contradictory findings in regard to the efficacy of silent reading and focused on the cognitive aspects of oral versus silent reading programs (Holmes, 1985; Juel & Holmes, 1981). Overall, these studies presented findings from comparing different modes of reading that perpetuated the debate over the relative effectiveness of silent reading instruction over oral reading as an unsettled issue (Allington, 1984; Armbruster & Wilkinson, 1991; McCallum, Sharp, Bell, & George, 2004). Research attention to student interests, motivations, and choices for reading gained prominence in the 1990s, soon adding valuable insights on the effect of student engagement on student achievement (Guthrie & Wigfield, 2000; Ivey & Broaddus, 2001; Pearson, 2002; Worthy, 1996).

In the meantime, oral reading instruction was still widely practiced in schools, especially for younger students and poor readers, and especially for assessment purposes (Allington, 1984; Armbruster & Wilkinson, 1991; Hoffman, 1987), at least until whole-language methods gained popularity in the 1980s and 1990s.

Silent Reading Pedagogy—An Ongoing Modern Debate

Silent reading secured a curricular beachhead for itself in several movements of the 1970s and 1980s. In schools that adopted individually guided education plans (Klausmeier, 1972), silent reading fit the ideal of differentiated instruction and individual pacing; these were often either "open" schools or schools with multi-age classrooms. After an initial burst of popularity and growth through the late 1970s, this model of schooling fell victim to another back-to-basics surge but survives today in the United States only in small pockets around the country (Kim, 2002). It was also a comfortable fit with the whole-language emphasis on helping individual students learn how to make important decisions for themselves, such as what to write, what to read, and how to demonstrate their own progress (see Pearson, 1989).

Perhaps the most welcoming curricular home was the literature-based reading movement, at least in its earliest stages, with its emphasis on a personalized reading component and prerogative for students to shape their own literacy identity and work (see Atwell, 1987, 1998). Ironically, in some iterations of literature-based reading, such as the literature-based basal readers that emerged in response to the state of California's call for adoption in the early 1990s, independent silent reading gave way to teacher read-alouds as whole-class instruction replaced ability groups in U.S. classrooms (McCarthey et al., 1994; Pearson, 2004). The price a teacher pays for assigning all students in a class the same literature selection is that many, and in some classrooms most, of the students will not be able to read the book on their own. Even highly regarded approaches such as book club (McMahon & Raphael, 1997) and literature circles (Daniels, 1994) must weigh the costs (i.e., lost opportunities) of reading books to and for students against the benefits of ensuring student access to the ideas and language of high-quality texts. The usual compromise is to retain the read-alouds for whole-class discussions but then to make sure that a part of each reading period is reserved for independent reading of books that are well within each reader's zone of competence (i.e., his or her instructional level).

Even though we lack definitive studies of the incidence of silent reading in classrooms across the decades, it is probably fair to conclude (from examinations of basal readers, standards, and curriculum guides) that from the 1960s through the early 2000s, silent reading played an important role in U.S. elementary classrooms in one or more of these instantiations:

- As independent text reading in anticipation of a group or whole-class shared or guided reading or discussion

- As a reserved time slot for independent reading, including sustained silent reading and its variations (e.g., DEAR—Drop Everything And Read)
- As the core reading program descending from the IRP approach championed after World War II
- As a free-time activity

With the publication of the National Reading Panel report (NRP; National Institute of Child Health and Human Development [NICHD], 2000), silent reading, at least as a regular classroom activity within the reading class, has met its most serious policy-related and curricular challenge. It is not that the NRP found that silent reading is not important and that it does not improve reading achievement. To the contrary, the panel admits that time spent reading is correlated with achievement gains (as documented by Anderson et al., 1988, for example). It is not even that the NRP concluded that independent silent reading during reading class time was not effective. What the panel actually concluded is that there was not enough credible research to warrant *any* policy conclusion about whether it worked. The meager body of evidence was simply inconclusive. The wholly unwarranted inference that many readers and, more important, many policymakers drew is that the practice of allocating class time to independent reading should cease and be replaced with instruction in various aspects of reading. If teachers want students to read more, the conclusions suggested, let them assign reading as homework. This is precisely the conclusion drawn by the authors of the popular, abridged version of the NRP report (Armbruster, Lehr, & Osborn, 2001).

This debate spawned by such interpretations of the NRP report (NICHD, 2000) played itself out in the pages of the International Reading Association's (IRA) newspaper, *Reading Today*, in 2006. Shanahan (2006), then IRA president and a member of the NRP, in trying to explain what the NRP really said, reiterated the idea that he was not suggesting that students should not read silently, only that the lack of credible evidence to support the practice of allocating class time for silent reading could result in a loss of crucial instructional time for other important reading skills and practices. Shaw (2006) and Krashen (2006), both proponents of independent silent reading in school, invoke Stanovich's (1986) Matthew effect concept to make an equity argument for silent reading in school—that it provides an opportunity for students, particularly poor students, to close the gap that divides them from rich students who have more silent reading opportunities at home.

A problem arises in sorting out the evidence from the rhetoric in this debate— research methodology and the press for basic decoding skills easily get confounded with the evidence about the effectiveness of independent silent reading. Those who advocate for less silent reading also happen to favor experimental paradigms and believe that phonics is important, thus permitting the inference that phonics will replace real reading. This confusion leaves us with little hope that the debate will be easily settled without some new evidence on the efficacy of silent reading as a school-based practice.

In this regard, there is hope in the middle. Some educators have argued on the basis of both research and best practice for some sort of balance; they would promote independent silent reading in school with student scaffolding and accountability measures built into the programs (Armbruster & Wilkinson, 1991; Reutzel, Fawson, & Smith, 2008). The Reutzel et al. (2008) study is interesting because it compares the guided oral reading practice that was championed in the NRP report with what they called scaffolded silent reading (i.e., lots of teacher guidance and monitoring), finding that the scaffolded approach was every bit as effective as the guided oral approach on a range of outcome measures. Such a finding necessarily softens, perhaps compromises, the common inference from the NRP report that silent reading has no place in the classroom.

Conclusions About Silent Reading as a Cultural and Pedagogical Practice

In taking an ecological stance in our historical journey, one that looks at broader cultural and social forces as well as at educational movements to understand silent reading, we have woven together strands of influence outside education—social norms, political events, economic factors, and literacy technologies that emerged over time in the larger society. We think technology, access, and social norms and goals are the key influences. Reading modes have always been influenced by technology. Nowadays we disparage (or champion) the computer, but surely each technology—the printing press, standardized spelling, the codex book form, punctuation, word spacing, or letters—had its proponents and opponents in its day. Reading modes have been similarly (perhaps even more greatly) influenced by access—the availability of books, time to read, and the skill to read without arduous effort. Reading modes have also been shaped by social norms and goals: When reading was a performance to be admired in social settings (the idea of powerful elocution on the way to speechifying), when the clergy discouraged idiosyncratic interpretation, even when classroom control was paramount in a classroom teacher's or Sunday school teacher's mind, oral reading dominated. When the communication of information and the transfer of technology were more important or when the needs and interests of the individual prevailed over those of the community, silent reading was preferred (Dooley, 1996).

We have neither the data nor the analytic tools required to pursue the issue, but we have always wondered whether there was a hidden agenda in the recurring "back to basics" movements. They always put an emphasis on lower level decoding skills, which means monitoring reading for accuracy, primarily at the word level. Could there be a subtext: In monitoring whether students say the words accurately, are we also monitoring to determine whether the students got the facts and nothing but the facts? It is an interesting hypothesis—one which is completely consistent with the motives of the clergy during periods of emphasis on oral reading in ecclesiastical settings—but one that others will have to pursue.

We can look back to elaborate on a past with multiple courses of change and use that perspective to ask questions about the courses of the future of reading pedagogy, especially in regard to finding a balanced approach (Pearson, 2000) to silent reading instruction. Balance (in the ecological sense of the balance of nature metaphor, for example) implies attention to factors affecting the instructional decisions involved in implementing oral reading and silent reading practices in the classroom, for both younger and older readers. It requires attention to issues of physical access to texts for all children, in and out of school, as well as to the provision of intellectual accountability to ensure both opportunity and achievement. A historical perspective on silent reading allows us to see the streams of language, text, technology, and practice that shape what we have done and are likely to do in the future. Perhaps the result will be an increasing pedagogical emphasis on practices that help students develop ever-greater competency to read and think by and for themselves.

QUESTIONS FOR PROFESSIONAL DEVELOPMENT

1. How has technology affected the prevalence of silent reading over time?
2. How has oral reading as a social practice related to instructional practices?
3. Would you use the 2000 National Reading Panel report to support or reject silent reading instruction in your classroom? Why?
4. Based on your reading of this chapter (and other chapters in this book, if you have already read them), which silent reading practices would you implement in your classroom or school?

NOTE

The authors of this chapter consider their contributions to be equal.

REFERENCES

Allington, R.L. (1977). If they don't read much, how they ever gonna get good? *Journal of Reading*, 21(1), 57–61. doi:10.1598/JAAL.21.1.10

Allington, R.L. (1984). Oral reading. In P.D. Pearson, R. Barr, M.L. Kamil, & P.B. Mosenthal (Eds.), *Handbook of reading research* (pp. 829–864). Mahwah, NJ: Erlbaum.

Allington, R.L. (2001). *What really matters for struggling readers: Designing research-based programs*. New York: Longman.

Anderson, R.C., Wilson, P.T., & Fielding, L.G. (1988). Growth in reading and how children spend their time outside of school. *Reading Research Quarterly*, 23(3), 285–303. doi:10.1598/RRQ.23.3.2

Armbruster, B.B., Lehr, F., & Osborn, J. (2001). *Put reading first: The research building blocks for teaching children to read*. Washington, DC: National Institute for Literacy.

Armbruster, B.B., & Wilkinson, I.A.G. (1991). Silent reading, oral reading, and learning from text (reading to learn). *The Reading Teacher, 45*(2), 154–155.

Asselin, M., & Doiron, R. (2008, March 26). *Towards a transformative pedagogy for school libraries 2.0.* Paper presented at the American Educational Research Association, New York, NY.

Atwell, N. (1987). *In the middle: Writing, reading, and learning with adolescents.* Portsmouth, NH: Heinemann.

Atwell, N. (1998). *In the middle: New understandings about writing, reading, and learning* (2nd ed.). Portsmouth, NH: Heinemann.

Bennett, S. (2003). *Libraries designed for learning.* Washington, DC: Council on Library and Information Resources.

Birkerts, S. (1996). Reading in the electronic era. *LOGOS, 7*(3), 211–215.

Bond, G.L., & Dykstra, R. (1967). The cooperative research program in first-grade reading instruction. *Reading Research Quarterly, 2*(4), 5–142. doi:10.2307/746948

Buswell, G.T. (1947). The subvocalization factor in the improvement of reading. *The Elementary School Journal, 48*(4), 190–196. doi:10.1086/458926

Chall, J.S. (1967). *Learning to read: The great debate.* New York: McGraw-Hill.

Cole, J.Y. (1993). *Jefferson's legacy: A brief history of the Library of Congress.* Washington, DC: Library of Congress.

Daniels, H. (1994). *Literature circles: Voice and choice in the student-centered classroom.* York, ME: Stenhouse.

Dooley, C. (1996). Approaches to individualized reading: A child-centered historical perspective. *Reading Psychology, 17*(3), 193–227. doi:10.1080/0270271960170301

Dresang, E.T. (1999). *Radical change: Books for youth in a digital age.* New York: H.W. Wilson.

Duke, N.K. (2000). 3.6 minutes per day: The scarcity of informational texts in first grade. *Reading Research Quarterly, 35*(2), 202–224.

English, J.F. (2005). *The economy of prestige: Prizes, awards, and the circulation of cultural value.* Cambridge, MA: Harvard University Press.

Fabos, B. (2004). *Wrong turn on the information superhighway: Education and the commercialization of the Internet.* New York: Teachers College Press.

Garrison, L.D. (1979). *Apostles of culture: The public librarian and American society, 1876–1920.* Madison: University of Wisconsin Press.

Gray, W.S. (1924). The importance of intelligent silent reading. *The Elementary School Journal, 24*(5), 348–356. doi:10.1086/455529

Gray, W.S., Artley, A.S., & Arbuthnot, M.H. (1952). *The new friends and neighbors.* Chicago: Scott Foresman.

Guthrie, J.T., & Wigfield, A. (2000). Engagement and motivation in reading. In M.L. Kamil, P.B. Mosenthal, P.D. Pearson, & R. Barr (Eds.), *Handbook of reading research* (Vol. 3, pp. 403–422). Mahwah, NJ: Erlbaum.

Hall, G.S. (1908). Children's reading: As a factor in their education. *Library Journal, 33*(4), 123–128.

Hoffman, J.V. (1987). Rethinking the role of oral reading in basal instruction. *The Elementary School Journal, 87*(3), 367–373. doi:10.1086/461501

Holmes, B.C. (1985). The effect of four different modes of reading on comprehension. *Reading Research Quarterly, 20*(5), 575–585. doi:10.2307/747944

Huey, E.B. (1898). Preliminary experiments in the physiology and psychology of reading. *American Journal of Psychology, 9*(4), 575–586.

Huey, E.B. (1968). *The psychology and pedagogy of reading.* Cambridge, MA: MIT Press. (Original work published 1908)

Hunt, L.C. Jr., (Ed.). (1967, May). *The individualized reading program: A guide for classroom teaching.* Proceedings of the 11th annual convention of the International Reading Association, Dallas, TX.

Ivey, G., & Broaddus, K. (2001). "Just plain reading": A survey of what makes students want to read in middle school classrooms. *Reading Research Quarterly, 36*(4), 350–377. doi:10.1598/RRQ.36.4.2

Juel, C., & Holmes, B. (1981). Oral and silent reading of sentences. *Reading Research Quarterly, 16*(4), 545–568. doi:10.2307/747315

Karp, M. (1943). Silent before oral reading. *The Elementary School Journal, 44*(2), 102–104. doi:10.1086/458260

Kearney, C.A. (2000). *Curriculum partner: Redefining the role of the library media specialist.* Westport, CT: Greenwood.

Kern, R. (2006). *Literacy, technology, and language learning: Where we've been and where we're headed.* Paper presented at the DigitalStream conference at California State University, Monterey Bay. Retrieved April 14, 2010, from

php.csumb.edu/wlc/ojs/index.php/ds/issue/
view/2

Kim, P. (2002). The rise and fall of individually guided education, 1969–1979. Paper presented at the annual meeting of the American Educational Research Association, New Orleans, LA.

Klausmeier, H.J. (1972). *Individually guided education: An alternative system of education.* New Haven, CT: Center for the Study of Education, Yale University.

Krashen, S. (1993). *The power of reading: Insights from the research.* Englewood, CO: Libraries Unlimited.

Krashen, S. (2006, August/September). SSR is a very good idea: A response to Shanahan. *Reading Today, 24*(1), 16.

Lankes, R.D., Silverstein, J., & Nicholson, S. (2006). *Participatory networks: The library as conversation.* Chicago: American Library Association.

Manguel, A. (1996). *A history of reading.* New York: Viking.

Mathews, M.M. (1966). *Teaching to read: Historically considered.* Chicago: University of Chicago Press.

McCallum, R.S., Sharp, S., Bell, S.M., & George, T. (2004). Silent versus oral reading comprehension and efficiency. *Psychology in the Schools, 41*(2), 241–246. doi:10.1002/pits.10152

McCarthey, S.J., Hoffman, J.V., Christian, C., Corman, L., Elliott, B., Matherne, D., et al. (1994). Engaging the new basal readers. *Literacy Research and Instruction, 33*(3), 233–256.

McCracken, R.A. (1971). Initiating sustained silent reading. *Journal of Reading, 14*(8), 521–524, 582–583.

McDade, J.E. (1937). A hypothesis for non-oral reading: Argument, experiment, and results. *Journal of Educational Research, 30*(7), 489–503.

McDade, J.E. (1944). Examination of a recent criticism of non-oral beginning reading. *The Elementary School Journal, 44*(6), 343–351

McMahon, S.I., & Raphael, T.E. (1997). *The book club connection: Literacy learning and classroom talk.* New York: Teachers College Press.

Mead, C.D. (1915). Silent versus oral reading with one hundred sixth-grade children. *Journal of Educational Psychology, 6*(6), 345–348. doi:10.1037/h0071709

Mead, C.D. (1917). Results in silent versus oral reading. *Journal of Educational Psychology, 8*(6), 367–368. doi:10.1037/h0067774

Michie, J.S., & Holton, B.A. (2005). *Fifty years of supporting children's learning: A history of public school libraries and federal legislation from 1953–2000* (NCES 2005-311). Washington, DC: National Center for Education Statistics.

Monaghan, E.J. (2005). *Learning to read and write in colonial America.* Amherst: University of Massachusetts Press.

Nagy, W.E., Herman, P.A., & Anderson, R.C. (1985). Learning words from context. *Reading Research Quarterly, 20*(2), 233–253. doi:10.2307/747758

National Institute of Child Health and Human Development. (2000). *Report of the National Reading Panel. Teaching children to read: An evidence-based assessment of the scientific research literature on reading and its implications for reading instruction* (NIH Publication No. 00-4769). Washington, DC: U.S. Government Printing Office.

Neuman, S.B., & Celano, D. (2001). Access to print in low-income and middle-income communities: An ecological study of four neighborhoods. *Reading Research Quarterly, 36*(1), 8–26. doi:10.1598/RRQ.36.1.1

Olson, D.R. (1994). *The world on paper: The conceptual and cognitive implications of writing and reading.* Cambridge: Cambridge University Press.

Olson, W.C. (1952). Seeking, self-selection, and pacing in the use of books by children. *The Packet, 7*(1), 3–10.

Pang, A.S. (2003). *Word spacing, silent reading, and cyborgs.* Retrieved June 18, 2003, from askpang.typepad.com/relevant_history/2003/06/word_spacing_si.html

Pearson, P.D. (1989). Reading the whole-language movement. *The Elementary School Journal, 90*(2), 230–241. doi:10.1086/461615

Pearson, P.D. (2000). Reading in the twentieth century. In T.L. Good (Ed.), *American education: Yesterday, today, and tomorrow: Yearbook of the National Society for the Study of Education* (pp. 152–208). Chicago: University of Chicago Press.

Pearson, P.D. (2002). American reading instruction since 1967. In N.B. Smith (Ed.), *American reading instruction* (pp. 419–486). Newark, DE: International Reading Association.

Pearson, P.D. (2004). The reading wars. *Educational Policy, 18*(1), 216–252.

Pearson, P.D., & Hamm, D.N. (2005). The assessment of reading comprehension: A review of practices—past, present, and future. In S.G. Paris & S.A. Stahl (Eds.), *Children's reading comprehension and assessment* (pp. 13–69). Mahwah, NJ: Erlbaum.

Printner, R., & Gilliland, A.R. (1916). Oral and silent reading. *Journal of Educational Psychology, 7*(4), 201–212. doi:10.1037/h0072173

Reutzel, D.R., Fawson, P.C., & Smith, J.A. (2008). Reconsidering silent sustained reading: An exploratory study of scaffolded silent reading. *The Journal of Educational Research, 102*(1), 37–50. doi:10.3200/JOER.102.1.37-50

Rideout, V.J., Foehr, U.G., & Roberts, D.F. (2010). *Generation M²: Media in the lives of 8- to 18-year-olds.* Menlo Park, CA: Kaiser Family Foundation.

Roberts, R.L. (2007). The evolving landscape of the learning commons. *Library Review, 56*(9), 803–810. doi:10.1108/00242530710831257

Saenger, P. (1982). Silent reading: Its impact on late medieval script and society. *Viator: Medieval and Renaissance Studies, 13*, 367–414.

Shanahan, T. (2006, June/July). Does he really think kids shouldn't read? *Reading Today, 23*(6), 12.

Shaw, M.L. (2006, August/September). Sustained silent reading: Another view. *Reading Today, 24*(1), 16.

Smith, C., Constantino, R., & Krashen, S. (1997). Differences in print environment for children in Beverly Hills, Compton and Watts. *Emergency Librarian, 24*(4), 8–9.

Smith, N.B. (2002). *American reading instruction.* Newark, DE: International Reading Association. (Original work published 1966)

Stanovich, K.E. (1986). Matthew effects in reading: Some consequences of individual differences in the acquisition of literacy. *Reading Research Quarterly, 21*(4), 360–407. doi:10.1598/RRQ.21.4.1

Taylor, B.M., Frye, B.J., & Maruyama, G.M. (1990). Time spent reading and reading growth. *American Educational Research Journal, 27*(2), 351–362.

Thorndike, E.L. (1917). Reading as reasoning: A study of mistakes in paragraph reading. *Journal of Educational Psychology, 8*(6), 323–332. doi:10.1037/h0075325

Venezky, R.L. (1991). The development of literacy in the industrialized nations of the west. In R. Barr, M.L. Kamil, P.B. Mosenthal, & P.D. Pearson (Eds.), *Handbook of reading research* (Vol. 2, pp. 46–67). New York: Longman.

Wade, S.E., & Moje, E.B. (2000). The role of text in classroom learning. In M.L. Kamil, P.B. Mosenthal, P.D. Pearson, & R. Barr (Eds.), *Handbook of reading research* (Volume 3, pp. 609–627). Mahwah, NJ: Erlbaum.

Weinberger, D. (2007). *Everything is miscellaneous: The power of the new digital disorder.* New York: Henry Holt.

Worthy, J. (1996). Removing barriers to voluntary reading for reluctant readers: The role of school and classroom libraries. *Language Arts, 73*(7), 483–492.

CHAPTER 2

Eye Movements Make Reading Possible

S. Jay Samuels
University of Minnesota Twin Cities

Elfrieda H. Hiebert
University of California, Berkeley

Timothy V. Rasinski
Kent State University, Ohio

The ability to read and understand printed words represents a remarkable human accomplishment. Although the ability to communicate through the spoken word seems to have been genetically hardwired into our species over the eons of time it has taken our species to develop (an estimated 5–8 million years), the skill of reading has been with us only for about 7,000 years. Because of the huge time differences between the development of language by ear versus language by eye, there appears to be some design flaws in the human eye that must be overcome before reading can occur. In essence, as remarkable an instrument as is the human eye, it is not ideally constructed for reading. An argument that we make in this chapter is that without eye movements, reading alphabetic texts would not be possible.

A century ago, the study of eye movements was one of the hottest topics in reading psychology. In the classic volume *The Psychology and Pedagogy of Reading*, Huey (1908/1968) devotes two chapters to eye movements. Despite this auspicious start, it is not the hot topic in reading that it once was, as evidenced in Cassidy and Cassidy's (2009) "What's Hot for 2009" survey in the United States. In this list, ocular-motor eye movement is not listed as a topic to be rated by the experts. Because of the critical role that eye movements play in the reading process, the topic should be of interest to educational leaders at all levels who desire to see improvements in reading achievement. This chapter on eye movements in reading should prove to be useful to educators in understanding how some reading problems that beginning readers encounter can be traced to faulty but correctable eye movements. When students' eye movements become more accurate and effective, schools can anticipate gains in reading achievement (Gelzer & Santore, 1968).

When reading scholars were asked to explain why eye movements are not hot today, responses indicated a perception of eye movements as purely mechanical,

Revisiting Silent Reading: New Directions for Teachers and Researchers, edited by Elfrieda H. Hiebert and D. Ray Reutzel. © 2010 by the International Reading Association.

unrelated to cognitive or social processes. It is true that eye movements seem purely mechanical when the reading process is going well. Eye movements, however, are influenced by cognitive factors, such as the need to locate information of personal interest or to reread a portion of the text to do a comprehension check (Just & Carpenter, 1980). These cognitive factors influence the duration of eye fixations and where the eye searches for information in texts.

Kaakinen and Hyönä (2008) examine how eye movements mirror the ongoing cognitive processing in which readers engage. In their study, half of the readers were told to read a passage about a house from the point of view of a burglar, while the other half were told to take the perspective of an interior designer. Both groups wore eye-tracking apparatus that indicated which parts of the text received attention and the duration of eye fixations. Those who read from a burglar's point of view had greater gaze duration time on words that dealt with how one might burglarize a house, while those who read from an interior designer's point of view spent more time on words that dealt with what made the house attractive.

In a similar study (Sipel & van den Broek, 2009) where the emphasis was on text comprehension, college students read a text that contained recently learned rare words, common words, and unknown words. Eye tracking revealed that students spent more time fixating on unlearned rare words than on recently learned rare words. The extra duration of eye fixations on the rare, unlearned words may also reflect greater cognitive emphasis on decoding and meaning generation of the rare, unlearned words. These studies strongly suggest that eye movements and gaze duration, rather than being purely mechanical and immutable, seem to be under the cognitive control of readers and influenced by factors such as personal interests and purpose for reading.

Numerous scholars have attempted to explain how reading is made possible. Given the number of different models of the reading process (see Ruddell & Unrau, 2004), one may rightfully wonder if we need yet another description of the reading process. The answer to this question may be found in the brilliant poem entitled "The Blind Men and the Elephant" (Saxe, 1873). In the poem, each of six blind men described the elephant from his perspective. Saxe claims that each blind man was partly in the right, though all were in the wrong. Like the blind men, each model of the reading process in the research literature on reading describes only a part of this complicated miracle called reading, and more information is needed to fill in the missing parts in the reading mosaic.

As remarkable as the human information processing system is, there are areas that can be considered to be design flaws insofar as reading is concerned. In essence, the eye was not designed for reading. In this chapter, we explain how eye movements and selective attention represent ways in which human beings overcame the information processing design flaws in the human eye. Furthermore, as we reviewed a considerable body of eye movement research, we became aware that most of it has been done using a convenience sample of adults. Keith Rayner (personal communication, May 10, 2009), one of the leading researchers in the field of eye movements, agrees that it is important that researchers learn more about the eye movements of beginning readers, especially young children. When, in the past, information that was derived from adults was used either to understand beginning reading or to justify the methods used in beginning reading instruction, it led to serious and regrettable consequences. Keeping this admonition in mind, we describe how ocular-motor eye movements make reading possible and, in fact, overcome some of the bottlenecks that are part of our human information processing system. To accomplish this goal, we begin by indicating how Javal's (1879) discovery set the stage for research on eye movements. Then we describe the physiology of the eye and the eye movements that enable reading to occur. In the final section, we suggest implications that can lead to enhanced reading achievement in classrooms.

Discovery of Eye Movements

More than a century ago, it was a commonly held belief that the eye uninterruptedly and smoothly took in information as it swept along a line of print or when looking at a scene outdoors. Contradicting this common belief, Javal (1879) found that the eye seemed to jump from spot to spot and then paused during reading. He concluded correctly that the eye took in information only when it paused. He called these ocular-motor eye movements saccades. Dodge (1900) supported Javal's conclusions indicating that when the eye movements were unbroken the observer was unable to tell what had been exposed. In fact, before an eye movement occurs, vision is suppressed to prevent the reader from seeing the blur that occurs during a saccade (Latour, 1962).

Whether the content is print or the view out of a window, eye movements occur in what Hochberg (1970) describes as installments. There are three types of ocular-motor eye movements that occur during reading:

1. Fixations—when the eye pauses momentarily on a line of print to take in information or integrate information across fixation pauses.
2. Forward saccades—when reading English script the eye seems to jump from left to right on a line of print to bring the eye to the next fixation pause.
3. Regressions and rereadings—where eye movements occur backward from right to left.

Generally, regressions go back about one word, whereas rereading allows the eye to reexamine a previously fixated portion of the text. If the saccade extends back several words, we identify this as a rereading saccade, not a regression. In rereading, a student moves quite a few words back to a prior section of a line and then proceeds in a usual manner to reread from that point forward as a comprehension check.

Human Eye Physiology

As depicted in Figure 2.1, the human eye contains three major parts. The first part is the cornea, located in the front of the eye. It acts like a window and allows light waves reflected from visual images on the printed page to pass through so they can settle upon the retina, which is located at the back of the eye. The second part is the retina, which primarily consists of two kinds of receptor cells: rods and cones. Some of these are sensitive to letter and word shape. The third part consists of a collection of communication wires called the optic nerve that carry information from the retina to the visual perceptions areas of the human brain.

The cornea of the eye contains a hole called the pupil through which visual information from the page passes through on its way to the retina. Surrounding the pupil is the colored portion called the iris, which contains muscles that alter the size of the opening of the pupil. Under dim light, the opening of the pupil is larger to admit more light and, under bright light, the opening is smaller to admit less light. Located directly behind the pupil is the lens that has the function of focusing the visual images from the page as sharply as possible on the retina. The retina contains cells that function like the film in a camera. These retinal cells are sensitive to particular bands of light wavelengths (i.e., red, blue, green) and fire only when the right wavelength causes the rhodopsin—a pigment in the retina— to react. The mosaic, or pixel-like, electrochemical impulses are sent to the brain via the optic nerve, where they are reconstructed to make an image. Some specialized parts of the brain, in turn, control the ocular-motor eye movements that we discuss shortly.

Figure 2.1. The Human Eye

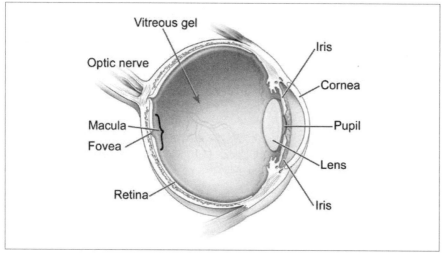

Graphic from National Eye Institute, National Institutes of Health.

A key idea in this chapter is that the human eye is not ideally designed for reading. Although the eyes are designed to move to perceive things, the typical perception pattern of a visual image differs from that of a line of print. Consequently, the eyes need to learn to make particular kinds of movements if proficient reading is to occur. Imagine that you are trying to identify the person who is standing in front of you. As you look at this person, all that is in focus is the person's nose and eyes. The rest is fuzzy, but you can detect shape. You rapidly shift your points of focus to other parts, so that in time the various parts of the individual are in focus. The difficulty in determining the identity of this person is somewhat similar to the problem of recognizing words when reading a text.

The problem with the eye when reading is that at any given moment only a tiny amount of printed material from a page is in enough focus to enable easy reading. Consequently, rapid eye movements are required to bring different parts of a text onto that tiny area on the retina that can see the letters and words clearly—the fovea. The retina of the eye contains two kinds of cells, rods and cones. Both kinds are important and have different reading functions. Cone cells provide the visual acuity that enables readers to see letters and words clearly. A major design flaw of the eye in regards to reading is that the cone cells that enable the reader to see letters most clearly are not evenly distributed across the retina but are concentrated in a tiny area called the fovea. There are about 10 million cone cells packed into the fovea of each eye where vision is most acute—where the reader can identify letters and words with precision. Because of the fovea's location in the middle of the retina, print has to be front and center and not off to the side.

Further, the parafoveal region surrounding the fovea also plays a critical role in reading. The parafovea contains the rod cells that are sensitive to word shape and word length. Information received in the periphery of the eye helps guide the eye to its next fixation destination (Rayner & Sereno, 1994). The spaces surrounding words are important clues as to word boundaries and length, and this information is used by peripheral vision to plan the distance the eye should jump with each saccade. In essence, the rod cells are part of the eye's guidance system.

Because the area of cone cell concentration is small, the number of letters that can be in focus within a single eye fixation is limited. We contacted two leaders in the field of eye movement research to get information on how many letters can be perceived by the fovea at any given time. Keith Rayner (personal communication, May 10, 2009) stated,

The number of letters falling in the fovea depends on letter size and viewing angle. In general, 3–4 letters usually occupy 1 degree of visual angle. Because the fovea is about 2 degrees, it would be 6–8 letters in the fovea.

The second expert, George McConkie (personal communication, May 10, 2009) stated,

The foveal region is the area where...visibility of letters drops off pretty fast as they move outward from the center of vision. Thus, the problem in answering this question is setting a "clarity" criterion. I suppose that a criterion might be even the most similar letters such as *v* and *u* or *o* and *c* can be distinguished at this distance.... What Keith and I were after in our original studies was to determine the region within which letter distinctions make a difference. We found this to be about four letters to the left and eight to the right of the directly fixated letter. The greater distance on the right is probably (there is some supportive evidence) an attentional factor rather than retinal resolution differences to left and right.

Legge et al.'s (2007) research suggests that only six or seven letters surrounding the fixation point on the fovea can be identified with 80% accuracy and, as the eye moves farther away from the fixation point, accuracy of identification decreases more. For example, within four letter spaces to the left of the fixation point, or eight letter spaces to the right of the fixation point, accuracy of identification drops to about 60%. In summary, the evidence from the experts is that the size of the perceptual span from which letters can be seen with accuracy and clarity falls in a range of six to eight letters. It also appears that the shape of the window is asymmetrical, with fewer letters in focus to the left of fixation and more letters in focus to the right of fixation. It is also commonly acknowledged that there is a rapid drop-off of acuity from the point of visual focus that makes word recognition difficult (Feinberg, 1949).

The experts make a good point when they say that there is no hard and fast rule about the number of letters that are in focus on the fovea. The number of letters in focus is a function of letter size and the distance at which they are being viewed. However, the experts agree that the number of letters in focus is not large. Thus, one bottleneck in the reading process is that only a small portion of the text on a line can be clearly identified. Other letters that fall to the right and left of the fovea experience a steady and rapid decline in clarity. One way to overcome this rapid loss of clarity is to shift focus through eye movements so that different parts of words that are not clear come into focus on the next eye movement. The problem of attempting to shift focus so that the desired part of the text is in focus on the fovea is somewhat analogous to the problem facing hunters who try to keep a moving target within the cross hairs of a riflescope. It is a difficult task, because eye movements make it easy to overshoot or undershoot and miss the target. Rod cells shift to the next eye fixation so that different parts of a text are in focus (Smith, 1971). While the cone cells aid in identifying letters and words, the rod cells help the brain plan the trajectory of how far to move the point of focus for each new eye fixation. In addition, when words are printed in lowercase letters, the words take on skyline and shape characteristics, and the rod cells are capable of picking up word shape information (Lee, Legge, & Ortiz, 2003).

The span of apprehension refers to the number of letters the eye can see in a single fixation. One might think that the span would be symmetrical around the fixation point, but this seems not to be the case. Instead, the span is asymmetrical with more letters recognizable to the right of fixation for those reading in English, whereas the span of apprehension is greater to the left of the fixation point for those reading in Hebrew or Arabic. These asymmetrical differences in the span of apprehension reflect how text is written and processed in each of the languages (e.g., English from left to right and Hebrew and Arabic from right to left). The span, then, is attention driven or learned rather than the result of a fixed pattern (Hebb, 1930). Moreover, if the words to be recognized are low frequency and unfamiliar to the reader, the span of apprehension is smaller than if the words are familiar high-frequency words (Rayner, 1998).

Eye Physiology and Cognitive Psychology

The eye has additional properties that are relevant to the reading process. Sperling's (1960) research convinced skeptical psychologists that the eye has a memory, or what has come to be called iconic memory. This memory buffer can be viewed in terms of four characteristics: (1) speed of input, (2) speed of output, (3) capacity, and (4) longevity. Speed of input and output refers to how fast the images in the visual field can be placed on the retina and how fast the images can be retrieved when needed. The capacity of the eye to take in the visual scene is huge and includes everything in a circular visual field. As Sperling's research indicates, however, the longevity of the image that is placed on the retina is short. The typical image lasts only for one or two seconds at most, and then the image is gone. Although the longevity of the word's image on the fovea is short, the reader can overcome this problem by fixating the same word several times. When this is done, image two can function as an erasing image and the second image can obliterate image one (Gilbert, 1953). With each repeated fixation of the same word, additional decoding occurs and the process is repeated until the word is recognized.

Because the capacity to take in information from the visual field is so huge, it presents a processing problem. The human brain can process only a limited amount of information in a short amount of time. In a single eye fixation, there is more information than the brain can handle. Consequently, the brain filters the unwanted information and focuses on what it needs. For example, when viewing a scene outside, the view is circular. In reading, however, the reader does not want circular information from the visual field because he or she would then be getting information from lines of print that are located above and below the line on which he or she is focusing. If the reader were aware of the information on lines of print above and below the fixation point, it would lead to confusion. Thus, the eye needs to filter out information above and below the line that is being processed (Willows, 1974).

Selective Attention

The mechanism the brain uses to filter out the unwanted information is selective attention (McConkie & Rayner, 1976; Posner, 1980). Selective attention is an internal mechanism that filters out of the visual field that which is not important, and by doing so it also allows the reader to focus attention on the areas that are important (LaBerge & Samuels, 1974). To illustrate the nature of selective attention, researchers have created laboratory analogs to what has been described as the "cocktail party phenomenon"—where an individual engaging in a conversation continues to maintain eye contact with another person even when he or she has switched his or her internal cognitive attention to an adjunct conversation. Even though the person is essentially filtering out the immediate conversation to attend to the adjunct one, there is no observable change in body position or receptors such as eyes or ears.

Evidence that the eye has a memory buffer that enables selective attention came from Sperling (1960). The experiment involved flashing 12 numbers on a screen in three rows of four numbers, one each at the bottom, middle, and top of the screen. As the 12 numbers disappeared from the screen, they were followed by a tone (e.g., high, middle, low) that signaled at which level the numbers were to be read back. This task is difficult on several levels. First, the number of numbers—12—exceeds the capacity of short-term memory, so they cannot be memorized. Second, subjects needed to read back the numbers even though they were no longer on the screen. Third, they needed to provide the tones that came after the visual image had disappeared. To succeed at this task, subjects had to do an internal scan using selective attention and read the numbers off their visual memory buffer. Subjects were successful with this task before the visual image disappeared from memory.

Several characteristics of selective attention allow it to be a useful companion to eye movements and reading. One feature is filtering out unwanted information, such as text above and below the line the reader is on. Although it is true that only about 6–8 letters that fall across the fovea can be seen clearly, surrounding letters can be discerned. Without resorting to another eye movement, the reader can do an internal attentional scan to read the other letters of interest. If, however, the letters cannot be identified, another eye movement is required. For readers who are not yet at the point where the entire word has become the unit of word recognition, selective attention allows them to attend to parts of words as they decode them (LaBerge & Samuels, 1974). Selective attention also allows readers to switch attention—whether on parts of a word or the entire word, on decoding and then on comprehension, or on the letters in focus and then on word shape in the periphery. Attention switching is fast, under cognitive control, and can be automatic or controlled (Shiffrin & Schneider, 1977).

Visual Unit of Word Recognition

If the processing problems created by the fact that only 6–8 letters strung across the fovea are seen with acuity were not enough, there is an additional problem that strikes hard on the beginning reader and less so on the skilled reader. This problem relates to the size of the visual unit used in word recognition. Cattell (1947), using a convenience sample of German graduate students, concludes that the unit of word recognition was the word. Gough (1971), on the other hand, concludes that the unit of word recognition was the letter, and each subsequent letter in a word added approximately 50 milliseconds (ms) to how long it took to recognize it. To determine which researcher was correct with regard to the size of the visual unit used in word recognition, the first author and colleagues (Samuels, LaBerge, & Bremer, 1978) devised an experiment in which words were shown on a computer screen. If the word on the screen was an animal word, the student pressed a handheld button, and the computer measured latency of response (i.e., reaction time) and accuracy. The animal words were all controlled for word frequency, and there were three-, four-, five-, and six-letter words.

The rationale for the study was simple. If Gough (1971) was correct and the unit of recognition was the letter, then the longer animal words should take more time to recognize, but if Cattell (1947) was correct, there should have been no difference in processing time related to word length because a chunk is a chunk and a word is a word. In our study, we had subjects from second, fourth, and sixth grades and college. Our results were fascinating, because Cattell and Gough were each correct, but for different age groups. The beginning readers were processing words letter by letter as Gough had predicted and longer words were taking them more time to process, while the sixth graders and the college students were using the whole word as the unit of recognition, supporting Cattell's contention that the unit of recognition was the whole word. For sixth graders and college students, there was no significant difference in processing time related to word length. In other words, they were processing words as entire units, and a chunk is a chunk. Fourth graders in this study showed increases in the size of the unit of word recognition. Their unit of word recognition was larger than the single letter but not yet whole word (Samuels et al., 1978).

There have been several replications of this study, including a significant change in method, and the results are robust and hold up. In fact, the research by Taylor (1971) on the number of eye fixations required to read a 100-word text supports the research findings on the size of the visual unit used in word recognition. By 11th grade, only 96 eye fixations were required, implying that with each eye fixation the unit of recognition was the word. In first grade, however, 224 fixations were required, suggesting that the unit of recognition was smaller than a word. As we have already discussed under selective attention, there is an internal scan mechanism that is used for processing the letters that are on the fovea and letters that extend slightly beyond.

The size of the visual unit used in word recognition is an important factor in eye movement. Imagine how hard it must be for the beginning reader to place the target word on the fovea and then to process a word unit that is smaller than the entire word. To add to the difficulty, the processing must be fast enough that the word fragments put into short-term memory are not lost (Peterson & Peterson, 1959). The student must figure out the meanings of the words that are placed in short-term memory in less than 10 seconds or what was placed there will be lost and the process must be repeated. In addition, the wrong part of the text may fall on the fovea with the fixation pause. Considering some of the processing bottlenecks that have been identified, such as the fact that only about six letters

Table 2.1. Development of Ocular-Motor Skills From 1st Through 12th Grades

Ocular-Motor Skills	1st Grade	12th Grade
Fixations (including regressions per 100 words)	224	96
Regression per 100 words	52	18
Average span of recognition in words	.45	1.06
Average duration of fixation in seconds	.33	.25
Reading rate with comprehension	80	250

are in focus in a single eye fixation, beginning readers may have difficulty with the accuracy of eye movements. Given these problems that must be overcome by beginning readers, it is not surprising that learning to read with skill takes time and practice. Table 2.1 shows the development of ocular-motor skills from first through 12th grades.

The Fixation Pause

Eye fixations in reading are critical because it is during a fixation that the eye takes in information from the printed page and begins to process it for meaning. The duration of the typical fixation pause is about 300 ms, which is about one third of a second (pauses can be as short as 100 ms or as long as 500 ms, which is ⅒ to ½ of a second). It is assumed that during longer fixations considerable cognitive processing is going on, such as attempting to grasp the meaning of a sentence or integrating information across several sentences. While the word *fixation* implies that the eye is motionless, this is not the case. There is a slight eye tremor that serves to activate the neurons in the retina so they will continue firing (Gilbert, 1959). Taking into account the brief amount of time it takes to make a forward saccade in which the eye moves from one fixation pause to the next, in a single second the eye can make approximately three fixations. When viewing a scene or a page of printed material, the typical person seems to be unaware that the information being processed by the brain has been coming in at a rate of three bursts a second and that each burst must be processed rapidly, because the visual image coming with each burst survives for less than a second and then it is lost. If, however, the processing is too slow and the visual image disappears from the retina, all is not lost. The reader can refixate the original image. The term *eye fixation pause* represents the time spent on a single fixation, whereas the term *gaze duration* suggests the total amount of time the reader spends on a word across several eye fixations.

Because of the rapid loss of the visual image from a fixated word or word part, what the reader must do is transform the visual image into its sound representation. For example, when the reader encounters the printed word *cat*, it is transformed into its phonological form /c-a-t/ and then placed in short-term memory.

The advantage gained by transferring visual into phonological information and placing the phonological information in short-term memory is that the shelf life of the acoustic information in short-term memory is about 10 seconds, which is considerably longer than the duration of visual information in iconic memory, which is less than 1 second (Peterson & Peterson, 1959). For the acoustic information that is in short-term memory, 10 seconds is usually sufficient time (in most cases) for skilled readers to complete tasks such as decoding the text, integrating sentence meaning, and finally, moving the information that was temporarily stored in short-term memory into long-term-semantic memory.

Because eye physiology is such that the eye takes in different kinds of information from three areas—foveal, parafoveal, or peripheral—the total span of information is large. Beginning readers have a span of apprehension that is 12 letters to the right and skilled readers have a span of 15 spaces, although we cannot assume that words can be recognized that far out, but word length and shape information is obtained (Ikeda & Saida, 1978; Rayner, 1998). Foveal information enables one to identify words, whereas the parafoveal area provides information about shape and length (Rayner, Well, & Pollatsek, 1986). McConkie and Rayner (1976) have shown that as skill increases the span of recognition increases, but not beyond one or two words.

To the person reading a text or viewing a scene outdoors, the entire operation appears to be seamless. It is the seamless nature of the operation that led to the mistaken belief before Javal's (1879) time that the eye continuously took in information and simultaneously processed it as the eye swept smoothly across a page of print. In terms of transfer of training, it seems as if several of the eye-movement mechanisms used in viewing a scene outdoors are also used in reading a text. The saccade serves as the setup to get the right information in focus. However, information is not taken in while the eye is in motion during a saccade. It is only during the fixation pause that the brain assembles information for processing. The number of fixation pauses per second for viewing a scene outdoors is about the same as for reading a text (Taylor & Robinson, 1963) and comes to about three fixations per second. According to Feinberg (1949), the number of letters that fall on the fovea that can be seen clearly comes to about four or five—the same as the number of letters in a high-frequency word. Thus, if the reader is skilled and the unit of word recognition is the word, he or she should be able to process three words per second and be able to read at a rate of about 180 words a minute with comprehension, which is a little short of the figure that Germane and Germane (1922) report as the silent reading rate for good readers in the eighth grade.

An important question that eye movement researchers have addressed is whether the eyes fixate on each word in a text or skip certain words. It appears that the eye skips certain words, and the words that are skipped are determined in part by word length and skill level. Short words, high-frequency words, and words that can be predicted from context may be skipped (Brysbaert & Vitu, 1998; Paulson & Goodman, 1999).

Gilbert (1940, 1959) notes that oral reading is slower than silent reading. This simple fact poses a problem in many classrooms where round robin reading is practiced. In round robin reading, one student reads orally from a text while the other students follow along reading silently from the same text. However, when a poor reader reads orally, with typical slow reading rate and lack of expression, it forces the better readers who are reading silently into twice as many eye fixations and regressions. Gilbert's concern was that this round robin reading practice was training poor ocular-motor habits in students. Gilbert cautions teachers that this common practice should be discontinued. The practice, however, was deeply entrenched in typical reading instruction.

One reason for the entrenchment of round robin reading in practice is that it provided a means whereby teachers could get a sense of how numerous students were progressing in their reading from day to day. Informal reading inventories, given in a one-to-one setting, might provide more valid information, but they were costly in terms of teachers' time and, consequently, given infrequently (Pikulski & Shanahan, 1982). Deno (1986) provides a viable alternative for monitoring that was not as costly in terms of teachers' time and, as a result, freed up instructional time for other forms of oral reading, such as choral or echo reading or even scaffolded silent reading. Deno's solution was to have students read orally for one minute and to count the number of correct words read in that brief period of time. By keeping a running record on each student's reading rate over a period of time, teachers could determine if there was improvement in rate up to some asymptote. As good as Deno's method is, there is a problem. The problem is that comprehension is not measured, only rate. Despite warnings that meaning should not be sacrificed for the sake of reading rate, some teachers continue to encourage rate and students fail to put attention on meaning. Because of the problems associated with using only reading rate to measure progress, the time has come for researchers to develop a testing method that focuses attention on comprehension as well as reading speed.

As we noted, the typical eye fixation pause lasts for about 300 ms, or about one third of a second. Even a pause this short can be separated into components representing the different processing tasks that must be performed to read with understanding (Abrams & Zuber, 1972). The typical pause comes at the end of an eye movement when the eye has just completed a rapid movement from one spot on a text to the next spot, somewhat like an automobile that comes to an abrupt stop at a stop sign. There is still residual motion that must be halted and stabilized, and in the case of the eye, it must be stabilized so that it can focus on the print.

Figure 2.2 is a simplified rendition of what takes place during an eye fixation of a skilled reader. Essentially, five tasks are performed with each fixation pause. The first task following a saccade is to stabilize the eye. Once the eye is stabilized sufficiently, the next task is to focus the visual images from the page on the fovea of the retina. With the visual image from the page focused on the retina, the third task is to engage in word recognition, or what many call the decoding process— converting the word into its sound representation. If the reader is highly skilled

Figure 2.2. Activities That Occur During a 400 Ms Eye Fixation by a Fluent Reader

←100 ms *stabilize and focus*→←100 ms *word recognition-decoding-200 ms-comprehension* and *plan next saccade*→
←————————————————400 ms a single eye fixation————————————————→

and automatic at word recognition, the task is done quickly and accurately, and it requires a minimal amount of cognitive resources and attention. Although the typical duration of an eye fixation is 0.33 seconds, in many instances it may take longer.

If a person is a skilled reader, the amount of time required for the word recognition process may be only 100 ms, leaving 200 ms for comprehension—the fourth task. In fact, the defining characteristic of fluency is the ability to decode and comprehend in the same eye fixation. For skilled fluent readers, the decoding task is done so quickly and requires so little of the cognitive resources that comprehension can take place at the same time (LaBerge & Samuels, 1974). The final task for the reader is to plan the next saccade (Abrams & Zuber, 1972). For fluent readers, the usual unit of word recognition is the word. A word is defined as a letter or series of letters surrounded by space. Space is a critical cue used by the rod cells in planning the trajectory for the next leap, which is probably the next word. For readers not at the automatic stage of word recognition, there are some important differences in what happens during an eye fixation. First, the word recognition process is usually slower, less accurate, and may use up all of the cognitive resources available at the moment. Thus, during that one eye fixation, the single major accomplishment for nonfluent readers is word recognition. To add to the complexity of word recognition for the nonfluent reader, the unit of word recognition is smaller than the entire word, leaving the student in the position of having to piece together the letter clusters that in combination make up the word. Because only 6–8 letters that are on the fovea are in focus along with some other letters to the right that are not so distinct, the student may resort to selective attention to process the letter cluster. However, once the student has recognized the word, his or her next task is to switch attention to the comprehension process. This constant switching of attention from decoding to comprehension places a heavy load on short-term memory and makes learning to read so much harder for the less skilled reader than for the accomplished reader.

Figure 2.2 is an important visual because it strikes at the heart of the debate on what is reading fluency. This visual shows that, within an eye fixation, skilled readers can decode and comprehend what is in the text. Unfortunately, beginning readers cannot do both tasks simultaneously. They first decode the text, and then they try to comprehend what they have decoded. The products of the dual process are stored briefly in short-term memory, but the decoding and comprehension tasks must be completed within 10 seconds of that memory system or what was briefly stored is lost. If beginning readers lose what was stored, they repeat the process. The second attempt is faster because of the previous encounter with the text.

During an eye fixation, exactly what part of the word the eye is focused on is important if the reader wants to infer the word using only partial information. Different parts of a word vary in the amount of information they provide the reader. Broerse and Zwaan (1966) found that not all parts of a word are equally informative for purposes of word recognition. They found that it is the beginning part that carries the most information for purposes of word recognition. For example, if the reader has already identified the following context "Father was cutting the green...," and the letter string on the fovea for the next eye fixation contains the following "gr_ _ _," it is an easy task to infer that the next word is *grass*. Paulson and Goodman (1999) believe that under certain conditions the reader may skip words in a text and, if context is strong enough, use partial information to infer the word. However, Taylor (1971) is of the opinion that typically the reader does not try to infer a word from its parts. Despite this claim, Paulson and Goodman report there are times when words are inferred and recognized through their parts. In planning an eye movement, the preferred location for a fixation is halfway between the beginning and middle of a word (McConkie, Kerr, Reddix, & Zola, 1988) because, given the span of apprehension, and the typical length of common words, the highly informative beginning of a word would be on the fovea.

An important question about the role of eye fixations in reading is how much information is taken in and processed with each fixation pause. The answer is that the eye provides the brain with information from three areas, the foveal, parafoveal, and the peripheral. Of the three, the foveal area is most important because it is here that the letters are in focus. The foveal area extends 2 degrees of visual angle for a maximum of 8 letter spaces asymmetrically distributed around the point of focus, with fewer letters in focus to the left of fixation and more to the right (McConkie & Rayner, 1976), but, as Feinberg (1949) has noted, beyond 4–5 letter spaces from the fixation point, there is a sharp drop-off in clarity. However, for skilled readers the amount of information that is available in a single eye fixation is usually sufficient to permit rapid identification of the word.

Although the parafoveal and peripheral areas do not provide sharp, detailed information, they provide important information in a number of ways. First, there is word length information (e.g., short words may be skipped). Word length information is provided by the spaces that skilled readers use in the decoding process. Second, there is word shape information. Words printed in lowercase have a characteristic shape or skyline that aids word recognition. In addition, the space surrounding words is used in planning the trajectory for the next saccade. To illustrate how difficult reading becomes when word shape and length information are eliminated, try reading the following sentence:

ONLYRECENTLYHAVEEYEMOVEMENTSANDEYEFIXATIONSBEENRECOGNIZEDF
ORWHATTHEYREALLYARETHEYAREUSEDINTHEWORDRECOGNITIONPROCESS

The division of printed words by spaces is a relatively recent invention that turns out to be a most useful cue to readers. Gaur (1992) has stated that the division of words and sentences developed only gradually, and these changes occurred between 600 and 800 AD. The majority of ancient scripts did not use space to divide words and sentences. The reason is that the scribes who wrote the texts were so well versed they did not need any aids as to word boundaries. It was not until about the year 1200 AD that monks preparing medieval manuscripts began to include spaces so that readers who were less skilled could determine where the word boundaries were, and it is this very word boundary information that is used today when the brain plans the next saccade. If the saccadic movement is incorrect and the eye overshoots the target, the flow of meaningful information can be interrupted and the reader may have to self-correct by means of regressive eye movements. Just as the duration of eye fixations varies as a function of reader skill, the number of eye fixations reflects reader skill as well. From Taylor's (1971) research, we learned that to read a 100-word text, 1st graders needed 224 eye fixations and 12th graders needed only 94 fixations. There are yet other factors that should influence eye fixations. For example, how do the goals of the reader influence eye movements? At times, the goal may be to study a text carefully to pass an exam, while at other times the reader desires only a casual, surface-level overview of a text. Surely, we might wonder how these differences in goals for reading influence visual factors such as duration of eye fixations, span of apprehension, the distribution of attention over the text, the length of a saccade, and regressions.

Regressions and Rereading

To advance through an English text from beginning to end, the direction of eye fixation advances from left to right. There are eye fixations when reading English texts that move in the opposite direction, and go from right to left. Fixations following right-to-left eye movements, excluding return sweeps from one line of print to the next, may be considered regressions. Some scholars differentiate between regressions and rereading. Taylor (1971) believes that some regressions that serve no purpose may reflect poor habits formed during the learning-to-read stage, and these inefficient habits may persist for long periods of time. Other regressions, however, may be purposeful and indicate that the reader has encountered an unanticipated word and is going back to do a comprehension check.

Regression may occur for any number of reasons. For example, in the earliest stages of learning to read, the student must learn how to adjust the accuracy of each eye movement. Pointing to the words is a strategy that many beginning readers—and even more proficient readers when the task is challenging—use (Ehri & Sweet, 1991). This aid (i.e., fingerpointing) is evidence that some young children are aware that they need to train themselves where and how to look at print.

Taylor's (1971) research uncovered sizable differences in the number of regressive eye fixations made as a function of reading skill. In 1st grade, for example, Taylor found that for every 100 words read, the students made 52 regressions while the 12th graders made only 17 regressions. How does one account for this large difference in backward eye movements between unskilled and skilled readers? One reason identified by researchers for such regressions pertains to poor habits that are acquired in the early grades that need to be overcome to some extent with increased skill in the later grades. A second reason acknowledges the need for comprehension checks, which may require regressions. A third reason to regress may occur when the eye misses its mark during a saccade and the reader tries to adjust with a regressive eye correction.

We suggest a fourth possibility. When beginning readers attempt to construct meaning from the text, they engage in a two-step process: They decode the words, and then they attempt to get their meanings. During this process, the decoded words or word parts are moved to short-term memory where they are held for 10 seconds before they are lost. Once lost, the readers must start the process again. Speed is of the essence in this process. We have all noticed during oral reading how beginning readers laboriously work their way through a sentence, stop, and then regress back to an earlier section of text and start over. What has happened is the students took too long and ran out of time, and what was temporarily stored in short-term memory was lost. Therefore, the students had to regress and start over.

Twelfth graders make only 17 eye regressions per 100 words read but first graders make about 52. Not only do less skilled readers make more backward eye movements but also the duration of each eye fixation is longer, which accounts in part for the slower reading speeds of the less skilled readers. Text difficulty also influences eye movements, with increases in text difficulty usually accompanied by increases in the duration of the fixation pause. Low-frequency, unfamiliar words in text are fixated longer, the distance the eye moves with each saccade decreases, and more regressions occur as more comprehension checks are needed.

Forward Saccades

When reading English, forward saccades are characterized by left-to-right eye movements. During an eye movement, vision is suppressed because the movement is so fast that the brain cannot process the information. The amount of time required to move the eye from fixation to fixation requires only $1/20$th of a second. The distance the eye moves in each forward saccade ranges between 1 and 20 letter spaces, with the average being 4–5 letter spaces—the length of a shorter word. It would appear, then, that for skilled readers, for whom the unit of word recognition is the word, the eye jumps from word to word. For skilled readers, what controls the distance the eye jumps with each saccade are the rod cells, which are sensitive to the spaces that mark word boundaries. Ideally, the saccade would place the image of the word so that the letters are spread across the fovea of the eye where letters are in focus. As we move away from the focal point, clarity of the letters decreases, and in fewer than 10 letter spaces out from the point of fixation, visual acuity has dropped by 45% and ease of word recognition becomes more of a problem (Feinberg, 1949; Legge et al., 2007). Consequently, as Rayner (1983) states, the planning of how far to move the eye with a forward saccade is critical.

It is by means of the forward eye movements that the reader is able to advance through a text from its beginning to its end. As important as the forward eye movements are, they exact a heavy price. The price is that they slow down reading speed and impair comprehension. It has been shown, for example, that when readers look at a point on a computer screen and all the words from a text are presented one at a time to that point, very high rates of reading accompanied by modest comprehension can be obtained—somewhere between 700 to 1,000 words per minute. This procedure, however, that requires no eye movements embodies a serious problem. It prevents the reader from making regressions that are essential for comprehension checks (Rayner & Pollatsek, 1989).

In summary, readers are able to overcome the limitations presented by the fact that in any given instant the eye can only see with clarity about one short word—or eight letter spaces—through several kinds of eye movements: forward saccades, regressions, and fixations. In the next section, we examine problems that readers can experience with eye movements.

What Educators Should Know About Eye Problems in Reading

Although there is some disagreement about the extent to which abnormalities of the eye itself and eye movement deficits lead to reading problems, we take the position that eye abnormalities and ocular-motor deficiencies can contribute to reading problems for inexperienced as well as experienced readers. Certainly, lack of visual acuity for distance viewing can be picked up through Snellen eye charts and corrected through properly fitted glasses, but the charts are not useful for detecting problems in the close-up viewing that is required in reading. Tracking can be a common and persistent source of difficulty, where readers have trouble maintaining the focus of the eye on a line of print. Some readers who have a tracking problem may skip entire lines. Even skilled readers may have this problem, especially when the lines of text are long. In fact, the tendency to lose one's place when reading long stretches of text across the page led many newspapers across the United States in the 1950s to adopt the practice of using narrow columns of text as a way to reduce eye-tracking problems in reading (Tinker, 1958).

Ideally, each eye should coordinate with the other, and both eyes should work as a team. When both eyes are working properly, we have binocular coordination. When there is a lack of binocular coordination, the effort it takes to read can become prohibitive. A somewhat related eye problem is convergence insufficiency. When reading, it is necessary for the eyes to turn inwards toward each other as well as to focus on the letters of the words that are being read. Convergence insufficiency is the condition whereby the ability of the eyes to converge and focus properly is compromised. If this occurs, students may experience blurred or double vision, headaches when trying to read, and burning and tearing of the eyes.

There can be other issues that stem from the fact that eye movements such as forward saccades and regressions are controlled by the muscles of the eye and, as such, are similar to motor activities found in skiing, golf, and tennis, all of which respond positively to training and practice. Each of these sports has a learning curve, starting with nonaccuracy and advancing with extended practice to mastery and beyond that to automaticity. When a skill reaches the automatic stage, it can be performed accurately and without conscious thought about its execution. Eye movements such as the forward saccades and regressions also require learning and practice to perform them accurately and automatically. These ocular-motor eye movements are difficult for the reader because he or she must estimate how far to move the eye from one fixation point to the next. Gauging how far the eye is to jump is not an automatic activity and is a complex skill that must be learned over an extended period of practice. The sports examples mentioned earlier may be easier to learn than gauging how far to move the eye, because skiing, tennis, and golf are open to observation by a coach who can see what is being done wrong and correct the athlete's mistakes. Under ordinary classroom conditions, the eye movements are invisible to the outsider. This "black box" phenomenon makes coaching the reader virtually impossible. The black box phenomenon is a term psychologists use to describe the workings of the mind that are hidden to an observer.

The sophisticated equipment that researchers such as Rayner and McConkie—the experts we contacted for this chapter—have used to study eye movements is unlikely to be affordable or practical in most classroom settings. However, digital technology is advancing rapidly, as video recording on cell phones and flip camcorders become cheaper and more accessible. The capacity of the technology will need to be matched with ways of analyzing eye movements. There is equipment that is more reasonable in cost and provides data almost as accurate as that of the equipment typically used in research settings (Spichtig, Vorstius, Greene, & Radach, 2009). It is unlikely that equipment such as this will be used routinely in classrooms but, for comprehensive diagnoses of struggling readers in particular, such information may well add insight that is not available from typical assessments. Diagnosis needs to be coupled with plans for addressing the inefficient patterns. There, too, digital programs hold promise in developing more productive eye movements that underlie efficient reading (Marrs & Patrick, 2002).

Conclusions About the Essential Role of Eye Movements in Reading

At one time it was thought that the eye of the reader swept along the lines of text and continuously processed texts for meaning. However, Javal's (1879) research more than a century ago showed that in reading the process was not characterized by a continuous uptake of information. Rather, it appeared as if the eye jumped from one point on a line of text to another, and the critical components of reading such as word recognition and comprehension occurred only during the brief fixation pauses. These fixation pauses occurred at a rate of about three fixations per second. Because the physiology of the eye is such that only about 6–8 letters at a time can be seen with clarity, eye movements are the means by which different parts of the text can be sequentially processed.

A critical aspect of eye movements is the guidance system used to gauge how far to move the eye from one focal point to the next. For skilled readers for whom the unit of word recognition is the word, the spaces surrounding words are used as cues to guide the jumps as the reader advances from one word to the next. For beginning and less skilled readers, however, the unit of word recognition is some unit that is smaller than the entire word. What guides the beginning reader is not clear, because the bulk of the eye movement research that has been done has used skilled adult readers. With the many advances that have come with eye-tracking equipment, the time has come to learn more about the ocular-motor processes of less skilled readers. One possibility as to how less skilled readers process a text is that in addition to the eye fixation pause when letters from a word are displayed in focus across the fovea, they rely partly on an internal shift of attention, or an internal scan, to process parts of words that are on their retina.

One thing seems certain when considering all involved in the learning-to-read process: effective and efficient eye movements are critical. Although many students master the complexities of eye movements on their own, there are many others who require additional help. Not only do less skilled readers need help with eye movements, but also even skilled readers working on advanced academic degrees can show marked improvement in their ocular-motor efficiency and reading achievement after receiving additional training and practice with eye movements.

QUESTIONS FOR PROFESSIONAL DEVELOPMENT

1. Why do the authors of this chapter believe that eye movements are essential aspects of reading?
2. What does the fluent reader do during an eye fixation that is different from what the nonfluent reader does?
3. Most of what we know about eye movements comes from adults. What do you think we might find that would be different if we looked at eye movements of beginning readers?

REFERENCES

Abrams, S.G., & Zuber, B.L. (1972). Some temporal characteristics of information processing during reading. *Reading Research Quarterly*, 8(1), 40–51.

Broerse, A.C., & Zwaan, E.J. (1966). Informative value of initial letters in the identification of words. *Journal of Verbal Learning and Verbal Behavior, 5*(5), 441–446. doi:10.1016/S0022-5371(66)80058-0

Brysbaert, M., & Vitu, F. (1998). Word skipping: Implications for theories of eye movement control in reading. In G. Underwood (Ed.), *Eye guidance in reading and scene perception* (pp. 125–148). Oxford, England: Elsevier.

Cassidy, J., & Cassidy, D. (2009, February/March). What's hot for 2009. *Reading Today, 26*(4), 1, 8–9.

Cattell, J. (1947). *Man of science: Psychological research.* Lancaster, PA: Science.

Deno, S.L. (1986). Formative evaluation of individual student programs: A new role for school psychologists. *School Psychology Review, 15*(3), 358–374.

Dodge, R. (1900). Visual perceptions during eye movement. *Psychological Review, 7*(5), 454–465. doi:10.1037/h0067215

Ehri, L.C., & Sweet, J. (1991). Fingerpoint-reading of memorized text: What enables beginners to process the print? *Reading Research Quarterly, 26*(4), 442–462. doi:10.2307/747897

Feinberg, R. (1949). A study of some aspects of peripheral visual acuity. *American Journal of Optometry and American Academy of Optometrics, 26*(2), 49–56.

Gaur, A. (1992). *A history of writing.* New York: Cross River.

Gelzer, A., & Santore, N.J. (1968). A comparison of various reading improvement approaches. *The Journal of Educational Research, 61*(6), 267–272.

Germane, C.E., & Germane, E.G. (1922). *Silent reading: A handbook for teachers.* Chicago: Row, Peterson & Co.

Gilbert, L.C. (1940). Effect on silent reading of attempting to follow oral reading. *The Elementary School Journal, 40*(8), 614–621. doi:10.1086/457813

Gilbert, L.C. (1953). Speed of processing visual stimuli and its relation to reading. *Journal of Educational Psychology, 50*(1), 8–14. doi:10.1037/h0045592

Gilbert, L.C. (1959). Saccadic movements as a factor in visual perception in reading. *Journal of Educational Psychology, 50*(1), 15–19. doi:10.1037/h0040752

Gough, P.B. (1971). One second of reading. In J.F. Kavanagh & I.G. Mattingly (Eds.), *Language by ear and by eye: The relationship between speech and reading* (pp. 331–358). Cambridge, MA: MIT Press.

Hebb, D.O. (1930). *Organization of behavior: A neuropsychological theory.* New York: John Wiley & Sons.

Hochberg, J. (1970). Components of literacy: Speculations and exploratory research. In H. Levin & J.P. Williams (Eds.), *Basic studies on reading* (pp. 74–89). New York: Basic.

Huey, E. (1968). *The psychology and pedagogy of reading.* Cambridge, MA: MIT Press. (Original work published 1908)

Ikeda, M., & Saida, S. (1978). Span of recognition in reading. *Vision Research, 18*(1), 83–88. doi:10.1016/0042-6989(78)90080-9

Javal, L.E. (1879). Essai sur la physiologie de la lecture [Essay on the physiology of reading]. *Annales d'Oculistique, 82*, 242–253.

Just, M.A., & Carpenter, P.A. (1980). A theory of reading: From eye fixations to comprehension. *Psychological Review, 87*(4), 329–354. doi:10.1037/0033-295X.87.4.329

Kaakinen, J.K., & Hyönä, J. (2008). Perspective-driven text comprehension. *Applied Cognitive Psychology, 22*(3), 319–334. doi:10.1002/acp.1412

LaBerge, D., & Samuels, S.J. (1974). Towards a theory of automatic information processing in reading. *Cognitive Psychology, 6*(2), 293–323. doi:10.1016/0010-0285(74)90015-2

Latour, P.L. (1962). Visual threshold during eye movements. *Vision Research, 2*(7–8), 261–262. doi:10.1016/0042-6989(62)90031-7

Lee, H.-W., Legge, G.E., & Ortiz, A. (2003). Is word recognition different in central and peripheral vision? *Vision Research, 43*(26), 2837–2846. doi:10.1016/S0042-6989(03)00479-6

Legge, G., Sing-Hang, C., Yu, D., Chung, S., Lee, H., & Owens, D. (2007). The case for the visual span as a sensory bottleneck. *Journal of Vision, 7*(2), 1–15.

Marrs, H., & Patrick, C. (2002). A return to eye-movement training? An evaluation of the Reading Plus program. *Reading Psychology, 23*(4), 297–322. doi:10.1080/713775286

McConkie, G.W., Kerr, P.W., Reddix, M.D., & Zola, D. (1988). Eye movement control during reading: I. The location of initial eye fixations on words. *Vision Research, 28*(10), 1107–1118. doi:10.1016/0042-6989(88)90137-X

McConkie, G.W., & Rayner, K. (1976). Asymmetry of the perceptual span in reading. *Bulletin of the Psychometric Society, 8*, 365–368.

Paulson, E., & Goodman, K. (1999). Eye movements and miscue analysis: What do the eyes do when a reader makes a miscue? *Southern Arizona Review, 1*, 55–62.

Peterson, L.R., & Peterson, M.J. (1959). Short-term retention of individual verbal items. *Journal of Experimental Psychology, 58*(3), 193–198. doi:10.1037/h0049234

Pikulski, J.J., & Shanahan, T. (1982). Informal reading inventories: A critical analysis. In J.J. Pikulski & T. Shanahan (Eds.), *Approaches to the informal evaluation of reading* (pp. 94–116). Newark, DE: International Reading Association.

Posner, M.I. (1980). Orienting of attention. *The Quarterly Journal of Experimental Psychology, 32*(1), 3–25. doi:10.1080/00335558008248231

Rayner, K. (1983). *Eye movements in reading: Perceptual and language processes.* New York: Academic.

Rayner, K. (1998). Eye movements in reading and information processing: 20 years of research. *Psychological Bulletin, 124*(3), 372–422. doi:10.1037/0033-2909.124.3.372

Rayner, K., & Pollatsek, A. (1989). *The psychology of reading.* Hillsdale, NJ: Erlbaum.

Rayner, K., & Sereno, S.C. (1994). Eye movements in reading: Psycholinguistic studies. In M.A. Gernsbacher (Ed.), *Handbook of psycholinguistics* (pp. 57–82). San Diego, CA: Academic.

Rayner, K., Well, A.D., & Pollatsek, A. (1986). Asymmetry of the effective visual field in reading. *Perception & Psychophysics, 27*(6), 537–544.

Ruddell, R.B., & Unrau, N.J. (Eds.). (2004). *Theoretical models and processes of reading* (5th ed.). Newark, DE: International Reading Association.

Samuels, S.J., LaBerge, D., & Bremer, C.D. (1978). Units of word recognition: Evidence for developmental changes. *Journal of Verbal Learning and Verbal Behavior, 17*(6), 715–720. doi:10.1016/S0022-5371(78)90433-4

Saxe, J.G. (1873). *The poems of John Godfrey Saxe* (Complete ed.). Boston: James R. Osgood.

Shiffrin, R.M., & Schneider, W. (1977). Controlled and automatic human information processing. *Psychological Review, 84*(2), 127–190. doi:10.1037/0033-295X.84.2.127

Sipel, B., & van den Broek, P. (2009). *Where readers look when reading recently learned and unknown words.* Unpublished manuscript. Holland: Leiden University.

Smith, F. (1971). *Understanding reading: A psycholinguistic analysis of reading and learning to read.* New York: Holt, Rinehart and Winston.

Sperling, G. (1960). The information available in brief visual presentations. *Psychological Monographs: General and Applied, 74*(11), 1–30.

Spichtig, A., Vorstius, C., Greene, A., & Radach, R. (2009, August). *Visagraph III and Eyelink2K: A comparison study.* Poster session presented at the 15th European Conference on Eye Movements, Southampton, UK.

Taylor, S.E. (1971). *The dynamic activity of reading: A model of the process.* New York: Educational Developmental Laboratories.

Taylor, S.E., & Robinson, H. (1963, February). The relationship of the oculo-motor efficiency of the beginning reader to his success in learning to read. Paper presented at the meeting of the American Educational Research Association, Chicago, IL.

Tinker, M.A. (1958). Recent studies of eye movements in reading. *Psychological Bulletin, 55*(4), 215–231. doi:10.1037/h0041228

Willows, D.M. (1974). Reading between the lines: Selective attention in good and poor readers. *Child Development, 45*(2), 408–415. doi:10.2307/1127962

CHAPTER 3

Why So Much Oral Reading?

Richard L. Allington

University of Tennessee, Knoxville

Anne McGill-Franzen

University of Tennessee, Knoxville

Why do we see so much oral reading in primary-grade classrooms? Why is oral reading a dominant practice in remedial reading and special education classes well beyond the primary grades? Why do high school teachers have students read aloud from their texts, often reading aloud terribly? These are all questions we hope to address in this chapter, for these are questions that, it seems to us, almost no one has ever asked.

Answers to Critical Questions About Oral Reading

Why Do We See So Much Oral Reading in Primary-Grade Classrooms?

We begin our chapter with this question, because the use of oral reading is a centerpiece of primary-grade reading lessons. You would be hard pressed to find a first-grade classroom where no oral reading takes place. But why is there a dominance of oral reading in first-grade classrooms? It is not because no one has ever explored the possibility that we could teach students to read without oral reading, ever.

Early last century (Smith, 1934/1965), the United States was moving toward a model of proficient reading as silent reading—up until the 1920s the focus was on developing oral reading proficiency alone. In a short period of time, at least two professional books for teachers were published that offered advice on how to teach silent reading (Smith, 1925; Watkins, 1922). Around the same time, some of the earliest research on reading was being published, research (Thorndike, 1917) indicating that oral reading proficiency had little to do with proficient comprehension after reading silently. This led to the development of the nonoral method of teaching beginning readers (McDade, 1937, 1941). This approach was compared in midwestern schools with the traditional method that involved primary-grade students mainly in the oral reading of texts (Buswell, 1945). Basically, oral reading

Revisiting Silent Reading: New Directions for Teachers and Researchers, edited by Elfrieda H. Hiebert and D. Ray Reutzel. © 2010 by the International Reading Association.

was never a practice that occurred in nonoral, silent reading classrooms. Buswell reports that both methods were equally successful in teaching students to read. However, while the traditional-method students read aloud more accurately, the students in the silent reading classrooms read with better comprehension. Perhaps because the study found no significant differences in reading achievement or because the emphasis in reading lessons until that time had been largely on oral reading opportunities, the study was ignored. Since that time, however, little further research has been directed to answer questions about the efficacy of primary-grade reading being dominated by oral reading activity.

So oral reading domination today in primary-grade classrooms seems to be most simply an adherence to a longstanding tradition that emerged when reading was largely defined as oral reading (prior to 1920). What seems in our minds, though, to be a significant increase in the amount of oral reading done in primary-grade classrooms over the past decade may reflect certain No Child Left Behind (NCLB) policies. In particular, the nearly universal acceptance of the Dynamic Indicators of Basic Early Literacy Skills (DIBELS) assessment system in Reading First schools refocused attention on oral reading accuracy and rate. The fact that there is good evidence that state Reading First directors were coerced by U.S. federal officials (Brownstein & Hicks, 2005; Office of the Inspector General, 2006) to include DIBELS as the assessment tool of choice meant that roughly 80% of all states put a DIBELS testing scheme in place. That testing regimen included oral response tests such as pseudoword reading rate and accuracy and oral text reading fluency, with the latter assessing not fluency but oral reading accuracy and rate. The fact that this assessment was new and largely untried in public schools makes it more understandable why independent scholars have found little relationship between DIBELS scores and scores on reading achievement tests (Pressley, Hilden, & Shankland, 2006; Samuels, 2007; Shelton, Altwerger, & Jordan, 2009). Nonetheless, having a test of oral reading accuracy and rate imposed on you meant that reading lessons changed, and one change was more time for students to practice reading aloud. That the Reading First program improved oral reading of pseudowords but had no effect on reading comprehension achievement may be surprising, but it really should not be (Gamse, Jacob, Horst, Boulay, & Unlu, 2008). It should not be surprising, because students are always more likely to learn what they are taught than what they are not taught. And what gets tested often dominates what gets taught.

In addition to the emphasis on reading rate and accuracy in the primary-grade NCLB classrooms, so was the use of grade-level core reading programs with all students, both those with above- and below-grade reading proficiencies. As McGill-Franzen (2009) has noted, however, "Contrary to the policy goals, the core reading program mandate did not enable the lowest quintile of students to achieve grade level standards, and may have, in fact, limited opportunities for these students by limiting teacher decision-making" (p. 256).

In other words, use of grade-level texts for all students, but especially for the struggling readers, runs counter to the evidence on the importance of matching students with appropriate texts, texts they can actually read with a high degree of accuracy and with comprehension (Ehri, Dreyer, Flugman, & Gross, 2007). So for the past few years, struggling readers in many NCLB classrooms were reading aloud from texts that were too difficult for them and made no real progress in developing reading proficiencies (Gamse et al., 2008).

In the end, what we as educators ultimately want are proficient silent readers. It may be that the best way to achieve this is by beginning with an emphasis on oral reading in the primary grades as we now do. But we do wonder, given McDade's (1937, 1941) and Buswell's (1945) arguments and evidence on the nonoral method. It may be time to reexamine that question and ask whether too much emphasis is currently placed on oral reading proficiency in the primary grades. Perhaps we could find a better blend of oral and silent practices for the primary grades. We can surely move away from the one-size-fits-all reading curriculum mandates that have become common and move toward research-based practices that would expand silent reading activity and increase opportunities for reading from texts of an appropriate level of difficulty. Hopefully, such changes will lead to earlier silent reading proficiency.

Why Is Oral Reading a Dominant Practice in Remedial and Special Education Classes Well After the Primary Grades?

Beyond the primary grades, about the only place you observe oral reading as common practice is in remedial and special education classes. Again, we cannot explain why oral reading dominates what little reading struggling readers do in these settings (Allington & McGill-Franzen, 1989; Allington, Stuetzel, Shake, & LaMarche, 1986; Vaughn, Moody, & Schumm, 1998); all you have to do is listen to fourth-grade struggling readers attempting to read aloud to understand that students really struggle with this practice. In addition, Leinhardt, Zigmond, and Cooley (1981) found that the time special education students spent reading silently predicted reading growth while time spent reading aloud did not. So why do we continue to have struggling readers read aloud?

Because remedial and special education programs are less than 50 years old, it does not seem that dominance here is the result of some 18th- or 19th-century tradition. And because oral reading is dominant in fourth- through eighth-grade remedial and special education classes, it does not seem likely that teachers are simply mimicking the reading instruction in first-grade classrooms in an attempt to match students with the sort of instruction usually offered at their reading levels because few struggling readers in these grades are still functioning at a first-grade level.

At a recent conference of several hundred remedial and special education teachers, one of us (Dick) asked members of the audience to write down how they would explain why struggling readers are asked primarily to read aloud. Many in the audience responded, and the most common responses were "If you don't have them read aloud, they won't actually read," and "I wouldn't be able to see if they were having problems if I didn't have them read aloud."

The first comment may be true, especially if the teacher selects the materials that struggling readers are supposed to read. The second comment leaves us wondering how teachers could possibly be teaching better readers anything, because they rarely read aloud after first grade. As for the second comment, there are, of course, a number of ways to determine whether students are having difficulty while reading silently and we would encourage teachers to make greater use of such schemes.

Choice of reading material is important for everyone. Ask yourself how many books you read last week because someone assigned you to read those books. Unless you are a student, the number of books you were assigned to read is likely zero. So why is it that only teachers feel the need to assign books to be read? Why not grocers? Or barbers? Or neighbors? These people may recommend books that you might read, but only teachers assign them. The best evidence for allowing students to self-select books comes from the meta-analysis of studies designed to improve reading comprehension and motivation done by Guthrie and Humenick (2004). What was striking was just how powerful student choice was (effect size [ES] = 1.20) in affecting both reading comprehension and motivation. Also powerful was improving access to interesting texts (ES = 1.64); powerful, we assume, because without an array of texts there is also no real choice.

It may be that what turns too many struggling readers off to reading is the dominant practice of having them read aloud from books someone has selected for them. It may be that access to interesting texts they can read is dramatically more restricted than that of better readers. Or perhaps it is all of this with powerful negative effects combining? If this is the case, then it is no wonder so few struggling readers ever become avid and able readers. In other words, it may be we, the teachers, who are the real problem that struggling readers face every day. It is teachers who too often select the too-hard texts that struggling readers struggle with every day. Given a choice, we imagine many struggling readers would select texts they could read accurately and fluently rather than selecting texts that are simply too hard for them to successfully read. The issue here is that we have designed whole graduate courses in reading diagnosis centered on finding out what is wrong with the students. Rarely, if ever, do such courses focus on examining the instructional environment these students are in.

Why Do High School Teachers Have Students Read Aloud From Their Texts, Often Reading Aloud Terribly?

Here again we can observe that oral reading in high school classrooms is more common in tracked classes of low-achieving students than in Advanced Placement classes. For more than 30 years, when we have asked secondary-grade teachers about having students read aloud from their textbooks, the most common response we have received is "I have them read it aloud, because they can't read it." Yes, that is right. "Because the students cannot read the book" is the most frequently given explanation for assigning struggling readers to read aloud in front of their classmates. Although this may make sense to you, we cannot understand how a poor oral reading of a text can possibly benefit struggling readers (either the reader or the listeners). We could better understand a high school teacher reading the text aloud to students (in a sort of admission they had the wrong text assigned). If the teacher read the assigned text aloud to students, it would at least provide struggling readers with a competent rendition of the text material.

Because so many high school struggling readers have texts they cannot read accurately, fluently, and with good comprehension, we ask, Who selected these textbooks? Step 1 in lesson planning is deciding what you are going to teach. Step 2 is finding appropriate materials to help you teach whatever it is you have decided to focus on in Step 1. When students have books they cannot read, it means the fundamental lesson planning process is broken (Allington, 2002).

Keep in mind that we are not referring to having an occasional student read aloud to emphasize a particular point, or to illustrate a particular structure or topic. What we are intending to discuss here is simply spending much of class time (except on test day) having students read aloud the assigned material. If the purpose of most high school classes is the dual development of key content area concepts and the ability to read independently to learn more about these concepts and perhaps many others, then having the students read the text aloud might work if the reading were reasonably accurate and fluent. But the read aloud practice seems most dominant in classrooms with many poor readers. In these situations, it is unlikely that either an accurate or fluent reading of the text is occurring. Thus, neither course concepts nor independence are being fostered in such situations.

Motivation to Read and Oral Reading

Across all grade levels discussed earlier, another theme emerges from discussions with teachers who assign lots of oral reading. That theme is simply thus: If they read it aloud, at least I know they've read it. Without oral reading, I never know whether they all have actually read what was assigned.

There are several problems here. First, in such cases it may be possible that these teachers are unaware of strategies for assessing whether someone has read something. Second, it is very possible that if given a difficult text (e.g., one written at several grade levels above a reader's reading level), students will not read it. The question here is, who created this problem? It was not the student. Having students attempt to read aloud from a too-difficult text is not the answer—replacing the curriculum materials is. Few schools, however, have policies that make it easy for teachers to acquire appropriate materials without spending their own money. That is the problem that needs to be solved.

The data in Table 3.1 reflect the reading levels of the bottom quartile of students at grades 4, 8, and 12 drawn from the national renorming of a standardized reading achievement test (Hargis, 2006). Notice that at each grade level, even after many of the lowest achieving students have dropped out of school, there are still many students reading well below grade level. One can easily observe that many

Table 3.1. Approximate Reading Levels of Bottom Quartile of Students at Three Grade Levels

Grade Level	25% Read Below This Grade Level
4th	2.8
8th	6.5
12th	9.0

Based on information presented in Hargis, C.H. (2006). Setting standards: An exercise in futility? *Phi Delta Kappan*, 87(5), 393–395.

12th-grade students read at the 6th-grade level or below. Many 8th-grade students read below the 4th-grade level, and many 4th-grade students read below the 2nd-grade level. It is these students who do most of the oral reading from texts as part of their school day. Why? Again, there seems to be no simple answer, just ineffective practice.

Changing Practice, More Evidence

We do not expect that primary-grade reading practices involving oral reading will change during our lifetime. That may be fine, because perhaps beginning reading instruction may best involve dominant oral reading practices. It does seem, though, that we need more research on different allocations of oral versus silent reading practices in the primary grades. But what of our practices with struggling readers, in both remedial and special education classes as well as in high school classes? We think we can make a persuasive argument for, largely, the elimination of oral reading once, say, students have attained a first-grade reading level. It is almost impossible, however, to use research to make this argument because we have little direct evidence comparing achievement from classes using oral reading practices with achievement from classes emphasizing silent reading and the use of appropriately difficult texts.

At the primary-grade level, however, we could begin by providing teachers with better information about the potential negative evidence on using round robin oral reading, for instance. Ash, Kuhn, and Walpole (2009) report that roughly two thirds of primary-grade teachers regularly use round robin oral reading, because they know little about the research on the procedure. They report that teachers believed that its use facilitated assessment of reading development and improved fluency. Neither, of course, is true, except that round robin reading does allow a teacher see to how well students can manage the public display of reading aloud in front of other students. We also know that during round robin reading, teachers respond to oral reading errors of struggling readers very differently than the way they respond to the same errors when better readers make them (Allington, 1980b). Teachers interrupt poor readers more quickly and more often and are more likely to pronounce the word for them. None of these actions supports reading fluency or even the development of problem-solving or self-regulating strategies necessary to become a good, independent reader.

In addition, we now know that expanding the volume of independent reading that poor readers do is more likely to foster fluency, vocabulary growth, and comprehension than round robin oral reading or even repeated readings of texts (Kuhn, 2005). However, having the research available does not mean that teachers are aware of it. In many respects, the dominant use of oral reading, and round robin oral reading in particular, with poor readers portends yet another problem in the design of their reading instruction. Not only do they engage in little silent reading practice, they also read much, much less than better readers during their reading lessons (Allington, 2009).

For instance, in our studies of reading lessons provided to good and poor readers in their primary-grade classrooms (Allington, 1980a, 1984; Allington & McGill-Franzen, 1989; McGill-Franzen & Allington, 1990), we found that the amount of words some poor readers read during their lessons was as low as 19 words per day. However, good readers read hundreds of words on the same day. The reason for this huge discrepancy was the dominance of round robin oral reading in the lessons offered to poor readers contrasted with the dominance of silent reading in the lessons offered to good readers. When reading aloud, only a single child is actually reading. Conversely, when silent reading dominated, all students were expected to be reading independently. Stanovich (1986) describes this as the Matthew effect (after the biblical Gospel of Matthew), meaning the rich get richer and the poor get poorer.

These data suggest that teachers understand how to teach reading using silent reading activities when working with good readers; they just rarely use these methods when working with poor readers. No matter what the source might be of these differences between the reading lessons provided to good and poor readers, the result is obvious. Poor readers continue to struggle and develop silent reading proficiencies later than good readers, if they develop them at all.

Further, the dominance of oral reading lessons that poor readers receive means they read less, far less, than good readers. As Stanovich (1986) concludes, "But the evidence available, I believe, supports my 30-year-old argument that reading volume matters" (p. 383). In other words, we have too often unintentionally designed and delivered reading lessons that create the struggling readers we have. Poor readers who have had little practice with silent reading cannot read silently in a proficient manner. In addition, providing poor readers with few lessons focused on comprehension strategies means that poor readers neither use nor know the sorts of strategies good readers use (Walczyk & Griffith-Ross, 2007).

Much of our diagnostic assessment of struggling readers is focused on their oral reading abilities rather than on their silent reading proficiency. Following the diagnostic workups, much of the instruction with poor readers is concentrated more on oral reading accuracy and fluency than on developing silent reading abilities. Perhaps because of the dominance of oral reading practices with poor readers, they come to understand reading as an oral reading performance, one in which they correctly pronounce all of the words as quickly as they can

We also argue that the dominance of oral reading practice is the key reason poor readers do not read much outside of school reading lessons. Anderson, Wilson, and Fielding (1988) report millions of word differences in how much out-of-school reading good and poor readers did across a school year. The number of words that students of different percentile levels reported reading is presented in Table 3.2. Students with reading achievement scores at the 20th percentile when compared with readers at the 70th percentile read roughly 1,500,000 fewer words that year. We can argue whether motivation to read plays an important role here, but we can also argue whether oral reading practice domination created differences in motivation to read. If reading aloud also requires a listener, then only limited amounts of oral reading will likely be done out of school. And it happens that "limited amounts" of reading are precisely what poor readers did.

There is also good research illustrating what has become known as the self-teaching hypothesis, or how reading proficiency develops without instruction but through extended independent reading. Much of this work focuses on the development of lower level skills, particularly decoding and vocabulary acquisition (Cunningham, Perry, Stanovich, & Share, 2002; deJong & Share, 2007; Share, 1995; Share & Stanovich, 1995). What these studies indicate is that students develop better decoding skills and larger reading vocabularies primarily as a result of reading independently and silently. While such development also occurred during assisted oral reading, finding that silent reading practice produced comparable learning suggests that the substantial differences in volume of reading the good and poor readers do outside of school is an important factor in the demonstrated differences in decoding proficiency and vocabulary size observed between these groups.

The question, however, is, How do we change the opportunities poor readers have to those that more closely approximate the opportunities good readers have? We have been considering this question since 1980. Books, articles, and speeches seem not to have made much difference in the reading lessons provided to poor readers. In the end, change will occur when teachers and administrators become more aware of how different lessons for poor readers are from those provided to good readers. However, as was mentioned earlier, these differences have been well documented for 30 years.

Table 3.2. Differences in the Volume of Out-of-School Reading in Fifth Grade

Reading Achievement Percentile	Numbers of Words Read
20th	155,000
50th	883,000
70th	1,719,000

Based on information presented in Anderson, R.C., Wilson, P., & Fielding, L. (1988). Growth in reading and how children spend their time outside of school. *Reading Research Quarterly, 23,* 285–303.

Will more evidence alleviate the problem? After careers as educational researchers, we are not optimistic that good research can change educational practices. For example, although we have 80 years of good research on the negative effects of retention in grade (Allington & McGill-Franzen, 1995; National Education Association, 1959; Otto, 1932; Shepard & Smith, 1989; Tanner & Galis, 1997), we today have whole states and many school districts in which retention is mandated for low achievers.

There is more than adequate research now available to suggest, at least, that the dominance of oral reading in lessons given to poor readers (from the primary grades through high school classes) needs to be reconsidered. We could design a large-scale study that documented positive effects for increasing the emphasis on silent reading for poor readers in grades K–12, but we are not at all sure that instructional design and delivery would change once we completed such a study, even if it demonstrated remarkable reading gains associated with ending the domination of oral reading practices.

Conclusions About Oral Reading and Future Directions

The heavy reliance on oral reading practices in lessons involving poor readers seems to stem more from tradition than from any evidence that the dominance of oral reading practice is a wise choice. Even when confronted with the evidence of the differences in reading lessons provided to good and poor readers, teachers often find reasons for continuing to use oral reading practices. As Ash, Kuhn, and Walpole (2009) note, oral reading practices give students minimal opportunities for reading connected texts, and the interruptive nature of taking turns provides a dysfluent reading model for students. Oral reading practices also have social and emotional effects, with many students, particularly poor readers, feeling embarrassed or stressed about being called on to read (Johnston, 1985). Again, while the research warning against using such practices exists, and has for a number of years, we continue to observe oral reading–dominated lessons in the primary grades and in remedial and special education classes.

It will not necessarily be easy to alter the dominant tradition in our view because, at least initially, many poor readers are less than enthusiastic about changing the practices they have become acquainted with. Silent reading requires engagement and understanding, while oral reading is less demanding in both regards. Silent reading also spreads the responsibility for reading to every student, while oral reading is typically an individual activity. When given the option of greater involvement and greater responsibility for understanding the texts versus less responsibility for either, poor readers will often elect the latter.

Nonetheless, it seems time to mount efforts that will reduce oral domination in reading lessons with poor readers. This will undoubtedly involve the use of professional development for teachers and, perhaps at the same time, a program of research documenting differences in student outcomes as oral reading is reduced. In the end, tradition is not evidence, and it is evidence on the effects of changing the nature of reading lessons that is needed.

QUESTIONS FOR PROFESSIONAL DEVELOPMENT

1. Observe classroom instruction in your school, paying particular attention to the lessons (activities) offered struggling readers. Did you observe greater reliance on oral reading in lessons focused on struggling readers? Did you observe oral reading activities that were focused on meaning? In the lessons you observed, did you observe immediate teacher attention to oral reading errors or was student-generated problem solving given precedent?

2. Have all students in your school been assigned books for all classes that are of an appropriate level of difficulty? In other words, does your school have a research-based curriculum plan? Select five struggling readers in your schools. Meet with these students individually and ask them to read aloud for one minute from each of the textbooks they have been given. Count the total number of words read during that minute and note the number of words each student mispronounced. Calculate each student's accuracy level. Do the students have books that they can read with 99% accuracy? Do they have books that they can read in phrases?

3. If, in the end, we want successful silent readers, describe what you have in place in your school to ensure that all students become effective silent readers. One aspect of being a good reader is the ability to select texts that are interesting and accessible. How does your school ensure that all students will be able to find such books for voluntary reading? Does your school expect teachers to rate (grade) students on their ability to self-select such texts? If not, why not? Describe a rating system for book self-selection skills that you could propose all teachers in your school use.

REFERENCES

Allington, R.L. (1980a). Poor readers don't get to read much in reading groups. *Language Arts,* 57(8), 872–877.

Allington, R.L. (1980b). Teacher interruption behaviors during primary-grade oral reading. *Journal of Educational Psychology,* 72(3), 371–377. doi:10.1037/0022-0663.72.3.371

Allington, R.L. (1984). Content coverage and contextual reading in reading groups. *Journal of Reading Behavior,* 16(2), 85–96.

Allington, R.L. (2002). You can't learn much from books you can't read. *Educational Leadership,* 60(3), 16–19.

Allington, R.L. (2009). If they don't read much...30 years later. In E.H. Hiebert (Ed.), *Reading more, reading better* (pp. 30–54). New York: Guilford.

Allington, R.L., & McGill-Franzen, A. (1989). School response to reading failure: Instruction for chapter 1 and special education students in grades two, four, and eight. *The*

Elementary School Journal, 89(5), 529–542. doi:10.1086/461590

Allington, R.L., & McGill-Franzen, A. (1995). Flunking: Throwing good money after bad. In R.L. Allington & S.A. Walmsley (Eds.), *No quick fix: Rethinking literacy programs in America's elementary schools* (pp. 45–60). New York: Teachers College Press.

Allington, R.L., Stuetzel, H., Shake, M.C., & LaMarche, S. (1986). What is remedial reading? A descriptive study. *Reading Research and Instruction, 26*(1), 15–30.

Anderson, R.C., Wilson, P., & Fielding, L. (1988). Growth in reading and how children spend their time outside of school. *Reading Research Quarterly, 23*(3), 285–303.

Ash, G.E., Kuhn, M.R., & Walpole, S. (2009). Analyzing "inconsistencies" in practice: Teachers' continued use of round robin reading. *Reading & Writing Quarterly, 25*(1), 87–103. doi:10.1080/10573560802491257

Brownstein, A., & Hicks, T. (2005). Special report: Reading First under fire. *Title I Monitor, 10*(9), 1, 3–12.

Buswell, G.T. (1945). *Non-oral reading: A study of its use in The Chicago Public Schools.* Chicago: University of Chicago Press.

Cunningham, A.E., Perry, K.E., Stanovich, K.E., & Share, D.L. (2002). Orthographic learning during reading: Examining the role of self-teaching. *Journal of Experimental Child Psychology, 82*(3), 185–199. doi:10.1016/S0022-0965(02)00008-5

deJong, P.F., & Share, D.L. (2007). Orthographic learning during oral and silent reading. *Scientific Studies of Reading, 11*(1), 55–71. doi:10.1207/s1532799xssr1101_4

Ehri, L.C., Dreyer, L.G., Flugman, B., & Gross, A. (2007). Reading Rescue: An effective tutoring intervention model for language-minority students who are struggling readers in first grade. *American Educational Research Journal, 44*(2), 414–448.

Gamse, B.C., Jacob, R.T., Horst, M., Boulay, B., & Unlu, F. (2008). *Reading First impact study final report* (NCEE 2009-4038). Washington, DC: National Center for Education Evaluation and Regional Assistance.

Guthrie, J.T., & Humenick, N.M. (2004). Motivating students to read: Evidence for classroom practices that increase motivation and achievement. In P. McCardle & V. Chhabra (Eds.), *The voice of evidence in reading research* (pp. 329–354). Baltimore: Paul H. Brookes.

Hargis, C.H. (2006). Setting standards: An exercise in futility? *Phi Delta Kappan, 87*(5), 393–395.

Johnston, P.H. (1985). Understanding reading disability: A case study approach. *Harvard Educational Review, 55*(2), 153–177.

Kuhn, M.R. (2005). A comparative study of small group fluency instruction. *Reading Psychology, 26*(2), 127–146. doi:10.1080/02702710590930492

Leinhardt, G., Zigmond, N., & Cooley, W. (1981). Reading instruction and its effects. *American Educational Research Journal, 18*(3), 343–361.

McDade, J.E. (1937). A hypothesis for non-oral reading: Argument, experiment, and results. *The Journal of Educational Research, 30*(7), 489–503.

McDade, J.E. (1941). *Essentials of non-oral beginning reading.* Chicago: Plymouth.

McGill-Franzen, A. (2009). Teachers using texts: Where we are and what we need. In E.H. Hiebert & M. Sailors (Eds.), *Finding the right texts: What works for beginning and struggling readers* (pp. 253–266). New York: Guilford.

McGill-Franzen, A., & Allington, R.L. (1990). Comprehension and coherence: Neglected elements of literacy instruction in remedial and resource room services. *Journal of Reading, Writing, and Learning Disabilities, 6*(2), 149–182.

National Education Association. (1959). *Pupil failure and non promotion.* Washington, DC: Author.

Office of the Inspector General. (2006). *The Reading First program's grant application process: Final inspection report.* Washington, DC: U.S. Department of Education.

Otto, H.J. (1932). Implications for administration and teaching growing out of pupil failures in first grade. *The Elementary School Journal, 33*(1), 25–32.

Pressley, M., Hilden, K., & Shankland, R. (2006). *An evaluation of end-of-grade 3 Dynamic Indicators of Basic Early Literacy Skills (DIBELS): Speed reading without comprehension, predicting little* (Tech. Rep.). East Lansing, MI: Literacy Achievement Research Center, Michigan State University.

Samuels, S.J. (2007). The DIBELS tests: Is speed of barking at print what we mean by reading fluency? *Reading Research Quarterly*, *42*(4), 563–566.

Share, D.L. (1995). Phonological recoding and self-teaching: *Sine qua non* of reading acquisition. *Cognition*, *55*(2), 151–218. doi:10.1016/0010-0277(94)00645-2

Share, D.L., & Stanovich, K.E. (1995). Cognitive processes in early reading development: Accommodating individual differences into a model of acquisition. *Issues in Education*, *1*(1), 1–57.

Shelton, N.R., Altwerger, B., & Jordan, N. (2009). Does DIBELS put reading first? *Literacy Research and Instruction*, *48*(2), 137–148. doi:10.1080/19388070802226311

Shepard, L.A., & Smith, M.L. (Eds.). (1989). *Flunking grades: Research and policies on retention*. New York: Falmer.

Smith, N.B. (1925). *One thousand ways to teach silent reading*. Yonkers, NY: World Book Co.

Smith, N.B. (1965). *American reading instruction: Its development and its significance in gaining a perspective on current practices in reading*. Newark, DE: International Reading Association. (Original work published 1934)

Stanovich, K.E. (1986). Matthew effects in reading: Some consequences of individual differences in the acquisition of literacy. *Reading Research Quarterly*, *21*(4), 360–407. doi:10.1598/RRQ.21.4.1

Tanner, C.K., & Galis, S.A. (1997). Student retention: Why is there a gap between the majority of research findings and school practice? *Psychology in the Schools*, *34*(2), 107–114. doi:10.1002/(SICI)1520-6807(199704)34:2<107::AID-PITS4>3.0.CO;2-N

Thorndike, E.L. (1917). Reading as reasoning: A study of mistakes in paragraph reading. *Journal of Educational Psychology*, *8*, 323–332.

Vaughn, S., Moody, S.W., & Schumm, J.S. (1998). Broken promises: Reading instruction in the resource room. *Exceptional Children*, *64*(2), 211–225.

Walczyk, J.J., & Griffith-Ross, D.A. (2007). How important is reading skill fluency for comprehension? *The Reading Teacher*, *60*(6), 560–569. doi:10.1598/RT.60.6.6

Watkins, E. (1922). *How to teach silent reading to beginners*. Philadelphia: J.B. Lippincott.

CHAPTER 4

Developmental Considerations in Transferring Oral Reading Skills to Silent Reading

Gary Wright
The University of Texas at Tyler

Ross Sherman
The University of Texas at Tyler

Timothy B. Jones
Sam Houston State University, Texas

There appears to be agreement in the field of literacy that the ability to read silently with adequate comprehension is an extremely important process to learn. More than a century ago, Huey (1908/1968) proclaimed that life reading was silent reading. Smith (1934/1965, 1934/1986) in her editions of *American Reading Instruction: Its Development and Its Significance in Gaining a Perspective on Current Practices in Reading*, noted that between the years 1918 and 1925 scientific investigations by various researchers provided evidence that silent reading was superior to oral reading both in comprehension and speed. The value educators began to place on silent reading was reflected in the fact that reading textbooks used to train teachers began to include the term *silent reading* in their titles (Germane & Germane, 1922; Stone, 1922).

However, the present emphasis on reading orally during guided reading lessons in the primary grades and the sporadic use of round robin reading in the secondary grades has produced a lack of direct practice of silent reading. Research evidence shows that the amount of time allocated to silent reading instruction is minuscule in the primary and middle grades (Anderson, Hiebert, Scott, & Wilkinson, 1985).

The National Reading Panel's report (National Institute of Child Health and Human Development, 2000), in its executive summary concerning reading fluency, focuses entirely on oral reading fluency. Based on a perusal of indexes included in elementary and secondary reading method books published since 2000, there appears to be a paucity of content related to silent reading processes and instruction. Of the approximate 2,845 pages of text in the three volumes of the *Handbook of Reading Research* (Barr, Kamil, Mosenthal, & Pearson, 1991; Kamil,

Revisiting Silent Reading: New Directions for Teachers and Researchers, edited by Elfrieda H. Hiebert and D. Ray Reutzel. © 2010 by the International Reading Association.

Mosenthal, Pearson, & Barr, 2000; Pearson, Barr, Kamil, & Mosenthal, 1984), the combined indexes refer to only 17 pages that specifically address the topic of silent reading. Simple observations of people reading to themselves provide ample evidence that more research, publication, and instructional time should be allocated to silent reading.

Have you ever been in an airport terminal, in a library reading room, in a physician's waiting room, or in your own classroom and observed individuals reading to themselves? If you have, you have probably noticed that not all individuals read silently when reading to themselves. You may have noticed the various read-to-oneself speech manifestations, such as subvocal and vocal speech. Such is the nature of the process referred to as silent reading.

Several questions can be posed from such casual observations in a variety of real-life circumstances in which silent reading is used. First, what speech manifestations may arise when one reads to oneself? Second, what are the implications of these manifestations for assessing silent reading behaviors? Third, what are the implications of these manifestations for teaching silent reading processes? Fourth, what if one does not read silently?

Speech Manifestations During Silent Reading

Subvocal Speech

Webster's Ninth New Collegiate Dictionary defines the word *silent* as "speechless, making no utterances" (Mish, 1983, p. 1096). Harris and Hodges (1981) define silent reading as a form of reading without vocalizing but they concede that subvocal activity could occur, which implies an inner link to speech.

Huey (1908/1968) directly links the accompanying subvocal activity during silent reading to speech, calling the activity *inner speech*. He contends that inner speech is a normal aspect of reading to oneself. Vygotsky (1934/1986) recognizes the phenomenon of inner speech and theorizes it is a form of autistic and logical thinking. Other terms have been used synonymously with inner speech, such as *silent speech*, *covert speech*, *implicit speech*, *inner vocalization*, and *subvocalization* (Cleland & Davies, 1963; Harris & Hodges, 1981, 1995). Nevertheless, each term denotes a direct link between inner speech—that is some form of subvocal activity—with silent reading.

There is a history of sophisticated research that links subvocalization and silent reading. Scheck (1925), using a small balloon and a pneumograph attached to a kymograph, and Edfeldt (1960), using rubber bulbs connected to an Elmquist Mingograph, recorded movement in subjects' larynges as they read to themselves. Hardyck and Petrinovich (1969), using sophisticated electromyographic instrumentation, also discovered muscular movement in the larynges of teenagers and adults during silent reading. In their review of inner speech, Rayner and Pollatsek (1989) conclude that published research data indicated that subvocalization is a normal aspect of silent reading.

Vocal Speech

The subvocal nature of inner speech, at times, manifests itself in more overt behaviors, especially in beginning readers and struggling readers. Quantz (1897) observes that lip movement accompanied inner speech of beginning readers. However, reading to oneself may produce manifestations that are vocal. Cole (1938) categorizes her direct observations of silent reading into five degrees of vocalization that ranged from loud whispering to soundless reading without lip movement and vibration of the throat. Cunningham (1978) observes what she called *mumble reading*, which she decided was a needed substitute for silent reading among beginning readers. Bruinsma (1980) also observes that beginning readers, when reading to themselves, moved their lips and exhibited various forms of vocalization.

Furthermore, Dixon-Krauss (1996) believes there was a parallel between Vygotsky's (1934/1986) theory of the development of thought and language and its relationship to speech. According to Dixon-Krauss, the initial stage of reading occurs via read-alouds with parents and teachers. Vygotsky viewed egocentric speech (i.e., vocalizing) as an intermediate and transformational stage from vocal to inner speech. Like Vygotsky's inner speech, Dixon-Krauss suggests that as children's literacy experiences accumulate, the tendency to vocalize while reading to themselves gradually internalizes and becomes inner speech.

Wright, Sherman, and Jones (2004) conducted research in two first-grade classrooms consisting of 56 students to identify early silent reading manifestations, ascertain the variance in these manifestations, and determine if there were sequential developmental stages consonant with these manifestations. The first graders were tested in October, February, and May, using the Durrell Analysis of Reading Difficulty, third edition (Durrell & Catterson, 1980). After reading a passage to themselves, the students' silent reading manifestations, silent reading rate, number and percentage of silent reading memories, and reading level were recorded.

In October, we observed all of the early reading manifestations, subvocal and vocal, addressed in the research literature. Five emergent silent reading manifestations were observed. The most pronounced observed behavior was that of blatant oral reading. Even when reminded to read the text silently to themselves, these first graders persisted in reading as if to an audience. Whisper reading appeared to be a refined version of the former behavior. Though each word whispered could be heard distinctly, the volume of the children's voices was such that it appeared the children were not intent on communicating the essence of the text to anyone but themselves. A less vocal manifestation observed was that of mumble reading. Definitely vocal, but unlike whisper reading, most of these readers' words were unintelligible. The movement of lips with no discernable sound was also observed among the first graders. Not surprisingly, there were first graders who read silently in October and who could retell the story content.

The first graders in this study confirmed what had been reported in the literature on silent reading manifestations, especially those reported by Cole (1938), which is that silent reading and its various observable subvocal and vocal manifestations were present when emerging readers read to themselves. Likewise, there was evidence that reading silently, over time, was developmental and strategic in nature. As emerging readers became more comfortable with the social context of their classrooms and became more proficient readers, and as they strove to become more efficient readers, vocalization strategies were often strategically altered in favor of subvocal strategies. However, the research also showed evidence that observed silent reading manifestations were strategically fluid and that they did not always move, over time, from vocal to subvocal. Depending on the complexity of the content and the readability of the text, some first graders were observed to move from subvocal to vocal strategies as they read to themselves.

Silent Reading and the Struggling Reader

There are researchers (Harris & Sipay, 1975; Pomerantz, 1971) who contend that a natural decrease in vocalization usually occurs without teacher intervention. However, there are students who fail to make the strategic transition from vocal to inner speech when reading silently. In essence, these students' silent reading behaviors remain similar to those of emergent readers in the primary grades.

Wright, Gilliam, Dykes, and Gerla (2009) tested the silent reading behaviors of 95 struggling readers ranging from 6th grade to 11th grade. The end-of-year testing revealed that less then half of these students (i.e., 38) read silently without lip movement or vocalization. They discovered that more than half of the students (i.e., 57) suffered from arrested development of their ability to read silently. Their observed silent reading manifestations during the testing sessions included loud oral reading, whispering, mumbling, and lip movement. There could be serious consequences for such students who vocalize when reading.

Consequences of Lip Movement and Vocalization During Silent Reading

Two primary goals of silent reading instruction and, conversely, for learning to read silently are those of efficiency and attitude. Efficiency refers to reading with adequate comprehension and rate. Attitude refers to engaging in and enjoying reading.

It appears that there may be many struggling readers in public and private schools who, because of various factors including instruction and practice, fail to develop mature subvocal, silent reading strategies. Quantz (1897) records that lip movement was a serious hindrance to the rate and comprehension of reading. Huey (1908/1968) stated that the inner speech of silent reading was faster than vocalizing what was being read for each individual he tested. Gray and Reese (1957) present data that by third grade, students' silent reading rates were considerably faster than oral (i.e., vocalizing) reading rates. Smith and Dechant (1961) suggested that once silent reading attains the maximum rate of oral reading, vocalizing inhibits further increases. Smith (1971, 1973) states that readers who voiced words or read with pronounced lip movement were not proficient readers.

Thus, there can be serious consequences for those students who vocalize as they read to themselves. These consequences entail a slower, more laborious, rate of comprehending text material and subsequently the developing of negative attitudes toward and a lack of interest in engaging in the activity of reading to oneself. Embarrassment is another consequence that may occur. Students who need to vocalize to comprehend printed text may choose to sit and stare at the text during allocated class time for silent reading and pretend to read the assignments, lest they feel embarrassed to be heard by classmates.

Assessment and Instructional Implications for Silent Reading

Because the process of silent reading appears to be developmental and strategic, there are classroom implications that need to be considered by literacy teachers at all grade levels. The implications should affect both literacy assessment procedures and literacy instructional activities.

Periodic, informal silent reading assessments akin to running records are a must. These assessments should be individually administered using either authentic classroom texts or commercial, informal reading inventories. During the assessment sessions, careful observations of students' employed speech strategies should be noted and recorded (e.g., blatant oral reading, whisper reading, mumble reading, lip movement, silent reading). Such recorded observations provide evidence as to the developmental level of the speech strategies employed by each student while trying to read silently.

Care must be taken in composing the language for the directions administered to the student being assessed. The teacher should use the following directions and language:

1. Read the story to yourself.
2. Read the story just once.
3. Look up when you finish the story.
4. Think about what you are reading, because I will ask you questions about the story.

The language in the first sentence (i.e., read to yourself) allows the student to choose the silent reading speech strategy that aids his or her reading comprehension. The second and third sentences allow the teacher to get an accurate reading rate for the student. The fourth sentence tells the student that his or her comprehension of the text content is the major purpose for reading.

Figure 4.1 is a suggested template for recording the various aspects of silent reading. As noted, there are places to record reading levels, vocal and subvocal manifestations, silent reading rates, and areas of improvement regarding specific comprehension skills. The comprehension skills listed are merely representative. Other comprehension skills could be included and those listed replaced.

Figure 4.1. Silent Reading Assessment Form

Student:
Age:
Grade:
Silent Reading Assessment Administered:

PLACEMENT LEVELS:
The student's estimated placement levels are as follows based on the results of the above silent reading assessment:

Instructional Reading Level(s):
Independent Reading Level(s):
Frustration Reading Level(s):

SILENT READING BEHAVIORS:
The following reading skills were observed as a result of the assessment:

Silent Reading Manifestations—Circle Manifestation(s) Observed

Vocalization Behaviors	Subvocalization Behaviors	Body Movement
1. Reading Aloud	1. Lip Movement	1. Head
2. Whisper Reading	2. Silent Reading	2. Finger Pointing
3. Mumble Reading		3. Arms
		4. Legs
		5. Feet

Silent Reading Rate—Circle/Fill in the Blank for the Rate Observed

1. The story was read at a silent reading rate of _____ WPM.
2. The above silent reading rate is high/normal/low considering the grade level of the student.

Silent Reading Comprehension

The following comprehension skills need special attention based on the results of the assessment:

_____	Main Idea
_____	Detail
_____	Sequence
_____	Cause/Effect
_____	Inference
_____	Vocabulary

Note. Designed by Gary Wright

Implications for Instructing Silent Reading Behaviors

The first implication is that more class time should be allotted to silent reading instruction and practice. One of the recommendations made in the Commission on Reading report in *Becoming a Nation of Readers* (Anderson et al., 1985) was that beginning readers should do more silent reading. However, once students, regardless of age and grade, are identified as those who vocalize when reading to themselves, a structured instructional program should be planned to help them become silent readers. On the other hand, several literacy researchers (Adams, 1994; Anderson & Dearborn, 1952; Davies, 1972; Edfeldt, 1960; McGuigan, 1970; Tinker, 1952) have warned that attempts to prematurely eliminate the manifestations of vocalizing or subvocalizing may be detrimental to comprehending the text being read.

Thus, the first instructional step is to inform students of the vocal or subvocal manifestation(s) in which they engage during read-to-yourself classroom sessions. The students need to be aware of the speech strategy they use when reading silently.

The second step is to set a goal to practice at the next speech level of vocalization or subvocalization. That is, if students exhibit the behavior of reading blatantly aloud, then practice whisper or mumble reading. If students whisper or mumble, then practice moving the lips without producing sound. If the students move lips without sound, then practice no lip movement, relying totally on inner speech.

Lip movers provide a special case, because they are already subvocalizing (i.e., relying on inner speech). However, lip movement slows the rate of comprehending and inhibits the individual from reading at a rate above a comfortable rate of speaking, which in turn, reduces reading efficiency.

Shanker and Cockrum (2009) recommend several instructional techniques to help students who move their lips while reading silently. The techniques are similar in that each employs a method of obstructing the lips from moving during the process of reading. These techniques include humming, pressing the teeth firmly together, holding a finger against the lips, and placing an object between the teeth.

Literacy research conducted in the 20th century and extending into the 21st century provides ample evidence that a knowledgeable teacher is the key component in helping students become efficient readers. Thus, literacy teachers who possess knowledge about the variable, developmental nature of silent reading and the procedures for assessing and teaching silent reading should be more successful in helping students become efficient and active silent readers. Knowledgeable literacy teachers should be able to answer the following questions about the students in their classrooms:

- Which students subvocalize and which students vocalize as they read to themselves?
- What assessment techniques are used to observe students and to record those observations?
- What instructional plans and procedures are employed to help students who move their lips or vocalize when reading to themselves?

Conclusions About Silent Reading and Recommendations for Future Research

Silent reading is such an important life skill that literacy teachers need to understand its process. It is the knowledgeable literacy teachers who have in their classrooms and in their schools the student resources to conduct significant action research that could provide needed information concerning the various aspects of the silent reading process. Classroom research could provide evidence about the incidence of vocalization and lip movement during silent reading among the grade levels. Classrooms are ideal for providing evidence concerning the relationship between vocalizing during silent reading and the rate and the level of comprehension. More research is needed to determine the best instructional procedures for helping students make the transition from vocalizing to subvocalizing when reading to themselves. The following are suggested areas for continued research related to subvocal and vocal speech manifestations exhibited during silent reading activities:

- Incidence of vocalization during silent reading activities among average and above-average students in 2nd grade through 12th grade
- Relationships between silent reading vocalization and rate of comprehension
- Relationships between silent reading vocalization and level of comprehension
- Instructional activities that aid readers who vocalize or move lips to make the transition to silent reading

It is the knowledgeable literacy teachers' classrooms that can have the most impact on extending and refining the current research on all aspects of silent reading.

QUESTIONS FOR PROFESSIONAL DEVELOPMENT

1. What is meant by the term *silent reading*?
2. Are silent reading behaviors really silent?
3. How do teachers assess students' developmental silent reading stage?
4. What should be observed when students are reading to themselves with narrative and expository text?
5. What do teachers need to do to develop silent reading behaviors and strategies?

REFERENCES

Adams, M.J. (1994). *Beginning to read: Thinking and learning about print.* Cambridge, MA: MIT Press.

Anderson, I.H., & Dearborn, W.F. (1952). *The psychology of teaching reading.* New York: Ronald Press.

Anderson, R.C., Hiebert, E.H., Scott, J.A., & Wilkinson, I.A.G. (1985). *Becoming a nation of readers: The report of the Commission on Reading.* Washington, DC: National Academy of Education, National Institute of Education; Champaign-Urbana, IL: Center for the Study of Reading.

Barr, R., Kamil, M.L., Mosenthal, P., & Pearson P.D. (Eds.). (1991). *Handbook of reading research* (Vol. 2). White Plains, NY: Longman.

Bruinsma, R. (1980). Should lip movements and subvocalization during silent reading be directly remediated? *The Reading Teacher, 34*(3), 293–295.

Cleland, D.L., & Davies, W.C. (1963). Silent speech—history and current status. *The Reading Teacher, 16*(4), 224–228.

Cole, L. (1938). *The improvement of reading, with special reference to remedial instruction.* New York: Farrar & Rinehart.

Cunningham, P.M. (1978). "Mumble reading" for beginning readers. *The Reading Teacher, 31*(4), 409–411.

Davies, W.C. (1972). Implicit speech—Some conclusions drawn from research. In R.C. Aukerman (Ed.), *Some persistent questions on beginning reading* (pp. 171–177). Newark, DE: International Reading Association.

Dixon-Krauss, L. (1996). *Vygotsky in the classroom: Mediated literacy instruction and assessment.* White Plains, NY: Longman.

Durrell, D.D., & Catterson, J.H. (1980). *Durrell analysis of reading difficulty: Manual of directions* (3rd ed.). New York: Psychological Corporation.

Edfeldt, A.W. (1960). *Silent speech and silent reading.* Chicago: University of Chicago Press.

Germane, C.E., & Germane, E.G. (1922). *Silent reading: A handbook for teachers.* Chicago: Row, Peterson.

Gray, L., & Reese, D.J. (1957). *Teaching children to read* (2nd ed.). New York: Ronald Press.

Hardyck, C.D., & Petrinovich, L.F. (1969). Treatment of subvocal speech during reading. *Journal of Reading, 12*(5), 361–368, 419–422.

Harris, A.J., & Sipay, E.R. (1975). *How to increase reading ability: A guide to developmental and remedial methods* (6th ed.). New York: Longman.

Harris, T.L., & Hodges, R.E. (Eds.). (1981). *A dictionary of reading and related terms.* Newark, DE: International Reading Association.

Harris, T.L., & Hodges, R.E. (Eds.). (1995). *The literacy dictionary: The vocabulary of reading and writing.* Newark, DE: International Reading Association.

Huey, E.B. (1968). *The psychology and pedagogy of reading, with a review of the history of reading and writing and of methods, texts, and hygiene in reading.* New York: Macmillan. (Original work published 1908)

Kamil, M.L., Mosenthal, P.B., Pearson, P.D., & Barr, R. (Eds.). (2000). *Handbook of reading research* (Vol. 3). Mahwah, NJ: Erlbaum.

McGuigan, F.J. (1970). Covert oral behavior during the silent performance of language tasks. *Psychological Bulletin, 74*(5), 309–326. doi:10.1037/h0030082

Mish, F.C. (Ed.). (1983). *Webster's ninth new collegiate dictionary.* Springfield, MA: Merriam-Webster.

National Institute of Child Health and Human Development. (2000). *Report of the National Reading Panel. Teaching children to read: An evidence-based assessment of the scientific research literature on reading and its implications for reading instruction* (NIH Publication No. 00-4769). Washington, DC: U.S. Government Printing Office.

Pearson, P.D., Barr, R., Kamil, M.L., & Mosenthal, P. (1984). *Handbook of reading research.* New York: Longman.

Pomerantz, H. (1971). Subvocalization and reading. *The Reading Teacher, 24*(7), 665, 667.

Quantz, J.O. (1897). Problems in the psychology of reading. *Psychological Review Monograph Supplements, 2*(1).

Rayner, K., & Pollatsek, A. (1989). *The psychology of reading.* Englewood Cliffs, NJ: Prentice Hall.

Scheck, M. (1925). Involuntary tongue movements under varying stimuli. *Proceeding of the Iowa Academy of Sciences, 32,* 385–391.

Shanker, J.L. & Cockrum, W.A. (2009). *Locating and correcting reading difficulties* (9th ed.). Boston: Allyn & Bacon.

Smith, F. (1971). *Understanding reading: A psycholinguistic analysis of reading and learning to read.* New York: Holt, Rinehart and Winston.

Smith, F. (1973). *Psycholinguistics and reading.* New York: Holt, Rinehart and Winston.

Smith, H.P., & Dechant, E.V. (1961). *Psychology in teaching reading.* Englewood Cliffs, NJ: Prentice Hall.

Smith, N.B. (1965). *American reading instruction: Its development and its significance in gaining a perspective on current practices in reading* (Rev. ed.). Newark, DE: International Reading Association. (Original work published 1934)

Smith, N.B. (1986). *American reading instruction: Its development and its significance in gaining a perspective on current practices in reading.* Newark, DE: International Reading Association. (Original work published 1934)

Stone, C.R. (1922). *Silent and oral reading: A practical handbook of methods based on the most recent scientific investigations.* Boston: Houghton Mifflin.

Tinker, M.A. (1952). *Teaching elementary reading.* New York: Appleton-Century-Crofts.

Vygotsky, L.S. (1986). *Thought and language* (A. Kozulin, Ed. & Trans.). Cambridge, MA: MIT Press. (Original work published 1934)

Wright, G., Gilliam, B., Dykes, F., & Gerla, J. (2009). *Silent reading manifestations of secondary student struggling readers.* Manuscript submitted for publication.

Wright, G., Sherman, R., & Jones, T.B. (2004). Are silent reading behaviors of first graders really silent? *The Reading Teacher, 57*(6), 546–553.

CHAPTER 5

Can Silent Reading in the Summer Reduce Socioeconomic Differences in Reading Achievement?

Thomas G. White
University of Virginia

James S. Kim
Harvard University, Massachusetts

In the years following entry into school, children of low socioeconomic status (SES) lose ground in reading relative to their high-SES peers. This widening achievement gap may be largely the result of different rates of learning during the summer months (e.g., Alexander, Entwisle, & Olson, 2001; Cooper, Nye, Charlton, Lindsay, & Greathouse, 1996; Heyns, 1978). Even small differences in summer learning can accumulate across years, resulting in a substantially greater achievement gap at the end of elementary school than was present at the beginning (Alexander, Entwisle, & Olson, 2004; see also Borman & Dowling, 2006; Lai, McNaughton, Amituanai-Toloa, Turner, & Hsiao, 2009). This leads us to the question, Can socioeconomic differences in reading achievement be reduced by programs that encourage silent reading in the summer months?

As Heyns (1978) suggested more than 30 years ago, increasing low-SES students' access to books and encouraging them to read in the summer might go a long way toward reducing seasonal differences in learning and achievement gaps. Although this powerful idea may be one whose time has finally come, it needs to be more fully developed and tested in a methodologically rigorous way. We need to know, for example, whether mere access to books is sufficient, and specifically how to encourage children to read during their summer vacation. We need experimental studies to establish the effectiveness of any interventions that are developed before they are widely implemented with children.

We have been pursuing the question of how to enhance silent summer reading while addressing socioeconomic differences in reading achievement for the past seven or eight years. In the process, we developed what we call a scaffolded summer reading program and conducted two randomized experiments to test its effectiveness (Kim, 2006; Kim & White, 2008). In the next three sections, to provide a backdrop, we review research on socioeconomic differences in reading

Revisiting Silent Reading: New Directions for Teachers and Researchers, edited by Elfrieda H. Hiebert and D. Ray Reutzel. © 2010 by the International Reading Association.

achievement and summer learning and some possible explanations of those differences. Then, in the heart of the chapter, we explain our thinking as we approached the task of developing the summer reading program, present the logic model underlying it, describe the experiments, give the details of the program, present findings, and describe related research and similar programs that are being implemented by others. We conclude with a set of recommendations for researchers and policymakers.

Socioeconomic Differences in Reading Achievement

Data from the nationally representative Early Childhood Longitudinal Study, Kindergarten Class of 1998–1999 (ECLS-K) show that low-SES children begin kindergarten with average reading scores that fall 0.58 standard deviation (SD) units below those of high-SES children, and that the gap between low-SES and high-SES students increases to 0.65 SD by the end of first grade and to 0.79 SD by the end of third grade (LoGerfo, Nichols, & Reardon, 2006, see Tables 3.9 and C1). Aikens and Barbarin (2008) analyzed ECLS-K reading growth trajectories from kindergarten through third grade by SES quintile, five categories based on father's (or male guardian's) education and occupation, mother's (or female guardian's) education and occupation, and household income. The difference between students in the highest and lowest SES quintiles increased from 11.3 points at kindergarten entry, or about 6 months of learning, to 27.2 points at the end of third grade, or about 16 months of learning. These studies demonstrate, in practical terms, that the SES gap in reading achievement is already large when children begin school, and it grows distressingly larger by the end of third grade.

Whether the SES gap in reading achievement continues to widen after third grade is not yet clear. Researchers are just beginning to examine the ECLS-K fifth- and eighth-grade data, and as of this writing, no studies have focused on the issue of whether SES differences increase beyond third grade. We do know that SES is associated with large differences in reading achievement in the upper elementary grades and beyond. For instance, results from the 2007 National Assessment of Educational Progress reading assessment show a gap of 0.83 SD at fourth grade and a gap of 0.73 SD at eighth grade between students who are eligible for free or reduced-cost lunch and those who are not (Lee, Grigg, & Donahue, 2007). The smaller gap at eighth grade may reflect underreporting of free-lunch eligibility at higher grade levels or a cohort effect. It seems implausible that socioeconomic differences in reading achievement decrease after third grade because vocabulary, knowledge, and comprehension demands increase (e.g., Becker, 1977; Chall, 1983), and low-SES students have smaller vocabularies and more limited knowledge (e.g., Chall, Jacobs, & Baldwin, 1990; Hart & Risley, 1995; White, Graves, & Slater, 1990). In addition, there is considerable evidence that low-SES students make less progress in reading than high-SES students in the summers following third through eighth grade, so an increasing achievement gap would be expected if there are no compensatory learning differences during the school year.

The Role of Summer Learning in the Development of SES Differences in Reading

In this section, we address two questions: (1) Do summer learning differences contribute to the SES achievement gap that is growing larger, almost certainly during the early years of schooling and probably in the later elementary and early middle school years as well? (2) If so, do school year or summer learning differences make a larger contribution to the growing gap?

Do Summer Learning Differences Contribute to the SES Achievement Gap?

Cooper et al.'s (1996) meta-analysis examined the effects of summer vacation on the reading achievement of first- through eighth-grade students (i.e., the summers following first through eighth grade). Combining grades, there was a significant effect of SES on summer learning. Middle-SES students made a nonsignificant gain (+0.06 SD in grade-level equivalents) while low-SES students showed a significant loss (−0.21 SD), based on 37 independent samples. The difference between grade-level equivalent scores in the fall and spring was +0.16 for middle-SES students and −0.19 for low-SES students, which is a difference of about three months of schoolyear learning.

The classic study of summer learning by Heyns (1978) was among the studies reviewed by Cooper et al. (1996). Heyns studied a stratified sample of public schools in Atlanta, Georgia, USA, that included several thousand sixth- and seventh-grade students who were tested, during the early 1970s, in the fall and spring of the school year and again in the following fall. The dependent variable in her analyses was the word knowledge subtest of the Metropolitan Achievement Test, a measure of reading vocabulary that was highly correlated with reading comprehension. Heyns (1978) found that (a) students of every income level learned at a slower rate during the summer than during the school year, (b) there were marked socioeconomic differences in learning, and (c) the socioeconomic differences were especially prominent during the summer months. High-SES sixth- and seventh-grade students with family incomes of at least $15,000 improved their reading skills in the summer, while low-SES students with family incomes of less than $9,000 either showed summer loss (sixth graders) or made no gain (seventh graders).

Another important study included in Cooper et al.'s (1996) meta-analysis was the Beginning School Study (BSS), a longitudinal study that followed students from first through fifth grade (e.g., Alexander et al., 2001, 2004; Entwisle, Alexander, & Olson, 1997). In the BSS, a standardized test of reading comprehension, the California Achievement Test (CAT-V), was given in the fall and spring of each year. Family SES was measured as a composite, including mother's and father's education and occupation and receipt of reduced-cost meals, and the composite was used to form three SES groups—high, medium, and low. The results of growth curve analyses by Alexander et al. (2001) show that during each school year, there were similar gains in reading for low-SES and high-SES students. There was, however, significant SES differentiation in the summer. Low-SES students showed small losses or very modest gains in the summer, whereas high-SES students gained. Figure 5.1 plots fall and spring CAT-V Reading Comprehension scores for the two SES groups. Between the spring and fall data points, the growth trajectories are clearly different, and the cumulative impact of summer loss or differentiation is apparent from the widening gap.

Kim (2004) followed a sample of ethnically diverse students who took reading tests in the spring of fifth grade and the fall of sixth grade in 18 schools in a suburban mid-Atlantic school district. He found that, holding constant spring scores and other background characteristics, low-SES students had significantly lower fall reading scores than high-SES students. Phillips and Chin (2004) analyzed

Figure 5.1. The Trajectory of CAT-V Reading

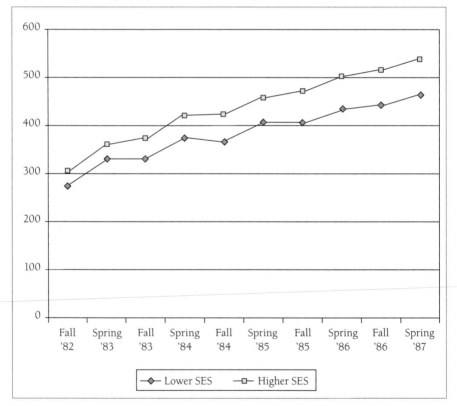

From Schools, Achievement, and Inequality: A Seasonal Perspective, by K.L. Alexander, D.R. Entwisle, & L.S. Olson, 2004, in *Summer learning: Research, policies, and programs*, pp. 25–51, edited by G.D. Borman & M. Boulay, Mahwah, NJ: Erlbaum. Reprinted with permission.

data for a subsample of students who were tested in the fall of second grade as well as spring of first grade as part of the congressionally mandated Prospects study conducted in the early 1990s in the United States. Students from families with incomes of less than $15,000 per year showed a small loss in reading vocabulary during the summer following first grade, and students from high-SES families showed a small gain.

Because the research of Heyns (1978) and others has suggested that there were seasonal differences in learning, the ECLS-K study tested participating students in the fall of their first-grade year in a random sample of 30% of the original ECLS-K schools. This subsample of about 4,000 students has allowed at least six sets of investigators to examine learning rates in the summer following kindergarten (Benson & Borman, 2007; Burkam, Ready, Lee, & LoGerfo, 2004; Cheadle, 2008; Downey, von Hippel, & Broh, 2004; LoGerfo et al., 2006; McCoach, O'Connell, Reis, & Levitt, 2006). These studies found no summer gains in reading for all students. However, there were significant differences in summer reading gains by SES group. High-SES students made reading gains while low-SES students lost ground in the summer. For example, in Burkam et al.'s (2004) study, students in the highest SES quintile gained 0.07 SD, whereas students in the lowest SES quintile lost 0.09 SD when compared with the middle-SES group.

In summary, Cooper et al.'s (1996) meta-analysis, Heyns's (1978) study, Alexander et al.'s (2001) study, Kim's (2004) study, and analyses of data from the ECLS-K (e.g., Burkam et al., 2004) and Prospects study (Phillips & Chin, 2004) are consistent in showing that there is significant SES differentiation in the summer months following kindergarten through eighth grade, such that low-SES students fall behind their high-SES peers in reading.

Do School Year or Summer Learning Differences Make a Larger Contribution to the Reading Gap?

In their analyses of ECLS-K data, Benson and Borman (2007), Cheadle (2008), Downey et al. (2004), LoGerfo et al. (2006, see Table 5.3), and McCoach et al. (2006) all found that high-SES students learned more than low-SES students during the school year as well as during the summer. They also found that there were larger socioeconomic differences in reading growth rates during the summer than during the school year. For example, in Benson and Borman's (2007) study, the gap between the highest and lowest SES quintiles increased by about 0.5 points per month in the summer between kindergarten and first grade and about 0.2 points per month in both kindergarten and first grade. They point out that the school year is longer than the summer (9.4 months vs. 2.6 months in their calculation), so the summer made a smaller contribution to SES differences overall, about 1.4 points compared with 1.9 points, or about 42% of the annual increase in the achievement gap.

In contrast to Benson and Borman (2007), Alexander et al. (2001) found that the summer months make the largest contribution to SES differences. In their growth curve analyses that included a summer adjustment term, the effect of SES was not significant and trivial in a negative direction. Thus, they stated that "the BSS conclusion is that *practically the entire gap increase across socioeconomic lines* [italics in the original] traces to summer learning differentials" (Alexander et al., 2001, p. 174; see also Entwisle et al., 1997, p. 38).

On the issue of school year versus summer learning differences, Heyns (1978) took a position that falls somewhere between Alexander et al. (2001) and Benson and Borman (2007). Unlike Alexander et al. (2001), she did find SES differentiation in the school year as well as the summer. The degree of differentiation varied with both grade level and ethnic group. The difference in gains, in grade-level equivalents, between students in the highest versus lowest income categories ranged from 0.04 to 0.35 in the school year and from 0.22 to 0.70 in the summer. Summer learning differences accounted for 39 to 95% of the annual increase in the SES gap. When Heyns (1978) looked at the increasing gap between U.S. norms and the total Atlanta sample comprised of students who were in general economically disadvantaged, she concluded that the summer differential "is responsible for perhaps 80% of the gap" (p. 68).

In sum, the answer to the question of whether school year or summer learning differences make the largest contribution to the SES gap in reading is that it depends on the sample. Based on the available evidence, summer learning differences account for as little as 40% to as much as 100% of the annual increase in the gap. In urban disadvantaged settings like those studied by Alexander et al. (2001) and Heyns (1978), it is apt to be closer to 100% than to 40%. What is clear in any event is that the *rate* of differentiation is greater during the summer months. For this reason, it makes sense to develop reading interventions for low-SES students that are designed to be implemented in the summer.

Why Do Low-SES Students Make Less Progress in Reading in the Summer Months?

We suggest, first, that spring-to-fall growth in reading achievement is affected by the amount of summer reading that students do. Second, the amount of reading that they do in the summer is influenced by (a) access to books and other reading materials in the home environment and outside of the home, and (b) family support for reading and literacy-related activities. Finally, access and family support are influenced by SES. In other words, the effect of SES on summer reading growth is mediated, at least in part, by access, support, and reading activity. So low-SES students make less progress in reading in the summer months than high-SES students because, among other factors, they have less access to books and less family support for reading and consequently read less. There is good evidence in the literature for the linkages between SES, access, and support, between access and amount of reading, and between amount of summer reading and fall reading achievement.

SES, Book Access, and Family Support

According to the "faucet theory" proposed by Entwisle et al. (1997), all children gain when they are in school because the resources needed for learning are available to them. But when school is not in session, the resource faucet is turned off, and inequalities in resources exert their effects, causing children from low-SES families to stop gaining or lose ground while children from high-SES families improve or at least maintain their skills. The faucet theory points to access to books and other reading materials as an important factor in attempting to explain why the summer months produce differential growth in reading.

Research has shown that there is a strong relationship between SES and access to books and other reading materials. In Bradley, Corwyn, McAdoo, and Coll's (2001) analysis of data from the National Longitudinal Survey of Youth (NLSY), children from low-SES families were far less likely than children from high-SES families to have 10 or more books. These SES differences also extend to the availability and quantity of books in stores, childcare centers, and local elementary school and public libraries (e.g., Neuman & Celano, 2001).

Family support for reading and literacy can be operationally defined in many different ways. One of the most straightforward and widely used measures, the frequency with which a parent reads to the child, is strongly associated with SES. Bradley et al. (2001) found that high-SES mothers were more likely than low-SES mothers to read to their children three or more times per week, with this difference being most pronounced in early childhood. Burkam et al. (2004) found that, compared with the middle-SES groups, low-SES parents were significantly less likely to read a book to their child in the summer between kindergarten and first grade, while high-SES parents were more likely to read a book to their child. A similar pattern was evident for taking the child to a library or bookstore.

An ethnographic study of fourth-grade students' summer activities by Chin and Phillips (2004) provides insight on the ways in which family support for literacy differs as a function of SES and how SES differences could contribute to summer learning differences. They found that the parents of low-SES children often went out of their way to obtain books and educational materials for their children to use in the summer. These parents, however, were less skilled at organizing and facilitating literacy-related activities and making them appealing for their children, and they were less knowledgeable about their children's capabilities than middle-SES parents. For example, a middle-SES mother organized a book club for her daughter and her friends and their mothers, whereas a low-SES mother purchased $45 worth of Harry Potter books for her daughter but did not realize that they were too difficult for her to comprehend.

Access and Amount of Summer Reading

Heyns (1978) found that the number of books sixth- and seventh-grade students read during the summer was related to both frequency of use of a public library and the distance from the student's home to the library. Kim (2004) surveyed students in the summer following fifth grade and found a significant relationship between access to books and number of books read. Access was measured on a 12-point scale that was based on students' responses (ranging from *strongly agree* to *strongly disagree*) to three statements: (1) "It's easy for me to find books to read at home during summer vacation," (2) "It's easy for me to find books to read at the public library during summer vacation," and (3) "It's easy for me to buy books to read during summer vacation." The number of books read was assessed by asking students to list as many as five titles they read and verifying each title in an electronic catalog of books for children and young adults. Only verified titles counted as a book read. Studies by Morrow (1992) and McQuillan and Au (2001) also indicate a relationship between access to books and amount of reading, although these studies focused on reading during the school year.

Summer Reading and Fall Reading Achievement

The crucial link is between summer reading and fall reading achievement, and it is well supported by research. In Heyns's (1978) landmark study, hours spent reading and books read were significantly related to fall reading achievement with spring reading achievement, family income, parental education, and household size controlled. Thus, the effect of reading was independent of SES, suggesting that "increasing access to books and encouraging reading may well have substantial impact on achievement" (Heyns, 1978, p. 172). Entwisle et al. (1997) also found that the number of books read in the summer predicted summer learning independent of SES.

Several studies have replicated Heyns's (1978) findings in recent years. Like Heyns (1978), all of these investigators controlled for spring scores and SES and they included a variety of additional covariates as controls (e.g., demographic characteristics, parents' expectations, teacher ratings, students' attitude toward reading). Phillips and Chin (2004) found that students who read more than 30 minutes per day in the summer had higher reading comprehension scores in the fall. Burkam et al. (2004) found a significant relationship between fall reading and a composite of seven literacy-related summer activities that included frequency of the student reading a book on his or her own and number of visits to a library or bookstore. Finally, Kim (2004) found a significant relationship between books read in the summer and fall reading comprehension scores. That study incorporated two significant improvements in methodology: Rising sixth-grade students were asked directly about their reading activities during the summer, and the book reading measure was validated against a list of actual titles. The other studies including Heyns (1978) relied on parents' retrospective reports of their children's summer reading that were collected after school began in the fall.

Other Variables

Other variables that could influence fall reading achievement include summer school attendance and summer activities not involving reading, such as taking a trip or visiting a museum. Some studies have found that attending summer school does not affect fall achievement whereas summer reading does (Burkam et al., 2004; Phillips & Chin, 2004). With regard to summer activities other than reading, both Heyns (1978) and Entwisle et al. (1997) found that taking a trip was related to summer gains. However, Heyns's results suggested that "the single summer activity that is most strongly and consistently related to summer learning is reading" (p. 161). This conclusion is supported by the findings of Burkam et al. (2004), who found no effect for summer trips, and Phillips and Chin (2004), who found only a weak effect of going to museums on summer learning ($p < 0.10$, weaker than reading).

Can Summer Silent Reading Programs Reduce the SES Reading Achievement Gap?

The explanation of why low-SES students make less progress in reading during the summer and the supporting evidence reviewed were, for us, a good start toward developing a summer intervention. It suggested that to improve the reading achievement of low-SES students, we needed to increase both their access to books and the volume of their summer reading. In addition, it suggested that it may be helpful to guide or structure the students' reading activities in some way, much as the middle-SES parents did in Chin and Phillips's (2004) ethnographic study. This, however, was only the first step in developing an effective program of silent summer reading.

Development of the Summer Reading Program

Development of our summer reading program began with this question: Were there any experimental studies of well-designed voluntary reading interventions that were successful in encouraging more reading and improving reading achievement among elementary school students? The National Reading Panel (NRP; National Institute of Child Health and Human Development [NICHD], 2000) had reviewed 14 experimental and quasi-experimental studies of sustained silent reading (SSR) and similar instructional approaches that typically involve asking students to select their own reading material, little monitoring, and no discussion or written follow-up assignment. The NRP's controversial conclusion was that there was little evidence that "encouraging reading has a beneficial effect on reading achievement" (p. 3-28). However, the panel members suggested that the dearth of experimental evidence "does not mean that procedures that encourage students to read more could not be made to work—future studies should explore this possibility" (p. 3-28). Thus, the NRP left open the possibility that voluntary reading could be made more effective and encouraged researchers to pursue the question of how.

Book Matching. One of the studies reviewed by the NRP was thought provoking. Carver and Leibert (1995) found that elementary school students who spent 15–30 hours reading library books in a school-based summer reading program did not gain in reading level, vocabulary, or reading rate. They interpreted this result as being due to the fact that the students read books that were too easy for them. Although most students were reading at the fifth-grade level, they chose to read books at the third- and fourth-grade levels. Other researchers had stressed the importance of text difficulty in silent or free reading (e.g., Byrnes, 2000; Stahl, 2004), and we knew that controlling the difficulty of text improves both oral reading fluency and reading comprehension (e.g., Shany & Biemiller, 1995). We concluded that the quality of the match between students' skill levels and the texts they are reading was a potentially important ingredient in an effective silent summer reading program. At the time, we were unaware of the work of Reutzel, Jones, Fawson, and Smith (2008) who were developing an instructional technique for teachers to use during the school year called scaffolded silent reading (ScSR). One of the key features of ScSR is teacher assignment of texts that are at students' independent reading levels.

We also believed that students should have an opportunity to read books that tap into their personal interests, because this enhances their motivation to read independently (Guthrie & Humenick, 2004). Thus, we concurred with Morrow's (2003) suggestion that providing high-interest books that match students' reading preferences as well as their reading levels is essential for encouraging voluntary reading outside school, and we adopted students' interests and preferences as a second potentially important element. We knew these principles had been applied previously in practical settings. For example, in a summer reading program described by Borduin and Cooper (1997), teachers assessed students' text reading levels and administered an interest survey to guide their selection of books.

Teacher and Parent Support. Kim (2004) found that students read more books over the summer when they fulfilled a teacher request to write about a book they had read. This suggested that teachers might encourage summer reading—an important but hardly novel idea. Chin and Phillips (2004) made a similar suggestion, based on their finding of a modest relationship ($p < 0.10$) between summer gains in reading comprehension and the frequency with which teachers had assigned reading-related projects in the spring (e.g., writing a report or making an oral presentation). Also, there were scattered reports in the literature of summer reading programs that incorporated teacher support. For instance, Baron (1999) described a Connecticut school in which teachers aimed to reduce the summer dip by mailing books to students and asking them to respond to the books on a postcard to be mailed to the teacher.

Kim (2004) also found that students read more books in the summer when their parents signed a form verifying that they had read at least one book from among a list of recommended titles. This indicated that parents as well as teachers might be enlisted to support summer reading, at minimum by monitoring it to provide a kind of accountability. At about the same time, Stahl (2004) pointed to monitoring as an important and often neglected component of SSR in classrooms.

Book Matching and Teacher and Parent Support. Kim (2007) studied the effects of a voluntary summer reading intervention for first- through fifth-grade students that incorporated book matching and teacher and parent support. In the late spring, the students took the reading portion of the Stanford Achievement Test (SAT) as a pretest and also completed a 20-item survey of their reading preferences. Then they were randomly assigned to a treatment condition in which they received 10 books during the summer vacation (i.e., last week of June to first week of September) or a control condition in which they received 10 books after readministration of the SAT reading test as a posttest in the fall. A fall reading survey administered after the posttest included questions about book ownership and summer reading activity.

The following procedures were used to accomplish book matching and provide teacher and parent support in Kim's (2007) experiment. A two-step computer algorithm identified books that matched (a) each student's reading preferences based on the reading survey and (b) each student's independent reading level based on a range of 50 Lexiles above to 100 Lexiles below students' scores on the SAT in the spring. Teachers supported the students' summer reading by conducting a lesson near the end of the school year where they explained that students in the program would receive 10 books during the summer or in the fall. Each book would be accompanied with a postcard with several questions to be answered before returning it: (a) Did you finish reading your new book? (b) Did you like reading this book? (c) Was this book easy to read? In addition, parents would receive a letter requesting that they remind their children to read the books.

In Kim's (2007) experiment, students in the treatment group reported reading significantly more books in the summer than did students in the control group, about three more books on average. Also, only 3% of the low-SES students in the treatment group reported owning 0–10 books (the lowest category on the survey), whereas 32% of the students in the control group did so. Further, the books were well matched to the students' interests and reading levels, and teachers and parents encouraged and supported the students' reading, although the level of support might be described as minimal. However, despite book matching and some teacher and parent support, and despite the observed impact of the treatment on summer reading and book ownership, there was no difference in reading achievement between the treatment group and the control group. It was clear that something more was needed.

Book Matching and Teacher and Parent Scaffolding. Kim (2007) suggested that to strengthen the efficacy of summer reading programs, teachers could scaffold silent reading activities by instructing students how to use strategies to monitor their comprehension of text (Pressley, 2002; Rosenshine & Meister, 1994). For example, during lessons conducted at the end of the school year, teachers could instruct students to use multiple strategies to improve their reading comprehension in the summer. If students were reminded to apply comprehension strategies in silent reading and they did so, this might also increase the degree to which they are actively engaged in reading and motivated to understand what they are reading, particularly if they know they will be explaining what they read to a parent.

Although the NRP (NICHD, 2000) found no convincing evidence of positive effects for voluntary reading, it did find that the use of multiple comprehension strategies produced significant gains on reading assessments. The NRP also found that guided oral reading of text improved reading comprehension. Our awareness of this second evidence-based instructional strategy led to the final development in our thinking about an effective summer reading program: Teachers could scaffold fluent oral reading in end-of-the-year lessons, and parents could scaffold summer reading by providing an opportunity for their children to practice oral reading of a text they had previously read silently. Thus, prior research suggested that students might benefit from summer reading if they were explicitly taught to use comprehension strategies during silent reading of text and instructed to practice oral reading with a family member.

Logic Model for Our Studies of Scaffolded Silent Summer Reading. Putting the pieces together, Figure 5.2 displays the logic model that underlies our studies of scaffolded silent summer reading. In essence, fall reading achievement is influenced by the amount of scaffolded silent summer reading of matched and interesting books that students do.

To provide scaffolding for students' summer reading, we ask teachers to implement several lessons at the end of the school year. In these lessons, the teacher instructs students to use comprehension strategies that they can apply at home during the summer when they are reading independently and silently. The teacher also provides oral reading fluency practice, encourages students to read aloud to

Figure 5.2. Logic Model for Studies of Scaffolded Silent Summer Reading

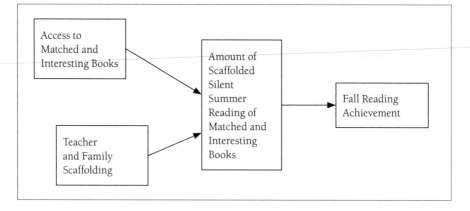

their parents over the summer, and shows them a simple procedure for doing so. We also ask parents to listen as their child tells them about a book he or she had read during the summer, listen as a short passage from a book is read out loud by the child, and provide feedback on the degree to which the child reads smoothly and with expression. Similarly, in Reutzel et al.'s (2008) ScSR procedure for classroom use, students read silently on their own, and they read aloud to the teacher.

The Experiments and the Program

In the first of our two experiments (Kim, 2006), fourth-grade students received lessons from their teacher at the end of the school year. In these lessons, the teacher modeled fluent oral reading and comprehension strategies for silent reading. The students practiced fluent oral reading in a paired-reading format and practiced using five reading comprehension strategies while reading silently on their own. In the summer, the treatment group received matched books and parent scaffolding that consisted of listening as the student talked about a book, listening as a 100-word passage from the book was read aloud and then reread, providing general feedback, and signing a postcard to be mailed to the researchers with an optional comment about the summer reading experience. The control group received no books and no parent scaffolding in the summer but did receive books in the fall after posttesting to satisfy ethical requirements.

Positive effects on reading achievement were observed in the Kim (2006) experiment, but considering the controversy over the benefits of silent reading, we believed that replication with a different sample of schools and additional grade levels was important. In addition, it is possible that the same results would have been obtained if students simply received the matched books without any support from their teachers or parents, or if students received only oral reading practice without comprehension strategies instruction. Therefore, we conducted a second experiment (Kim & White, 2008) with four groups of students in third through fifth grades:

1. Matched books only (Books Only)
2. Matched books and oral reading (Books With Oral Reading Scaffolding)
3. Matched books, oral reading, and comprehension strategies instruction (Books With Oral Reading and Comprehension Scaffolding)
4. Control group receiving books in the fall after posttesting and no teacher or parent scaffolding (Control)

Participants. Both experiments were conducted in a large, suburban school district in the mid-Atlantic region of the United States. In the first experiment, the participants were 34 teachers and 486 students who were completing fourth grade in one of 10 elementary schools. Non-Caucasian ethnic minorities (e.g., African American, Hispanic, Asian) were predominant (67%), and 39% of the students were receiving free or reduced-cost lunch. In the second experiment, the participants were 24 teachers and 400 students who were completing third, fourth, or fifth grade in one of two elementary schools. The students' characteristics were similar: 69% non-Caucasian and 38% receiving free or reduced-cost lunch. Students with special education needs who could not be tested under standard conditions were excluded from the experiments. About 8% of the students tested were classified as learning disabled.

Prior research informed our decision to target the intervention to students in the third through fifth grades. Most voluntary reading interventions have focused on students who are old enough to have mastered basic decoding skills and are capable of improving their reading through reading (Byrnes, 2000; Share, 1999). For example, 12 of the 14 studies on voluntary reading reviewed by the NRP involved students in third grade or higher. Although Kim (2007) found no significant effects for summer reading, treatment–control differences were larger in the third and fifth grades than in the first and second grades.

Treatment and Control Groups. In the first experiment, all students—including those in the control group—received the three end-of-year lessons. (We assumed—and this assumption was later borne out by the data—that there would be minimal lesson effects for the control group because the students received no books in the summer and, thus, no opportunity to practice what they were taught in the lessons.) Within each of the participating teachers' classes, students were randomly assigned to either the treatment group or the control group. The treatment group received matched books and parent scaffolding of oral reading in the summer. The control group received books in the fall after the posttests were administered and no parent scaffolding. In the second experiment, both teachers and students were randomly assigned to one of the four groups—Books Only, Books With Oral Reading Scaffolding, Books With Oral Reading and Comprehension Scaffolding, and Control. The Control group received no end-of-year lessons from their teacher, no books in the summer, and no parent scaffolding.

Measures. To determine the reading preferences we used to match books with students, teachers administered a survey that asked students how much they enjoyed reading books from one of 25 categories. The categories were initially developed from the Adventuring with Books list for pre-K to grade 6 students published by the National Council of Teachers of English (McClure & Kristo, 2002), validated using other published surveys of students' reading preferences (e.g., Galda, Ash, & Cullinan, 2000; Ivey & Broaddus, 2001), and reviewed and refined by four elementary teachers. To find out whether the intervention increased reading activity at home or access to books at home during the summer, teachers administered a survey in September in which students were asked to rate how often they had engaged in each of five reading activities and how many books there were in their homes.

To measure growth in the students' reading achievement over the summer, teachers administered the appropriate level of the vocabulary and reading comprehension tests from the Iowa Tests of Basic Skills (ITBS) in the second week of June and the second week of September. Different forms of the test were used in June and September. The vocabulary and reading comprehension test scores were combined to get a total reading score that was used in analyzing gains from pretest to posttest. The ITBS is highly reliable (KR-20 coefficients above 0.93 and equivalent form estimates of 0.86 or higher), and the levels are vertically equated to yield a continuous measure of reading achievement.

The Program. The program was implemented in four stages: teacher training, end-of-year lessons, book matching, and parent/family member support for summer reading. In early June, teachers attended a two-hour training session conducted by an experienced elementary language arts teacher. This teacher trainer had developed the lessons to meet our specifications and field tested them in a fourth-grade class prior to training. During training, she modeled a series of three lessons using an engaging, well-illustrated children's storybook, *The Wreck of the Zephyr* by Chris Van Allsburg.

The end-of-year lessons were carried out over the course of several days by the participating classroom teachers, following training. Each lesson was fully scripted and required no more than 45 minutes of class time. Lesson 1 focused on comprehension strategies. The teacher began by explaining to the students that they would be receiving books and postcards over the summer, and they would need to know what to do when they received them. She asked for the students' help in generating a list of five strategies that good readers use to help them understand what they are reading: reread, predict, ask questions, make connections, and summarize. These were strategies the teachers had already introduced and taught, so it was not difficult to elicit them. The teacher then read *The Wreck of the Zephyr* aloud, stopping at appropriate points to model one of the strategies. As each strategy was modeled, the students were asked to identify it, and the teacher rephrased their responses so they exactly matched the phrases they would see on the postcard. Next, the teacher demonstrated on an overhead transparency how to complete the questions on a postcard like the one the students would be receiving with their books. In the last part of the lesson, students selected a book, attached sticky notes where they used a comprehension strategy, shared their examples of strategy use with the class, and practiced answering the questions on the postcard. The fourth question asked them to place a check mark by each comprehension strategy they used.

In Lesson 2, the focus was fluency practice. Following a review of comprehension strategies, the teacher stated, "Another thing that good readers do is read smoothly and with good expression when they are reading aloud." She asked the students how they knew if someone was a good reader when they read aloud, accepted their answers, and said, "Yes, when someone reads aloud with good expression and at just the right speed without mistakes, we call that fluent reading." She wrote *fluent reading* on the board and beneath it, *smooth*, *good expression*, and *correct*. Then she explained that she would read a 100-word passage from *The Wreck of the Zephyr* several times, and the students would rate her reading. The first reading was poor, with lots of pauses and miscues; the second reading was better, with shorter pauses and no miscues but flat and expressionless; and the third reading was her best reading—smooth, full of expression, and errorless. Next, the teacher used an overhead transparency of the postcard to demonstrate how the students would be answering an additional question that was not discussed the day before: a three-part question that asked whether they read more smoothly, knew more words, and read with more expression. Finally, the teacher pointed out that postcard asked for a family member's signature and optional comment.

Lesson 2 continued with students pairing up, counting 100 words from a passage in a book, and practicing reading with their partners. One student read the passage aloud while the other gave feedback using the postcard rating categories, then the roles were reversed for a second reading. After paired reading, the students "mailed" their postcards by returning them to the teacher. They were given a homework assignment to independently read a book for 15 minutes, read aloud a 100-word passage to a family member twice, complete the questions on the postcard, and obtain a family member's signature.

Lesson 3 provided additional teacher modeling and practice with a nonfiction book. The teacher elicited and modeled comprehension strategies as before, modeled completion of the postcard questions, and modeled counting out 100 words and reading aloud with improvement shown. The students then practiced on their own (for silent reading and comprehension strategies) and with a partner (for oral reading and fluency practice).

In the first experiment, all students received all three end-of-year lessons exactly as described earlier. In the second experiment, only the students in the Books With Oral Reading and Comprehension Scaffolding group received all three lessons. Students in the Books With Oral Reading Scaffolding group received two lessons that did not include comprehension strategies; and students in the Books Only group received a single lesson that included neither oral reading nor comprehension strategies instruction. For students in the Control group, the teacher prepared an alternative reading activity to use in place of the lessons.

In both experiments, matched books were selected for each student by a computer algorithm that merged data from two files. One file contained a text difficulty (Lexile) level and preference categories for each of 240 available book titles. The second file contained each student's Lexile range from the June ITBS and reading preference ratings for the categories on the June survey. The algorithm generated a list of the eight books that represented the best matches for each student, those with high preference ratings within the student's Lexile range. For students in the treatment groups, one matched book was mailed each week for eight successive weeks from early July until the end of August. Students in the control group received all eight of their matched books at once in September after the posttests.

Along with each book that was mailed, there was a postcard for the student and a letter for the parent or other family member (translated into Spanish, Urdu, Arabic, or Vietnamese for parents who spoke one of these languages). The letter asked the parent to encourage their children to read and requested return of the postcard. Except for students in the Books Only group of the second experiment, the parent letter suggested that "It will help your child if he or she reads out loud to you, or to an older brother or sister" and requested that "After you listen to your child reading out loud a second time, tell him or her how they improved." The postcard was modified as needed to implement the Books Only and Books With Oral Reading Scaffolding treatment conditions in the second experiment (e.g., the postcard had no questions asking the student about his or her use of comprehension strategies).

Findings

First Experiment

Table 5.1 displays the posttest mean total reading scores on the ITBS for all students in the treatment and control groups. The posttest scores were adjusted for pretest scores by means of an ANCOVA. Overall reading achievement was higher for the treatment group ($M = 207.9$) than the control group ($M = 205.9$). The difference of 2.0 points was just 0.01 short of the conventional 0.05 level of statistical significance at $p < 0.06$ but it represented 1.3 additional months of school learning, so it is clearly significant in practical terms. We calculated additional months of school learning by dividing the difference between the treatment and control group means by 1.56, because students gain 14 points from the spring of fourth grade to the spring of fifth grade according to the test publisher's norm sample, or 1.56 points per month during a nine-month school year. Research (e.g., Cooper et al., 1996) suggests that achievement scores do not increase during the summer, so we divided 14 by 9, not 12.

Table 5.1. ITBS Results of the First Experiment

Participants	N (Total for Both Groups)	SD (Combining Groups)	Treatment Group Mean (ITBS Total Reading)[a]	Control Group Mean (ITBS Total Reading)[a]	Additional Months of Learning[b]
All students (including "other" ethnicity)	486	24.1	207.9	205.9	+1.3
Caucasian	160	24.3	221.8	219.2	+1.6
African American	93	19.6	201.5	196.3	+3.3
Hispanic	125	18.6	197.2	193.9	+2.1
Asian	85	22.0	203.1	207.2	−2.6
Low SES	183	20.3	199.8	198.5	+0.8

[a]Adjusted for pretest scores. [b]See text for explanation.

Table 5.1 also displays the ITBS results for low-SES students and each ethnic group regardless of income. African American and Hispanic students derived the greatest benefit from the summer reading program, showing treatment effects that were about twice as large as the overall effect. For African American students, the difference between treatment and control conditions (5.2 points) represents 3.3 additional months of learning. For Hispanic students, the treatment–control difference is the equivalent of 2.1 additional months of learning. For Asian students, the control group performed better than the treatment group. This anomalous result may be related to the fact that the control group included a much higher proportion of females than males. It is possible that these Asian females were avid readers before the experiment began. Thus, the results for Asian students may reflect selection effects—that is, the overrepresentation of Asian females in the control group—rather than differences due to the effects of the intervention.

Other data collected in the first experiment indicated that many of the students did read their books with a parent or family member. Slightly more than half of the students in the treatment group in each of the ethnic groups returned a postcard indicating that they read at least one book, and all but a few of the returned postcards had been signed by a parent or family member. Also, on two survey items measuring oral reading with a family member, the treatment group had significantly higher scores than the control group.

Second Experiment

As in the first experiment, there was evidence that the intervention had an impact on the students' summer reading activity. On a scale that combined results from five items, there was a significant difference favoring the Books With Oral Reading and Comprehension Scaffolding group over the Control group. About half of the students in each treatment group returned at least one postcard indicating they had read at least one book, and about 25% returned four or more postcards indicating they had read at least four of the eight books.

As expected, students in the Books Only group ($M = 203.6$) performed similarly to those in the Control group on ITBS total reading ($M = 203.1$). Thus, as in the Kim (2007) experiment, simply providing matched books did not have a significant positive effect on reading achievement. The lack of positive effects for books only did not seem to result from the students having not read the books. The percentage of students who reported reading part or all of at least one book was actually higher for the Books Only group (55%) than for the Books With Oral Reading and Comprehension Scaffolding group (49%), as was the percentage of students who reported reading four or more of the eight books, 34% and 23%, respectively.

Students in the full-treatment group, Books With Oral Reading and Comprehension Scaffolding ($M = 207.0$) significantly outperformed students in the Control group on the ITBS ($M = 203.1$, $p < 0.03$). The difference in posttest scores of 3.9 points represents a learning advantage of 2.5 months.

Table 5.2. ITBS Results of the Second Experiment

Participants	N (Total for Both Groups)	SD (Combining Groups)	Treatment Group Mean (ITBS Total Reading)[a,b]	Control Group Mean (ITBS Total Reading)[a,b]	Additional Months of Learning[c]
All students (including "other" ethnicity)	207	28.3	207.0	203.1	+2.5
Caucasian	72	25.4	221.6	222.4	−0.5
African American	50	26.2	201.0	198.4	+1.7
Hispanic	61	24.3	196.0	188.1	+5.1
Low SES	77	22.6	195.6	189.3	+4.0

[a]Books with oral reading and comprehension scaffolding only; other treatment groups, books only, and books with oral reading scaffolding are excluded to make Tables 5.1 and 5.2 comparable. [b]Adjusted for pretest scores. [c]See text for explanation.

Students in the Books With Oral Reading Scaffolding group ($M = 204.8$) performed better than those in the Control group ($M = 203.1$) on the ITBS, and this difference was larger for students who were below the median on the fluency pretest ($M = 204.8$ vs. 200.7), but differences were not statistically significant. Thus, the second experiment did not provide clear evidence on whether oral reading scaffolding alone produces better reading outcomes.

Table 5.2 presents the main ITBS results for low-SES, African American, Caucasian, and Hispanic students, comparing the Control group with the full-treatment group, Books With Oral Reading and Comprehension Scaffolding. These data are directly comparable to the data in Table 5.1. The largest positive effects, ranging from 1.7 to 5.1 additional months of learning, were observed for African American, Hispanic, and low-SES students. Low-SES students gained an average of 4.0 months. Notably, this is enough to offset 100% of the summer loss shown by low-SES students in Cooper et al.'s (1996) meta-analysis of studies of the effect of summer vacation on achievement, 0.34 grade-level equivalents or about 3 months.

Related Research and Similar Programs Implemented by Others

In our studies, the intervention lasted for a single summer only, and we found that it was sufficiently effective to offset the amount of summer loss that is typically seen in low-SES students. In subsequent summers, however, the low-SES students who benefited from the program are likely to have slipped behind their high-SES peers. Thus, to make a significant dent in the SES achievement gap, it may be necessary to implement a multiyear program of silent summer reading. In the only study of the impact of increasing access to books over consecutive summers on students' reading achievement that we are aware of, Allington and McGill-Franzen (2008) randomly assigned primary school students in 17 high-poverty schools to a treatment group or a control group. Treatment-group students received 12 self-selected paperback books for three consecutive summers. Students were encouraged to keep a book log each summer. After the third summer, the treatment group scored 0.14 SDs higher than the control group on the Florida Comprehensive Assessment Test, and the effect size was somewhat larger for the lowest SES students (0.21 SD).

Since the conclusion of our two experiments, numerous school districts have implemented similar programs of silent summer reading. For example, in 2008, Communities in Schools (a dropout prevention organization) and MetaMetrics, Inc. (a North Carolina-based testing firm) partnered with local school administrators and teachers in Durham, North Carolina, USA, to implement a silent summer reading program based on our earlier experimental studies. The study involved third- and fourth-grade students from two schools who were below reading level as measured by the North Carolina end-of-grade assessments in reading. These students were administered a pretest and posttest comprehension measure developed by MetaMetrics (Vitiello, 2008). Students' Lexile levels ranged from 120L to 990L (Lexiles), which corresponded to the mean reading level of students in first to sixth grades.

Book fairs were held to select matched and interesting books for students to read during the summer. Since the book fairs were held after the school year ended, dinner was provided for parents and their children to increase participation. Approximately 230 books that accommodated the wide range of reading levels were purchased from Barnes & Noble and Scholastic. The books were organized into one of six Lexile levels ranging from (1) below 300L, (2) 300–400L, (3) 401–500L, (4) 501–600L, (5) 601–700L, and (6) above 700 Lexiles. Books were color coded to correspond to the appropriate Lexile zone. Staff and volunteers used Lexile scores from the pretest reading measure to direct students to one of the six Lexile zones, and students were allowed to choose eight books within their zone that interested them. The students were informed that their chosen books would be mailed to them in July and August, and they were also encouraged to return a postcard after reading each book.

Staff from MetaMetrics examined whether pretest to posttest reading Lexile gains were related to the number of books students reported reading as measured by their postcard return rate. The results revealed a moderate relationship between reading growth in Lexiles and the number of books students reported reading during the summer. Students who read more than half of their books (5 to 8 books) had an average gain of more than 80 Lexiles, whereas students who read less than half of their books (0 to 4 books) lost ground during the summer. For example, students who read only 0 to 1 book underwent a decline of approximately 50 Lexiles, on average. Because there was no comparison group and students were not randomly assigned to receive different numbers of books, no firm causal conclusions can be drawn.

Despite the limitations of correlational evidence, the Durham program provides an example of adapting a silent reading program to fit within the resource constraints of a local school district. It is important to note that the Durham program did match books to readers, but the strategy for doing so—a leveled book fair—was different from the strategy we had employed in our two experiments. Equally important, there was also an effort to evaluate the efficacy of the program.

Conclusions About Summer Reading and Recommendations for Researchers and Policymakers

In future years, we suspect that policymakers and practitioners will become more interested in adopting scaffolded silent summer reading programs. Given the budget deficits at all levels of government, school districts are unlikely to have the resources to implement costly summer school programs. At the same time, federal and state accountability mandates will continue to hold schools responsible for reducing achievement gaps, especially those based on socioeconomic status. Both budget constraints and accountability demands are likely to fuel the debate about the most cost-effective approaches to reduce achievement gaps and implement silent summer reading programs. We conclude this chapter by offering several recommendations for researchers and policymakers pursuing these goals.

First, researchers and policymakers should continue to examine the question of whether increasing the quantity and quality of silent summer reading activities improves reading achievement for low-SES students. As noted in the first part of this chapter, sociological research suggests that students must have access to books at home to enjoy gains in reading comprehension during the summer months. The Allington and McGill-Franzen (2008) study is exemplary in its use of a longitudinal design to test the impact of increasing access to books across multiple summers. Findings from this experimental study suggest that a longer intervention spanning multiple summers may enhance the efficacy of silent reading programs. In future work, researchers should continue to pursue the question of whether a multiyear silent summer reading program can generate long-term, cumulative, and practically significant effects on reading achievement.

Our research has suggested that *qualitative* differences in students' silent reading activities also matter. The quality of students' silent reading experiences, as measured by the match between readers and texts, may be as important as *quantitative* differences in students' access to books and opportunities to read. We are certainly not alone in pointing to the match between text and reader (e.g., Hiebert & Sailors, 2009). In the Allington and McGill-Franzen (2008) study, students were allowed to self-select books without regard to their difficulty. From our perspective, their positive results are somewhat surprising. But the point we wish to emphasize is that, to date, there has been no study of a silent summer reading program that increased access to matched books for multiple summers.

Second, researchers and policymakers should articulate a clear logic model for their silent summer reading program. Our logic model (Rossi, Lipsey, & Freeman, 2004) describes the critical program components through which a silent summer reading program may improve reading achievement. Based on our review of research, we proposed that increasing students' access to matched books and teacher and family scaffolding are needed to increase silent reading activities in the summer and to improve reading achievement. An important goal of our two experimental studies was to test the logic model outlined in Figure 5.2. Results from our two studies indicated that both program components—access to matched books and teacher and family scaffolding—were needed to improve students' reading comprehension.

A logic model can also predict the conditions under which an intervention may *not* improve student outcomes. Kim and Guryan (2010) allowed 400 low-SES Hispanic students who had just completed fourth grade to self-select 10 books for summer reading at an end-of-year book fair. Most students did not choose 10 books that were matched to their reading level. Specifically, 67% of the students selected 10 books with a mean readability level above their independent reading level. In addition, many parents and children did not attend the family literacy events that were offered in an attempt to increase parent support or scaffolding for summer reading. Consistent with the logic model in Figure 5.2, students who received 10 books and whose parents were invited to the family literacy events scored no higher on the Gates–MacGinitie Reading Test administered in the fall than students who received no books in the summer.

Third, policymakers should insist on evaluation of any silent summer reading programs that are implemented to determine if they are effective, particularly in reducing socioeconomic disparities in reading achievement. Evaluation is critical, because there is no guarantee that positive results from a silent reading intervention in one district will be easily replicated in a district with different groups of students. Local adaptations of silent reading programs will inevitably lead to variations in program design, and these variations (e.g., the strategy for matching books to readers, the duration of the intervention, and the English proficiency of the students in the program) are likely to affect the results. The Durham program is noteworthy, because there was not only an intervention to address the problem of summer reading loss but also a plan to collect data on students' summer reading activity and progress in reading comprehension. We encourage other school districts to intervene to address the problem of summer loss and to simultaneously evaluate their efforts by measuring students' reading skills and the amount of summer reading.

QUESTIONS FOR
PROFESSIONAL DEVELOPMENT

1. What are some reasons why low-SES students fall behind in reading during summer vacation?

2. How could the results of the two experiments inform the design of a scaffolded silent reading program in your school?

3. How could you determine whether the core components of the logic model are being implemented with high fidelity?

4. How could you evaluate your silent reading program to determine if it is working well or is in need of additional modifications?

NOTE

Some of the material in this chapter has been adapted from White and Kim (2008).

REFERENCES

Aikens, N.L., & Barbarin, O. (2008). Socioeconomic differences in reading trajectories: The contribution of family, neighborhood, and school contexts. *Journal of Educational Psychology, 100*(2), 235–251. doi:10.1037/0022-0663.100.2.235

Alexander, K.L., Entwisle, D.R., & Olson, L.S. (2001). Schools, achievement, and inequality: A seasonal perspective. *Educational Evaluation and Policy Analysis, 23*(2), 171–191. doi:10.3102/01623737023002171

Alexander, K.L., Entwisle, D.R., & Olson, L.S. (2004). Schools, achievement, and inequality: A seasonal perspective. In G.D. Borman & M. Boulay (Eds.), *Summer learning: Research, policies, and programs* (pp. 25–51). Mahwah, NJ: Erlbaum.

Allington, R., & McGill-Franzen, A. (2008). Got books? *Educational Leadership, 65*(7), 20–23.

Baron, J.B. (1999). *Exploring high and improving reading achievement in Connecticut.* Washington, DC: National Education Goals Panel.

Becker, W.C. (1977). Teaching reading and language to the disadvantaged—What we have learned from field research. *Harvard Educational Review, 47*(4), 518–543.

Benson, J.G., & Borman, G.D. (2007). *Family and contextual socioeconomic effects across seasons: When do they matter for the achievement growth*

of young children? (WCER Working Paper No. 2007-5). Madison: Center for Education Research, University of Wisconsin.

Borduin, B.J., & Cooper, E.D. (1997). Summer reading pals. *The Reading Teacher, 50*(8), 702–704.

Borman, G.D., & Dowling, N.M. (2006). Longitudinal achievement effects of multiyear summer school: Evidence from the Teach Baltimore randomized field trial. *Educational Evaluation and Policy Analysis, 28*(1), 25–48. doi:10.3102/01623737028001025

Bradley, R.H., Corwyn, R.F., McAdoo, H.P., & Coll, C.G. (2001). The home environments of children in the United States part I: Variations by age, ethnicity, and poverty status. *Child Development, 72*(6), 1844–1867. doi:10.1111/1467-8624.t01-1-00382

Burkam, D.T., Ready, D.D., Lee, V.E., & LoGerfo, L.F. (2004). Social-class differences in summer learning between kindergarten and first grade: Model specification and estimation. *Sociology of Education, 77*(1), 1–31. doi:10.1177/003804070407700101

Byrnes, J.P. (2000). Using instructional time effectively. In L. Baker, M.J. Dreher, & J.T. Guthrie (Eds.), *Engaging young readers: Promoting achievement and motivation* (pp. 188–208). New York: Guilford.

Carver, R.P., & Leibert, R.E. (1995). The effect of reading library books at different levels of difficulty upon gain in reading ability. *Reading Research Quarterly*, 30(1), 26–48. doi:10.2307/747743

Chall, J.S. (1983). *Stages of reading development*. New York: McGraw-Hill.

Chall, J.S., Jacobs, V.A., & Baldwin, L.E. (1990). *The reading crisis: Why poor children fall behind*. Cambridge, MA: Harvard University Press.

Cheadle, J.E. (2008). Educational investment, family context, and children's math and reading growth from kindergarten through the third grade. *Sociology of Education*, 81(1), 1–31. doi:10.1177/003804070808100101

Chin, T., & Phillips, M. (2004). Social reproduction and child-rearing practices: Social class, children's agency, and the summer activity gap. *Sociology of Education*, 77(3), 185–210. doi:10.1177/003804070407700301

Cooper, H., Nye, B., Charlton, K., Lindsay, J., & Greathouse, S. (1996). The effects of summer vacation on achievement test scores: A narrative and meta-analytic review. *Review of Educational Research*, 66(3), 227–268.

Downey, D.B., von Hippel, P.T., & Broh, B.A. (2004). Are schools the great equalizer? Cognitive inequality during the summer months and the school year. *American Sociological Review*, 69(5), 613–635. doi:10.1177/000312240406900501

Entwisle, D.R., Alexander, K.L., & Olson, L.S. (1997). *Children, schools, and inequality*. Boulder, CO: Westview.

Galda, L., Ash, G.E., & Cullinan, B.E. (2000). Children's literature. In M.L. Kamil, P.B. Mosenthal, P.D. Pearson, & R. Barr (Eds.), *Handbook of reading research* (Vol. 3, pp. 361–379). Mahwah, NJ: Erlbaum.

Guthrie, J.T., & Humenick, N.M. (2004). Motivating students to read: Evidence for classroom practices that increase reading motivation and achievement. In P. McCardle & V. Chhabra (Eds.), *The voice of evidence in reading research* (pp. 329–354). Baltimore: Paul H. Brookes.

Hart, B., & Risley, T.R. (1995). *Meaningful differences in the everyday experience of young American children*. Baltimore: Paul H. Brookes.

Heyns, B. (1978). *Summer learning and the effects of schooling*. New York: Academic.

Hiebert, E.H., & Sailors, M. (Eds.). (2009). *Finding the right texts: What works for beginning and struggling readers*. New York: Guilford.

Ivey, G., & Broaddus, K. (2001). "Just plain reading": A survey of what makes students want to read in middle school classrooms. *Reading Research Quarterly*, 36(4), 350–377. doi:10.1598/RRQ.36.4.2

Kim, J. (2004). Summer reading and the ethnic achievement gap. *Journal of Education for Students Placed at Risk*, 9(2), 169–188. doi:10.1207/s15327671espr0902_5

Kim, J.S. (2006). Effects of a voluntary summer reading intervention on reading achievement: Results from a randomized field trial. *Educational Evaluation and Policy Analysis*, 28(4), 335–355. doi:10.3102/01623737028004335

Kim, J.S. (2007). The effects of a voluntary summer reading intervention on reading activities and reading achievement. *Journal of Educational Psychology*, 99(3), 505–515. doi:10.1037/0022-0663.99.3.505

Kim, J.S., & Guryan, J. (2010). The efficacy of a voluntary summer book reading intervention for low-income Latino children from language minority families. *Journal of Educational Psychology*, 102(1), 20–31.

Kim, J.S., & White, T.G. (2008). Scaffolding voluntary summer reading for children in grades 3 to 5: An experimental study. *Scientific Studies of Reading*, 12(1), 1–23. doi:10.1080/10888430701746849

Lai, M.K., McNaughton, S., Amituanai-Toloa, M., Turner, R., & Hsiao, S. (2009). Sustained acceleration of achievement in reading comprehension: The New Zealand experience. *Reading Research Quarterly*, 44(1), 30–56. doi:10.1598/RRQ.44.1.2

Lee, J., Grigg, W.S., & Donahue, P.L. (2007). *The nation's report card: Reading 2007* (NCES 2007-496). Washington, DC: National Center for Education Statistics, Institute of Education Sciences, U.S. Department of Education.

LoGerfo, L., Nichols, A., & Reardon, S.F. (2006). *Achievement gains in elementary and high school*. Washington, DC: Urban Institute.

McClure, A.A., & Kristo, J.V. (2002). *Adventuring with books: A booklist for pre-K–grade 6* (13th ed.). Urbana, IL: National Council of Teachers of English.

McCoach, D.B., O'Connell, A.A., Reis, S.M., & Levitt, H.A. (2006). Growing readers: A hierarchical linear model of children's reading growth during the first 2 years of school. *Journal of Educational Psychology, 98*(1), 14–28. doi:10.1037/0022-0663.98.1.14

McQuillan, J., & Au, J. (2001). The effect of print access on reading frequency. *Reading Psychology, 22*(3), 225–248. doi:10.1080/027027101753170638

Morrow, L.M. (1992). The impact of a literature-based program on literacy achievement, use of literature, and attitudes of children from minority backgrounds. *Reading Research Quarterly, 27*(3), 251–275. doi:10.2307/747794

Morrow, L.M. (2003). Motivating lifelong voluntary readers. In J. Flood, D. Lapp, J.R. Squire, & J.M. Jensen (Eds.), *Handbook of research on teaching the English language arts* (2nd ed., pp. 857–867). Mahwah, NJ: Erlbaum.

National Institute of Child Health and Human Development. (2000). *Report of the National Reading Panel. Teaching children to read: An evidence-based assessment of the scientific research literature on reading and its implications for reading instruction* (NIH Publication No. 00-4769). Washington, DC: U.S. Government Printing Office.

Neuman, S.B., & Celano, D. (2001). Access to print in low-income and middle-income communities: An ecological study of four neighborhoods. *Reading Research Quarterly, 36*(1), 8–26. doi:10.1598/RRQ.36.1.1

Phillips, M., & Chin, T. (2004). How families, children, and teachers contribute to summer learning and loss. In G.D. Borman & M. Boulay (Eds.), *Summer learning: Research, policies, and programs* (pp. 255–278). Mahwah, NJ: Erlbaum.

Pressley, M. (2002). *Reading instruction that works: The case for balanced teaching* (2nd ed.). New York: Guilford.

Reutzel, D.R., Jones, C.D., Fawson, P.C., & Smith, J.A. (2008). Scaffolded silent reading: A complement to guided repeated oral reading that works! *The Reading Teacher, 62*(3), 194–207. doi:10.1598/RT.62.3.2

Rosenshine, B., & Meister, C. (1994). Reciprocal teaching: A review of the research. *Review of Educational Research, 64*(4), 479–530.

Rossi, P.H., Lipsey, M.W., & Freeman, H.E. (2004). *Evaluation: A systematic approach* (7th ed.). Thousand Oaks, CA: Sage.

Shany, M.T., & Biemiller, A. (1995). Assisted reading practice: Effects on performance for poor readers in grades 3 and 4. *Reading Research Quarterly, 30*(3), 382–395. doi:10.2307/747622

Share, D.L. (1999). Phonological recoding and orthographic learning: A direct test of the self-teaching hypothesis. *Journal of Experimental Child Psychology, 72*(2), 95–129. doi:10.1006/jecp.1998.2481

Stahl, S.A. (2004). What do we know about fluency? Findings of the National Reading Panel. In P. McCardle & V. Chhabra (Eds.), *The voice of evidence in reading research* (pp. 187–211). Baltimore: Paul H. Brookes.

Vitiello, C. (2008). *Durham READS: Summer reading results.* Durham, NC: MetaMetrics.

White, T.G., Graves, M.F., & Slater, W.H. (1990). Growth of reading vocabulary in diverse elementary schools: Decoding and word meaning. *Journal of Educational Psychology, 82*(2), 281–290.

White, T.G., & Kim, J.S. (2008). Teacher and parent scaffolding of voluntary summer reading. *The Reading Teacher, 62*(2), 116–125. doi:10.1598/RT.62.2.3

Silent Reading:
Instruction and Opportunity

CHAPTER 6

Engaged Silent Reading

Emily A. Swan
University of Utah

Cassandra S. Coddington
Georgia State University

John T. Guthrie
University of Maryland

Out of all of the concerns educators have, one of the most crucial is how to motivate their students to read and do the required work assigned in class (Wagner, 2008). This concern is not surprising, given the evidence that children's and adolescents' intrinsic motivations for reading are low (Guthrie, McRae, & Klauda, 2007). The problem is that students' reading attitudes, value for, and motivations to read begin to decline in the fourth grade and continue to decline each subsequent year (Meece & Miller, 1999), reaching their lowest point in high school (Zusho & Pintrich, 2001). This is often referred to as the fourth-grade slump (Chall, 1983). By fourth grade, the amount and breadth of reading required of students is much higher than in the primary grades, and the focus of instruction is no longer about formally teaching students how to read. By fourth grade, students are expected to know how to read and the focus is now on reading to learn (Swan, 2003).

Students in fourth grade are required to read substantially more content, including history, science, and literature, in addition to their regular reading and math instruction. The kinds of books or textbooks students read become denser and more difficult, and they contain more information on a variety of topics. Thus the volume of reading increases, as does the domain, content knowledge, and text difficulty. All of these factors, coupled with the fact that formal classroom reading instruction may actually decrease because of increased content demands on the teacher, may depress students' motivation to read. Also in fourth grade and beyond, the demands of school are felt more acutely because there is more emphasis on extrinsic motivations such as grades, points, and competition than there is in the primary grades. This shift in instructional focus may lead not only to decreased motivation or work avoidance, which is the desire to avoid reading activities, but also to a decrease in students' reading comprehension, time spent reading, volume of reading, and overall academic achievement.

Revisiting Silent Reading: New Directions for Teachers and Researchers, edited by Elfrieda H. Hiebert and D. Ray Reutzel. © 2010 by the International Reading Association.

In a 2005 U.S. survey of representative fourth graders, 65% of the students did not list silent reading as a favorite activity. In this same survey, 59% of the students claimed that they did not think they learned very much when reading books. So it is not surprising that 73% of these students did not read frequently for enjoyment (Guthrie et al., 2007). This survey indicated that a substantial number of fourth graders are not intrinsically motivated to read silently. Despite the potential for a downward spiral when it comes to students' reading motivation, there is good news.

The good news is that when students are motivated to engage in silent reading for intrinsic reasons (e.g., enjoyment, involvement, curiosity, challenge) as opposed to extrinsic reasons (e.g., grades, rewards, competition), their reading comprehension increases (Cox & Guthrie, 2001; Guthrie, Hoa, Wigfield, Tonks, & Perencevich, 2006). This has been shown, in turn, to result in increased reading time and volume, improved academic achievement, or both (Baker & Wigfield, 1999; Wang & Guthrie, 2004). Intrinsic motivation to read is when reading is done for its own sake (Wigfield & Guthrie, 1997). Reading for enjoyment or as a favorite activity is considered an intrinsic motivation for reading because the locus of control is internal. In this chapter, however, we move a step beyond reading silently simply for enjoyment to a deeper level of intrinsic reading we call *engaged silent reading*.

In this chapter, we first explain our definition of engaged silent reading and how this level of silent reading significantly influences students' amount of reading, time spent reading, and academic achievement. Second, we present the current and ongoing research that supports engaged silent reading. Third, we suggest six instructional practices that increase students' engaged silent reading in the classroom. Fourth, we offer suggestions for future research in this area.

What Is Engaged Silent Reading?

We define engaged silent reading as intrinsically motivated, strategic reading. Reading silently for fun and recreation can be intrinsically motivated reading. However, such reading is not fully engaged unless it entails the use of strategies when they are necessary for comprehension. When reading silently is automatic and easy, it may not require higher order systems of processing, such as reasoning or self-correcting. Conversely, when students read silently to extend their learning from text, they are reading for knowledge, which may require more strategic reading from the students. For reading silently to be truly strategic, the process of reading may be slow and deliberate and take conscious effort when students need to clarify meaning or build knowledge. Self-discipline is necessary for strategic reading because extended reading requires reasoning, identifying key points, organizing information, and linking new information to prior knowledge to build deep, meaningful, conceptual knowledge. Students who read silently to learn are often required to understand difficult or complicated texts, integrate information from multiple sources, write explanations, and share this knowledge with others. This process is *engaged* reading because it requires both strategic processing *and* intrinsic motivation. Engaged silent reading is more purposeful and more determined than simply reading for enjoyment, and it leads to greater comprehension (van den Broek & Kendeou, 2008). When students' purpose is to learn and to share their knowledge with others, their motivation increases, their time spent reading increases, and ultimately, improved academic achievement follows.

Factors Affecting Engaged Silent Reading and Reading Achievement

The study of reading motivation includes many aspects and conceptualizations of what motivates students to read silently. Much of the literature on reading motivation focuses on aspects of motivation, which also increase students' reading achievement, such as intrinsic motivation and students' sense of self-efficacy as readers. Intrinsically motivated students are interested in reading for reading's sake and choose reading among many alternative activities. They like to read. In comparison, self-efficacious readers have positive beliefs about their ability to read competently. Research has shown that students who believe they are competent readers are more likely to persevere in the face of difficulties or challenges when they read silently. Therefore, much motivation research has focused on ways to foster intrinsic motivation and self-efficacy when reading silently.

In a recent qualitative interview study of reading engagement, researchers interviewed 260 middle school students in two separate interviews for 30 minutes each. Interviewers and students were matched by sex and ethnicity. For example, an African American female interviewed African American female students. Equal numbers of males and females and students from three levels of achievement were evenly distributed in the sample. The resulting 9,000 pages of interview transcripts were coded using a detailed coding rubric to capture seventh-grade students' perspectives and attitudes toward silent reading. A second research project with the same subject pool investigated the association between motivation and reading comprehension more quantitatively. Cognitive tests and motivation questionnaires were administered to approximately 1,250 seventh-grade students at the beginning of their seventh-grade year. The results of both the qualitative interviews and quantitative research study were revealing (Guthrie, Klauda, & Morrison, in press).

In these two studies, researchers found that intrinsic motivation and self-efficacy for reading silently are positively associated with reading achievement (Coddington, 2009; Guthrie, Coddington, & Wigfield, 2009). This positive association between intrinsic motivation and reading achievement was true for school and nonschool reading only when the reading genre or content was not specified. This result confirms the fact that increasing intrinsic motivation and self-efficacy for silent reading has a positive impact on student achievement.

However, in the interview portion of the study with these same seventh-grade students, when they were told to think specifically about the informational books they read in school, the results differed. When students focused on only the informational books, their intrinsic motivation was negatively associated with achievement. This means that students who were typically the highest achievers in reading overall reported a lack of interest or motivation to read informational texts in school. In other words, these students were not interested in reading their textbooks.

Students' reading engagement predicts reading achievement as measured by standardized tests of reading comprehension and reading/language arts grades (Baker & Wigfield, 1999). Recent research of seventh-grade students' intrinsic motivation and self-efficacy demonstrated that reading motivation is positively correlated with scores on the Gates–MacGinitie reading comprehension subtest and reading/language arts grades (Coddington, 2009). This positive association indicates that students who reported higher levels of intrinsic motivation and self-efficacy for silent reading were more likely to receive higher scores on the Gates–MacGinitie test and higher grades in reading/language arts class than students who reported lower levels of reading motivation. This was true even after controlling for inference ability and other strategic processing variables (Coddington, 2009). Overall, student self-efficacy for reading was the strongest predictor of reading ability as measured by both the standardized test of comprehension and reading/language arts grades. This finding is revealing, as it relates to silent reading and amount of reading students do. Competent readers are more likely to be truly engaged when reading silently, and these students read more frequently than students who do not believe they are competent readers.

Amount of reading has long been linked to higher academic achievement (Coddington, 2009). The results from the study of seventh graders reemphasize this point. Amount of reading, as measured by student self-reports of reading activities such as textbooks, workbooks, class notes, websites, handouts, and whiteboard and overhead readings was significantly associated with reading achievement, even when controlling for students' level of poverty (Guthrie et al., in press). Therefore, the amount of time students spent in silent reading activities was significantly associated with higher performance on reading comprehension tasks. So the time spent reading silently, whether in or outside of the classroom, is positively linked to high achievement. Self-efficacy may be a more important variable in determining the amount that students choose to read than students' intrinsic interest in the reading activity. More research is needed to determine if this is true.

These two studies indicate that there are factors more important than intrinsic motivation to read silently. This becomes relevant when students are not particularly interested in reading informational texts in school. These interview studies, as well as the questionnaires collected during the quantitative portion of this study, reveal that students are not intrinsically interested in reading the books and materials that are required for school. If students' interest in the topic or act of reading for school is not the motivator of above-average middle school students, what is motivating them to complete the work? We know that above average students are doing the reading somehow. What motivates above-average students who believe they are competent readers, but who have absolutely no interest or intrinsic motivation for reading required books and materials? We suggest that these above-average middle school students are motivated by their *dedication* to be good students and to complete their schoolwork. Dedication is very important to certain students.

Dedicated Readers Are Engaged Readers

Dedication to reading, at the most basic level, refers to students' willingness to persist even when what they are reading is not particularly interesting to them. Students who are dedicated complete the reading activities that are expected of them at school thoroughly and consistently. Dedication is closely related to the notion of "grit." Grit is defined as "perseverance and passion for long-term goals" (Duckworth, Peterson, Matthews, & Kelly, 2007, p. 1087). There are various aspects of perseverance and passion that are captured in grit, such as "working strenuously towards challenges, maintaining effort and interest over years despite failure, adversity, and plateaus in progress" (Duckworth et al., 2007, pp. 1087–1088).

The principle of dedication as described in Concept-Oriented Reading Instruction (CORI; Guthrie, Wigfield, & Perencevich, 2004; Swan, 2003) shares many similarities with Duckworth et al.'s (2007) definition of grit. Dedication as defined in our research refers to academic perseverance and goals, whereas grit has been used to investigate this kind of perseverance in multiple occupational, educational, and competitive settings, but with more widely valued general goals. Students complete homework assignments and participate in classroom activities involving silent reading despite having little or no interest in the actual reading content itself. There are many potential explanations for why dedicated students persist in their silent reading schoolwork despite having little or no interest in the readings themselves. First, dedicated students tend to be high achievers and good students overall. This is an important aspect of their self-identity. Although they are not inherently interested in the content texts or materials, completing the silent reading assignment is an expectation of the teacher and important to the student because it fulfills the requirements of being a good student. Long-term goals are equally important to the dedicated student. Dedicated students know that being successful in school now will pay off in the future. Dedicated students are also competent readers. They do read silently on their own with topics of personal interest.

Many of the seventh-grade students in the interview study discussed the connection between completing silent reading assignments that were expected in school and long-term goals such as doing well in high school, getting into a good college, and eventually getting a good job. It should be no surprise then that dedication is positively correlated with reading achievement in both content reading and standardized reading tests, both of which are done silently. Dedicated readers read more texts silently, both fiction and nonfiction, than do undedicated students. The majority of reading is completed independently during silent reading time either in the classroom or at home. Students who are dedicated, therefore, spend more time engaged in independent silent reading activities, and these reading activities include more genres of texts than those typically discussed. Dedicated readers are not simply readers of fiction novels, but they are readers of many kinds of texts and genres.

If dedication is the ultimate outcome, how do we foster dedication or reading engagement in students? Evidence from a meta-analysis of 11 quasi-experimental studies in which CORI was compared with one or more control groups indicates that CORI increases the amount of time students spend reading silently (Guthrie et al., 2007). In addition, elementary students who received the CORI intervention showed an increase in their intrinsic motivation for reading silently and their willingness to read challenging books. At the middle school level, the CORI principles of choice, relevance, collaboration, success, and thematic units led to increased dedication for content book reading (Guthrie et al., in press; Guthrie et al., 2004; Swan 2003). CORI provides a framework for fostering dedication for reading in students. As dedicated students are more likely to read both fiction and content books for school independently, using the CORI principles may be one way to increase the amount of time students spend reading silently.

The link between amount of engaged silent reading and achievement was also strengthened through the interview data. In Figure 6.1, you can see that when comparing low readers to high readers, the amount of engaged silent reading that the high readers report is almost twice that of the low readers. Amount of engaged reading in this study included reading that required a significant time commitment from students. So high frequency of reading also means that students were spending a considerable amount of time engaged in silent reading activities. To change low readers into high readers, the amount of time spent reading must increase. The amount of time reading does not increase when students are avoiding reading.

The current research clearly demonstrates the connection between motivation, amount of reading, and reading achievement. Teachers who foster reading engagement instructionally in the classroom increase the amount of time students spend reading silently and their reading achievement. The most recent research also reveals that teachers who do not focus on fostering engagement in the classroom are actually hindering their students by increasing avoidance behaviors in the classroom. By avoiding reading, these students decrease the amount of time they spend reading and therefore prevent themselves from becoming better readers. So it is not simply a matter of providing instruction that fosters silent reading engagement, but also of providing instruction that thwarts avoidance behaviors in the classroom.

Our perspective on reading silently and the body of research about how to motivate students to read silently has helped us to identify six instructional practices that will satisfy students' needs for competence, autonomy, and belonging

Figure 6.1. Association of Amount of School Reading With Achievement for Two Ethnic Groups

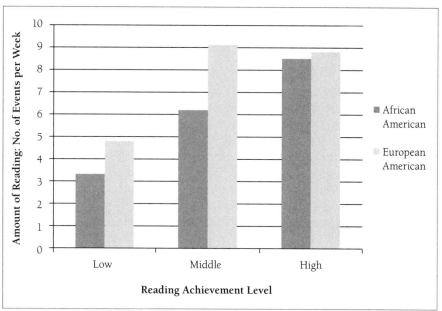

(Deci & Ryan, 1985). These practices also increase reading comprehension and engaged silent reading when implemented.

Instructional Practices That Foster Engaged Silent Reading

There is a need for strong instructional contexts to foster engaged silent reading development for all students. If we know what changes occur in students during the acquisition of reading motivation, teachers can more easily and effectively create classroom contexts to support this motivational development (Guthrie et al., 2004, 2006; Swan, 2003). The body of research is expanding on the topic of which instructional practices are best to increase elementary and secondary school students' motivation to read. Guthrie and Humenick (2004) conducted a meta-analysis of 22 investigations, which reported experimental evidence for six classroom practices that lead to improvements in reading engagement. This meta-analysis, combined with a book of treatments on this issue (Stipek, 2002), qualitative studies of motivating teachers (Dolezal, Welsh, Pressley, & Vincent, 2003), and the synthesis of research on characteristics of engaging schools (National Research Council & The Institute of Medicine, 2004), gives us insight on this important topic. These six practices are as follows: (1) emphasizing mastery goals based on content concepts, (2) providing choice and control, (3) making content and tasks relevant, (4) providing interesting texts, (5) providing opportunities for social collaboration, and (6) encouraging success.

Emphasizing Mastery Goals Based on Content Concepts

We believe that when instruction is taught around broader conceptual content, there is a greater opportunity for students to gain deeper knowledge and expertise in the content area. In addition, multitiered curriculum helps students see the connections across the topics from week to week as the teacher helps to build conceptual content knowledge. Students are also more likely to be involved and enjoy learning (Guthrie et al., in press; Swan, 2003). Also, when the curriculum is based on broader content concepts or themes, it is easier for students to set their own mastery goals for reading within the teacher's goals.

Using mastery goals for reading instruction expands students' interest and engagement. Content goals also build knowledge and conceptual understanding. Content goals for reading include the most important aspect of the content to be learned from the text. These content goals, which are provided by the teacher, help students focus on the purpose of the assignment. This builds students' competence. When teachers write daily goals on the board and explain what these goals for reading are, students pay attention. Students want to be successful. Much of the guesswork is eliminated when students know what is expected and what the purpose for the assignment is. Instruction that allows students to focus on what they will learn about a topic, why it is important to know, and the means for how to be successful is motivating. Students can then focus on gaining knowledge from the text and making connections to their lives, rather than on gaining rewards or worrying about the exact skills they used. For example, when fifth-grade students received content-mastery goals for reading, they increased their reading comprehension more than when they received performance goals of scoring well on a test (Grolnick & Ryan, 1987).

Not only must goals be related to content, but when mastery goals are emphasized more than performance goals, students' motivation increases. Learning is valued as an end in itself. Students with mastery goal orientations do things such as read to learn and gain knowledge from text; understand stories at a deeper level; grasp the essence of literary texts, such as poetry or folk tales; persist at difficult tasks; prefer and choose challenging tasks; seek forms of help that promote independent problem solving; and use cognitive strategies that enhance conceptual understanding (Meece & Miller, 1999). Mastery goal orientations are aligned with engaged silent reading.

We offer a caveat in relation to mastery goals versus tangible rewards such as prizes or grades in the classroom. We all know that extrinsic motivations will always exist in schools. Teachers often ask, How do I motivate my students intrinsically if my students are always getting paid for their grades or there is constant competition between students for points or rewards? How will mastery goals survive in a school climate of competition? These are real concerns. One suggestion is to focus first on the mastery goals and teach students what performance looks like when a mastery goal is adopted. For example, when students are engaged readers who are reading to gain conceptual knowledge and become more competent readers, we believe that they produce quality work, put forth more effort, are willing to help others to be successful, are able to articulate how they arrived at their answers or conclusions based on textual evidence, and turn in their assignments on time.

Rewards are not wholly bad things. We are certain that serious athletes focus on performance; winning, for them, is the name of the game. But in school, when teachers and students focus on mastery goals first, students gain knowledge, their performance is exhibited in quality and thorough work, and then the good grades follow. Often in classrooms, educators believe they have to bribe their students with points, stickers, or competition, which oftentimes undermines students' motivations to read. Student may perceive the reading to be a chore to endure until they can get the reward (Worthy, 2002). We must be careful to reward students with the behavior we want to improve. When students do well in reading, they should receive extra time to read or more books to choose from, not a new toy or a pizza party. These kinds of rewards contribute to the notion of a bribe. We want to encourage reading, so the rewards must align with reading. An extrinsic motivation that can be very effective includes praise that is specific, succinct, and sincere (Wlodkowski, 1985). The reality is that it takes a combination of intrinsic and extrinsic motivations to create lifelong learning (Guthrie & Anderson, 1999). The problem with rewards is that "While...they may actually lend themselves to successful academic performance in the short term...they do not lend themselves to the types of...learning characteristics associated with self-regulated learning" (Nichols, Jones, & Hancock, 2003, p. 77).

Providing Choice and Control

It seems the older students get, the less control over their learning and the fewer choices they have at school. Think of kindergarten or first-grade classes where young, excited children get to choose between fun reading center activities, with whom they will partner to read, which book to read, and what story they will write. As children move into upper grades, they seem to have fewer choices and less control, not more. Imagine a middle school student who is now rushing from one class to another, managing six or seven different classes and teachers each day. These students are often sitting alone, in rows, listening to a teacher lecture for 45 minutes or longer, being told which chapter to read, which questions to answer, when the assignment is due, and the exact details of how long their responses should be. For even the most engaged student, this can be a demotivating experience. For struggling readers or students in high-risk populations, this situation contributes to their disengagement and boredom. Why is this scenario all too common? Researchers have discovered from questioning students that many teacher actions are actually quite disengaging for students (Assor, Kaplan, & Roth, 2002; Skinner, Wellborn, & Connell, 1990). For example, students report that the following practices are disengaging:

- The teacher tells students what to do all the time
- The teacher listens only to students who share his or her opinions
- The teacher makes students stop reading when they are reading something interesting

Conversely, students report that the following practices are engaging:

- The teacher relates material to them
- The teacher allows them to choose what they learn
- The teacher helps them find their own ways to learn
- The teacher listens to all opinions and voices his or her own opinion
- The teacher lets them finish if they are writing something interesting

Ironically, teachers often view giving students a choice as an all-or-nothing proposition. Many teachers believe that if they give their students choices, they lose complete control or their class will turn into utter chaos. Given these teacher and student perceptions, we believe the following suggestions will foster and promote motivation while giving students more choice and control over their own learning. First, help students have ownership over *what they read*. This may be as simple as allowing students to choose what book to read, what supplemental material to add to their textbook reading, what novel to read, or what website to choose when researching a topic. If these options are still too large, simplify them by giving students a choice about which part or chapter of the informational book to read or which character in a novel to focus on, while reading it all. By allowing students to choose what they read, within the context of the curriculum, project guidelines, book club offerings, or homework options, they will feel more empowered and successful.

Second, give students choices about *how they learn* from text. When teachers teach students multiple ways to learn from text, students will choose the option that works best for them, which might not be the same as someone else. For example, teachers can teach students different reading strategies such as the following:

- How to ask questions and change them into different types of questions that yield more information when answering
- How to make a diagram, outline, graphic organizer, or concept map of what students are reading so it makes more sense
- How to highlight, use sticky notes, or take notes to hold onto students' thinking while they read

- How to summarize or synthesize what students read so they can remember the main ideas for longer periods of time or combine information from multiple sources

- How to use a character map or text structure diagram to help students determine important information while reading narrative or expository texts

These are several ways in which teachers can encourage students to get the most out of what they read and also help them cultivate a lifelong reading habit.

Third, teachers can help motivate students by allowing them to choose topics of interest within the curriculum. For example, in a unit on the American Revolutionary War, students might focus on a person who played a role in the war, such as Paul Revere. Another option might be an event, so students might choose to study a specific battle, like the Battle of Lexington, if that is of particular interest to them. Students become more engaged when they can select something that interests them within the curriculum. Oftentimes, teachers allow small choices, such as choosing a person, an event, or a place associated with the American Revolution. This allows students to focus their choice within three given options selected by the teacher. Limited choices are easy for teachers to provide and are engaging for students.

Fourth, allow students to choose how to demonstrate their knowledge at the end of a book or unit of instruction. Whether it is a written or oral report, detailed poster that explains a content concept, handmade book, PowerPoint presentation or slideshow, writing and performing a one-act play based on a short story, or student-created exam questions for the class, students will rise to the occasion.

Fifth, allow students to provide input about grading or evaluating work. This can be helpful to the teacher for creating rubrics or guides for projects. Student input allows for common agreement on what a quality report, research project, or book report looks like.

Finally, teachers can share control with students in inquiry or research projects. Allowing students to select topics from a list, books to read on a topic, and how they will display their knowledge incorporates three kinds of choices into one project. Sometimes a combination of two or three areas into one project gives the student a heightened sense of control over their own learning. Our suggestion is to start small, with limited choice, and gradually expand the choices or the number of different choices. Every teacher has his or her own style, so what works for one may look different for another. When students feel that teachers support their autonomy, they are more likely to value the task and have positive feelings toward it, which has a positive impact on their achievement (Grolnick, Ryan, & Deci, 1991).

Making Content and Tasks Relevant

One way to increase interest in a topic is to make the content and tasks relevant to the students' lives. This can be done by providing hands-on, stimulating activities or tasks that create situational interest in the topic (Anderson, 1998). For example, bringing in a hermit crab or a red-eared slider turtle is a great way to have students think about what kinds of animals live in fresh water and the kind of environment they need to survive (Anderson, 1998). Another example is to role-play whether taxes were a form of tyranny in the time prior to the American Revolutionary War by giving students a cup full of M&Ms and taxing them with predetermined, arbitrary fees such as using a pencil, wearing denim, eating candy or something sweet, or reading a book, which allows students to experience firsthand what it may have been like to be a colonist being taxed without representation. When you have students play the roles of King George III, tax collectors, members of Parliament, and colonists, they get a sense of what it means to be taxed. Students can also judge whether the colonists were fairly taxed and under what conditions by King George III. These activities lead to a heightened sense of attention and can create curiosity (Schiefele, 1999). Creating relevance also builds background knowledge, which can prime students for additional learning. It can also spur spontaneous questioning (Ross, 1988), which can ultimately lead to deeper learning through texts.

Providing Interesting Texts

After students have experienced a stimulating task or relevant activity, their interest is piqued and they often have many questions. The situational interest and curiosity can have a longer lasting effect on motivation and comprehension if the activity is immediately connected to further knowledge by reading interesting texts (Anderson, 1998). Texts are considered interesting when a topic is rated as interesting (Schiefele, 1999); when the format is appealing to students and there are vivid details, photographs, or diagrams; or when the text is relevant and accessible to students' purposes for reading and gaining knowledge (Schraw, Bruning, & Svoboda, 1995). When these factors are present, interest and motivation increase.

For example, when students observe real animals, their curiosity about these animals is piqued. What does the hermit crab's body look like inside the shell? Can we take the crab out of the shell? What if the crab cannot find another shell? These kinds of questions cannot simply be answered through observation only. Students need to read about hermit crabs. Therefore, the books provided to students are full of information about hermit crabs—their shells, their bodies, and how they live and grow. The books' photographs and diagrams of hermit crab bodies provide answers to questions that students are not able to gain through observation alone. The observation, however, stimulates students' questions. The hands-on activity creates relevance, interest, and curiosity in the topic while the texts provide the information and answers through silent reading. The readings can also lead to additional questions, requiring further observation and then more silent reading.

The combination of hands-on activities and interesting texts provides a dynamic process that is highly engaging.

In the Revolutionary War simulation, students became curious about why the colonists were taxed on sugar and paper. Small-group and whole-class discussions about what people are taxed on today is a conversation that usually follows this simulation. Students realize that when their parents buy them clothing, a book, or candy, they pay a sales tax on these items. Also, when students are given random amounts of M&Ms at the beginning of the activity, some cannot resist eating a few. Then, when they run out of "M&M money" and cannot pay their taxes, another great discussion ensues. What did the colonists do if they could not pay their taxes? What jobs did colonists have that were lucrative? These kinds of questions create great interest; students cannot wait to read about these topics generated from their own or their peers' questions.

Providing Opportunities for Social Collaboration

We are social beings. The popularity of Facebook and Twitter websites are evidence. In fact, according to a 2007 survey by the National School Boards Association (NSBA; 2007), 96% of students with online access reported using social networking technologies, and those online generally spent 9 hours per week chatting, text messaging, blogging, and visiting online communities. Social goals or cooperative learning situations for classroom reading activities improve students' motivation and achievement (Isaac, Sansone, & Smith, 1999). Practices such as having open discussions, student-led discussions, text-based collaborative reasoning, or debate increase students' motivations to read and participate in whole-class reading activities (Antonio & Guthrie, 2008; Guthrie, 2008). Students need a sense of belonging (Deci & Ryan, 1985) to be self-determined learners in addition to their need for autonomy and competence.

For example, when students are interested in a particular battle of the American Revolution, such as the Battle of Lexington, and they realize that three other peers are also interested in this battle, they feel a sense of belonging. When teachers then allow these students to work together to research this topic, learn about it in depth, and then present their findings to the class, they create a way for these students to feel connected to one another and to the curriculum, and students become motivated and knowledgeable. Learning for them is social and academic. They are working toward a common goal of learning about the Battle of Lexington but they are doing the work based on their personal interest. The control over their learning is theirs. This autonomy is empowering for students.

Encouraging Success

As an instructional practice, success refers to "assuring that students perform meaningful classroom tasks proficiently" (Guthrie et al., 2007, p. 243). For teachers, part of this process involves providing students with opportunities to form short- and long-term goals with accurate feedback of their progress. Providing opportunities for students to achieve success in reading with teacher support helps students to read independently. There are many strategies that teachers can employ to foster success in reading. For example, teachers can help students self-evaluate their reading ability with accuracy, select level-appropriate texts, and gain knowledge from text. All of these practices help to foster a sense of efficacy for reading in students. In addition to fostering self-efficacy, practices that facilitate student success also teach students the relationship between effort and success. By providing feedback at the completion of a task, teachers encourage students to attribute either success or failure to their efforts (Guthrie et al., 2007).

Conclusions About Motivation and Silent Reading and Suggestions for Future Research

Engaged silent reading plays a crucial role in education. When students are motivated to read to answer their own questions, extend their thinking, and make deeper connections among and between texts and topics, they are empowered as learners. Engaged reading provides students with skills and practice to become knowledgeable and informed. This process of learning is exactly what they need to prepare them to be active citizens and contribute to society in meaningful ways. Everyone needs an opportunity to practice the skills necessary for participation in future endeavors. Just like student teaching empowers preservice teachers, the internship awakens the developing physician, disciplined practice helps perfect the focus of the Olympic athlete, and credits from stage experiences give backbone to a theater candidate. Engaged silent reading is the enculturation into a knowing society. The culture of literacy in the United States and throughout the world enables youths to become information processors and self-determining participants in a global society. Engaged silent reading fosters acquisition of the questions of why, who, when, and what of reading. From guided lessons, students learn the how. But active, purposeful, engaged silent reading employs and embraces skills in purposeful quests for knowledge and social participation.

Questions for future research in this area may include the following: (a) Are specific intrinsic motivational constructs such as self-efficacy more powerful than general intrinsic motivations to read silently? (b) To what extent does extrinsic motivation decline when engaged silent reading factors are implemented in the classroom? (c) What is the effect of academic achievement on students who are in CORI classrooms for multiple years in a row? (d) Can the fourth-grade slump reverse?

QUESTIONS FOR
PROFESSIONAL DEVELOPMENT

1. What does the professional development model for Concept-Oriented Reading Instruction (CORI) look like?
2. Where can your school or district learn more about implementing CORI principles in your classrooms?
3. Are long-term and short-term professional development options available?
4. What are the costs of professional development for CORI?
5. What is a great resource for content area texts to use with students at a variety of reading levels?

REFERENCES

Anderson, E. (1998). *Motivational and cognitive influences on conceptual knowledge acquisition: The combination of science observation and interesting texts.* Unpublished doctoral dissertation, University of Maryland, College Park.

Antonio, D., & Guthrie, J.T. (2008). Reading is social: Bringing peer interaction to the text. In J.T. Guthrie (Ed.), *Engaging adolescents in reading* (pp. 49–63). Thousand Oaks, CA: Corwin.

Assor, A., Kaplan, H., & Roth, G. (2002). Choice is good, but relevance is excellent: Autonomy-enhancing and suppressing teacher behaviours predicting students' engagement in schoolwork. *British Journal of Educational Psychology, 72*(2), 261–278. doi:10.1348/000709902158883

Baker, L., & Wigfield, A. (1999). Dimensions of children's motivation for reading and their relations to reading activity and reading achievement. *Reading Research Quarterly, 34*(4), 452–477. doi:10.1598/RRQ.34.4.4

Chall, J.S. (1983). *Stages of reading development.* New York: McGraw-Hill.

Coddington, C.S. (2009). *The effects of constructs of motivation that affirm and undermine reading achievement inside and outside of school on middle school students' reading achievement.* Unpublished doctoral dissertation, University of Maryland, College Park.

Cox, K.E., & Guthrie, J.T. (2001). Motivational and cognitive contributions to students' amount of reading. *Contemporary Educational Psychology, 26*(1), 116–131. doi:10.1006/ceps.1999.1044

Deci, E.L., & Ryan, R.M. (1985). *Intrinsic motivation and self-determination in human behavior.* New York: Plenum.

Dolezal, S.E., Welsh, L.M., Pressley, M., & Vincent, M.M. (2003). How nine third-grade teachers motivate student academic engagement. *The Elementary School Journal, 103*(3), 239–267. doi:10.1086/499725

Duckworth, A.L., Peterson, C., Matthews, M.D., & Kelly, D.R. (2007). Grit: Perseverance and passion for long-term goals. *Journal of Personality and Social Psychology, 92*(6), 1087–1101. doi:10.1037/0022-3514.92.6.1087

Grolnick, W.S., & Ryan, R.M. (1987). Autonomy in children's learning: An experimental and individual difference investigation. *Journal of Personality and Social Psychology, 52*(5), 890–898.

Grolnick, W.S., Ryan, R.M., & Deci, E.L. (1991). Inner resources for school achievement: Motivational mediators of children's perceptions of their parents. *Journal of Educational Psychology, 83*(4), 508–517. doi:10.1037/0022-0663.83.4.508

Guthrie, J.T. (Ed.). (2008). *Engaging adolescents in reading.* Thousand Oaks, CA: Corwin.

Guthrie, J.T., & Anderson, E. (1999). Engagement in reading: Processes of motivated, strategic, knowledgeable, social readers. In J.T. Guthrie & D.E. Alvermann (Eds.), *Engaged reading:*

Processes, practices, and policy implications (pp. 17–45). New York: Teachers College Press.

Guthrie, J.T., Coddington, C.S., & Wigfield, A. (2009). Profiles of reading motivation among African American and Caucasian students. *Journal of Literacy Research, 41*(3), 317–353. doi:10.1080/10862960903129196

Guthrie, J.T., Hoa, L.W., Wigfield, A., Tonks, S.M., & Perencevich, K.C. (2006). From spark to fire: Can situational reading interest lead to long-term reading motivation? *Reading Research and Instruction, 45*(2), 91–117.

Guthrie, J.T., & Humenick, N.M. (2004). Motivating students to read: Evidence for classroom practices that increase reading motivation and achievement. In P. McCardle & V. Chhabra (Eds.), *The voice of evidence in reading research* (pp. 329–354). Baltimore: Paul H. Brookes.

Guthrie, J.T., Klauda, S., & Morrison, D. (in press). Adolescents' engagement in academic literacy. London: Bentham.

Guthrie, J.T., McRae, A., & Klauda, S.L. (2007). Contributions of concept-oriented reading instruction to knowledge about interventions for motivations in reading. *Educational Psychologist, 42*(4), 237–250.

Guthrie, J.T., Wigfield, A., & Perencevich, K.C. (Eds.). (2004). *Motivated reading comprehension: Concept-oriented reading instruction.* Mahwah, NJ: Erlbaum.

Isaac, J.D., Sansone, C., & Smith, J.L. (1999). Other people as a source of interest in an activity. *Journal of Experimental Social Psychology, 35*(3), 239–265. doi:10.1006/jesp.1999.1385

Meece, J.L., & Miller, S.D. (1999). Changes in elementary school children's achievement goals for reading and writing: Results of a longitudinal and an intervention study. *Scientific Studies of Reading, 3*(3), 207–229. doi:10.1207/s1532799xssr0303_2

National Research Council & The Institute of Medicine. (2004). *Engaging schools: Fostering high school students' motivation to learn.* Washington, DC: National Academies Press.

National School Boards Association. (2007). Creating and connecting: Research and guidelines on online social—and educational—networking. Alexandria, VA: National School Boards Association. Retrieved October 15, 2007, from www.nsba.org/site/view.asp?CID=63&DID=41340

Nichols, W.D., Jones, J.P., & Hancock, D.R. (2003). Teachers' influence on goal orientation: Exploring the relationship between eighth graders' goal orientation, their emotional development, their perceptions of learning, and their teacher's instructional strategies. *Reading Psychology, 24*(1), 57–87. doi:10.1080/02702710308236

Ross, J.A. (1988). Controlling variables: A meta-analysis of training studies. *Review of Educational Research, 58*(4), 405–437.

Schiefele, U. (1999). Interest and learning from text. *Scientific Studies of Reading, 3*(3), 257–279. doi:10.1207/s1532799xssr0303_4

Schraw, G., Bruning, R., & Svoboda, C. (1995). Sources of situational interest. *Journal of Reading Behavior, 27*(1), 1–17.

Skinner, E.A., Wellborn, J.G., & Connell, J.P. (1990). What it takes to do well in school and whether I've got it: A process model of perceived control and children's engagement and achievement in school. *Journal of Educational Psychology, 82*(1), 22–32. doi:10.1037/0022-0663.82.1.22

Stipek, D. (2002). Good instruction is motivating. In A. Wigfield & J.S. Eccles (Eds.), *Development of achievement motivation* (pp. 309–332). San Diego, CA: Academic.

Swan, E.A. (2003). *Concept-oriented reading instruction: Engaging classrooms, lifelong learners.* New York: Guilford.

van den Broek, P., & Kendeou, P. (2008). Cognitive processes in comprehension of science texts: The role of co-activation in confronting misconceptions. *Applied Cognitive Psychology, 22*(3), 335–351. doi:10.1002/acp.1418

Wagner, T. (2008). *The global achievement gap: Why even our best schools don't teach the new survival skills our children need—and what we can do about it.* New York: Basic.

Wang, J.H., & Guthrie, J.T. (2004). Modeling the effects of intrinsic motivation, extrinsic motivation, amount of reading, and past reading achievement on text comprehension between U.S. and Chinese students. *Reading Research Quarterly, 39*(2), 162–186. doi:10.1598/RRQ.39.2.2

Wigfield, A., & Guthrie, J.T. (1997). Motivation for reading: Individual, home, textual, and classroom perspectives. *Educational Psychologist, 32*(2), 57–134. doi:10.1207/s15326985ep3202_1

Wlodkowski, R.J. (1985). *Enhancing adult motivation to learn: A guide to improving instruction and increasing learner achievement*. San Francisco: Jossey-Bass.

Worthy, J. (2002). What makes intermediate-grade students want to read? *The Reading Teacher, 55*(6), 568–569.

Zusho, A., & Pintrich, P.R. (2001). Motivation in the second decade of life: The role of multiple developmental trajectories. In T. Urdan & F. Pajares (Eds.), *Adolescence and education: General issues in the education of adolescents* (pp. 163–200). Greenwich, CT: Information Age.

CHAPTER 7

Sustained Silent Reading:
An Update of the Research

Maryann Manning

University of Alabama at Birmingham

Marta Lewis

Nexus Treatment Facilities, Minnesota

Marsha Lewis

Kenansville Elementary School, North Carolina

Reading is to the mind what exercise is to the body.

Richard Steele, *The Tatler*

Wˉhen interviewed about silent reading, second-grade students shared the following thoughts on the topic:

"Reading silently is just reading in your mind and not saying a word out loud. I like to go to the reading loft with a few other kids."

"Sometimes we read the same book, but most of the time we read our own books that we choose in the library."

"Mrs. Lewis talks to us about what we read, and sometimes she has us do a project like make a different cover for the book."

"I'm so glad she lets us read silently because we read books that we like to read. If we had a teacher who didn't let us read a book we like, we might have to read easy books with everybody else."

Their teacher, Marsha Lewis, shared her students' insights on the value and joys of reading. In her journal, Marsha wrote, "Using SSR has saved two of my students who were diagnosed [with] ADHD. Nothing else was working, so I got them interested in and excited about time for reading in class. To my surprise and that of others in my school, and the [students'] parents, they made three years' growth during one year in my classroom."

Revisiting Silent Reading: New Directions for Teachers and Researchers, edited by Elfrieda H. Hiebert and D. Ray Reutzel. © 2010 by the International Reading Association.

Definition of and Background on Sustained Silent Reading

Sustained silent reading (SSR) is a reading program originally outlined by Hunt (1966) at the proceedings of the International Reading Association Annual Convention and, later, in a 1970 article from *The Reading Teacher* (Hunt, l970). SSR is a daily established period of time during the school day when all students and their teachers read silently. An important goal of the activity is to develop a positive reading attitude and the emphasis is on enjoyment, so there are no reading assessments conducted during this period or afterwards. By providing time for students to enjoy reading and modeling good habits of reading, teachers promote lasting literacy behaviors. SSR can be used as part of the reading curriculum, or it can be adapted to extracurricular and after-school activities that promote extensive reading.

Considerable research has been conducted around the world on SSR, and websites that support and promote extensive reading and provide assistance with free downloadable materials and information on implementing extensive reading programs are being developed. The literature uses many terms to describe this practice, such as *silent reading time, independent reading, self-selected reading, voluntary reading, extensive reading, exposure to text, leisure reading, recreational reading,* or *free reading* (Lewis, 2002). According to Krashen (2000), the first published study of silent reading was done by Boney and Agnew (1937) and the first controlled study was published by Sperzl (1948). Since then, more studies have examined the relationship between time spent reading and reading achievement. Since the early 1980s, there have also been 11 reviews of the literature on silent reading practices.

Moore, Jones, and Miller (1980) report a lack of implementation consistency and differences in the amount of time set aside for reading as well as in the length of the programs examined. They conclude that, overall, SSR has a positive effect on attitude toward reading and on reading comprehension when combined with a program of reading instruction. They also note that studies that did not report significant differences were all of short duration (i.e., five months or less).

Sadoski (1980) established that reading is a skill that develops with practice. He finds SSR to be neither more nor less effective than other approaches to reading. He also reports a positive effect on attitude toward reading and concludes that benefits are likely to be in the form of long-term progress and gains.

Schaudt (1983) determined that SSR is an effective practice. She emphasizes that it is an addition to and not a substitution for reading instruction.

Wiesendanger and Birlem (1984) found the effect of SSR on achievement inconclusive. They note that some studies reported no differences in achievement whether students had independent in-school reading time; other researchers found significant differences. They conclude that the effects of SSR on attitude were more consistent; almost all studies indicated a positive effect on motivation to read. They state that silent reading time was most effective when combined with some form of systematic skills instruction, and benefits were most likely long term.

Manning-Dowd (1985) agreed that the overall effects of reading on reading ability were inconclusive, although she found overall effects on attitude positive. She also noted that positive results were found in long-term studies of six months or more, and that the benefits of independent reading time are likely realized long term.

Tunnell and Jacobs (1989) concluded that literature-based programs are successful in helping a wide range of students learn to read and to enjoy reading. They found that when children read an extensive variety of good literature, they have a reason to read and they develop good literacy habits.

Krashen (1994) concluded that voluntary reading increases competence and is the only way to literacy. He also states his belief that silent reading time can take the place of, rather than supplement, more traditional skills-based reading instruction.

Meyers (1998) found evidence for the benefits of silent reading on both achievement and attitude. He reports mixed results but concludes that the overall effect of silent reading on reading achievement was positive, even if results were not always statistically significant. He also believes that the benefits of independent reading time were achieved long term.

Chow and Chou (2000) reported mixed conclusions on the effects of silent reading time on reading achievement. They found that gains in reading achievement were generally positive, but longer studies were more likely to produce statistically significant results. They also conclude that changes in attitude were positive.

The National Reading Panel (NRP; National Institute of Child Health and Human Development, 2002) found no evidence to support the benefits of silent reading time in improving reading skills and achievement. They found no significant statistical support for a relationship between independent reading practice and increases in reading achievement. They also found no empirical studies of high methodological quality that clearly demonstrated a positive relationship between the amount of reading students do and improved performance on measures of achievement.

Lewis (2002) and Lewis and Samuels (2005) found that students who have in-school independent reading time do significantly better on measures of reading achievement. Lewis concludes that silent reading time was especially beneficial for students at earlier stages of reading development: students in lower grades, those experiencing difficulties learning to read, and those learning English as a second language.

In summary, several conclusions were reached by most of the reviews of the silent reading literature: reading is a skill that improves with practice; longer studies show more positive results in reading achievement; time spent reading is a positive and effective practice, though not always significantly so; more research is needed to determine how best to combine reading instruction and practice; and more long-term studies are needed.

Current Review of Sustained Silent Reading

The studies selected for this review came from journals, unpublished doctoral dissertations, and other ERIC documents. Study design included experimental research, quasi-experimental designs, and correlational studies. Including studies from a variety of sources provides converging evidence for the benefits of silent reading time in school and avoids any potential positive bias from including only journal articles that are more likely to report positive results.

Criteria for selection included the following conditions: studies had to examine either SSR or some equivalent type of independent classroom based reading program and its influence on reading achievement, SSR was measured in time spent reading, the reading component had to be independent of a larger reading or school-based program or able to be separately examined, and subject samples were limited to students in grades K through 12. This eliminated studies of summer and out-of-school recreational reading programs, studies that used number of books read or measures of print exposure, studies with adult readers, and other reading programs such as computerized reading systems, guided and oral reading, and repeated reading. Programs such as Success For All, the school enrichment reading model, and reading programs where independent reading time was embedded in a larger language arts program or combined with reading response activities were also eliminated from this review.

Twenty-nine studies met these criteria. They fell into two groups: those that reported statistical results that could be used in a quantitative overview and those that reported either insufficient statistical data or only the overall direction of results as either positive, negative, or no benefit. Twelve studies fell in the second category of reporting directional results with little or no statistical tests or data.

Evans and Towner (1975) compared two fourth-grade classes for a 10-week period. Both classes had a traditional reading program; one class had an additional 20 minutes of SSR while the other class had 20 minutes of supplementary basal activities. There were no significant differences at either pretest or posttest on the reading subtest of the Metropolitan Achievement Test (MAT).

Oliver (1976) compared the achievement scores of matched groups of fourth, fifth, and sixth graders assigned to one of three interventions. Students had traditional reading instruction only, traditional instruction with daily independent reading time, or three days a week of traditional instruction and two days of independent reading practice. After one month, no significant differences on measures of comprehension, vocabulary, speed, and accuracy were found.

Reed (1977) studied the effects of SSR on 14 high school English classes with one half of the students receiving SSR one day a week and the other half receiving no SSR. After five months, there were no differences between the two groups of students on the reading comprehension and word-knowledge subtests of the MAT.

Cline and Kretke (1980) examined the results of a three-year SSR program with junior high students. The 111 students who received three years of SSR scored the same as 138 comparable students who received no SSR. There were, however, positive attitude changes reported in the SSR group.

Minton (1980) studied the reading growth of 550 ninth graders before and after a 15-minute SSR period was implemented. During the fall semester prior to SSR, students showed a growth of seven months in reading speed and accuracy on the Gates–MacGinitie Reading Test and no changes on vocabulary or comprehension. After a semester of SSR, students improved six months on accuracy and speed, three months on vocabulary, and four months on comprehension.

Kefford (1981) conducted a study of seventh graders in a Welsh school. For six months, one class period a day was set aside for SSR. Students made substantially greater pretest to posttest gains than expected and greater improvement than national norms of similar students.

Schon, Hopkins, and Davis (1981) examined the effects of SSR on Hispanic students' reading abilities and attitudes. Forty-nine students in second, third, and fourth grades were given 60 minutes of free reading time to read books in Spanish in addition to reading instruction in Spanish. The control group received reading instruction in English and received no in-class SSR. After eight weeks, on comparable measures in English and Spanish, the students given time to read outperformed the control group on measures of speed, comprehension, and attitude. The instruction-only students had higher vocabulary scores.

Farrell (1982) examined the total reading scores of average-level readers in junior high who read for 42 minutes daily. After eight months, 90% of the students gained one to two years on the Gates–MacGinitie Reading Test. Of the remaining students, 5% made slight gains only, but 5% had three to five years of growth in reading achievement scores.

Green (1984) conducted a 24-week study of fourth and fifth graders, comparing the effects of two variants of SSR with no silent reading time. In addition to regular instruction, one group received 20 minutes of silent reading time four days a week plus prereading (e.g., reading about different genres), while the other group had only silent reading time. The control group had no reading time, only regular reading instruction. All three groups improved on measures of reading comprehension and attitude; no one practice was more effective. Teachers reported that students engaged in SSR were reading more and reading a wider variety of materials.

Manning and Manning (1984) compared fourth graders in three classrooms for one school year with three models of recreational reading practice: SSR, peer-interaction book discussion, and teacher conference on self-selected books. All students received traditional reading instruction. Scores increased in all three groups, but the peer-interaction model was most effective in raising both reading achievement and attitude.

Dwyer and Reed (1989) examined the effects of SSR on the reading ability and attitude of fourth- and fifth-grade students. The experimental group had 15 minutes of daily SSR. The control group had additional reading instruction instead of reading time. The reading level of both groups was the same at pretest. After six weeks, the students given reading time had a grade equivalent of 8.3 whereas the students given additional reading instruction had a grade equivalent of 6.7. The experimental group's attitude toward reading decreased 1.78 points over the duration of the study, compared with a decrease of 0.57 for the control group.

Machet and Olen (1996) examined the effects of SSR on English as a Second Language (ESL) students in fourth through seventh grades. The experimental group of 139 students had designated time for SSR; the control group did not. After eight months, students in all grades who had reading time showed greater improvement on a test of reading comprehension than did control group students. Differences were significant only for fourth- and sixth-grade students.

To summarize, results in six of these studies showed little or no difference in reading achievement between students who did and did not have in-school reading time. The other six studies showed positive results for students who engaged in SSR. With the exception of one study, a small number also reported that students who had SSR had positive attitude changes toward reading, their amount of reading increased, and they read a wider range of materials.

The remaining 17 studies reviewed reported statistical tests of the effects of reading time on reading skills and achievement. Fifteen studies compared an SSR group to a non-SSR group, one study examined a single group of students given SSR from pretest to posttest, and one was a correlational study of the relationship between time spent reading and reading achievement. They can be quantitatively evaluated and summarized using the effect size statistic. Effect size quantifies the difference between two groups; it is not affected by sample size and provides a measure of practical significance as opposed to results reported as either statistically significant or nonsignificant.

Wilmot (1975) investigated the effects of a seven-month SSR program on the reading achievement of second-, fourth-, and sixth-grade students. Reading achievement was measured with the Gates–MacGinitie Reading Test. Schools were randomly assigned to the experimental or control group and used a range of similar reading instruction practices. Experimental-group classes had in-school reading time, increasing from a few minutes to 30 minutes a day. Control-group classes received regular reading instruction only. Results on measures of vocabulary and comprehension were positive but not significant.

Bartelo (1979) examined the effects of a seven-month program of daily silent reading time on the achievement of seventh-grade students who were reading two or more years below grade level and were enrolled in compensatory reading programs. Students read self-selected materials for 15 minutes daily. They made significant pretest to posttest gains in comprehension and total reading score.

Summers (1979) compared the reading achievement of students who participated in a five-month SSR program to a group of similar students who did not receive SSR. Equivalent schools participated, and there were no significant differences on pretest MAT comprehension and vocabulary scores. Reading time increased from 10 minutes two days a week to 25–30 minutes four to five days a week. Overall, the control group made greater gains on the MAT vocabulary and comprehension subtests, but differences between the two groups were not significant.

Summers and McClelland (1982) compared the reading achievement of fifth- and sixth-grade students in a school that implemented an SSR program to the achievement of students in a school that did not have an independent reading program. Attempts were made to keep groups equivalent on characteristics such as student ability, teacher characteristics and experience, and student attitude toward reading. Reading time increased from several minutes a day to 20–25 minutes a day, four to five days a week. All students received similar reading instruction. After five months, SSR students outperformed non-SSR students on the MAT vocabulary and comprehension subtests, but differences were not significant.

Collins (1980) looked at the effect of daily silent reading on the achievement of students in second through sixth grade. There were no significant differences at pretest on the Gates–MacGinitie Reading Test. Treatment group students read 10 to 30 minutes every day for 15 weeks in addition to regular reading instruction. Control-group students had regular reading instruction and spent the additional time on English and spelling. Students given reading time achieved greater gains on the Gates–MacGinitie vocabulary test and the Iowa Test of Basic Skills (ITBS) reading test; differences were not significant.

Higgins (1981) examined the effects of an SSR program on fifth graders. Students in the experimental group had 20 minutes of daily independent reading time for six months. The control group had higher pretest scores on all reading measures. Students given daily reading time made greater gains on the Gates–MacGinitie speed and accuracy subtest and on the Stanford Achievement Test (SAT) comprehension subtest. Students given reading instruction only made greater gains on the SAT vocabulary subtest; differences were not significant.

Langford and Allen (1983) examined the effects of a silent reading program on the reading achievement of fifth- and sixth-grade classes randomly assigned to the experimental or control group. While experimental-group students read for 30 minutes a day, control-group students participated in a variety of nonreading activities. After six months, students who read every day performed significantly better on the Slosson Oral Reading Test of reading achievement.

Elley and Mangubhai (1983) compared a Book Flood program and Shared Books program to traditional English instruction with students in Fiji. Book Flood is an extensive reading program that provides books and time to read; Shared Books involves shared reading of storybooks by the teacher. The traditionally taught students had no independent reading time. After eight months, the two groups of students exposed to the storybooks made twice the gains as did the group with the conventional curriculum. Book Flood students who read independently made greater gains than the students in the shared books group, but differences were not significant. Increased gains were still evident after 20 months.

Lund (1983) looked at the effects of silent reading time on the reading achievement of junior high remedial class students randomly assigned to four 40-minute periods of skills-only instruction, or two periods of skills instruction and two periods of silent reading time every week. They were assessed after nine months with the vocabulary and comprehension subtests of the California Reading Test.

Skills-only students did better on vocabulary measures whereas skills-plus-reading-time students did better on comprehension measures. Neither difference was significant.

Box (1984) looked at the effects of 13 weeks of independent reading time on the reading achievement of third-grade students of varying abilities. The experimental group read for 10 minutes a day in addition to regular reading instruction; the control group had regular reading instruction only. There were two low-, two average-, and two high-level classes in each group. Overall, students who had reading time did significantly better on the vocabulary subtest of the California Achievement Test (CAT). Their comprehension scores were also higher, but differences were not significant. Low-level readers appeared to benefit the most, outperforming nonreaders on all measures. Average-level readers outperformed nonreaders only on vocabulary. High-level readers outperformed nonreaders on all measures, but differences were not significant.

Denslow (1985) examined the effects of independent reading time on the reading achievement of first through sixth grade below-level readers. Ten randomly selected students from each class read self-selected materials for 15 to 20 minutes a day for seven months. Control-group students were randomly picked from another school. There were no significant differences among students prior to the study. Experimental-group students performed significantly better on the vocabulary and comprehension subtests of the ITBS than did control-group students. Students who read more than 7,000 pages made greater gains than those who read less than 3,000 pages, but these differences were not significant.

Parker (1986) compared the reading achievement of inner-city, below grade level seventh graders given independent reading time to that of seventh graders from the previous year who had not participated in an independent reading program. Students read for one 50-minute class period a week for seven months. Reading achievement was measured with the CAT vocabulary subtest and total reading scores. Students given independent reading scored significantly higher than did students who had no reading time.

Rossman (1986) explored the relationship between reading time, reading achievement, and automaticity in a correlational study with students in first, third, and fifth grades. The relationship between reading time and all Gates–MacGinitie Reading Test subtests was positive and significant. Based on the fact that 92% of automatic readers read 210 or more minutes weekly and 96% of nonautomatic readers read less, he concluded that a critical minimum amount of three and a half hours per week reading time is needed to develop automaticity.

Everett (1987) examined the effects of independent reading time on the reading comprehension of African American, inner-city eighth graders. Students were randomly divided into two groups. Both groups received daily developmental reading instruction. For three weeks, one group read self-selected materials for 15 minutes a day while the other group copied a math assignment during that time. Overall, pretest to posttest scores on the Burns and Roe Informal Reading

Inventory increased in the reading group and decreased in the nonreading group; differences were not significant.

Melton (1993) examined the effectiveness of daily silent reading time for learning disabled third- and fourth-grade students. He compared the reading achievement of students who had 10 minutes of reading time every day for six months to the achievement of students who had regular reading instruction only. Differences between groups were significant on measures of word recognition in context and reading comprehension; differences on word recognition from word lists were not significant.

Sheu (2003) conducted an extensive reading program for 45 minutes a week with junior high students at a beginning level of English proficiency. There were two experimental groups; one read graded readers and the other read authentic English books. The control group received traditional English instruction only. There were no appreciable differences between groups on any measures at pretest. Both experimental groups made significant gains on measures of reading comprehension, vocabulary, and grammar; the control group's scores decreased significantly. All groups made considerable gains in reading rate, but the experimental groups' gains were three to four points higher than the control group's gains. The attitude scores for all groups decreased.

Cho and Kim (2004) examined the effects of two different reading programs with sixth-grade English as a Foreign Language (EFL) students in Korea. For 16 weeks, the experimental group received one 40-minute session of EFL instruction and one session for reading English-language storybooks on the Internet. Control-group students received text-based English instruction during both sessions. Students given reading time performed substantially better on vocabulary and comprehension measures. They also showed a significantly higher increase in interest in reading and confidence in their reading ability.

What We Can Conclude From These Studies

None of the SSR studies reviewed reported that students who had reading time scored significantly lower on any reading achievement measure than did students who had regular reading instruction with no added reading time. In almost all instances, students who read had higher scores than their nonreading counterparts. The pre–posttest study and the correlational analysis reported a statistically significant relationship between SSR and reading achievement. Overall, results were generally not statistically significant for heterogeneously grouped readers, or for average- and high-level readers. For lower level readers and those learning English as a second language, readers' scores were significantly higher than nonreaders' scores on all reading measures except one measure of vocabulary in junior high students.

Results for studies of SSR are neither consistent nor particularly clear using measures of statistical significance as a yardstick for success. Effect size gives us a measure of practical significance, a means of quantifying and evaluating the results of one study or a group of studies that examined a similar construct. For our purpose, effect size provides a practical measure of the difference between students who are given independent reading time as part of the reading curriculum and those not given in-class reading time. Researchers have provided several means of interpreting effect size. According to Cohen (1988), 0.10 reveals a small effect, 0.25 a medium effect, and 0.40 a large effect. Borg and Gall (1989) state that in educational settings, an effect size larger than 0.30 has practical significance; the intervention is large enough to make a worthwhile difference in the outcome measure. Coe (2002) provides a table for interpreting effect size as a percentage of subject scores in one group that fall below the average score in the other group. For example, a positive effect size of 1.0 would mean that the score of the average person in the experimental group is higher than 84% of the scores in the control group.

Tables 7.1 and 7.2 illustrate the results for vocabulary and comprehension measures in studies that compared readers with nonreaders. The last column interprets the effect size according to Coe (2002), indicating the percentage of scores in the lower group that fall below the average person's score in the higher group. Results indicate little or no difference between readers and nonreaders for high-level readers, student sample groups that were not separated by reading level, and, surprisingly, low-level readers in a mixed, junior high seventh- through ninth-grade group. For low-level readers in first through sixth grades, a separate below-level seventh-grade group, and EFL students, effect sizes were in the large range. This provides support for the practical significance of SSR as a valuable intervention that can make a worthwhile difference in reading achievement. The average reader in these reader groups scored higher than 66% to 86% of the students in the comparable nonreader control groups.

Results for measures of reading comprehension were similar. The same student groups of readers and nonreaders showed little or no difference, including the junior high low-level readers. The separately examined low-level readers in first through seventh grades, the EFL students, the average-level third-grade readers, and the fifth-grade heterogeneous-group readers all outperformed nonreaders at a level of practical significance.

Only a few studies reported a total reading score or assessed word recognition and reading accuracy. These results showed the same distribution. High-level and heterogeneous groups of readers and nonreaders showed little difference in outcome measures; lower level readers and EFL students significantly outperformed nonreaders. Results for student attitude toward reading were mixed. Readers and nonreaders in mixed-ability groups showed little difference in attitude toward reading; other groups of readers had a more positive attitude than their nonreading peers, but differences were in the small-to-medium range. This does not mean that some readers like reading more than nonreaders, only that SSR may not have had a substantial impact on existing student attitudes. In most instances, teachers reported that students who were given time to read enjoyed

Table 7.1. Vocabulary Results in Studies Comparing Readers With Nonreaders

Student Sample	Study Length Weekly Reading Time	Effect Size	Treatment vs. Control
Grade 3 High-level readers	13 weeks 10 minutes daily	−0.10	Control > 53% of treatment
Grades 7, 8, 9 Low-level readers	9 months 40 minutes, 2 days	−0.07	Control > 53% of treatment
Grade 7 All reading levels	5 months 25–30 minutes, 4–5 days	−0.001	Treatment > 50% of control
Grade 6 All reading levels	5 months 25–30 minutes, 4–5 days	0.003	Treatment > 50% of control
Grades 2, 4, 6 All reading levels	7 months 30 minutes daily	0.006	Treatment > 50% of control
Grades 5, 6, 7 All reading levels	5 months 20–25 minutes daily	0.01	Treatment > 50% of control
Grade 5 All reading levels	5 months 25–30 minutes, 4–5 days	0.07	Treatment > 53% of control
Grade 5 All reading levels	6 months 20 minutes daily	0.10	Treatment > 53% of control
Grades 1–6 Low-level readers	7 months 15–20 minutes daily	0.41	Treatment > 66% of control
Grade 6 EFL	16 weeks 50 minutes, 1 day	0.47	Treatment > 68% of control
Grade 3 Average readers	13 weeks 10 minutes daily	0.68	Treatment > 75% of control
Grade 7 Low-level readers	7 months 50 minutes, 1 day	0.73	Treatment > 77% of control
Grade 3 Low-level readers	13 weeks 10 minutes daily	0.78	Treatment > 78% of control
Junior High EFL	9 months 45 minutes, 1 day	1.11	Treatment > 86% of control

it, read more and different books, and wanted to continue having independent reading time in class.

Although results show support for the effectiveness of silent reading, overall conclusions should be cautious and conservative. Fewer silent reading studies have been conducted since the NRP published their conclusions on the value of independent reading and its relationship to reading ability and performance than in decades prior to the report. There are several possible reasons for this. Under No Child Left Behind directives, independent reading in the United States may have fallen by the wayside in many classrooms, as teachers work harder than ever to

Table 7.2. Comprehension Results in Studies Comparing Readers With Nonreaders

Student Sample	Study Length Weekly Reading Time	Effect Size	Treatment vs. Control
Grade 3 High-level readers	13 weeks 10 minutes daily	−0.28	Control > 61% of treatment
Grade 5 All reading levels	5 months 25–30 minutes, 4–5 days	−0.13	Control > 55% of treatment
Grade 7 All reading levels	5 months 25–30 minutes, 4–5 days	−0.03	Control > 51% of treatment
Grades 7, 8, 9 Low-level readers	9 months 40 minutes, 2 days	0	Treatment > 50% of control
Grades 2, 3, 4, 5, 6 All reading levels	15 weeks 10–30 minutes daily	0.05	Treatment > 52% of control
Grade 6 All reading levels	5 months 25–30 minutes, 4–5 days	0.07	Treatment > 53% of control
Grades 5, 6, 7 All reading levels	5 months 20–25 minutes daily	0.07	Treatment > 53% of control
Grades 2, 4, 6 All reading levels	7 months 30 minutes daily	0.14	Treatment > 56% of control
Grade 5 All reading levels	6 months 20 minutes daily	0.29	Treatment > 62% of control
Grade 4 EFL	1 academic year 20–30 minutes daily	0.37	Treatment > 65% of control
Grade 3 Average readers	13 weeks 10 minutes daily	0.40	Treatment > 66% of control
Grades 1–6 Low-level readers	7 months 15–20 minutes daily	0.43	Treatment > 67% of control
Grade 4 EFL	1 academic year 20–30 minutes daily	0.58	Treatment > 73% of control
Grade 3 Low-level readers	13 weeks 10 minutes daily	0.62	Treatment > 73% of control
Junior High EFL	9 months 45 minutes, 1 day	1.36	Treatment > 91% of control
Grades 3, 4 Students with learning disabilities	6 months 10 minutes daily	6.57	Treatment > 99.9% of control

meet required student achievement standards. Administrators and teachers are so busy meeting mandates that they may be reluctant to take valuable classroom time to facilitate research. Administrators may also be disinclined to allow researchers access to school data because of media attention.

Those educators who are strong proponents of the value of silent reading as an instructional tool may not want to conduct experimental studies in their classrooms, especially if they feel this may deny some students reading time for the sake of experimental rigor. Unfortunately, more real-world classroom projects that follow student performance over the school year are less experimentally "gold standard" and so are frequently criticized as not producing quality results. Despite this, we strongly believe that teachers should continue to document student progress and report on both their successful and unsuccessful efforts. It is important for educators to remain aware of and share information and ideas for student success. It is this collaboration and cooperation among teachers that stimulates and improves the practice. Garan and DeVoogd (2008) summarize what many educators already believe when they state, "If we don't allow students to read in school at the same time that we tout the wonders of reading, what message are we sending to students about our values?" (p. 341).

Teachers know students, and students know what they like. Marsha's students express the value and joy of reading in ways that cannot be measured by tests or rigorous statistical methods:

> "When I read a book silently, I feel I'm going to pop, it makes me feel so good."

> "Silent reading makes your brain work harder than watching television or playing video games or stuff like that."

> "If a book is good enough, I can read for more than an hour without taking time off."

> "I feel really good inside when I read a good book. When I finish it, I just want to start another book by the same author."

> "You know, you are one of the book's characters when you read a good book silently."

> "When you read a really good book silently, it makes you feel like a king. You can go anywhere and do anything, and that feels really good."

Recommendations for Future Research

Although the majority of the studies discussed in this chapter show that independent reading is a positive and constructive instructional practice, there are still questions and issues that need to be addressed. More research needs to be done that examines the effects of prereading activities, such as the availability of and guidance selecting appropriate books, and reading response activities such as writing, discussion, and teacher conference in conjunction with independent reading time. Teachers deal with a wide variety of students and issues in classrooms today. Future studies need to look at the effects of independent reading programs for students at all grades and reading abilities. Ongoing research is needed with students who have reading and learning disabilities, the deaf and hearing impaired, second-language learners in the United States as well as abroad, high-ability students, and other special-needs groups. What materials, reading activities, and practices are most effective? Is there an optimum reading time? Additional research that examines varying amounts of reading time, along with other activities and practices, is especially critical in today's schools, where every minute counts, and teachers are faced with increasing expectations for student success and achievement. Finally, teachers are as essential a component of reading research as their students and should be included in reading research. What teacher characteristics, education, training, collaboration, mentoring, and professional practices contribute to effective learning and reading achievement?

QUESTIONS FOR PROFESSIONAL DEVELOPMENT

1. In comparing varying amounts of independent reading time, McGroarty (1982) found no consistent trends; more time did not always result in higher reading achievement scores. He concluded that this relationship is positive and significant, but neither simple nor linear. How can teachers determine a constructive amount of time for reading, and what teacher and student characteristics and instructional practices have an impact on reading time?

2. Studies by Oliver (1973), Manning and Manning (1984), Davis (1988), Elley (1991), and Reedy (1994) examined the effects of silent reading time, with and without reading response activities, on reading achievement. How can reading response activities enhance reading time? What are some specific reading response activities that could be used to augment the usefulness of silent reading time for students of differing abilities and in different grades?

3. Rodriguez and Lira (1998) found that ESL students showed the most benefit of silent reading time but were also more likely than other students to choose books at their instructional rather than independent level. This suggests that what students read is as important as the fact that they are reading. How can teachers help students choose books that are interesting as well as challenging? How do they know that students are benefiting from the books they read?

4. In a study of at-risk students, Dully (1989) found that students given time to read tested 1.38 grade levels higher than a similar group who had no reading time; differences were not statistically significant. This brings up the issue of the practical value of reading practice. Is a small amount of time given to reading practice worth a statistically small gain in reading level? How do we assess the practical value of reading time?

5. As noted earlier, teachers today have greater teaching obligations and outcome requirements to meet in a school day that has not changed in many years. As a teacher today, how can you engage your students in reading, help them realize the value and enjoyment of reading, and implement effective reading time in classrooms without sacrificing other subjects? How can independent reading time with self-selected materials be used in other subject classes?

REFERENCES

Bartelo, D.M. (1979). *The effect of silent reading practice on reading achievement and attitudes in reading.* Blacksburg, VA: Virginia Polytechnic Institute and State University. (ERIC Document Reproduction Service No. ED194887)

Boney, C.D., & Agnew, K. (1937). Periods of awakening or reading readiness. *Elementary English Review, 14,* 183–187.

Borg, W.R., & Gall, M.D. (1989). *Educational research: An introduction* (5th ed.). New York: Longman.

Box, L. (1984). *A study of achievement and attitudes of high-achieving, average-achieving, and low-achieving third grade students involved in daily sustained silent reading.* Unpublished doctoral dissertation, Mississippi State University.

Cho, K., & Kim, H. (2004). Recreational reading in English as a foreign language in Korea: Positive effects of a sixteen-week program. *Knowledge Quest, 32*(4), 36–38.

Chow, P., & Chou, C. (2000). Evaluating sustained silent reading in reading classes. *The Internet TESL Journal, 6*(11). Retrieved May 5, 2010, from iteslj.org/Articles/Chow-SSR.html

Cline, R.K.J., & Kretke, G.L. (1980). An evaluation of long-term SSR in the junior high school. *Journal of Reading, 23*(6), 503–506.

Coe, R. (2002, September). *It's the effect size, stupid: What effect size is and why it is important.* Paper presented at the annual conference of the British Educational Research Association, Exeter, England.

Cohen, J. (1988). *Statistical power analysis for the behavioral sciences* (2nd ed.). Hillsdale, NJ: Erlbaum.

Collins, C. (1980). Sustained silent reading periods: Effect on teachers' behaviors and students' achievement. *The Elementary School Journal, 81*(2), 108–114. doi:10.1086/461213

Davis, Z.T. (1988). A comparison of the effectiveness of sustained silent reading and directed reading activity on students' reading achievement. *The High School Journal, 72*(1), 46–48.

Denslow, O.F. (1985). *Effects of a recreational reading program on language use and reading progress of elementary students.* Unpublished doctoral dissertation, Brigham Young University, Provo, UT.

Dully, M. (1989). *The relation between sustained silent reading to reading achievement and attitude of the at-risk student.* Unpublished master's thesis, Kean College, Union, NJ.

Dwyer, E.J., & Reed, V. (1989). Effects of sustained silent reading on attitudes toward reading. *Reading Horizons, 29*(4), 283–293.

Elley, W.B. (1991). Acquiring literacy in a second language: The effect of book-based programs. *Language Learning, 41*(3), 375–411. doi:10.1111/j.1467-1770.1991.tb00611.x

Elley, W.B., & Mangubhai, F. (1983). The impact of reading on second language learning. *Reading Research Quarterly, 19*(1), 53–67. doi:10.2307/747337

Evans, H.M., & Towner, J.C. (1975). Sustained silent reading: Does it increase skills? *The Reading Teacher, 29*(2), 155–156.

Everett, I. (1987). *Recreational reading effects on reading comprehension achievement.* Unpublished master's thesis, Kean College, Union, NJ. (ERIC Document Reproduction Service No. ED283123)

Farrell, E. (1982). SSR as the core of a junior high reading program. *Journal of Reading, 26*(1), 48–51.

Garan, E.M., & DeVoogd, G. (2008). The benefits of sustained silent reading: Scientific research and common sense converge. *The Reading Teacher, 62*(4), 336–344. doi:10.1598/RT.62.4.6

Green, H.R.H. (1984). *A comparison of the effects of sustained silent reading with and without stimulant experiences on attitudes toward reading and reading achievement of fourth- and fifth-grade students.* Unpublished doctoral dissertation, East Texas State University, Commerce.

Higgins, K.J. (1981). *Sustained silent reading in the fifth grade: The effects of sustained silent reading on speed, comprehension, word study skills, and vocabulary.* Unpublished doctoral dissertation, Brigham Young University, Provo, UT.

Hunt, L.C., Jr. (Ed.). (1966). The individualized reading program: A guide for classroom teaching. *Proceedings of the 11th annual convention of the International Reading Association, 11*(3).

Hunt, L.C., Jr. (1970). The effect of self-selection, interest, and motivation upon independent, instructional, and frustrational levels. *The Reading Teacher, 24*(2), 146–151.

Kefford, R. (1981). Assessing reading gains in a scheme based on sustained silent reading. *Australian Journal of Reading, 4*(4), 212–216.

Krashen, S.D. (1994). An answer to the literacy crisis: Free voluntary reading. *School Library Media Annual, 12,* 113–122.

Krashen, S.D. (2000). Foreword. In J.L. Pilgreen (Ed.), *The SSR handbook: How to organize and manage a sustained silent reading program* (pp. vii–xi). Portsmouth, NH: Boynton/Cook.

Langford, J.C., & Allen, E.G. (1983). The effects of U.S.S.R. on students' attitudes and achievement. *Reading Horizons, 23*(3), 194–200.

Lewis, M. (2002). *Read more—read better? A meta-analysis of the literature on the relationship between exposure to reading and reading achievement.* Unpublished doctoral dissertation, University of Minnesota, Twin Cities.

Lewis, M., & Samuels, S.J. (2005). *Read more—read better? A meta-analysis of the literature on the relationship between exposure to reading and reading achievement.* Minneapolis: University of Minnesota.

Lund, J.M. (1983). *Sustained silent reading with junior high school remedial readers.* Unpublished doctoral dissertation, Yeshiva University, New York.

Machet, M., & Olen, S. (1996, July). *Determining the effect of free voluntary reading on second language readers in South Africa.* Paper presented at the annual meeting of the International Association of School Librarianship, Ocho Rios, Jamaica. (ERIC Document Reproduction Service No. ED403738)

Manning, G.L., & Manning, M. (1984). What models of recreational reading make a difference? *Reading World, 23*(4), 375–380.

Manning-Dowd, A. (1985). *The effectiveness of SSR: A review of the research* (Report No. CS008607). (ERIC Document Reproduction Service No. ED276970)

McGroarty, J.J. (1982). *The effect of varied amounts of sustained silent reading (S.S.R.) on selected aspects of reading/thinking skills and attitude toward reading.* Unpublished doctoral dissertation, Temple University, Philadelphia.

Melton, E.J. (1993). *SSR: Is it an effective practice for the learning disabled?* Scranton, PA: Marywood College. (ERIC Document Reproduction Service No. ED397569)

Meyers, R. (1998). *Uninterrupted sustained silent reading* (Exit Project, EDSE 695). Long Beach: California State University. (ERIC Document Reproduction Service No. ED418379)

Minton, M.J. (1980). The effect of sustained silent reading upon comprehension and attitudes among ninth graders. *Journal of Reading, 23*(6), 498–502.

Moore, J.C., Jones, C.J., & Miller, D.C. (1980). What we know after a decade of sustained silent reading. *The Reading Teacher, 33*(4), 445–450.

National Institute of Child Health and Human Development. (2000). *Report of the National Reading Panel. Teaching children to read: An evidence-based assessment of the scientific research literature on reading and its implications for reading instruction* (NIH Publication No. 00-4769). Washington, DC: U.S. Government Printing Office.

Oliver, M.E. (1973). The effect of high intensity practice on reading comprehension. *Reading Improvement, 10*(2), 16–18.

Oliver, M.E. (1976). The effect of high intensity practice on reading achievement. *Reading Improvement, 13*(4), 226–228.

Parker, L.G. (1986). *A study of the effects of sustained silent reading on reading achievement scores of inner city middle school students.* Unpublished doctoral dissertation, University of Connecticut, Storrs.

Reed, K. (1977). *An investigation of the effect of sustained silent reading on reading comprehension skills and attitude toward reading of urban secondary school students.* Unpublished doctoral dissertation, University of Connecticut, Storrs.

Reedy, J.D. (1994). *Effects of a sustained silent reading program with literature response journals on third graders' attitude, reading achievement, and writing.* Unpublished doctoral dissertation, Baylor University, Waco, TX.

Rodriguez, C., & Lira, J.R. (1998). *A study of eighth grade students from a South Texas middle school who participated in 30-minute required reading periods of self-selected books.* Laredo: Texas A&M International University. (ERIC Document Reproduction Service No. ED416452)

Rossman, A.D. (1986). *The effect of uninterrupted sustained silent reading strategies on the attainment of automaticity in reading.* Unpublished doctoral dissertation, Northwestern University, Evanston, IL.

Sadoski, M.C. (1980). Ten years of uninterrupted sustained silent reading. *Reading Improvement, 17*(2), 153–156.

Schaudt, B.A. (1983). Another look at sustained silent reading. *The Reading Teacher, 36*(9), 934–936.

Schon, I., Hopkins, K.D., & Davis, W.A. (1981, April). *The effects of books in Spanish and free reading time on Hispanic students' reading abilities and attitudes.* Paper presented to the American Educational Research Association, Los Angeles, CA. (ERIC Document Reproduction Service No. ED204096)

Sheu, S.P. (2003). Extensive reading with EFL learners at beginning level. *TESL Reporter, 36*(2), 8–26.

Sperzl, E. (1948). The effect of comic books on vocabulary growth and reading comprehension. *Elementary English, 25,* 109–113.

Summers, E.G. (1979). *An evaluation of the effects of a program of sustained silent reading (SSR) on reading achievement and attitude toward reading in intermediate grades: Final report.* Vancouver, Canada: University of British Columbia. (ERIC Document Reproduction Service No. ED169473)

Summers, E.G., & McClelland, J.V. (1982). A field-based evaluation of sustained silent reading (SSR) in intermediate grades. *The Alberta Journal of Educational Research, 28*(2), 100–112.

Tunnell, M.O., & Jacobs, J.S. (1989). Using "real" books: Research findings on literature based reading instruction. *The Reading Teacher, 42*(7), 470–477.

Wiesendanger, K.D., & Birlem, E.D. (1984). The effectiveness of SSR: An overview of the research. *Reading Horizons, 24*(3), 197–201.

Wilmot, M.P. (1975). *An investigation of the effect upon the reading performance and attitude toward reading of elementary grade students, of including in the reading program a period of sustained silent reading.* Unpublished doctoral dissertation, University of Colorado, Boulder.

CHAPTER 8

Scaffolded Silent Reading: Improving the Conditions of Silent Reading Practice in Classrooms

D. Ray Reutzel
Utah State University

Cindy D. Jones
Utah State University

Terry H. Newman
Fairfield Area School District, Pennsylvania

Research has consistently shown that time spent reading is highly correlated with student reading achievement (Anderson, Hiebert, Scott, & Wilkinson, 1985; Cunningham & Stanovich, 1998; Hepler & Hickman, 1982; Krashen, 1993; National Institute of Child Health and Human Development [NICHD], 2000). In an effort to increase the amount of time students spend reading in school classrooms, many teachers allocate a block of time for students to read silently. This type of reading practice has been referred to as Sustained Silent Reading (SSR), Drop Everything and Read (DEAR), Super Quiet Reading Time (SQUIRT), Wonderful Exciting Books (WEB), Daily Independent Reading Time (DIRT), and a variety of other acronyms intended to promote interest in time spent reading (Jarvis, 2003; Jensen & Jensen, 2002; Routman, 1991). During SSR and other similar reading practice routines, students read independently and silently from self-selected texts. Typically, the teacher also reads independently and silently during this time.

Stemming largely from the National Reading Panel report (NRP; NICHD, 2000), independent, silent reading practice routines such as SSR have come under increased critical scrutiny. After the NRP announced that research evidence was insufficient in quantity and quality to offer an unqualified endorsement of independent, silent reading practice routines, many school administrators and classroom teachers began to shy away from providing students with time for practicing reading either independently or silently on a regular basis in classrooms. This recent reticence toward providing independent, silent reading practice is particularly evident in early elementary grades but also exists in intermediate elementary grades and secondary schools. Given the current environment of teacher and

Revisiting Silent Reading: New Directions for Teachers and Researchers, edited by Elfrieda H. Hiebert and D. Ray Reutzel. © 2010 by the International Reading Association.

student accountability for meeting benchmarks, standards, and growth targets, educators are becoming increasingly leery of educational practices that do not have substantial empirical evidence of effectiveness.

Why then was independent, silent reading found to be less than uniformly effective in classrooms using the conditions and procedures typically associated with SSR and DEAR? Let us consider another situation similar to learning to read in which students must practice a great deal to acquire a critical set of skills. For this example, we turn to the universal learning situation found in many high school settings—learning to drive an automobile in driver's education. Picture for a moment what kind of drivers might emerge from a driver's education course if the practice conditions used in SSR or DEAR were also applied to learning to drive.

Imagine that the instructor of this driver's education class thought it best that when students initially practiced driving they would be allowed to choose any car or truck on any car lot in town to heighten the motivation to learn that is associated with choice. Continue to imagine that student drivers can take this car or truck onto any road, under any traffic or weather conditions they choose for driving practice.

What about the driver's education instructor? Where is he or she during practice? Well, the driver's education instructor is driving his or her own car to model the fact that the instructor can drive and does drive. In fact, to emphasize the value of driving, the instructor and other school personnel all drive at the same time daily to exhibit which cars they choose to drive in a program called Drop Everything and Drive (DEAD). Of course, the DEAD program fails to provide students much in the way of teacher modeling, teacher instruction, or teacher–student interaction about *how* to drive or guided practice for those learning to drive, especially those who struggle. The expectation is that students would practice driving daily for at least 20 minutes, but there would be *no* accountability for whether students actually practiced their driving. Students would not receive any feedback, guidance, support, or monitoring from their instructor during practice time to help them become better drivers. The real beauty of this kind of practice for student drivers is they could engage in unsupervised driving practice on a daily basis while their instructor took off driving his or her own car for the same period of time. (Remember how motivating learning to drive is compared with learning to read!)

We suspect by now you might be snickering about, if not getting quite a good laugh out of, this scenario. On a sober note, if the practice conditions just described for learning to drive were obviously ineffective, why then did we believe that such practice conditions when used for practicing reading in classrooms would be any more or less effective? Of course for those students who could already drive and love to drive, this approach might provide certain benefits as it did for some readers who were motivated to read. But many students are not so motivated, nor are they sufficiently skilled to practice reading in unguided or unsupervised settings.

Recently, scholars have roundly criticized the conditions of practice associated with independent, silent reading (Kelley & Clausen-Grace, 2006; Reutzel, Fawson, & Smith, 2008; Stahl, 2004). In the next section of this chapter, we look into the research on independent, silent reading, especially studies associated with SSR, DEAR, and other programs using similar practice conditions in an effort to lay the groundwork for determining more effective conditions of independent, silent reading practice than those used in the past.

Conditions for Effective Reading Practice in Independent, Silent Reading

Because SSR has been so widely promoted in many teacher education programs, preservice teacher textbooks, and reading education journals as an effective way to increase time spent reading and thus increase student competencies in fluency, comprehension, reading engagement, and other reading skills, a thorough vetting of the practice conditions associated with SSR and the accompanying effects seem warranted. SSR or similar reading practice conditions have been implemented throughout schools in the United States and countries such as Canada, Japan, Korea, New Zealand, Hong Kong, and Singapore. As previously noted, a major discrepancy existed between the findings of the NRP regarding effective research-based instructional practices and the independent, silent reading time actually taking place in many classrooms. This contradiction left many educators unsure of which course to follow. Some openly discouraged the use of silent reading time in the classroom, and others encouraged teachers to support at-home reading rather than allocate valuable classroom time to SSR (Armbruster, Lehr, & Osborn, 2001). Some chose to discontinue the use of SSR altogether, possibly depriving students of any reading practice time during the school day. Others continued the status quo of using SSR.

The practice of SSR has been a topic of reading discussions for more than 40 years. In the mid-1960s, Hunt (1965) presented the *Philosophy of Individualized Reading* stating that a reader needs periods of continuous, uninterrupted silent reading. In later publications (Hunt, 1970, 1971a, 1971b), Hunt provided details about this silent reading time, which he referred to as Uninterrupted Sustained Silent Reading (USSR). Hunt presented USSR as the definitive act of high-quality reading instruction and the setting where student reading skills were combined to achieve the ultimate goal of reading—independently gaining meaning from the reading of text. USSR emphasized an important characteristic of a true reader: reading stamina. In the final analysis, *sustained* silent reading was viewed as representing the personal stamina of a reader to continue gaining important information from a text for extended amounts of time. The hallmark of an accomplished and engaged reader is the ability and disposition to read from self-selected texts for extended periods, focusing on important ideas in the text while disassociating himself or herself from distractions.

The notion of allocating in-school instructional time for SSR caught hold. Soon, others offered guidelines for effectively implementing SSR in classrooms (McCracken, 1971). Some of these guidelines contrasted sharply with Hunt's ideas.

Over the years, numerous ideas have been presented about the use of SSR as a way to practice independent, silent reading; but as Stahl (2004) so aptly points out—all practice is not equally effective! As educators and researchers continued to investigate the use of SSR, concerns converged on four factors: (1) student self-selection of reading materials, (2) student engagement and time on task, (3) accountability of students, and (4) interactions of teachers and students around text. By addressing these concerns, we can identify specific modifications for SSR that might provide students with better reading practice conditions to develop reading proficiency.

Student Self-Selection of Reading Materials

A proficient reader is able to choose texts that are of interest and at a level of appropriate difficulty. Teacher guidance in selection of appropriately challenging and interesting reading materials can help develop these important skills for those who are becoming proficient readers. When outlining the procedures associated with SSR, Hunt (1965) recognizes the importance of teacher guidance in student selection of reading materials and states that teacher guidance was needed to help students choose books of an appropriate value of content, level of difficulty, and interest appeal. He argued for a flexible framework that allowed for "pupil choice and teacher judgment" (p. 147).

A factor commonly associated with the use of SSR is for students to have unlimited free choice when selecting reading materials. Although choice can be motivating and increase student engagement (Deci & Ryan, 1985; Turner 1995), being able to determine if a book is either too hard or too easy to read is essential to "sustain" reading. Unfortunately, research has shown that those readers who need to practice reading the most, struggling readers, often select books they cannot read (Donovan, Smolkin, & Lomax, 2000; Fresch, 1995). Educators who used SSR in the past often failed to teach students useful strategies for selecting appropriately challenging reading materials that span the genres. Students who select easy books time after time experience little growth in reading ability (Baker & Wigfield, 1999; Carver & Leibert, 1995). Conversely, students who continuously select books that are too hard become frustrated, lose interest, and are less engaged (Anderson, Higgins, & Wurster, 1985).

Students who select texts that match their ability level are more likely to sustain their reading and consequently increase the volume of reading, which in turn increases vocabulary growth and achievement (Stanovich, 1986). Teachers can nurture students' ability to select appropriately leveled texts by establishing and maintaining a well-designed classroom library that includes high-interest texts from a variety of genres and levels of difficulty (Reutzel, Jones, Fawson, & Smith, 2008). In fact, reading widely has been shown to be the most motivating path to obtain a reading incentive among the following four: (1) reading widely, (2) number of pages, (3) number of books, and (4) number of minutes (Fawson, Reutzel, Read, Smith, & Moore, 2009).

Student choice of reading materials can increase motivation and engagement with text (Spaulding, 1992; Turner & Paris, 1995). However, unguided choice can become a negative force. It is important for students to read from a variety of texts to increase reading competencies (Kuhn & Stahl, 2000). Left on their own, students usually select reading materials from a limited base of genres and topics. Students may also chronically self-select reading material that is either too easy or too hard (Kelley & Clausen-Grace, 2006; Stahl, 2004). Worthy and Broaddus (2001) note that these typically occurring behaviors during self-selection of texts could result in negative reading attitudes and behaviors for gifted readers and struggling readers. In fact, self-selection time can be used as an avoidance time. Some students can spend the entire designated SSR block choosing materials to read. Just as the student finds the "right" book, reading time ends. To address this avoidance tactic, some teachers have implemented rules such that students must select a book before reading time and they must remain in the same place during reading time so students can only "sit and pretend to read or sit and read" (Kelley & Clausen-Grace, 2006). This reading avoidance can become a habit that spills over to home reading as well (Chua, 2008).

Teacher guidance in selection of reading texts helps students learn to recognize material that is of interest, draws from a variety of text genres and topics, and is an appropriate level of difficulty (Greenleaf, Schoenbach, Cziko, & Mueller, 2001; Parr & Maguiness, 2005; Reutzel, Jones, et al., 2008; Trudel, 2007). Because time spent reading with appropriate texts leads to improvement in word reading and comprehension (Kuhn et al., 2006), selection of text is an important consideration for effective implementation of SSR.

Student Engagement and Time on Task

One widely accepted idea that seems to be extremely intuitively appealing among educators is that the more you read the better a reader you become (Allington, 1977; Chambliss & McKillop, 2000). However, simply allocating time for reading is not sufficient for increasing student reading engagement. Teachers must provide time and instructional practices that foster motivation to read (Kamil, 2008). Even if students are going through the motions of reading, how does a teacher know if a student *really* is reading silently or just pretending to read? It is difficult to know just how much time students are actually reading during SSR (Garan & DeVoogd, 2008; Kelley & Clausen-Grace, 2006; Stahl, 2004). If students are not fully engaged in the practice of reading during SSR, is this the best use of instructional time or the best type of practice to develop proficiency in reading?

Hunt (1965, 1971a, 1971b) recognizes the importance of engagement and time on task during SSR and warns that this time could be unproductive until students are taught responsibility for the task and reading endurance. He warns of the students who would exhibit evasive or disruptive behaviors to avoid reading such as the following: (a) "the gossips," students who talk instead of read; (b) "the wanderers," students who spend most of their time searching for something to read; and (c) "the squirrels," students who are so busy collecting books they have little time to read. Hunt emphasizes the importance of teacher guidance to firmly establish principles of high productivity during SSR. Recently, researchers have also noted the importance of appropriate reading behaviors for SSR, as readers learn and establish beliefs about self-efficacy and reading abilities, including viewing themselves as reluctant readers and nonparticipants (Alvermann, 2001; Chua, 2008; Greenleaf et al., 2001; Parr & Maguiness, 2005).

Frequently, SSR is not presented to students as an important time for *practicing* reading skills; perhaps this lack of direction regarding a dedicated purpose for SSR is one its downfalls. It makes sense that as readers are working to build SSR stamina, teachers should guide practice time and students should be accountable for their practice of reading.

Accountability of Students

Accountability of students for reading practice during SSR should serve to build reading stamina and proficiency. A lack of accountability may again call into question the efficacy of SSR. Researchers have noted that although students may appear to be engaged, because they are not held accountable some students can be "reading" the same book day after day, week after week (Kelley & Clausen-Grace, 2006; Worthy & Broaddus, 2001). Hunt (1965, 1971a, 1971b) addresses the need for accountability and suggests that teachers periodically complete observational checklists of students' reading performance and abilities. Hunt also emphasizes the importance of student self-evaluation. Finally, he cautions that accountability tasks completed by students (including book reports) should be time efficient so that they do not spend more time on record keeping than on reading.

Several methods for establishing accountability have been proposed by those studying the use of SSR in the classroom, such as student reading logs, anecdotal records, documentation of wide reading among genres, and reader response notebooks (Garan & DeVoogd, 2008; Newman, 2000; Reutzel, Jones, et al., 2008; Trudel, 2007; Worthy, Turner, & Moorman, 1998). Stahl (2004) emphasizes that the teacher should actively monitor student reading activity and progress during independent, silent reading time. SSR can be a time when the teacher helps students make the transition between guided, oral reading and independent, silent reading when standards and accountability are established and maintained for this reading practice.

Interactions of Teachers and Students Around Text

Interactions around text are another important component of reading practice in the development of a proficient reader. The effectiveness of reading practice is increased when interactions around text are a consistent, integral part of SSR. Interactions around text provide a purpose for reading and for authentic use of reading skills. Researchers have reported that social interactions about text were highly important to motivation for wide, frequent reading and for selection of books to read, even for reluctant readers (Gambrell, 1996; Palmer, Codling, & Gambrell, 1994; Parr & Maguiness, 2005; Worthy & Broaddus, 2001). Discussions about text also increased appreciation and understanding of literature and reading achievement (Atwell, 2007; Cole, 2003; Garan & DeVoogd, 2008; Lee-Daniels & Murray, 2000).

Interactions around text can take place through teacher–student discussions and student–student discussions of thought-provoking and engaging issues centered on the book being read. Hunt (1965, 1971a, 1971b) views the inclusion of interactions around text through conferences and book talks as the heart of silent reading time. This was a time for teacher and student to discuss ideas and implications of the book, to assess if the student comprehended the text, and to provide on-the-spot instruction. This was also a time for students to share their readings with each other through discussions, performances, and other creative means.

Traditionally implemented SSR presents little opportunity for students to collaborate and share. Social interaction among peers is an important aspect of reading motivation. Research has demonstrated that social collaboration among students promotes development of higher level literacy skills and increases students' intrinsic motivation to read and write (Almasi, 1995; Guthrie, Schafer, Wang, & Afflerbach, 1995; Jongsma, 1990; Slavin, 1990). Discussions around text should focus on higher level questions that engage students in synthesizing and evaluating key concepts and ideas. Students who are involved in a community of readers and discuss literature with peers or the teacher are likely to be socially motivated to read (Wigfield & Guthrie, 1997). The interaction and sharing of literature in classrooms creates an opportunity to expose students to a variety of genres. It also empowers the students with a sense of ownership, because they often feel proud and important as they share what they have read, thus making the activity meaningful to them.

The importance of interactions around text directly affects the role of the teacher during SSR. It has been suggested that during SSR, teachers are to model reading by silently reading in their own book (McCracken, 1971). This practice was thought to be motivating to students and to increase student engagement, as they were able to observe a model reader. However, Widdowson, Dixon, and Moore (1996) found that teacher modeling does not increase student engagement for all ability levels, specifically above-average readers. In a more recent study, above-average fifth-grade students reported that the traditional role of the teacher is not a motivating factor for them to read during SSR (Newman, 2007). Many in the teaching profession agree on the importance of the teacher as a reading model. However, a teacher holding a book and reading during silent reading is a passive model, not an explicit, effective model of what it means to be a reader (Gambrell, 1996). A teacher becomes a reading model by enthusiastically introducing books to students, reading great books aloud, discussing books, and promoting and teaching the skills and joys of reading.

One of the most universal concerns about SSR is whether students are adequately engaged in reading. Stahl (2004) questions the use of teacher modeling, because it limits the social interaction between teacher and student. In the traditional SSR, students are not held accountable for what they read, and because teachers are expected to be modeling the proper reading behavior, they are not able to monitor the students. The lack of teacher–student interaction prohibits the teacher from knowing if the student is reading, what the student is reading, and the progress the student is making with the text. Bryan, Fawson, and Reutzel (2003) found that brief teacher–student conferences during SSR would keep even the most disengaged students engaged in reading for up to three weeks.

Worthy and Broaddus (2001) suggest that teachers use SSR for instruction and assessment. Garan and DeVoogd (2008), similar to Manning and Manning (1984), note an increased effectiveness of SSR by including reading conferences and minilessons. Other researchers suggest that interactions around text are especially important for reluctant readers (Parr & Maguiness, 2005). Many teachers have already made this modification and conduct individual student conferences and promote student discussions during SSR (Gambrell, 2007).

The ability to read for extended periods of time from appropriately challenging and interesting self-selected texts to gain important ideas may indeed be the hallmark of a proficient reader. However, gaining proficiency for any skill is made easier with expert guidance. Providing readers with important scaffolds needed to aid their development of reading proficiency through independent, silent reading time requires a major revision of many of the conditions associated with this practice time. Several researchers have begun to design and investigate independent, silent reading routines that address the weaknesses associated with SSR and other similar routines for providing independent, silent reading practice (Kelley & Clausen-Grace, 2006; Reutzel, Fawson, et al., 2008; Reutzel, Jones, et al., 2008). Because Kelley and Clausen-Grace (2006) describe their makeover of SSR in Chapter 10 of this volume, we confine our discussion to the revisions made to SSR identified in a new routine for providing independent, silent reading practice: Scaffolded Silent Reading.

Scaffolded Silent Reading

Scaffolded Silent Reading (ScSR; Reutzel, Fawson, et al., 2008; Reutzel, Jones, et al., 2008) is an approach to reading fluency practice that specifically addresses many of the previously described weaknesses associated with traditionally implemented SSR. ScSR makes use of silent reading practice of independent-level texts selected with teacher guidance from among varied genres. Periodic teacher monitoring of and interaction with individual students is coupled with accountability through completed book response assignments.

ScSR begins with teachers carefully arranging the classroom library to support and guide students' reading choices toward appropriately challenging books. Because students receive less feedback and support in independent, silent reading than in other forms of reading practice, students should practice reading texts they can process accurately and effortlessly (Stahl & Heubach, 2006). Teachers can guide students' book selections by placing reading materials on clearly labeled shelves or in plastic bins as shown in Figure 8.1.

To further assist students, teachers can color code book levels within the classroom library collection using cloth tape on the book binding or stickers in the upper right-hand corner of the covers. Students are then taught to select and practice reading books marked by a specific color code representing their individual independent reading levels (95% or more accuracy level is typically used in school settings). Instruction about comprehension monitoring is also useful in helping students manage their book selections. Students need not be confined to their color levels if they have high levels of interest and are willing to persist in reading and sharing the books they select. Color coding is merely a guide to augment their strategies for selecting books they can and do read.

In addition, teachers guide their students to read widely from a variety of literary genres. Students are asked to choose books for reading practice using a reading genre wheel, as shown in Figure 8.2. Thus, with this method, students' book selections are guided by level and across genres to encourage wide reading at appropriately challenging levels of text difficulty. Students in ScSR are expected to read a minimum of five books every nine weeks of the school year, across the genres represented on the wheel. Once students have completed reading books

Figure 8.1. Book Storage in Classroom Library by Levels and Genre

Figure 8.2. Reading Genre Wheel

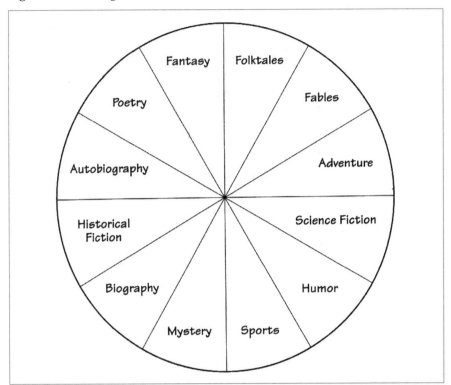

From *Your Classroom Library: New Ways to Give It More Teaching Power*, by D.R. Reutzel & P.C. Fawson, 2002, New York: Scholastic. Reprinted with permission.

from all of the genres on the wheel, they can begin again and select books from previously read genres. Students in ScSR are expected to read enough books each year to complete two reading genre wheels.

Because teachers have carefully planned the organization, display, and storage of books in the classroom library, they introduce ScSR by planning and teaching a series of explicit book selection strategy lessons (Reutzel & Fawson, 2002). During these book selection strategy lessons, students are taught the "three finger" or "five finger" rule, dependent upon grade levels (i.e., three fingers in primary grades and five fingers in intermediate and secondary grades). These rules, as described by Allington (2006) and others, involve students in counting on one hand the number of words they do not recognize on a page. If students hold up three (or five) fingers, the text is considered to be too difficult for independent reading. Unless students are very interested in or motivated by the topic or theme of the book, they should be encouraged to select another book. A sample book selection strategy lesson for ScSR in the primary grades is explained in Figure 8.3.

Figure 8.3. Example Book Selection Strategy Lesson

Objective: To help students learn the location and organization for leveled books in the classroom library, as well as to demonstrate the use of the "three finger" rule for evaluating the appropriate difficulty of a book.

Needed Supplies:
- Different colored dots to use on book covers or cloth tape on book spine
- Different colored plastic bins or book storage boxes
- A poster showing the students' names and colored dots that correspond to their individual independent reading levels
- A strategy poster for using the "three finger" rule to evaluate a book's difficulty

Explanation: Tell the students that soon they will be allowed to select books from the classroom library for their own reading, but before doing so they need to learn about how the classroom library is organized to support their book selections. Today, students will be learning about the way the different levels of books are arranged and stored in the classroom library.

Modeling: Seat the students in and around the classroom library so they can see the shelves. Show them the poster with their names and the book colors that represent their independent levels. Each book level is represented by a different colored dot that matches the color of dots on the book storage bins or boxes and on the books inside them. Demonstrate how if you were one of the students (pick a name), you would look at the poster showing your name and the colored dot indicative of your independent reading level. Next, show where that color of bin or box is located on the library shelves. Then, show students that each book also has a colored dot, which is the same as on the outside of the bin or box. Remind them that they are to choose a book that represents one of the genres on the reading genre wheel. Demonstrate how you might select a book about Babe Ruth as an example of a biography. Next, show students the three-finger rule poster and model reading aloud a single page from the Babe Ruth book. Show them how many words on the page you did not know. Inform students that if they hold up three or more fingers, they should choose another book either from this level or ask you for another book level color they might select from that would be a bit easier.

Application: Continue modeling with the help of one or two students who role-play the selection of an appropriately leveled book with decreasing amounts of guidance from you. Tell the students you will be allowing them to go to the classroom library to select an appropriately leveled reading book one at a time. This will be their chance to show that they have listened and understand what you have taught them before they can go to the classroom library on their own in the future.

Monitoring for Success: Monitor each student's book selection level and his or her ability to use the three-finger rule.

Daily ScSR practice time begins with short, five- to eight-minute lessons that include an explanation and modeling of an element of fluent reading or how to use a comprehension strategy. For example, the teacher might model a brief lesson on comprehension monitoring using a strategy of "click or clunk," where readers determine if the meaning of the text is clicking or clunking (Carr, 1985). If the meaning clicks, they keep on reading. If the meaning clunks, they are shown several fix-up strategies they can use when reading silently. Following these brief lessons, students are dismissed to select a new book or retrieve a previously selected book. Students are then free to choose an area in the classroom library, on the carpet, or at their seats for ScSR. During ScSR, students engage in 20 minutes of independent, silent reading each day.

As students read, the teacher conducts teacher–student reading conferences, completing at least one conference each week per student. During each conference, the teacher asks the student to read aloud from the book while making a running record analysis of his or her reading. Recent research has established that an average of three running record analyses within the same level of text difficulty provides a reliable assessment of students' reading progress (Fawson, Ludlow, Reutzel, Sudweeks, & Smith, 2006). After the student reads aloud for one or two minutes, the teacher initiates a discussion with the student about the book. To monitor comprehension, the teacher might prompt the student by saying, "Please tell me about what you just read." This prompt is typically followed with a brief (two-minute) discussion of the text, focusing on higher level questions posed by the student and the teacher. Finally, the teacher asks the student to set a goal date to finish the book. The student is also asked to think about how to share the book with other students from a displayed menu of book response projects, such as drawing and labeling a "character wanted" poster, generating a story map, adding elements of a story to a story comparison bulletin board, or filling in elements of a graphic organizer. After each teacher–student conference, the teacher completes the student's running record, notes the student's comprehension of the book, records the goal date for book completion, and indicates the selected book response project on a tracking form, shown in Figure 8.4.

During the allocated 20-minute ScSR session, the teacher continues individual teacher–student reading conferences, meeting with four or five students per day, allowing the monitoring of individual students' reading progress weekly. In this way, the teacher better ensures that students are engaged and accountable for the time spent reading silently, addressing a major criticism of traditionally implemented SSR (Stahl, 2004). At the end of the 20-minute daily ScSR time, students quietly return their books and reading folders containing their genre wheel and personal response projects to their leveled bins in the classroom library or to the storage crates around the room and move to the next part of the daily routine.

How Well Does ScSR Work?

To examine the effectiveness of ScSR, Reutzel, Fawson, and Smith (2008) compared ScSR to the NRP's (NICHD, 2000) recommended reading practice of Guided Repeated Oral Reading with Feedback (GROR), using a dominant–less dominant mixed-methods design (Creswell & Plano-Clark, 2007; Tashakkori & Teddlie, 1998).

Figure 8.4. Tracking Form for Individual Student Reading Conferences

Student Name _____

Date of Reading Conference _____

Title of Book Student Is Reading _____

_____

Part A: Fluency
Teacher's Running Record of Student's One- to Two-Minute Reading Sample

Number of Words Read _____

Number of Errors _____

Word Read Correctly Per Minute _____

Part B: Comprehension

Oral Retelling

Narrative Text:
☐ Setting   ☐ Characters   ☐ Problem   ☐ Goals   ☐ Episode(s)   ☐ Resolution

Expository Text:
☐ Topic   ☐ Main Idea   ☐ Supporting Detail(s)   ☐ Use of Vocabulary Terms

Discussion Questions

Narrative: Ask story structure questions about setting, characters, problem, and so forth.

Expository: Ask about the topic, main idea, supporting details, and so forth.

Part C: Goal Setting
Book Completion Goal Date _____

Goal Pages to Be Read by the Next Reading Conference _____

Part D: Book Sharing
Book Response Project Selected and Approved by Teacher _____

_____

_____

The study involved four classrooms, four third-grade teachers, and 72 third-grade students in two elementary schools. The two schools in which the study was conducted were designated high-poverty, low-performing schools with approximately 35–50% diversity (i.e., African American, Asian, and Hispanic) and more than half of the students in the schools qualifying for free or reduced-cost lunch. All four teachers in the study rotated through teaching the ScSR and GROR treatment approaches during the year of this study. All third-grade students' spring-administered (i.e., end of second grade), state-criterion referenced, end-of-level reading test scores were listed from high to low and divided into three achievement strata: high, medium, and low. Students were randomly assigned from within their achievement strata using a computer-generated table of random numbers. There were two ScSR classrooms ($n = 40$) and two GROR classrooms ($n = 40$). During the school year in which this study was conducted, 8 of the original randomly assigned students moved from the school either during the summer after random assignment or during the study, leaving 72 students for the final data collection and analysis. Attrition was equal in the two treatment groups.

Teachers had received classroom-based coaching weekly and were also given monthly professional development workshops or in-class reading instruction and practice demonstrations by the district's technical assistant, a university professor in early literacy. Reading coaches conducted weekly study groups for one to two hours on scientifically based reading research. The participating third-grade teachers received two days of professional development on effective fluency instruction and practice using training materials drawn from a variety of professional sources.

Two pretest and posttest passages (a total of four passages) from the third-grade level Dynamic Indicators of Basic Early Literacy Skills (DIBELS) Oral Reading Fluency (ORF) test were used to assess students' fluency and comprehension growth over the yearlong study (Good & Kaminski, 2002): "Pots" and "The Field Trip" (pretest passages) and "My Parents" and "Planted a Garden" (posttest passages). Recognizing the withering criticisms of the ill-fated uses of the DIBELS ORF, this was selected by the schools and the researchers as the test for progress monitoring reading fluency based on the ORF's demonstration of adequate test reliability and predictive validity and its pervasive use in school settings. The school-based literacy coaches were trained to score the four test passages using the standardized approach for giving the DIBELS ORF. Reading expression was judged using the Multi-dimensional Fluency Scale (MFS), which assesses volume, phrasing, smoothness, and pacing. Zutell and Rasinski (1991), the developers, report a 0.99 inter-rater reliability coefficient for the MFS. Student oral retellings of the four third-grade DIBELS ORF passages were used as the measure of student comprehension. We did not use the DIBELS oral retelling scoring protocols, because these demonstrated inadequate validity or reliability evidence. Instead, we produced a template text-base scoring protocol for each DIBELS third-grade passage by parsing the passages into idea units (i.e., number of independent clauses or meaning units). To establish reliability of the comprehension oral retelling scoring process, 10 randomly selected student audiotapes of the post-passage oral retellings were scored independently by two members of the research team using the text-base oral retelling protocol template. The obtained Pearson r was 0.94, indicating a high percentage of agreement (89%). To correct for the potential limiting effect of the number of words read correctly in one minute on each student's reading comprehension oral retelling scores, a proportional score was used in the analysis. This was done so that the comprehension scores reflected the amount of recalled idea units attenuated by the proportion of the number of words read correctly.

Each teacher's fluency instruction was observed weekly by the school-based literacy coach for the full length of the practice session (i.e., 25 minutes) using a five-item observation rating scale. On a monthly basis, the research team and the district language arts coordinator observed in each teacher's classroom using the same observation scale to assure fidelity to the experimental treatments and to problem solve implementation issues with the teachers. Observations revealed high degrees of fidelity in the two treatments. Problems generally were of a minor nature and quickly solved by supplying on-the-spot training or access to additional requested practice materials when necessary. A random sample of four monthly ratings using the five-item observation scale completed by the district language arts coordinator and a member of the research team revealed a 97% agreement on treatment quality and fidelity.

Individual copies of a Teacher Response Journal (TRJ) were created for each of the four third-grade teachers. The first section of the TRJ contained 28 weekly response pages that required answers to three written questions, with space for each response along with an open response area:

1. What difficulties are you encountering with the two fluency practice treatments?
2. What is going well for you with the fluency practice treatments?
3. What effects, if any, are you noticing on your students with each fluency practice treatment?

The second section of the TRJ requested a written response for sharing overall impressions and teacher conclusions about the study.

At the outset and conclusion of the experiment, students were asked to answer the following three questions:

1. How do you think your reading aloud sounds?
2. If you do not think your reading aloud sounds good, what will you do to fix it?
3. What does a good reader sound like to you?

There was no traditional control group that simply continued the regular reading instruction time without the benefit of either ScSR or GROR. A true control group of "no treatment" is difficult to implement within the ecologically valid context of a school setting. The teachers who participated in this research did so believing they would be doing something ultimately helpful to their students rather than simply doing more of the norm. The norm was not a sufficient enticement for teachers to participate. Given this limitation, we decided to analyze the results of the study using gain scores from pretest to posttest scores for the two treatment groups to determine if students in the two treatment groups made progress in fluency and comprehension during the year.

Quantitative data were analyzed using ANOVA for gain scores between the ScSR and GROR treatment groups on accuracy, rate, expression, and comprehension on two DIBELS ORF third-grade passages. The subjects were used as analysis unit, because no treatment by teacher interactions was found for any of the measures when tested in a nested ANOVA as potential teacher effects were controlled by design.

Qualitative observational data were analyzed to assess the degree to which ScSR and GROR were implemented with fidelity in the four classrooms. Classroom observations were also periodically videotaped to provide researchers with intact records of actual practice sessions and the accompanying dialogue between teachers and students. These data were used along with written observations to construct the classroom instructional and procedural descriptions in this report. TRJs were collected to gain insights on the teacher's perceived struggles and triumphs in working with the varied reading fluency practice routines. Student answers to prestudy and poststudy structured questions provided insight on students' perceptions of ScSR and GROR.

The quantitative analyses demonstrated no significant differences in the pretest to posttest gain scores made between the ScSR or GROR treatment groups at the end of the yearlong experiment on three of the four outcome measures— accuracy, rate, or comprehension. The exception was the ScSR group's gains in expression for the "My Parents" passage, $F(1, 70) = 8.0$, $p = 0.006$, which were significantly greater than the GROR group's expression ratings on a single posttest passage.

Thus, average gains made by the ScSR and GROR treatment groups from the beginning-of-year to end-of-year growth in accuracy, rate, expression, and comprehension from the fall to spring of the third-grade year were similar. Over the course of the yearlong study, ScSR and GROR approaches resulted in a 21% average reduction in the number of reading errors, a 27% average increase in the mean number of words read correctly per minute, and a 20% average increase in expressive reading qualities, including phrasing, volume, smoothness, and pacing. ScSR and GROR approaches also resulted in a 43% average increase in the proportion of idea units recalled. Students in the ScSR treatment group made progress equivalent to students in the scientifically validated (NICHD, 2000) comparison reading practice condition of GROR in reading accuracy, rate, expression, and comprehension.

All students responded to the structured interview questions. Across both groups, student responses to the first question were brief at the beginning of the school year. In the spring, student responses in both groups were still brief but had shifted from negative comments to positive comments. In the fall, student responses from both groups to the second question evoked responses such as "read more often," "practice," "read louder," "read it again over and over," "read the words correctly," and "read it over until it sounds right." In the spring, students in both groups offered more elaborated responses to this question. Students in the ScSR group responded with "Read more, practice," "Practice silently, then read out loud every day," "Read more, read slower to understand the words, not just go through it quickly," and "Slow reading down, think more, and take a big breath and read to the comma or end punctuation." In the spring, student responses to the third question showed similar patterns of elaborated understanding of the concept of good reading. Across both groups, student responses were similar, with students saying that a good reader is "Someone who goes back and fixes mistakes," "Someone who reads smooth, clearly, and loud enough that others can hear," "Someone who reads lots of books," and "Someone who watches commas and exclamation points."

Reflections recorded in the TRJs about the ScSR practice condition included narrative comments such as "The students who love to read are enjoying this time," "More students are reading chapter books and seem to be really enjoying them," and "Kids are really enjoying and getting more expressive in their oral reading." One teacher wrote, "I appreciate the quiet time of ScSR. What is wrong with letting students read? I think it is beneficial." Another remarked, "Some students who did not enjoy reading before are completing their books!" In the GROR practice condition one teacher wrote, "The students are reading, practicing, and performing. Rereading has become automatic to some students. I heard one child ask her partner if what they [sic] read made sense. Her partner read the sentence again and they continued." Another teacher stated, "I have noticed the expression of my students is improving. They are stopping and rereading with greater expression."

Finally, ScSR teacher responses to the third question included initial complaints about student participation during silent reading. One teacher wrote, "I notice now that some students just do not read during the 20 minutes of practice." Another wrote, "Students who really want me to hear them practice are developing good skills. I notice that some students do not like to be heard or perform." Still another teacher reported, "They like to read. I enjoy hearing the students tell me about their reading. The excitement and energy is contagious when they read a book they enjoy!"

Recommendations and Conclusions for Reading Independently and Silently

Hiebert (2006) has repeatedly asserted that fluency practice must, at some point, provide opportunities for transferring students' oral reading skills to silent reading. One simple reason is that most of adult reading is done silently for private purposes. In addition, reading texts repeatedly must give way to reading widely across genres of interest to meet personal needs for acquiring information or for pure enjoyment. Few adult readers read texts repeatedly unless it is necessary to do so comply with procedures or rituals.

It is clear from the research on ScSR, as well as from makeovers of other silent reading practice routines, that reading independently and silently in school requires several important conditions for practice to be effective (Kamil, 2008; Kelley & Clausen-Grace, 2006; Newman, 2007; Reutzel, Fawson, et al., 2008; Reutzel, Jones, et al., 2008). We summarize our chapter by briefly reviewing those conditions of independent, silent reading practice that demonstrate real utility in classroom settings.

Independent, silent reading practice actively involves teachers in structuring, guiding, teaching, interacting with, monitoring, and holding students accountable for time spent reading independently and silently. Effective teachers provide students with guidance and instruction on how to select appropriately challenging and interesting books. Similarly, highly effective teachers monitor students' ability to read the books they select. They also monitor students' stamina to remain engaged in reading during allocated silent reading practice time. Such monitoring can be accomplished through well-structured, brief one-on-one reading conferences between teachers and students. Students also set reading goals for completing books in a timely manner to help themselves remain engaged in their reading and to promote the development of reading stamina.

Students are held accountable to share what they are reading with other students or the teacher. This can be accomplished through brief book club meetings at the end of silent reading time. Students talk about or orally read an interesting part of the book they were reading that day. Students can also share after a book is finished by completing a self-selected book response project.

In conclusion, simply sending students off to read on their own without guidance, interaction, instruction, monitoring, or accountability has not been shown to promote effective, sustained, independent, silent reading practice in school. Teachers should resist the seductive practice of going off by themselves, silently and independently "modeling" that they can read and do read, and showing what they read. If teachers are compelled to model reading for students, they should offer daily interactive read-alouds and book talks to build or heighten students' interests in reading. Reading aloud provides an excellent setting for teachers to share through "think-alouds"—authentic modeling of the thinking processes and comprehension strategies successful readers use to enjoy and understand texts.

The intuitive appeal of reading practice was a correct understanding for educators to have and to promote regularly in classrooms. However, all practice is not equally effective—remember our driver's education example. Consequently, educators across the spectrum of grades and special services within schools need to know that when independent, silent reading practice time is accompanied by active teacher instruction, guidance, interaction, and monitoring along with classroom structure of the environment and procedures, student reading development and engagement flourishes. When left to the independent, silent reading practices of yesteryear in which everyone "does their own thing" without teacher intervention, structure, monitoring, and accountability, the current evidence is anything but convincing that such reading practice conditions will produce either able or motivated readers.

QUESTIONS FOR PROFESSIONAL DEVELOPMENT

1. How could teachers productively engage students in brief one- or two-minute conversations, reading aloud, and sharing of their books to conclude the daily ScSR experience?

2. How might teachers remove the color-coded book-level scaffolds and gradually release to students the opportunity to select appropriately challenging book levels on their own?

3. What might a menu contain that would detail how students could meaningfully respond to and share the books they have read during ScSR?

REFERENCES

Allington, R.L. (1977). If they don't read much, how they ever gonna get good? *Journal of Adolescent & Adult Literacy, 21*(1), 57–61. doi:10.1598/JAAL.21.1.10

Allington, R.L. (2006). *What really matters for struggling readers: Designing research-based programs* (2nd ed.). Boston: Allyn & Bacon.

Almasi, J.F. (1995). The nature of fourth graders' sociocognitive conflicts in peer-led and teacher-led discussions of literature. *Reading Research Quarterly, 30*(3), 314–351. doi:10.2307/747620

Alvermann, D.E. (2001). Reading adolescents' reading identities: Looking back to see ahead. *Journal of Adolescent & Adult Literacy, 44*(8), 676–690.

Anderson, G., Higgins, D., & Wurster, S.R. (1985). Differences in the free-reading books selected by high, average, and low achievers. *The Reading Teacher, 39*(3), 326–330.

Anderson, R.C., Hiebert, E.H., Scott, J.A., & Wilkinson, I.A.G. (1985). *Becoming a nation of readers: The report of the Commission on Reading*. Washington, DC: National Academy of Education, National Institute of Education; Champaign-Urbana, IL: Center for the Study of Reading.

Armbruster, B.B., Lehr, F., & Osborn, J. (2001). *Put reading first: The research building blocks for teaching children to read: Kindergarten through grade 3*. Washington, DC: National Institute for Literacy.

Atwell, N. (2007). *The reading zone: How to help kids become skilled, passionate, habitual, critical readers*. New York: Scholastic.

Baker, L., & Wigfield, A. (1999). Dimensions of children's motivation for reading and their relations to reading activity and reading achievement. *Reading Research Quarterly, 34*(4), 452–477. doi:10.1598/RRQ.34.4.4

Bryan, G., Fawson, P.C., & Reutzel, D.R. (2003). Sustained silent reading: Exploring the value of literature discussion with three non-engaged readers. *Reading Research and Instruction, 43*(1), 47–73.

Carr, E.M. (1985). The vocabulary overview guide: A metacognitive strategy to improve vocabulary comprehension and retention. *Journal of Reading, 28*(8), 684–689.

Carver, R.P., & Leibert, R.E. (1995). The effect of reading library books at different levels of difficulty upon gain in reading ability. *Reading Research Quarterly, 30*(1), 26–48. doi:10.2307/747743

Chambliss, M.J., & McKillop, A.M. (2000). Creating a print- and-technology-rich classroom library to entice children to read. In L. Baker, M.J. Dreher, & J.T. Guthrie (Eds.),

Engaging young readers: Promoting achievement and motivation (pp. 94–118). New York: Guilford.

Chua, S.P. (2008). The effects of the sustained silent reading program on cultivating students' habits and attitudes in reading books for leisure. *The Clearing House, 81*(4), 180–184. doi:10.3200/TCHS.81.4.180-184

Cole, A.D. (2003). *Knee to knee, eye to eye: Circling in on comprehension.* Portsmouth, NH: Heinemann.

Creswell, J.W., & Plano-Clark, V.L. (2007). *Designing and conducting mixed methods research.* Thousand Oaks, CA: Sage.

Cunningham, A.E., & Stanovich, K.E. (1998). What reading does for the mind. *American Educator, 22*(1/2), 8–15.

Deci, E.L., & Ryan, R.M. (1985). *Intrinsic motivation and self-determination in human behavior.* New York: Plenum.

Donovan, C.A., Smolkin, L.B., & Lomax, R.G. (2000). Beyond the independent-level text: Considering the reader-text match in first graders' self-selections during recreational reading. *Reading Psychology, 21*(4), 309–333.

Fawson, P.C., Ludlow, B.C., Reutzel, D.R., Sudweeks, R., & Smith, J.A. (2006). Examining the reliability of running records: Attaining generalizable results. *Journal of Educational Research, 100*(2), 113–126.

Fawson, P.C., Reutzel, D.R., Read, S., Smith, J.A., & Moore, S.A. (2009). The influence of differing the paths to an incentive on third graders' reading achievement and attitudes. *Reading Psychology, 30*(6), 564–583.

Fresch, M.J. (1995). Self-selection of early literacy learners. *The Reading Teacher, 49*(3), 220–228.

Gambrell, L. (1996). Creating classrooms that foster reading motivation. *The Reading Teacher, 50*(1), 14–25.

Gambrell, L. (2007, June/July). Reading: Does practice make perfect? *Reading Today, 24*(6), 16.

Garan, E.M., & DeVoogd, G. (2008). The benefits of sustained silent reading: Scientific research and common sense converge. *The Reading Teacher, 62*(4), 336–344. doi:10.1598/RT.62.4.6

Good, R.H., & Kaminski, R.A. (2002). *DIBELS Oral Reading Fluency Passages for first through third grades* (Tech. Rep. No. 10). Eugene: University of Oregon.

Greenleaf, C.L., Schoenbach, R., Cziko, C., & Mueller, F.L. (2001). Apprenticing adolescent readers to academic literacy. *Harvard Educational Review, 71*(1), 79–129.

Guthrie, J.T., Schafer, W., Wang, Y.Y., & Afflerbach, P. (1995). Relationships of instruction to amount of reading: An exploration of social, cognitive, and instructional connections. *Reading Research Quarterly, 30*(1), 8–25. doi:10.2307/747742

Hepler, S.I., & Hickman, J. (1982). "The book was okay. I love you"—Social aspects of response to literature. *Theory Into Practice, 21*(4), 278–283. doi:10.1080/00405848209543019

Hiebert, E.H. (2006). Becoming fluent: Repeated reading with scaffolded texts. In S.J. Samuels & A.E. Farstrup (Eds.), *What research has to say about fluency instruction* (pp. 204–226). Newark, DE: International Reading Association.

Hunt, L.C., Jr. (1965). Philosophy of individualized reading. In J.A. Figurel (Ed.), *Reading and inquiry: Proceedings of the International Reading Association Conference, 10,* 145–147. Newark, DE: International Reading Association.

Hunt, L.C., Jr. (1970). The effect of self-selection, interest, and motivation upon independent, instructional, and frustrational levels. *The Reading Teacher, 24*(2), 146–151, 158.

Hunt, L.C., Jr. (1971a, April). *The psychological and pedagogical bases for individualized reading.* Paper presented at the annual convention of the International Reading Association, Atlantic City, NJ.

Hunt, L.C., Jr. (1971b). Six steps to the individualized reading program (IRP). *Elementary English, 48*(1), 27–32.

Jarvis, D.H. (2003). RED time stories: Fostering or forcing literacy across the curriculum? *The Ontario Action Researcher, 6*(3). Retrieved June 8, 2009, from www.nipissingu.ca/oar/archive-Vol6No3-V631E.htm

Jensen, T.L., & Jensen, V.S. (2002). Sustained silent reading and young adult short stories for high school classes. *The ALAN Review, 30*(1), 58–60.

Jongsma, K.S. (Ed.). (1990). Collaborative learning [Questions & answers dept.]. *The Reading Teacher, 43*(4), 346–347.

Kamil, M.L. (2008). How to get recreational reading to increase reading achievement. In Y. Kim et al. (Eds.), *57th yearbook of the National*

Reading Conference (pp. 31–40). Oak Creek, WI: National Reading Conference.

Kelley, M., & Clausen-Grace, N. (2006). R⁵: The sustained silent reading makeover that transformed readers. *The Reading Teacher, 60*(2), 148–156. doi:10.1598/RT.60.2.5

Krashen, S. (1993). *The power of reading: Insights from the research.* Englewood, CO: Libraries Unlimited.

Kuhn, M.R., Schwanenflugel, P.J., Morris, R.D., Morrow, L.M., Woo, D.G., Meisinger, E.B., et al. (2006). Teaching children to become fluent and automatic readers. *Journal of Literacy Research, 38*(4), 357–387. doi:10.1207/s15548430jlr3804_1

Kuhn, M.R., & Stahl, S.A. (2000). *Fluency: A review of developmental and remedial practices* (CIERA Report No. 2-008). Ann Arbor, MI: Center for the Improvement of Early Reading Achievement.

Lee-Daniels, S.L., & Murray, B.A. (2000). DEAR me: What does it take to get children reading? *The Reading Teacher, 54*(2), 154–155.

Manning, G.L., & Manning, M. (1984). What models of recreational reading make a difference? *Reading World, 23*(4), 375–380.

McCracken, R.A. (1971). Initiating sustained silent reading. *Journal of Reading, 14*(8), 521–524, 582–583.

National Institute of Child Health and Human Development. (2000). *Report of the National Reading Panel. Teaching children to read: An evidence-based assessment of the scientific research literature on reading and its implications for reading instruction* (NIH Publication No. 00-4769). Washington, DC: U.S. Government Printing Office.

Newman, T. (2000). Accountability strategies for reading. *Schools in the Middle, 9*(5), 30–32.

Newman, T.H. (2007). *Factors that motivate fifth-grade students to read during sustained silent reading (SSR).* Unpublished doctoral dissertation, University of Maryland, College Park.

Palmer, B.M., Codling, R.M., & Gambrell, L.B. (1994). In their own words: What elementary students have to say about motivation to read. *The Reading Teacher, 48*(2), 176–178.

Parr, J.M., & Maguiness, C. (2005). Removing the *silent* from SSR: Voluntary reading as social practice. *Journal of Adolescent & Adult Literacy, 49*(2), 98–107. doi:10.1598/JAAL.49.2.2

Reutzel, D.R., & Fawson, P.C. (2002). *Your classroom library: New ways to give it more teaching power.* New York: Scholastic.

Reutzel, D.R., Fawson, P.C., & Smith, J.A. (2008). Reconsidering silent sustained reading: An exploratory study of scaffolded silent reading. *The Journal of Educational Research, 102*(1), 37–50. doi:10.3200/JOER.102.1.37-50

Reutzel, D.R., Jones, C.D., Fawson, P.C., & Smith, J.A. (2008). Scaffolded silent reading: A complement to guided repeated oral reading that works! *The Reading Teacher, 62*(3), 194–207. doi:10.1598/RT.62.3.2

Routman, R. (1991). *Invitations: Changing as teachers and learners K–12.* Portsmouth, NH: Heinemann.

Slavin, R.E. (1990). *Cooperative learning: Theory, research, and practice.* Englewood Cliffs, NJ: Prentice Hall.

Spaulding, C.L. (1992). The motivation to read and write. In J.W. Irwin & M.A. Doyle (Eds.), *Reading/writing connections: Learning from research* (pp. 177–201). Newark, DE: International Reading Association.

Stahl, S.A. (2004). What do we know about fluency? Findings of the National Reading Panel. In P. McCardle & V. Chhabra (Eds.), *The voice of evidence in reading research* (pp. 187–211). Baltimore: Paul H. Brookes.

Stahl, S.A., & Heubach, K. (2006). Fluency-oriented reading instruction. In K.A.D. Stahl & M.C. McKenna (Eds.), *Reading research at work: Foundations of effective practice* (pp. 177–204). New York: Guilford.

Stanovich, K.E. (1986). Matthew effects in reading: Some consequences of individual differences in the acquisition of literacy. *Reading Research Quarterly, 21*(4), 360–407. doi:10.1598/RRQ.21.4.1

Tashakkori, A., & Teddlie, C. (1998). *Mixed methodology: Combining qualitative and quantitative approaches.* Thousand Oaks, CA: Sage.

Trudel, H. (2007). Making data-driven decisions: Silent reading. *The Reading Teacher, 61*(4), 308–315. doi:10.1598/RT.61.4.3

Turner, J., & Paris, S.G. (1995). How literacy tasks influence children's motivation for literacy. *The Reading Teacher, 48*(8), 662–673.

Turner, J.C. (1995). The influence of classroom contexts on young children's motivation for literacy. *Reading Research Quarterly, 30*(3), 410–441. doi:10.2307/747624

Widdowson, D.A.M., Dixon, R.S., & Moore, D.W. (1996). The effects of teacher modelling of silent reading on students' engagement during sustained silent reading. *Educational Psychology, 16*(2), 171–180. doi:10.1080/0144341960160206

Wigfield, A., & Guthrie, J.T. (1997). Relations of children's motivation for reading to the amount and breadth of their reading. *Journal of Educational Psychology, 89*(3), 420–432. doi:10.1037/0022-0663.89.3.420

Worthy, J., & Broaddus, K. (2001). Fluency beyond the primary grades: From group performance to silent, independent reading. *The Reading Teacher, 55*(4), 334–343.

Worthy, J., Turner, M., & Moorman, M. (1998). The precarious place of self-selected reading. *Language Arts, 75*(4), 296–304.

Zutell, J., & Rasinski, T.V. (1991). Training teachers to attend to their students' oral reading fluency. *Theory Into Practice, 30*(3), 211–217.

CHAPTER 9

Are Students Really Reading in Independent Reading Contexts? An Examination of Comprehension-Based Silent Reading Rate

Elfrieda H. Hiebert
University of California, Berkeley

Kathleen M. Wilson
University of Nebraska–Lincoln

Guy Trainin
University of Nebraska–Lincoln

After a recent presentation by one of the authors (Kathleen), a teacher asked, "My students act like they are reading when reading silently, but how do I know if they are really reading?" This teacher's question reflects a concern of many teachers. Recently, however, teachers have not been the only ones asking questions about the efficacy of silent reading. As a result of the conclusions of the National Reading Panel (NRP; National Institute of Child Health and Human Development, 2000) that sustained silent reading has not proven particularly effective in increasing fluency and comprehension, policymakers and administrators have raised questions about the effectiveness of silent reading during instructional time. The NRP's conclusions regarding the efficacy of oral, guided repeated reading have meant an emphasis on oral reading experiences in the primary grades as evident in classroom observations (Brenner, Hiebert, & Tompkins, 2009) and in textbook programs (Brenner & Hiebert, 2010). At the same time, the Panel's conclusions regarding the lack of substantive empirical literature that confirms the efficacy of independent, silent reading experiences on comprehension have meant, at least in the primary grades, a deemphasis on silent reading (Brenner et al., 2009).

Ultimately, however, most of the reading that adults, adolescents, and even middle- and upper elementary–grade students do is silent. Unarguably, the ability to read extended texts on one's own (i.e., silently) with comprehension is the foundation of proficient reading. The products and processes of comprehension are frequently the focus of researchers and educators. However, one dimension that is infrequently addressed is the rates at which students are reading with meaning. The topic of rate of silent reading has often been equated with speed reading. We are not suggesting a return to the speed-reading craze of the 1960s, nor are we advocating the obsession with speed that has become the interpretation of oral reading fluency during the last decade.

There can be little doubt that demands for efficient and effective silent reading have increased as the amount of information available to citizens of the digital–global age increases. The form of reading in which we are interested has comprehension at its center. Within a focus on comprehension, we believe that there is room for attention to the rates at which students are reading, particularly whether students are reading at appropriate rates. The digital revolution has meant that there are potential ways to address these reading rates and for determining whether they are appropriate for the tasks confronting students. We have termed the construct in which we are interested as comprehension-based silent reading rate (CBSRR).

Teachers in our graduate courses and workshops have asked numerous questions about CBSRR, such as the one that introduces our chapter. We delved into the research literature to answer these questions as well as our own questions. Our search for answers, however, produced few definitive responses. With only a few exceptions (e.g., Carver, 1990, 1992), researchers have not addressed CBSRR over the past decades. While the lack of a robust research surprised us, it also served as an impetus. We initiated a study that considered several persistent questions about CBSRR. We could not address all of the critical questions in a single study, so we raise some of our many remaining questions at the end of the chapter. We were able, however, to provide preliminary answers to some critical questions about CBSRR in the study we describe here.

This chapter provides a summary of responses to the three foci of our study: (1) How do students of different quartiles vary in their CBSRR? (2) How well do students sustain their CBSRR across an extended text? (3) How consistent is the CBSRR of students in a digital context relative to a paper-and-pencil context? Before describing the design and findings of this study, we provide an overview of what is and is not known about CBSRR and our three foci.

A Review of CBSRR

The term *comprehension-based* is central to our definition of CBSRR. The digital age has made an abundance of information available to human beings, unlike any volume experienced by previous generations. While offering unique opportunities for learning and communication, this surfeit of information places demands on readers for higher level comprehension processes more than those demands of previous eras. Full participation in the digital–global marketplace and community demands deep and broad background knowledge and comprehension skills that are finely honed to evaluate and integrate information. A fast reading rate without higher order comprehension skills falls far short of the literacy standards needed for full participation.

The term *silent reading rate* is also a critical consideration in developing readers who can participate fully in the tasks of the digital–global age. Readers who stop and tediously sound out numerous words in texts are unlikely to have the cognitive resources to employ higher level comprehension processes. They are also individuals who will likely not have the stamina to read and integrate information from several sources or read extended texts.

Literacy researchers have shown an interest in two of the words within these terms—*comprehension* and *rate*. There has been substantial research on comprehension and comprehension processes (e.g., Duke & Pearson, 2002) and considerable work on rate. Almost all of this work, however, has been done on oral reading rate (e.g., Fuchs, Fuchs, Hosp, & Jenkins, 2001; Kame'enui & Simmons, 2001). Rarely, however, have the two constructs been examined in the same study. In particular, attention on the rates at which students are reading with meaningful comprehension has been scant.

When the topic of silent reading rates is raised among literacy researchers, the general response is one of skepticism (e.g., Brozo & Johns, 1986) or disinterest (see, e.g., Cassidy & Cassidy, 2009). In our case, especially for the two of us who have been teachers or teacher educators in U.S. contexts since the early 1970s, we know that this describes our perspective. As teachers and graduate students, we watched with skepticism the claims of and the techniques on speed reading (e.g., Frank, 1992). Continued spurious claims of speed-reading programs, such as that of reading 25,000 words a minute, have only reinforced a sense of skepticism for a new generation of researchers. As a result, the study of rate, with respect to silent reading at least, has not been a popular topic for research.

Although there are several sets of oral reading norms (e.g., AIMSweb, 2008; Good & Kaminski, 1996; Hasbrouck & Tindal, 2006), there is a single set of silent reading norms that are based on data gathered in the late 1950s and reported in 1960 (Taylor, Frankenpohl, & Pettee, 1960). These silent reading norms are presented in Table 9.1. This set, although based on a large sample, is for the 50th percentile. How the 25th or 75th percentile groups do in comparison is uncertain. Such generic norms stand in contrast to the oral reading norms like those of Hasbrouck and Tindal (2006) that are also included in Table 9.1. As is the case with the various oral reading norms that have proliferated over the past 20 years in the wake of the advent of curriculum-based measurement (CBM; Deno, 1985), these oral reading norms are not based on assessments that include comprehension. Although dated and not as detailed as the Hasbrouck and Tindal (2006) oral reading norms, the silent reading norms (Taylor et al., 1960) are based on comprehension. This distinction is an important one, and it served as a primary incentive for our interest in CBSRR rather than simply on silent reading rate.

How Do Students of Different Quartiles Vary in Their CBSRR?

Although the Taylor et al. (1960) comprehension-based silent reading norms do not give an indication of the variation across a cohort of students, all available

Table 9.1. Silent Reading and Oral Reading Rates

	Percentile	Grade												
		1	2	3	4	5	6	7	8	9	10	11	12	College
Silent reading rates (Taylor et al. (1960)	50th	80	115	138	158	173	185	195	204	214	224	237	250	280
Oral reading rates (Hasbrouck & Tindal, 2006)	25th	23	65	87	92	100	122	123	124	NA				
	50th	54	94	114	118	128	150	150	151	NA				
	75th	82	117	137	153	168	177	177	177	NA				

evidence leads to the expectation that differences across students within a cohort would be great. On the National Assessment of Educational Progress (NAEP; Lee, Grigg, & Donahue, 2007), the differences within a cohort of students in their comprehension performances on a silent reading test are substantial.

There is evidence that rate figures into these performance differences on the NAEP silent reading assessments, insofar as the evidence comes from oral reading assessments. In a special study associated with the NAEP, researchers had a representative sample of students read orally the texts on which their silent reading comprehension had been assessed (Pinnell et al., 1995). Oral reading rate correlated moderately well with comprehension. Differences in students' word recognition accuracy were not statistically significant. Differences in students' oral reading rates were substantially different, with students who comprehended less well having much slower oral reading rates than students whose comprehension was higher. Similar patterns were found in a recent replication of the Pinnell et al. study (Daane, Campbell, Grigg, Goodman, & Oranje, 2005).

Table 9.1 includes the rate of growth that occurs in words per minute (wpm) in oral reading for students at three percentile levels across first through eighth grades, according to the Hasbrouck and Tindal (2006) norms. What is remarkable is the degree of consistency across the percentile groups once students move beyond first grade. They start at different points in first grade, but their growth occurs at the same pace after this point. Once students get to the middle grades, they level off. This rate of oral reading—150 wpm—is the same as the typical speech production rate of adults in the United States (Schmidt & Flege, 1995). The students in the 75th percentile have attained a level slightly higher than this rate, but the 50th percentile is on target in terms of speech production speed. The 25th percentile, at least through eighth grade, performs approximately 25 words slower than the average speech production rate.

In considering the potential patterns of CBSRR for readers at different levels, it is critical to recognize the differences between oral and silent reading. Oral reading is a performance-based situation. If a word is unknown, students cannot gloss over it in the manner that is possible in silent reading. Further, oral reading speed is governed by the speed with which individuals talk. Humans can speak faster than 150 wpm, and students can likewise read faster orally, especially if there is no concern with prosody or comprehension. These higher than expected rates may be the case as a result of the assessment expectations and practices of the past decade. Typically, as the norms in Table 9.1 indicate, proficient oral reading keeps pace with the rate at which human beings speak.

The oral production factor and the need to produce each word when reading orally, especially to a teacher or evaluator, leads to the suggestion that there may be more similarities among individuals in oral reading than in silent reading. Silent reading contexts, however, also have constraints. There are limits to what the brain can do (Cunningham, Stanovich, & Wilson, 1990) and what the eye can do (see Chapter 2, this volume). Claims that someone can take a mental photograph of a page of text at 25,000 words a minute do not require extensive investigation to be deemed as spurious (McNamara, 2000).

What is clear from the data in Table 9.1 is that, not long into the reading acquisition process, silent reading rates surpass oral reading rates. The comparison of students at the 50th percentile in oral and silent reading attest to this conclusion, even at first grade. By fourth grade, silent reading for 50th percentile students is approximately one third faster than it is for oral reading. Further, once oral reading rates stabilize (reflecting the oral production factor) at the end of elementary/middle school, silent reading rates continue to increase. By the time they are in college, readers at the 50th percentile read silently at almost twice the rate that they read orally.

With a greater range in reading rates, as is the case with silent reading, there may be greater variability among students of different proficiency levels. One factor that has sometimes created problems in the measurement of silent reading is the tendency for struggling readers to inflate their self-reports of reading rates (Fuchs et al., 2001). By making comprehension performances the ultimate criterion for determining appropriate rates, we are eliminating the potential of "fake" reading (Griffith & Rasinski, 2004).

How Well Do Students Sustain Their CBSRR Across an Extended Text?

We are especially interested in a construct called "reading stamina"—the ability to sustain attention and proficiency across a text. Even though educators refer to stamina as a critical aspect of reading (e.g., Johnson, Freedman, & Thomas, 2008; Qualifications and Curriculum Authority, 2005), it is rarely addressed directly in research. For example, in reviewing the three volumes of the *Handbook of Reading Research*, we found no references to or descriptions of stamina. Despite this lack of attention, a strong case can be made for hypothesizing that stamina could be an issue in both oral and silent reading. Students, particularly those in the bottom quartile, may quickly become fatigued when asked to read longer texts. Conversely, it could be argued that once students become familiar with the content and the vocabulary of an extended text, their reading rates would increase. Texts are frequently written so that the principal ideas—and the vocabulary that represents those ideas—are presented early in a text. Once students have been introduced to a text's vocabulary and principal ideas, their reading rates might increase as they move through the remainder of the text.

Another perspective is that stamina would be challenged most directly in silent reading. Silent reading involves managing one's strategies and comprehension. A strategy that illustrates such comprehension management is clarifying confusing parts of text, one of a handful of strategies that has been found to distinguish proficient and challenged readers (Brown & Smiley, 1978). Thus, slow silent reading may be an indication of comprehension monitoring. Evidence for this hypothesis is limited. There is a need to find out more about silent reading rates, especially those of students in different proficiency groups. Rather than glossing over silent reading, interventions may need to focus directly on the nature of dysfluent silent reading patterns of low-performing students.

Stamina may be a particularly critical construct to consider in relation to the "iGeneration" (Rosen, 2010). For these students, whose lives have involved a barrage of information presented in several modalities simultaneously, attending to the fine print in rather solitary situations may be challenging. These students may have high levels of word recognition and may be facile with a variety of background knowledge. What may be challenging for them is sustained involvement with a text. The average length of a text on the fourth-grade NAEP is 800 words (Lee et al., 2007), while the average length of texts in the fourth-grade anthology of a widely used core reading program is approximately 2,000 words (Afflerbach et al., 2007).

A particular shortcoming of assessments that have typified the CBM movement, whether the mode is oral or silent reading, is the brevity of assessments—one minute or two minutes at most. The oral reading norms summarized in Table 9.1 reflect the shorter tasks. The silent reading norms, by contrast, reflect substantially longer tasks.

How Consistent Is the CBSRR of Students in a Digital Context Relative to a Paper-and-Pencil Context?

Teachers' interest in answers to this question derive from the recognition that reading in digital contexts is central to success in the digital–global age. Reading in digital contexts involves a myriad of issues that are not present in paper-and-pencil contexts (see Chapter 13, this volume). Even elementary students need to make numerous choices as they negotiate online reading tasks. In the face of a paucity of information on students' comprehension and rate of reading, our interest was straightforward: We wanted to know if students were able to read with similar levels of comprehension and at similar rates when they were reading texts presented digitally and in conventional contexts with printed texts.

Students' ability to transfer their reading skills to a new and critical context was one reason for including this component in our study. As researchers, we had a second reason. If teachers are going to support students' stamina and capture whether students are improving in their CBSRR, they need ways to gather information on students' CBSRR regularly and with *authentic* data. At the present, the typical form of assessment that is used for capturing CBSRR is the maze technique (Deno, 2003). The maze technique emanates from the CBM perspective that also spawned the widely used one-minute oral reading assessments (e.g., Good & Kaminski, 1996). A maze assessment for the primary grades consists of a passage slightly longer than what is anticipated would be read by the fastest grade-level readers (e.g., 300 words for second grade). Every seventh word (although the number can be varied) is replaced with a blank, and three or four words are listed underneath. The choices include the correct word as well as words that vary in their semantic, syntactic, or graphophonemic similarity to the target word. Students mark their choices. Their CBSRR is based on the number of words represented by their correct choices. As with oral reading fluency assessment, the typical length of time is one minute.

Studies have been conducted on the reliability of the maze relative to other assessments and have shown that the maze is positively related to performances on standardized tests (Shin, Deno, & Espin, 2000). Questions of validity have persisted around the maze, such as the effects of needing to stop and mark choices (Guthrie, Siefert, Burnham, & Caplan, 1974; Parker, Hasbrouck, & Tindal, 1992). Maze developers have identified particular rules for guessing, but the technique's success depends on carefully crafted alternatives for the target words.

The crafting of questions is a challenge for any assessment, but we are interested in the use of comprehension texts and questions that are typical of those used in classroom experiences, including typical tests. The tests that currently form such a central part of the classroom lives of students and teachers often contain highly crafted questions. Unfortunately, information from such tests is reported as summary scores, usually in the form of norms. If data on CBSRR are to be brought to bear on instruction, teachers and students require information about specific texts and questions. They also require this information quickly to make informed instructional decisions—in hours rather than in the weeks or even months it can take to get back test results.

Because recent advances in digital environments have been notable (PytlikZillig, Bodvarsson, & Bruning, 2005), we believe that new technologies offer a viable approach to the problem of assessing CBSRR. In particular, the interactivity of the computer "page" could permit educators to measure students' CBSRR reliably, frequently, and with authentic texts and tasks. A question that remained unanswered was whether students would perform with similar rates and comprehension when reading text on a computer screen and in the more typical school contexts of a printed text.

Designing and Implementing a Project to Answer Questions About CBSRR

In the study that we designed to address our questions about CBSRR, we had students representing a range of reading proficiencies read silently sections of an extended text in two different reading contexts. Our interest lay in similarities or differences in the performances of students of different quartile groups, at different points in reading an extended text, and between two contexts (digital and paper and pencil).

Method

Eighty-three students from five fourth-grade classrooms in a Midwestern, urban school district participated in the study. The participants were 65% Caucasian, 13% African American, 12% Asian American, and 9% Hispanic. More than 60% of the students in the schools receive free- or reduced-cost lunch. Participants included 15% English Learners and 13% special education students (i.e., those with speech-language disorders or specific learning disabilities).

We wrote two comparable sets of informational texts, each containing 1,000 words. Each set consisted of five texts connected by a common theme. The content of both themes came from a similar domain—communication. The underlying theme of one set of texts had to do with the role of posters in the past and present (e.g., posters as a source of information and announcements before the printing press). The theme of the second set was on nonverbal language (e.g., military hand signals, Braille).

Texts were created over numerous iterations to ensure that the two sets were as comparable as possible on several measures. The first was sentence length. As the readability levels for the Flesch-Kincaid and Fry indicate in Table 9.2, texts were comparable on that dimension. A second consideration in the creation of the texts was the comparability of vocabulary. Data on the distribution of words in word zones established by frequency of appearance in written English (Hiebert, 2005) indicate that the distribution of words that were highly frequent (i.e., Word Zones 0–2), moderately frequent (Word Zones 3–4), and rare (Word Zones 5–6) was comparable across the two sets of texts.

The readability levels on both the Flesch-Kincaid and Fry suggest that the texts were approximately 1.5–2.5 grade levels above the mid-fourth-grade (the grade-level placement of students in the study). This difficulty level, however, is an artifact of a feature of readability formulas that has long been recognized as inflating the difficulty of informational texts (Cohen & Steinberg, 1983). This feature is that each appearance of a word counts in the establishment of readability with formulas such as the Flesch-Kincaid or Fry. In informational texts, rare (and often multisyllabic words) are repeated frequently when they are central to the content. Thus, informational texts typically are assigned high readability levels.

Table 9.2. Features of Texts Used in Study

Feature	Text A (Posters)	Text B (Nonverbal Language)
Number of words	1,000	1,000
Flesch-Kincaid readability	6.1	5.9
Fry readability	7	7
Unique words:		
Word Zones 0–2	85%	83%
Word Zones 3–4	13%	16%
Word Zones 5–6	1.5%	1%
Type-token ratio	.28	.28

The texts in this study had been written to be representative of informational texts and to comply with components of the TExT model (Hiebert, 2002) in which cognitive load (i.e., the ratio of unique words to total words or type-token ratio) and the percentage of rare words (i.e., Word Zones 5–6) are seen to influence text difficulty. The texts, as can be seen in Table 9.2, had type-token ratios of 0.28. A typical assessment text, such as those on the Dynamic Indicators of Basic Early Literacy Skills (DIBELS; Good & Kaminski, 1996) has a type-token ratio of 0.50 or higher (Hiebert, Stewart, & Uzicanin, 2010). Further, the percentages of rare words were low (1–1.5%) and the percentages of words in the 1,000 most frequent words (i.e., Word Zones 0–2) of 83–85% were high, leading to the expectation that most fourth graders should be able to read the majority of words.

To accompany the two text sets, we created two short sample passages of 200 words, each on familiar informational subjects: U.S. parks and dinosaurs. Each sample passage had two multiple-choice comprehension questions. As with the main text sets, the vocabulary in the sample passages was controlled. The purpose of the sample passages was to familiarize the participants with the assessment's format.

Each passage within a theme was immediately followed by four comprehension questions specific to the passage that students needed to answer before continuing to the next passage. Each set of passages, therefore, included 20 questions. Each set of questions for a passage included two literal questions, one inferential, and one interpretive.

We conducted a pilot study to ensure the validity and reliability of the comprehension questions and to ensure that the special Internet-based application that had been created for the computer condition of the study was student friendly. The pilot study sample consisted of two fourth-grade classes with demographics similar to those in the main study. One class of students ($n = 19$) was administered the full texts with comprehension questions in the computer context. A second class ($n = 21$) responded to the questions about the texts without exposure to the texts. The data from the pilot study was used to refine both the computer program and the comprehension questions. For example, questions that students in the latter group could answer with high levels of success were eliminated from the final test set.

Students were assessed in spring of fourth grade. Computer administration was conducted in the school's computer lab with two observers who read directions, assisted with technical problems, and redirected students. The individualized paper-and-pencil administration followed the same format and organization but added a third observer who aided in recording students' start and stop times for text sections.

Texts were counterbalanced for order of administration (i.e., computer vs. paper-and-pencil) and topic (i.e., nonverbal language vs. posters). Comprehension scores were corrected for guessing. Reliability of the 20-item comprehension items for each set of passages was established using coefficient α. The reliability for both scales was 0.74, an acceptable range for research measures.

Results

Outlier analysis showed that there was a group of students with extremely high reading rates and very low comprehension performances. The performances of the outlier students can be seen in Figure 9.1. The observers who had been present during the task administration to ensure students' ease with the computer interface confirmed that particular students appeared to move rapidly through the task. As a result of this analysis, the data used in the subsequent analyses was limited to 65 students.

Descriptive statistics that appear in Table 9.3 indicate that silent reading rates were precisely the same on the two different sets of passages. This silent reading rate of approximately 154 wpm is similar to the average of 158 wpm reported by Taylor et al. (1960) for fourth graders almost 50 years ago. Comprehension performances were slightly lower on the posters text than that on nonverbal language.

A repeated-measures ANOVA was used to compare performances in the paper-and-pencil and computer administrations. For reading comprehension, there were no significant differences: $F(1, 77) = 1.19$, $p = 0.28$ $MSE = 6.32$. For silent reading rate, there was a significant effect for mode of presentation $F(1, 61) = 5.43$, $p = 0.02$ $MSE = 873$. This difference was not massive, but the context in which the slightly faster rate occurred is of interest—the computer context as is evident in Figure 9.1. Further, the lack of significant differences in comprehension indicates that this somewhat higher rate did not compromise comprehension.

The next set of analyses considered differences across quartile groups. Quartile groups were established on the basis of comprehension scores. Repeated-measures ANOVA revealed that rates for different comprehension quartiles were significantly different overall $F(3, 72) = 2.7$, $p = 0.05$ $MSE = 210035$.

The interpretation of rates by different groups is difficult because of different patterns of performance by the quartile groups on different parts of the texts. These

Figure 9.1. Average Reading Rate by Group and Context

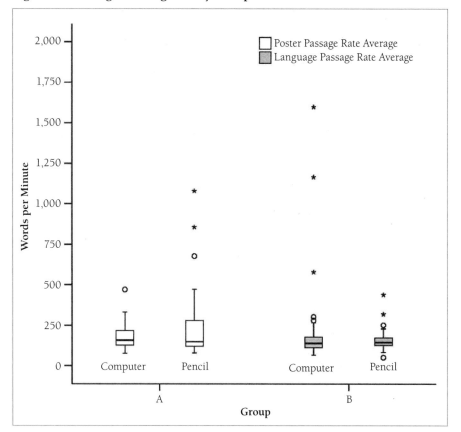

Table 9.3. Descriptive Statistics for Comprehension and Silent Reading Rate for Texts

	Mean	SD
Corrected comprehension score Text A (posters)	6.3	4.1
Corrected comprehension score Text B (nonverbal language)	7.9	3.7
Silent reading rate Text A	153.5	63
Silent reading rate Text B	153.5	60

patterns are provided for the first text (Posters) in Figure 9.2. For the first section of the assessment, the highest quartile performed approximately 30 wpm faster than the other three quartiles. The rates of Quartiles 1 and 2 were slightly lower than those of Quartile 3 but not substantially so on the first section of the text.

Figure 9.2. Silent Reading Rate for Text A (Posters) by Section

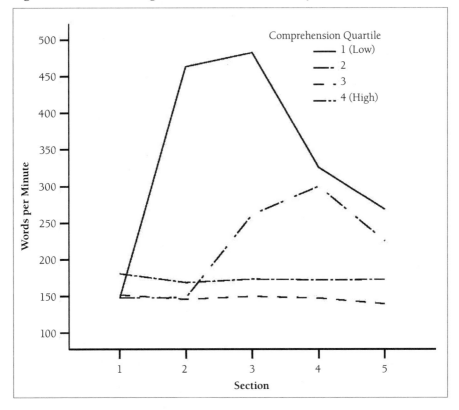

A repeated-measures ANOVA verified the pattern that can be seen in Figure 9.2 of performances of different quartile groups across sections of the text. Although students in the two lower quartiles started out at a reasonable rate, their rates changed dramatically over the sections of the assessment (but not with increases in comprehension). The effect was nonlinear. The lowest quartile readers increased their speed after one passage (but without commensurate gains in comprehension). The second-lowest quartile increased their speed after two sections (again, without commensurate gains in comprehension). The students in the top two quartiles had stable rates that changed very little across sections of the text. Further, their comprehension remained stable.

Some Conclusions About Silent Reading

Silent reading has been an area in which educational practices have swung from one extreme to another (see Chapter 1, this volume). At particular times, all reading—even for first graders—was mandated or advocated to be silent. The opposite swing of the pendulum has been evident in the past decade, when oral reading has been emphasized as the primary mode. When one solution is found wanting, it is replaced by another solution. In a domain as complex as reading, single solutions will always be found wanting. A single study on CBSRR cannot produce all of the answers to a very complex set of issues. We can, however, give some tentative answers to a critical set of questions. These answers are offered in the spirit of continuing investigation, both by researchers and teachers, of what works best with particular kinds of texts and at particular points in development.

We begin by answering the question that we raised in the title of this chapter—are students really reading in independent reading contexts? The answer: Yes, most students are. Many students read at fairly consistent rates across different sections of a text. They comprehend at a fairly consistent level as well. Their rate is somewhat faster when they are reading digital text rather than a paper text, but with similar levels of comprehension.

This pattern—where most students are reading consistently in different silent reading contexts—is an important one to consider when thinking about the design of instruction. We are in the midst of the greatest knowledge revolution in human history. In a world where knowledge is the critical commodity, reading is a primary means whereby knowledge is acquired. We are not suggesting by any stretch of the imagination that all reading should be silent reading (see the Conclusion for an expansion on the functions of oral and silent reading). Oral reading serves several essential roles, particularly at critical periods in students' reading acquisition. By the same token, to limit silent reading opportunities of all students because a portion of a cohort struggles with the task does a great disservice to all students. For struggling readers, such prohibitions mean that there is no opportunity to develop capacity in silent reading. For proficient readers, opportunities to learn are constrained when silent reading is limited.

Consider the greater amount of new vocabulary that students can acquire through silent rather than oral reading. If fourth graders read orally for 30 minutes daily at a speed of 118 wpm, they will read approximately 3,540 words daily or 637,200 words over a school year of 180 days. If they spend the same length of time reading silently, they will read 4,590 words daily or 826,200 words over the school year—approximately 189,000 more words. Based on existing research, it is estimated that 2–5% of these words will be unknown to students (Stahl, 1999) and, of these unknown words, students can be expected to remember approximately 5–10% from a single reading (Nagy, Anderson, & Herman, 1987). Using estimates of 3.75% unknown words and 7.5% remembered words, students will learn approximately 532 additional words in silent reading contexts. In that it is estimated that fourth graders acquire approximately 2,000 new words a year (Graves, 2006), this amount is significant. Further, because a primary way in which oral reading occurs is through round robin reading (Brenner et al., 2009), it is not at all clear that students will be attending to the texts to the same degree during oral reading as in silent reading.

But not all students' performances are consistent and reliable in silent reading contexts. Approximately 20% of the students did not stay "on the page." Another group of students read the first one or two texts conscientiously but changed their strategy at that point, moving quickly to answer the comprehension questions without careful reading of the text. Considerable attention is required on the kind of experiences that underlie consistency in silent reading, particularly the stamina that is required to sustain interest and monitor comprehension through extended texts. We hypothesize that stamina is part of the cycle of poor reading that Stanovich (1986) describes. As poor readers read less, their skills become increasingly inadequate for new developmental tasks such as reading chapter-long texts. Even if the texts are not overly difficult (which was the case with the texts in the present study), poor readers approach reading tasks with low levels of motivation and interest. As Swan, Coddington, and Guthrie (see Chapter 6, this volume) describe, these students have poor identities of themselves as readers and low levels of intrinsic motivation.

Effective silent reading habits are not automatic outcomes of proficient word recognition and oral reading fluency. There are aspects of silent reading that make it unique from oral reading: vocalization, the need for self-monitoring, stamina, and interest. Numerous chapters in this volume highlight the components of instruction that support these components of effective silent reading. We will not review all of these components, but we do underscore one point: Just as the development of poor reading habits occurs over an extended period of time, so too development of good reading habits likely reflects many experiences over an extended period of time.

For the students who engage in what Griffith and Rasinski (2004) have described as "fake reading" behaviors, efforts to develop proficiencies such as self-monitoring, stamina, and interest are interwoven with the need to develop students' identities as readers and their intrinsic motivation. Most students have acquired fundamental word recognition by the end of second grade (Hiebert et al., 2010) and definitely by the middle of fourth grade (Pinnell et al., 1995). For a significant portion of these students (approximately a third of a grade cohort), this recognition is tedious and time consuming. They have not developed perseverance or stamina for the task. They need considerable support if they are to sustain attention to the texts and tasks of daily classroom life.

There are likely limits to what teachers can do—especially in classrooms where large groups of students have such behaviors. Hiebert, Menon, Martin, and Bach (2009), in considering the research on silent reading, suggest that digital contexts may be one means whereby support can be provided for struggling readers. In a computer context, the text can be fine tuned. The length of time can be monitored. Content can be chunked and periodic check-ins can be made. The architecture can be designed so that the length of time, the accessibility of text, and the tasks can be carefully adjusted to students' growing capacity as readers. Not much data have been gathered on current efforts, especially for struggling readers, but there is suggestive evidence that digital technology may provide the scaffolding that supports struggling readers in becoming stronger readers (Moran, Ferdig, Pearson, Wardrop, & Blomeyer, 2008).

At least in terms of our interest in providing classroom teachers with authentic and reliable assessments, the findings of this study leave us optimistic that digital contexts can serve as a means for providing teachers and students with consistent and usable information. Students responded well to the digital context with overall reading rates higher in that context than in the paper-and-pencil context. What we found to be particularly encouraging about this result is that students' faster rates did not compromise comprehension. This finding of students' somewhat superior performances in the digital context also bodes well for their flexibility as readers and their adaptation to a context that will be a critical one in their futures.

The study that we report in this chapter offers a window on variations of silent reading rate and comprehension of fourth-grade students when they are asked to read informational text. There are numerous questions that remain: How does this relationship change when similar assessments are administered to students in other elementary grades? Will the rates level off, as has been observed with oral reading fluency as the grades increase? Will reading rates change when comparing matched narrative and informational texts? When is it possible to gather reliable data based on students' developmental reading patterns? How should meaningful benchmark reading rates across the grades be created that are related to comprehension performance? Are students reading at appropriate rates? Are there optimal silent reading rates? Does oral reading practice improve CBSRR? Although this list of unanswered questions is sizable, it is not exhaustive. It illuminates the need for much more work in the area of silent reading assessment. Educators at all levels would benefit from a more nuanced understanding of the factors that affect students' learning when reading silently. Greater understanding of this little-studied reading mode will help to inform the instructional choices teachers make as students progress across the grades.

QUESTIONS FOR
PROFESSIONAL DEVELOPMENT

1. Given the emphasis on the assessment of oral reading rates and practice of oral reading fluency in today's elementary classrooms as a result of the No Child Left Behind legislation, how might teachers better integrate a variety of reading contexts into the instructional experiences that they offer to students?

2. How might grade-level teams approach silent reading fluency and comprehension assessment in their classrooms? What might teachers in these teams gain from the data gathered from such assessments?

3. It is important to communicate that students need to work at comprehending what they read. How might this concept be incorporated in engaging silent and oral reading fluency assessment and instruction?

REFERENCES

Afflerbach, P., Blachowicz, C.L.Z., Boyd, C.D., Cheyney, W., Juel, C., Kame'enui, E.J., et al. (2007). *Scott Foresman Reading Street: Grade 4* (4th ed.) [Student edition]. Glenview, IL: Scott Foresman.

AIMSweb Assessment and Data Management for RTI. (2008). *Establishing curriculum-based measurement oral reading fluency performance standards to predict success on local and state tests of reading achievement.* Retrieved June 22, 2010, from www.aimsweb.com/uploads/news/id19/orf_benchmarks.pdf/

Brenner, D., & Hiebert, E.H. (2010). If I follow the teachers' editions, isn't that enough? Analyzing reading volume in six core reading programs. *The Elementary School Journal, 110*(3), 347–363. doi:10.1086/648982

Brenner, D., Hiebert, E.H., & Tompkins, R. (2009). How much and what are third graders reading? Reading in core programs. In E.H. Hiebert (Ed.), *Reading more, reading better* (pp. 118–140). New York: Guilford.

Brown, A.L., & Smiley, S.S. (1978). The development of strategies for studying texts. *Child Development, 49*(4), 1076–1088.

Brozo, W.G., & Johns, J.L. (1986). A content and critical analysis of 40 speed reading books. *Journal of Reading, 30*(3), 242–247.

Carver, R.P. (1990). *Reading rate: A review of research and theory.* San Diego: Academic.

Carver, R.P. (1992). Reading rate: Theory, research, and practical implications. *Journal of Reading, 36*(2), 84–95.

Cassidy, J., & Cassidy, D. (2009). What's hot for 2009: National Reading Panel influence wanes in 13th annual survey. *Reading Today, 26*(4), 1, 8–9.

Cohen, S.A., & Steinberg, J.E. (1983). Effects of three types of vocabulary on readability of intermediate grade science textbooks: An application of Finn's transfer feature theory. *Reading Research Quarterly, 19*(1), 86–101. doi:10.2307/747339

Cunningham, A.E., Stanovich, K.E., & Wilson, M.R. (1990). Cognitive variation in adult college students differing in reading ability. In T.H. Carr & B.A. Levy (Eds.), *Reading and its development: Component skills approaches* (pp. 129–159). San Diego, CA: Academic.

Daane, M.C., Campbell, J.R., Grigg, W.S., Goodman, M.J., & Oranje, A. (2005). *Fourth-grade students reading aloud: NAEP 2002 special study of oral reading* (NCES 2006-469). Washington, DC: Institute of Education Sciences, U.S. Department of Education.

Deno, S.L. (1985). Curriculum-based measurement: The emerging alternative. *Exceptional Children, 52*(3), 219–232.

Deno, S.L. (2003). Developments in curriculum-based measurement. *The Journal of Special Education, 37*(3), 184–192. doi:10.1177/00224669030370030801

Duke, N.K., & Pearson, P.D. (2002). Effective practices for developing reading comprehension. In A.E. Farstrup & S.J. Samuels (Eds.), *What research has to say about reading instruction* (3rd ed., pp. 205–242). Newark, DE: International Reading Association.

Frank, S.D. (1992). *Remember everything you read: The Evelyn Wood 7-day speed reading and learning program.* New York: Avon.

Fuchs, L.S., Fuchs, D., Hosp, M.K., & Jenkins, J.R. (2001). Oral reading fluency as an indicator of reading competence: A theoretical, empirical, and historical analysis. *Scientific Studies of Reading, 5*(3), 239–256. doi:10.1207/S1532799XSSR0503_3

Good, R.H., & Kaminski, R.A. (1996). *DIBELS: Dynamic Indicators of Basic Literacy Skills.* Longmont, CO: Sopris West.

Graves, M.F. (2006). *The vocabulary book: Learning and instruction.* New York: Teachers College Press; Newark, DE: International Reading Association; Urbana, IL: National Council of Teachers of English.

Griffith, L.W., & Rasinski, T.V. (2004). A focus on fluency: How one teacher incorporated fluency with her reading curriculum. *The Reading Teacher, 58*(2), 126–137. doi:10.1598/RT.58.2.1

Guthrie, J.T., Siefert, M., Burnham, N.A., & Caplan, R.I. (1974). The maze technique to assess, monitor reading comprehension. *The Reading Teacher, 28*(2), 161–168.

Hasbrouck, J., & Tindal, G.A. (2006). Oral reading fluency norms: A valuable assessment tool for reading teachers. *The Reading Teacher, 59*(7), 636–644. doi:10.1598/RT.59.7.3

Hiebert, E.H. (2002). Standards, assessments, and text difficulty. In A.E. Farstrup & S.J. Samuels (Eds.), *What research has to say about reading instruction* (3rd ed., pp. 337–369). Newark, DE: International Reading Association.

Hiebert, E.H. (2005). In pursuit of an effective, efficient vocabulary curriculum for the elementary grades. In E.H. Hiebert & M.L. Kamil (Eds.), *The teaching and learning of vocabulary: Bringing scientific research to practice* (pp. 243–263). Mahwah, NJ: Erlbaum.

Hiebert, E.H., Menon, S., Martin, L.A., & Bach, K.E. (2009). *Online scaffolds that support adolescents' comprehension*. Seattle, WA: Apex Learning.

Hiebert, E.H., Stewart, J., & Uzicanin, M. (2010, July). *A comparison of word features affecting word recognition of at-risk beginning readers and their peers*. Paper to be presented at the annual conference of the Society for the Scientific Study of Reading, Berlin, Germany.

Johnson, H., Freedman, L., & Thomas, K.F. (2008). *Building reading confidence in adolescents: Key elements that enhance proficiency*. Thousand Oaks, CA: Corwin.

Kame'enui, E.J., & Simmons, D.C. (2001). Introduction to this special issue: The DNA of reading fluency. *Scientific Studies of Reading, 5*(3), 203–210.

Lee, J., Grigg, W.S., & Donahue, P.L. (2007). *The nation's report card: Reading 2007* (NCES 2007-496). Washington, DC: National Center for Education Statistics, Institute of Education Sciences, U.S. Department of Education.

McNamara, D.S. (2000). *Preliminary analysis of photoreading* (ODURF File No. 193021). Moffett Field, CA: NASA Ames Research Center. Retrieved April 27, 2010, from ntrs.nasa.gov/archive/nasa/casi.ntrs.nasa.gov/20000011599_2000009345.pdf

Moran, J., Ferdig, R.E., Pearson, P.D., Wardrop, J., & Blomeyer, R.L., Jr. (2008). Technology and reading performance in the middle-school grades: A meta-analysis with recommendations for policy and practice. *Journal of Literacy Research, 40*(1), 6–58. doi:10.1080/10862960802070483

Nagy, W.E., Anderson, R.C., & Herman, P.A. (1987). Learning word meanings from context during normal reading. *American Educational Research Journal, 24*(2), 237–270.

National Institute of Child Health and Human Development. (2000). *Report of the National Reading Panel. Teaching children to read: An evidence-based assessment of the scientific research literature on reading and its implications for reading instruction* (NIH Publication No.

00-4769). Washington, DC: U.S. Government Printing Office.

Parker, R., Hasbrouck, J.E., & Tindal, G. (1992). The maze as a classroom-based reading measure: Construction methods, reliability, and validity. *The Journal of Special Education, 26*(2), 195–218. doi:10.1177/002246699202600205

Pinnell, G.S., Pikulski, J.J., Wixson, K.K., Campbell, J.R., Gough, P.P., & Beatty, A.S. (1995). *Listening to children read aloud: Data from NAEP's Integrated Reading Performance Record (IRPR) at grade 4*. Washington, DC: National Center for Education Statistics, U.S. Department of Education.

PytlikZillig, L.M., Bodvarsson, M., & Bruning, R.H. (2005). *Technology-based education: Bringing researchers and practitioners together*. Greenwich, CT: Information Age.

Qualifications and Curriculum Authority. (2005). *English: 2004/05 annual report on curriculum and assessment* (QCA/05/2167). Coventry, England: Author. Retrieved April 27, 2010, from www.ttrb.ac.uk/attachments/31f8ef70-0516-4a54-878e-c4f268ef85c2.pdf

Rosen, L.D. (2010). *Rewired: Understanding the iGeneration and the way they learn*. New York: Palgrave Macmillan.

Schmidt, A.M., & Flege, J.E. (1995). Effects of speaking rate changes on native and nonnative speech production. *Phonetica, 52*(1), 41–54. doi:10.1159/000262028

Shin, J., Deno, S.L., & Espin, C. (2000). Technical adequacy of the maze task for curriculum-based measurement of reading growth. *The Journal of Special Education, 34*(3), 164–172. doi:10.1177/002246690003400305

Stahl, S.A. (1999). *Vocabulary development*. Cambridge, MA: Brookline.

Stanovich, K.E. (1986). Matthew effects in reading: Some consequences of individual differences in the acquisition of literacy. *Reading Research Quarterly, 21*(4), 360–407. doi:10.1598/RRQ.21.4.1

Taylor, S.E., Frankenpohl, H., & Pettee, J.L. (1960). *Grade level norms for the components of the fundamental reading skills* (EDL Research and Information Bulletin No. 3). Huntington, NY: Educational Development Laboratories.

CHAPTER 10

R⁵: A Sustained Silent Reading Makeover That Works

Michelle J. Kelley
University of Central Florida

Nicki Clausen-Grace
Carillon Elementary School, Florida

Absently flipping the pages of a book, staring blankly at the printed page, and frequently switching books are a few common behaviors disengaged readers exhibit during silent reading. Other, more overt avoidance tactics include talking and what we have described as the "anything-but-reading shuffle" typically to the restroom or the bookshelf and back again (Kelley & Clausen-Grace, 2007). Less obvious are those students who fly under the radar by appearing to read, even though they have really selected inappropriate texts and are unable to fully engage in silent reading. Also disturbing are those readers who read only when told, even though they actually like it (Kelley & Clausen-Grace, 2008a).

Although the behaviors and reasons for failing to engage in silent reading differ, the effect is the same. All of these students have difficulty engaging in independent reading. A lack of student engagement is not the only barrier to effective independent reading. Lack of time can be a roadblock to successfully implementing any teaching approach, but it is especially true for independent reading (Kelley & Clausen-Grace, 2008a). Teachers are continually expected to cover more material and accomplish more despite the fact that the school day has not been extended. This pressure has left some educators feeling as though they do not have enough time for independent reading or that independent reading is a low priority in the face of other mandated instructional practices.

Unfortunately, the implementation of independent reading itself, such as sustained silent reading (SSR), can also be problematic. Sometimes teachers use this time to complete administrative tasks rather than to guide student book selection, monitor progress, or provide students with feedback regarding their reading (Kelley & Clausen-Grace, 2008a; Reutzel, Jones, Fawson, & Smith, 2008). Any instructional method that is poorly executed will not yield desired results. Another concern is the National Reading Panel's (National Institute of Child Health and Human Development, 2000) controversial position regarding independent

Revisiting Silent Reading: New Directions for Teachers and Researchers, edited by Elfrieda H. Hiebert and D. Ray Reutzel. © 2010 by the International Reading Association.

reading, which has led to a general lack of support for SSR in schools. This less than stellar endorsement, coupled with the previously mentioned concerns, has led many teachers to eliminate independent reading from the school day (Garan & DeVoogd, 2008; Kelley & Clausen-Grace, 2008a).

However, research has found numerous positive benefits for independent reading (Garan & DeVoogd, 2008). Independent reading is a classroom practice vital to developing motivated independent readers (Kelley & Clausen-Grace, 2009). In addition, there are other benefits of independent reading, such as increases in vocabulary (Anderson, 1996; Baumann & Kame'enui, 1991; Brozo & Hargis, 2003), reader self-confidence (Clay, 1991), writing and reading competence (Gallik, 1999; Guthrie, Wigfield, Metsala, & Cox, 1999), and positive attitudes toward reading (Arthur, 1995; Gambrell, 1996, 2001; Valeri-Gold, 1995). Furthermore, independent reading can serve as an instructional transition from oral to silent reading (Hiebert, 2006).

Rather than eliminating independent reading, we acknowledge that the current model of SSR does not meet the needs of most students. In response, we initiated an action research project in 2004–2005 to determine how we could remodel independent reading to better engage independent readers. The result was R^5: Read, Relax, Reflect, Respond, and Rap. This chapter describes R^5 in detail, including how the structure supports different types of readers. In addition, we report on our recent work successfully connecting at-home reading to school through R^4: Read, Relax, Reflect, and Respond.

Different Readers, Different Needs

Although a handful of fake readers, ranging from low ability to gifted, are what challenged us to rethink independent reading in our classroom, we wanted to increase membership in the Avid Readers' Club for all students. Our goal as teachers was to develop habitual readers who chose to read for pleasure, the criteria for being in the Avid Readers' Club (Kelley & Clausen-Grace, 2008a). To do this, we looked more closely at our readers and realized that they were disengaged for different reasons. We had students who never read, had difficulty reading, could not choose a book they were both interested in *and* able to read, and read only when instructed. In addition, our engaged readers exhibited a huge range of reading preferences and habits (Kelley & Clausen-Grace, 2008a, 2009), and we recognized that we would need to address each of them when redesigning independent reading. This led us to identify categories of readers that exhibited common attributes (see Table 10.1). These categories are not intended to be used as static labels but as a way for teachers to quickly identify how they can support each reader and move him or her toward fuller engagement (see Figure 10.1). In R^5, the level of teacher support is differentiated according to the student's level of independence (Kelley & Clausen-Grace, 2008a, 2009).

Table 10.1. Types of Readers and Their Behaviors

Type of Reader	Behaviors Exhibited
Fake	• Avoid reading • Pretend to read • Cannot find a book they like • Do not really read
Challenged	• Read and comprehend well below grade level • May or may not want to be in the Avid Readers' Club • Have physical, cognitive, or social issues that make independent reading difficult
Unrealistic or wannabe	• Consistently choose books well beyond their reading level • Frequently discard books before completing them • Frequently report their progress to the teacher (e.g., "I'm on Chapter 3 now," "I'm almost done with Chapter 2") • Boast untruthfully about reading accomplishments
Compliant	• Read only when required • Do not have a text preference • Are ambivalent towards reading
Does nonfiction count?	• Prefer nonfiction • Have trouble focusing on narrative storylines • Often do not see themselves as readers • Might appear fake or disengaged if they are forced to read only narrative texts
I can but don't want to (even though I enjoy it)	• Can choose books they enjoy • Read only the required amount • Take a long time to finish reading a book • Do not choose to read
Stuck in a genre (or series)	• Have a narrow range of interests • Read only from one genre or series for a period of more than a month
Bookworms	• Choose to read when given the choice • Read a variety of genres but usually have a preference • Read a lot • Have to be told twice to put their books down when it is time to move on

Description of R⁵

As previously stated, R^5 is an independent reading block originally conceived to support engagement and encourage strategic reading (Kelley & Clausen-Grace, 2006). The structure of R^5 is divided into three phases: Read and Relax, Reflect and Respond, and Rap. The total time spent in the three phases of R^5 averages between 30 and 40 minutes, but the time in each phase varies from the beginning of the year to the end of the year, as students take on more responsibility for their

Figure 10.1. Continuum of Readers

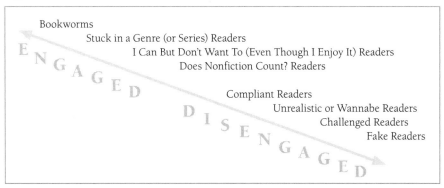

From *R⁵ in Your Classroom: A Guide to Differentiating Independent Reading and Developing Avid Readers*, by M. Kelley & N. Clausen-Grace, 2008, p. 18, Newark, DE: International Reading Association.

reading, build the stamina to read independently, and are able to more fully engage with their reading. This practice assists students in transferring reading skills that have been learned during direct instruction from basic awareness to independence (Kelley & Clausen-Grace, 2008b). In addition, R⁵ has led students to read more widely and contributed to increased reading proficiency (Kelley & Clausen-Grace, 2006, 2007, 2008a, 2008b). R⁵ contains five key elements as described by Trudel (2007):

1. Teacher assists with book selection.
2. Students keep track of their reading.
3. Students complete a response about their reading.
4. Teacher and students engage in discussion.
5. Teacher does not read during independent reading.

In addition to helping students engage during R⁵, three simple rules are enforced (Kelley & Clausen-Grace, 2006, 2007):

1. Students must have reading materials selected prior to the beginning of R⁵.
2. Students cannot get up for any reason during R⁵ (restroom and water breaks are provided before).
3. Students cannot talk to others, unless in a teacher conference or during Rap.

Read and Relax

During the Read and Relax phase of R⁵, each student chooses a location to read. While the students get comfortable and settle in to read, the teacher completes a brief status-of-the-class (Atwell, 1989) to monitor book selection, determine reading progress, and provide brief feedback (Kelley & Clausen-Grace, 2006, 2007, 2008a). Keeping a simple record of conferences (Kelley & Clausen-Grace, 2007, 2008a) along with a status-of-the-class helps the teacher determine with whom to confer. Typically, these more formal one-on-one conferences take about 10 minutes and occur on a monthly basis. During a conference, the teacher records information on a form, which makes the conference highly predictable for both teacher and student. Students bring their book and reading folder to the conference. The reading folder contains a running log of books read and daily strategy reflections, a copy of the current strategy goal-setting plan, and any documents that might be used for honing strategy use, such as lists of strategy components. The teacher asks the student to share something about the book being read, including the title, a brief summary of what has been read, and knowledge about the book's genre. If needed, the teacher probes to clarify and assist with recall. Then, the teacher has the student describe how he or she has used their strategy plan (developed on the basis of the cognitive unit taught during direct instruction) while reading. If the plan has not been used, it may not be well thought out. Therefore, the teacher reviews the plan and, if necessary, assists in its revision. If the student appears to lack strategy awareness, the teacher may prod for any evidence of strategy use. After strategy discussion, the teacher asks how he or she can help the student become a better reader. Next, the teacher and student collaborate to set a student goal to work on until the next conference. Throughout, the teacher provides positive feedback based on the student's growth.

Reflect and Respond

After 10–20 minutes of reading and relaxing, students begin to Reflect and Respond. The student writes a brief response in his or her reading log. The log serves two purposes: (1) to record what has been read (including the title, author, and genre) and (2) to allow students to process through writing something they read. There are response stems at the top of the log that prompt students to reflect on what was read and any cognitive strategies used while reading. For example, one stem, "I can see a clear picture...," encourages readers to remember any visualizing they did as they read. Reflecting and responding takes only a few minutes and guides the discussion during the final phase of R^5, Rap.

Rap

The Rap phase has two parts. In the first part, the teacher places students in pairs to discuss their books and reflections. After a few minutes, the teacher pulls the class together for the second part, a whole-class share. The teacher calls on a pair to take turns telling the class what the partner shared. The teacher then asks the other students to identify strategy(ies) mentioned in the share. This gives students strategy practice and immediate feedback each day. The time spent in Rap is usually 10–15 minutes.

How R⁵ Meets the Needs of Different Readers

Motivation: Interest and Choice

We believe that promoting the motivation to read in a classroom is as important as scaffolding the internalization of reading skills. When students are motivated to read and are interested in the text, they are more likely to continue reading (Hidi & Baird, 1986; Wigfield & Guthrie, 1997; Williams, Hedrick, & Tuschinski, 2008). Giving students the option to read self-selected texts is one way to foster intrinsic motivation and encourage students to read independently (Johnson & Blair, 2003; Schraw, Flowerday, & Reisetter, 1998). Furthermore, research suggests that students can read texts far above their grade level when they are interested, and when allowed to choose their own reading materials, students are more likely to engage in and enjoy reading (Darigan, Tunnell, & Jacobs, 2002).

Johnson and Blair (2003) purport that "enjoyment of a book cannot be forced on a child; it must come naturally" (p. 184). They further suggest that when students are given the opportunity "they will make positive selections based on both interest and ability" (p. 184). We believe this is true with some students, especially those who have exposure and access to texts and can read independently. But many students still have difficulty choosing books they can read that also sustain their interest. Those who do not have exposure, access, or ability are even more likely to struggle in text selection. These readers continue to select from a narrow range of authors, topics, and genres or consistently choose books that are too difficult for them. Even engaged readers, such as the Stuck in a Genre or Series group, sometimes need help with selection. They might read every single copy of The Baby-Sitters Club series even when surrounded by a tempting array of other books. Many of our disengaged readers have taught us that providing time to read self-selected texts was not enough to help them develop into engaged readers (Bryan, Fawson, & Reutzel, 2003). Therefore, although students are encouraged to self-select texts during R⁵, the teacher carefully monitors to determine whether students are having issues with engagement caused by book selection. If necessary, the teacher guides students to more appropriate text.

An example occurred during a conference with a fourth-grade student who repeatedly selected books from the Junie B. Jones series for independent reading. He was representative of the Compliant Readers we have encountered. He could read above grade level, yet he continually chose texts with little connection to his interests—skateboarding and football—because he felt he should be reading chapter books and had been exposed to the series through teacher read-aloud in the primary grades. He read to please the teacher, not himself. He had not yet experienced a text aesthetically, and no matter how much time he was given to read independently, without teacher guidance he would have continued to read books for others. Instead, Nicki introduced him to *Hatchet* by Gary Paulsen during teacher read-aloud. This led him to explore other survival books written by Gary Paulsen, and by the end of the year he had added the entire Chasing the Falconer series by Gordon Korman to his reading repertoire. This did not happen naturally for this reader. Nicki used an Interest and Wide Reading Inventory (Kelley & Clausen-Grace, 2007) to determine topics or genres that might pique his interest, then chose a read-aloud geared specifically to him. Knowing his interests, strengths, and needs allowed Nicki to help him select compelling texts he wanted to read.

One behavior all of our Bookworms—founding members of the Avid Readers' Club—exhibit is the ability to repeatedly choose engaging, accessible texts from a wide variety of authors, genres, and topics. This is one key to their success as independent readers. The Rap phase allows these readers to showcase this skill. With some guidance, particularly during the Read and Relax phase, we can help all students get closer to this ideal.

Monitoring and Accountability

Many disengaged readers need some sense of accountability for their reading. The monitoring aspects of R^5 are particularly helpful for those readers that we have characterized as Fake and Challenged Readers. As described at the beginning of this chapter, these students run the gamut from outright defiant to extremely discreet. The status-of-the-class is a tool used daily during the Read and Relax phase for monitoring and serves as a form of subtle accountability. On the status-of-the-class, the teacher keeps track of each student's book selection by logging the title and page number being read. When students frequently switch (i.e., abandon) books or devour books, the teacher can provide guidance or feedback right away. The teacher can also flag a student who might need a conference.

The teacher–student conference during Read and Relax is another more explicit form of accountability. When the teacher confers with a student during R^5, the purpose of the conference is to coach, monitor, or facilitate the reader (Kelley & Clausen-Grace, 2007). Most of the beginning-of-year conferences require some sort of an intervention, typically centered on book selection. The teacher uses his or her knowledge of the students' interests, experiences, and general reading abilities to guide students toward texts they will enjoy and be able to read.

The Rap phase also provides accountability. When the students are paired to discuss their books, it is nearly impossible for them to have a conversation if they have not engaged while reading. These conversations help students construct meaning and create a community of readers. All disengaged readers, especially Fake and Compliant Readers, need a strong sense of purpose beyond "because the teacher told me to." Rap helps to set an additional purpose for reading.

Response and Social Interaction

In R⁵, students respond to texts in many ways. These include conferring with the teacher, reflecting and then writing a response, rapping with a peer, and participating in the whole-class share. The Rap phase, as already described, offers many opportunities for students to collaborate. Rap creates moderate peer pressure, because students cannot fake read and have a discussion about their book. In addition, if students do not focus on their partner during the first part of Rap, they will have nothing to say when the teacher calls on them. For many students it is the enthusiasm for books shared by the Bookworms during Rap that makes them want to join the Avid Readers' Club. This connectedness is especially important for the I Can But Don't Want To (Even Though I Enjoy It) Readers. The peer discussion aspect gives these readers permission to enjoy text, rather than simply reading to answer teacher questions (Asselin, 2004).

Classroom Environment

In addition to the structure of R⁵ providing support to all readers, the teacher must create a comfortable classroom environment (Reutzel & Cooter, 1992) with a well-stocked library to entice students to read (Routman, 2003). Consistent engagement with independent reading and other related literacy practices, such as read-alouds and book talks, sends the message that literacy is valued, thus encouraging risk taking and building a community of readers (Fresch, 1995).

Including a variety of genres in reading lessons and stocking the classroom library with a multitude of texts is especially inviting for the Does Nonfiction Count? Readers. These readers often lack self-confidence, because their school and classroom libraries often highlight fiction and narrative texts rather than the nonfiction texts that attract them. Holding enthusiastic nonfiction book talks, expressing a genuine interest in nonfiction texts a student reads, and naming him or her your nonfiction "expert" go a long way in validating these readers. They can quickly become Bookworms once they feel valued.

Scaffolding Book Selection

Because our goal is developing lifelong readers, we have also learned that many students need strategies to help them in book selection. This is particularly helpful for Wannabe Readers. Wannabe Readers want to be in the Avid Readers' Club so much that they consistently choose books far above their grade level. They lovingly pick up every book you highlight and peruse the bookshelves several times a day. Unfortunately, they need to do this because their love affair with each book lasts only a few minutes. These students are perhaps the most tragic. They want in and have no idea how to get there. Sometimes they need to learn what it means to really read, other times there is something physical getting in the way of their comprehension. Sometimes they have learned the "anything-but-reading shuffle" from teachers who sent the message that you could do what you wanted during independent reading time as long as you were quiet and allowed them to do their work. Whether it is the Goldilocks Strategy (Ohlhausen & Jepsen, 1992) or the Five Finger and a Palm Strategy (Allington, 2006; Kelley & Clausen-Grace, 2007, 2008a; Routman, 2000), strategies that help students identify books that are too difficult, too easy, or just right usually based on the number of unknown words on a page, these students need specific techniques to support them with book selection.

R^4: Connecting At-Home Reading to School

During the 2006–2007 school year, it became apparent that we needed to do something about at-home reading. We had not ignored it per se, and of course we encouraged it, but we were hesitant to *require* it. Our apprehensions stemmed from past experiences. Previous at-home reading approaches had as many, if not more, issues than in-school independent reading. But when several students during R^5 conferences repeatedly suggested that the way Nicki could help them become better readers was to have them read more at home, we decided we could no longer avoid it. The only question was how we would address the problems with at-home reading. Some of these problems were as follows:

- Lack of access to books
- Little to no accountability
- Little to no feedback
- Lack of purpose (other than because the teacher told them to)
- Lack of parental support

The answer became R^4: Read, Relax, Reflect, and Respond. It was important for us to make at-home reading enjoyable and meaningful, and we thought if we followed a format that complemented R^5, we could accomplish this (Kelley & Clausen-Grace, 2008a). During R^4, students were asked to read 80 minutes per week. The title of the book read and time spent reading were logged and verified by a parent. Students could break the reading into manageable chunks, or they could read 80 minutes all at once. Students were encouraged to read more than 80 minutes but not required to do so. Students completed a weekly response based on their reading. Prompts were provided to help students think deeply about their reading, but they could create their own. Unlike the shorter R^5 responses, the R^4 response was expected to be at least a half page in length. Once a week, students turned in their folder for us to check and provide feedback. In addition to written feedback, we publicly acknowledged students who had exceeded the 80-minute requirement and identified quality log responses to be shared and discussed in class.

During the year that R^4 was first implemented, 2007–2008, it became clear that the feedback aspect was crucial to its success. Furthermore, Nicki felt that she needed to include social interaction to the response aspect of R^4. She added the element of written dialogue. Before students turned in their R^4 folder, they exchanged their response with a partner. Partners read each other's responses then wrote a response. These messages contained connections, clarifying questions, and even questions designed to help the partner more fully comprehend what they read. The only conversations in the room at this time were on paper, and students wrote back and forth three times before turning in the log. Nicki carefully matched partners for various reasons, such as to harbor a mentor–mentee relationship, broaden perspectives or reading choices, or initiate literary friendships among students. She also coached them in the art of written dialogue. This 15 minutes on Monday morning was important to students, and even those who sometimes forgot other homework made sure they had their prompt done so they could participate.

Another integral component that led to the success of R^4 was parent involvement. During the 2008–2009 school year, Nicki spent part of Curriculum Night explaining R^4, reviewing the purposes and expectations in person rather than sending home a written explanation. Comments during subsequent parent conferences led us to seek parent feedback (see Figure 10.2 for Parent Survey) prior

Figure 10.2. Parent Survey

R^4 Survey of At-Home Reading

Name (optional) _____

Directions: Please write your responses to the following questions. Your input helps us evaluate the effectiveness of our at-home reading program and make adaptations as needed.

1. Describe your child's at-home reading habits related to the following probes:

   a. How often does your child read? (every day, almost every day, only a few days, etc....)

   _____

   b. Where does your child like to read? Do they have a favorite place?

   _____

   c. What types of books or other reading materials does your child typically read at home?

   _____

2. Has your child's at-home reading changed as a result of R^4? Circle YES or NO.

   a. If YES, please describe the changes you have noticed in your child's at-home reading.

   _____

   b. If NO, please explain why you think your child's at-home reading has not changed.

   _____

3. What is the best part of R^4?

   _____

4. Do you have any recommendations to improve R^4? Do you have any questions about R^4 or at-home reading?

   _____

to the winter break. We wanted to know from the parents' perspective what their children's reading habits were and whether they felt they had changed as a result of R^4. We also wanted to know what aspects of R^4 they felt were most important and what they would change.

Seventy-nine percent of the parents reported that their child read every day or almost every day and that their child's reading had positively changed because of R^4. Some changes they identified included reading more, increased motivation, better comprehension, and more ownership. Of the 21% that stated their child's reading had not changed because of R^4, half noted their child already read a lot at home.

Based on parent responses, most students read in their room (74%), although students also read in the car, on the couch, or in the kitchen. When reporting on types of books students read, no text preference was prevalent. All genres and materials were mentioned. When asked to describe what was the best part of R^4, parents identified increased volume of reading, more responsibility, exposure to books, more interest in reading, and the importance of written reflection. Although most parents (84%) did not have any recommendations to improve R^4, two parents suggested increasing the amount of required reading time and one parent proposed having all students read the same book.

At the end of the school year, students helped tally the number of minutes each of them logged while reading during R^4 and then how much time the entire class read. The class averaged reading 3,577 minutes, with one student reading 1,905 minutes and one student reading 15,903 minutes. Combined, the students read 78,691 minutes at home. In addition to the increased volume of at-home reading, we were impressed by the student interactions during the written dialogue. Providing time in class for students to take part in a written dialogue became invaluable because they were probing each other for ideas, clarifying ideas, and demanding thoughtful responses. In an excerpt from a student's log pertaining to the fantasy book she was reading, she wrote, "I'm wondering what a glow worm is? The reason why I am wondering that is because I have never heard of a glow worm before. Also, I'm wondering what a mu shield [sic] is?..." Her partner responded, "What do you think those words mean depending on the sentence it's in? Do you still understand the story? Where does the story take place?" Through the written dialogue, students were scaffolding reading for each other, further extending the learning for all.

Recommendations and Conclusions About Sustained Reading Engagement

Something that has become evident to us is that there is a huge difference between momentary reading engagement and sustained reading engagement. Although most of our readers have sustained their engagement beyond an R^5 classroom, some students have become disengaged when in a classroom that did not support independent reading. In addition, maintaining reading growth is of interest to us, as we know that summer reading, or lack of summer reading, plays an important role in sustaining growth. The question remains, How long does it take to move a student from momentary engagement to sustained engagement? How can we continue the level of engagement exhibited at the end of the year through summer?

So is independent reading an important part of developing an engaged reader? We believe it is. But, like many instructional practices, it is not worth doing if used incorrectly. In fact, some common practices, such as leaving students completely to their own devices during this time, can help them learn to be disengaged. Instead of eliminating the practice of independent reading, we engaged in professional dialogue characterized by reflection and research to develop and improve independent reading in school and at home. When structured independent reading is executed well in a conducive environment, monitored, and supported both at school and at home, it is an indispensable part of a quality reading program.

QUESTIONS FOR PROFESSIONAL DEVELOPMENT

1. What are some problems you have experienced with traditional independent reading?
2. What can be gained from structured independent reading, such as R^5 in school and R^4 at home?
3. What are the elements of a classroom environment conducive to engaged reading?

REFERENCES

Allington, R.L. (2006). *What really matters for struggling readers: Designing research-based programs* (2nd ed.). Boston: Allyn & Bacon.

Anderson, R.C. (1996). Research foundations to support wide reading. In V. Greaney (Ed.), *Promoting reading in developing countries* (pp. 55–77). Newark, DE: International Reading Association.

Arthur, J.E. (1995). *What is the effect of recreational reading on reading achievement of middle grade students?* (ERIC Document Reproduction Service No. ED391143)

Asselin, M. (2004). Supporting sustained engagements with texts. *Teacher Librarian, 31*(3), 51–52.

Atwell, N. (1989). *In the middle: Writing, reading, and learning.* Portsmouth, NH: Heinemann.

Baumann, J.F., & Kame'enui, E.J. (1991). Research vocabulary instruction: Ode to Voltaire. In J. Flood, J.M. Jensen, D. Lapp, & J.R. Squire (Eds.), *Handbook of research on teaching the English language arts* (pp. 604–632). New York: Macmillan.

Brozo, W.G., & Hargis, C.H. (2003). Taking seriously the idea of reform: One high school's efforts to make reading more responsive to all students. *Journal of Adolescent & Adult Literacy, 47*(1), 14–23. doi:10.1598/JAAL.47.1.3

Bryan, G., Fawson, P.C., & Reutzel, D.R. (2003). Sustained silent reading: Exploring the value of literature discussion with three non-engaged readers. *Reading Research and Instruction, 43*(1), 47–73.

Clay, M.M. (1991). *Becoming literate: The construction of inner control.* Portsmouth, NH: Heinemann.

Darigan, D.L., Tunnell, M.O., & Jacobs, J.S. (2002). *Children's literature: Engaging teachers and children in good books.* Upper Saddle River, NJ: Prentice Hall.

Fresch, M.J. (1995). Self-selection of early literacy learners. *The Reading Teacher, 49*(3), 220–227.

Gallik, J.D. (1999). Do they read for pleasure? Recreational reading habits of college students. *Journal of Adolescent & Adult Literacy, 42*(6), 480–488.

Gambrell, L.B. (1996). Creating classroom cultures that foster reading motivation. *The Reading Teacher, 50*(1), 14–25.

Gambrell, L.B. (2001). What we know about motivation to read. In R.F. Flippo (Ed.), *Reading researchers in search of common ground* (pp. 129–143). Newark, DE: International Reading Association.

Garan, E.M., & DeVoogd, G. (2008). The benefits of sustained silent reading: Scientific research and common sense converge. *The Reading Teacher, 62*(4), 336–344. doi:10.1598/RT.62.4.6

Guthrie, J.T., Wigfield, A., Metsala, J.L., & Cox, K.E. (1999). Motivational and cognitive predictors of text comprehension and reading amount. *Scientific Studies of Reading, 3*(3), 231–256. doi:10.1207/s1532799xssr0303_3

Hidi, S., & Baird, W. (1986). Interestingness—A neglected variable in discourse processing. *Cognitive Science, 10*(2), 179–194. doi:10.1016/S0364-0213(86)80003-9

Hiebert, E.H. (2006). Becoming fluent: Repeated reading with scaffolded texts. In S.J. Samuels & A.E. Farstrup (Eds.), *What research has to say about fluency instruction* (pp. 204–226). Newark, DE: International Reading Association.

Johnson, D., & Blair, A. (2003). The importance and use of student self-selected literature to reading engagement in an elementary reading curriculum. *Reading Horizons, 43*(3), 181–202.

Kelley, M., & Clausen-Grace, N. (2006). R⁵: The sustained silent reading makeover that transformed readers. *The Reading Teacher, 60*(2), 148–156. doi:10.1598/RT.60.2.5

Kelley, M.J., & Clausen-Grace, N. (2007). *Comprehension shouldn't be silent: From strategy instruction to student independence.* Newark, DE: International Reading Association.

Kelley, M.J., & Clausen-Grace, N. (2008a). *R⁵ in your classroom: A guide to differentiating independent reading and developing avid readers.* Newark, DE: International Reading Association.

Kelley, M.J., & Clausen-Grace, N. (2008b). To read or not to read: Connecting independent reading to direct instruction. *Florida Reading Quarterly, 44*(4), 6–11.

Kelley, M.J., & Clausen-Grace, N. (2009). Facilitating engagement by differentiating independent reading. *The Reading Teacher, 63*(4), 313–318. doi:10.1598/RT.63.4.6

National Institute of Child Health and Human Development. (2000). *Report of the National Reading Panel. Teaching children to read: An evidence-based assessment of the scientific research literature on reading and its implications for reading instruction* (NIH Publication No. 00-4769). Washington, DC: U.S. Government Printing Office.

Ohlhausen, M.M., & Jepsen, M. (1992). Lessons from Goldilocks: "Somebody's been choosing my books but I can make my own choices now!" *The New Advocate, 5*(1), 31–46.

Reutzel, D.R., & Cooter, R.B., Jr. (1992). *Teaching children to read: From basals to books.* New York: Macmillan.

Reutzel, D.R., Jones, C.D., Fawson, P.C., & Smith, J.A. (2008). Scaffolded silent reading: A complement to guided repeated oral reading that works! *The Reading Teacher, 62*(3), 194–207. doi:10.1598/RT.62.3.2

Routman, R. (2003). *Reading essentials: The specifics you need to teach reading well.* Portsmouth, NH: Heinemann.

Schraw, G., Flowerday, T., & Reisetter, M.F. (1998). The role of choice in reader engagement. *Journal of Educational Psychology, 90*(4), 705–714. doi:10.1037/0022-0663.90.4.705

Trudel, H. (2007). Making data-driven decisions: Silent reading. *The Reading Teacher, 61*(4), 308–315. doi:10.1598/RT.61.4.3

Valeri-Gold, M. (1995). Uninterrupted sustained silent reading is an effective authentic method for college developmental learners. *Journal of Reading, 38*(5), 385–386.

Wigfield, A., & Guthrie, J.T. (1997). Relations of children's motivation for reading to the amount and breadth of their reading. *Journal of Educational Psychology, 89*(3), 420–432. doi:10.1037/0022-0663.89.3.420

Williams, L.M., Hedrick, W.B., & Tuschinski, L. (2008). Motivation: Going beyond testing to a lifetime of reading. *Childhood Education, 84*(3), 135–141.

CHAPTER 11

Sharing the Stage: Using Oral and Silent Wide Reading to Develop Proficient Reading in the Early Grades

Paula J. Schwanenflugel
The University of Georgia

Melanie R. Kuhn
Boston University

Gwynne Ellen Ash
Texas State University–San Marcos

In fluency-oriented reading classrooms, oral reading often takes center stage. In our own work in second-grade classrooms, we have focused on programs designed to provide extensive, scaffolded oral reading practice to promote oral reading fluency. By scaffolded practice, we simply mean practices that provide the right amount of support in the decoding of texts. These scaffolding practices gradually release responsibility for reading the texts from the teacher to the students. Scaffolded oral reading practice provides a connection between the social origins of reading (i.e., being read to by an adult) and reading on one's own (Prior & Welling, 2001). The point of these scaffolded practices is to enable students to receive accurate and timely feedback for decoding struggles, so the focus of the activity can be on the oral reading itself, and comprehension of the passage, rather than the decoding activities. These scaffolded practices allow students to read texts that would be too difficult to read on their own. Ultimately, our goal is to encourage the development of quick, accurate, and expressive reading to pave the way to effective silent reading. We believe that good oral reading fluency will necessarily be the foundation on which good silent reading skills are built.

An emphasis on extensive oral reading practice may have particular benefits as compared with silent reading as a developmental classroom practice for students who are learning to read. Oral reading seems to enhance the comprehension of early elementary school students learning to read compared with silent reading (Fuchs, Fuchs, & Maxwell, 1988; Holmes & Allison, 1985; Miller & Smith, 1985, 1990; Mullikin, Henk, & Fortner, 1992). Oral reading provides a certain degree of discipline to prevent students from skipping over difficult words while reading the text

Revisiting Silent Reading: New Directions for Teachers and Researchers, edited by Elfrieda H. Hiebert
and D. Ray Reutzel. © 2010 by the International Reading Association.

(Juel & Holmes, 1981). It may also help to amplify the phonological memory code (i.e., the voice in our heads that we hear as we read) to maintain information in short-term memory long enough so that the student can assemble the message (Gathercole & Baddeley, 1993). In fact, it is not at all unusual for adults to switch to the oral reading mode when they are having difficulty understanding a particularly troublesome piece of text (Hardyck & Petrinovich, 1969). We believe that oral reading may help students better deal with processing difficulties engaged by complex texts.

Our work in classrooms was inspired originally by the Fluency-Oriented Reading Instruction approach (henceforth, FORI) developed by Stahl, Heubach, and Holcomb (2005). They designed FORI for classrooms where the majority of students were reading below grade level with the goal of accelerating fluency's development so that students are quickly able to read texts at grade level. FORI focused on scaffolded reading and extensive repeated readings of the grade-level texts, texts that were at the frustration level for the targeted group of young readers. Using FORI, teachers in the study who were highly schooled in the techniques and who had considerable input in the program's development, brought most of students up to grade level in their reading skills. Unfortunately, despite the enormous success of the Stahl et al. (2005) study, evidence from other repeated reading studies using similar approaches has been more uneven.

In some studies, improved oral reading fluency has been found for some but not all measures (Kuhn, 2005; Kuhn et al., 2006). In others, no improvement in fluency over control groups was found at all (Kuhn & Schwanenflugel, 2007; Rasinski, Padak, Linek, & Sturtevant, 1994; Schwanenflugel et al., 2009). One of our own studies found benefits for FORI on reading fluency (Morrow, Kuhn, & Schwanenflugel, 2006), but that study also had a detailed emphasis on an at-home reading component, so it is unclear whether the effectiveness could be attributed to the well-established benefits of parental involvement on child academic achievement or to the program itself.

Subsequently, our attention has turned to a program developed for small groups by Kuhn (2005) and expanded for whole-class use by Kuhn et al. (2006), which has been more consistent in improving the oral reading fluency of young children. The approach, which we call Wide FORI (Kuhn & Schwanenflugel, 2007), stands for Wide Fluency-Oriented Reading Instruction. Wide FORI bears both similarities to and differences from the basic FORI. Like basic FORI, it emphasizes extensive scaffolded oral and silent reading practice. Unlike basic FORI, it emphasizes reading a wide variety of grade-level texts (Kuhn, 2005; Kuhn et al., 2006), rather than a limited number of texts repeatedly. In Wide FORI, students engage in scaffolded oral and silent reading as they participate in shared reading along with the teacher and with a partner in attempting new texts, or while they practice previously introduced text. In Wide FORI, scaffolded oral and silent reading share the stage.

In this chapter, we describe the Wide FORI approach as implemented in research. We discuss theories underlying Wide FORI that we believe explain its effectiveness. We also explore how to incorporate silent reading into an elementary classroom focused on the development of fluent readers. Finally, we discuss various ways to incorporate silent reading into classroom instruction and how to introduce text for silent reading practice, in independent or partner reading.

What Is Wide Fluency-Oriented Reading Instruction?

Developed to combat standard instructional practice in which young readers actually spend very little time each day reading connected text (cf. Gambrell, 1984; Leinhardt, Zigmond, & Cooley, 1981), Wide FORI seeks to increase the amount of time that students spend reading text to improve both their fluency and comprehension. Yet unlike basic FORI, which focuses on multiple readings of the same text, Wide FORI research suggests that students can experience similar growth in reading skills by spending a similar amount of time reading a variety of texts through scaffolded practice (Kuhn, 2005; Kuhn et al., 2006). A previous meta-analysis carried out by Kuhn and Stahl (2003) has found that, although repeated reading was the primary classroom practice recommended in research for enhancing fluency, extensive oral reading of a wide variety of text often produced much the same result. Consequently, Wide FORI emphasized the reading of three texts per week, presented with the appropriate scaffolding practices, rather than merely one text.

Wide FORI also emphasized the selection of complex texts that are above students' current reading level, rather than the simple texts that teachers usually select for students' fluency practice. The understanding is that, with appropriate scaffolding, students will be able to read texts that have the potential to provide greater long-term reading growth than do simple texts. We discuss the important implications of this view later.

Wide FORI as described by Kuhn et al. (2006) and Schwanenflugel et al. (2009) followed a basic weekly lesson plan (see Table 11.1 for the short version of this plan). On Monday, teachers were asked to introduce a text to the class by engaging in shared reading practice. Teachers were told to read the passage aloud to the class with good expression. Students were to follow the teachers' reading by reading along silently to themselves. The teachers were to roam the classroom while reading to ensure that students were attending to the print. This essentially provided appropriate scaffolds for silent reading practice. Teachers then carried out comprehension activities for the story as they might normally do. This might entail introducing difficult vocabulary, asking literal and inferential comprehension questions, completing graphic organizers, and so forth. Often, students needed to refer back to the text to address these comprehension activities, introducing yet another opportunity for silent reading practice. This generally took teachers 25–40 minutes within their literacy block.

On Tuesday, teachers were asked to echo read the story. Teachers were to read two or three sentences from the story, and students were asked to echo the readings back. Basically, the amount of text that teachers read aloud in their turn of this echo reading was designed to fully exceed the limits of working memory for

Table 11.1. Wide-Reading Approach (Wide FORI) Weekly Lesson Plan

	Monday	Tuesday	Wednesday	Thursday	Friday
Wide-reading instruction lesson plan	Teacher introduces Text 1. Teacher reads story to class, class reads along silently, then discusses story. Option: Teacher develops graphic organizers. Option: Class does activities from basal.	Students echo read story. Option: Students partner read if time allows.	Students do extension activities; these may include writing in response to story, etc. Option: Teacher keeps running records of students' reading.	Option: Students echo read or choral read Text 2. Option: Students partner read story. Option: Students do prereading or extension activities (writing, etc.).	Option: Students echo read or choral read Text 3. Option: Students partner read story. Option: Students do prereading or extension activities (writing, etc.).
Home reading	Students read 15–30 minutes per day in a book of their choosing.	Students take story home and read to parents (or other).	Students read 15–30 minutes per day in a book of their choosing.	Students read 15–30 minutes per day in a book of their choosing.	Students read 15–30 minutes per day in a book of their choosing.

Approach as implemented in "Teaching Children to Become Fluent and Automatic Readers," by M.R. Kuhn, P.J. Schwanenflugel, R.D. Morris, L.M. Morrow, D.G. Woo, E.B. Meisinger, et al., 2006, *Journal of Literacy Research*, 38(4), 357–387.

the students. In this way, they had to focus on the readings and silently read along with the teacher so they could be ready to read it aloud when it was their collective turn to echo the reading back. If there was time, this could be followed up by a partner reading. This partner reading was carried out following recommendations of Meisinger, Schwanenflugel, Bradley, and Stahl (2004). First, students were paired according to contrasting skills (i.e., that there was a student in the pair who might need assistance with the text and a student that could provide it) and friendship patterns (i.e., that students would be able to get along with each other). Second, students took turns reading alternate pages aloud. Note that the side effect of this partner reading practice is that, while one student is reading aloud, the other reads along silently to catch and quickly assist in correcting reading errors. The combined oral practice on the text should take no less than 20 minutes.

On Wednesday, teachers carried out extension activities on the story. Again, these activities should refer often to the text so that students have continued practice in oral or silent reading. These activities should take no less than 20 minutes.

On Thursday, the students echo read a second new text along with the teacher. Again, as with Monday's story, teachers introduced the new story with the appropriate comprehension activities and carried out a discussion of it. If there was time, a partner or choral reading of it could occur as well.

On Friday, the teacher introduced a new third text and carried out an echo reading of it. As with the previous day's text, if there was time, other oral reading practice such as choral or partner reading could be carried out.

Some features should be noted about this wide-reading approach. First, directed oral and silent reading occur in Wide FORI in nearly equal measure. Students read silently along with the teacher as the teacher reads a segment of the text. Then they read the same segment aloud. They first read along silently with their partner. Then they carry out a read-aloud of the next page. Unlike long periods of uninterrupted silent reading, such as found in sustained silent reading practices, however, this silent reading is scaffolded to ensure correct reading of the passage. At all times, the students have been provided with a good model of reading to ameliorate decoding and phrasing issues. Second, the introduction of three new passages a week virtually ensures that teachers will spend at least 20 minutes on oral and silent reading practice of connected text daily. Finally, Wide FORI incorporates the elements of repeated readings, but the emphasis on repetition is not excessive, boring, or unmotivated. With the complexity of the texts used and the constant rotation to new texts, students need the minimal repetition that occurs.

Why Use Wide Reading?

Put simply, wide reading is effective in improving reading fluency. In studies carried out by Kuhn et al. (2006) and Schwanenflugel et al. (2009), which together involved more than 60 classrooms and 800 second-grade students, Wide FORI had a broad impact on the development of reading skills. When used over the school year, the approach led to improved fluency over control group instruction on standardized assessments. It had the added benefit of improving word recognition skills as well (Kuhn, 2005; Kuhn et al., 2006).

Wide reading had implications for other aspects of the reading process. Wide reading was also associated with improved reading comprehension both immediately (Kuhn et al., 2006) and one year later (Schwanenflugel et al., 2009), as could be anticipated if fluency is truly the bridge to comprehension that it is supposed to be. Moreover, participation in wide reading was linked to positive changes in students' reading self-concept, or their perceptions of their own competence as readers (Schwanenflugel et al., 2009), when compared with controls. Indeed, developing good reading skills is related to the development of good reading self-concept (Chapman & Tunmer, 2003). Moreover, a student who considers himself or herself to be a good reader may choose to read more, promoting a cycle of greater fluency (Quirk, Schwanenflugel, & Webb, 2009).

The Wide FORI approach also changed the way classrooms looked. Teachers who used the Wide FORI approach spent more than twice as much time in their

Figure 11.1. Important Components of the Wide-Reading Approach

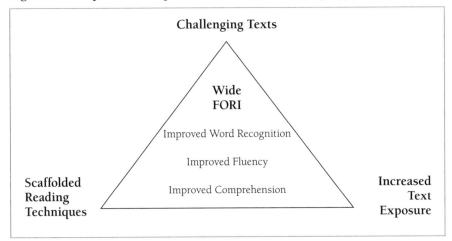

classrooms engaging students in extensive oral reading practice (choral, echo, partner. and repeated read-alouds) than did the control teachers. Ultimately, this meant there was more actual "reading" going on in the reading block.

To what do we attribute the growth of fluency and other reading skills from wide reading? We believe that the benefits from the Wide FORI program are the result of a number of solid principles underlying reading growth (see Figure 11.1). First, the approach encourages the use of scaffolded reading techniques that provide immediate feedback as to the accuracy of the oral reading. Second, students spend a significant amount of time (i.e., 20–40 minutes per day) reading connected text. Third, there was some degree of repetition to enable the development of automaticity. Fourth, and finally, the program encouraged the use of texts that promoted not only reading growth but also conceptual and vocabulary growth in students. We deal with each of these points in greater detail in the following sections.

Scaffolded Reading Practices Assist Reading Growth

As noted, Wide FORI uses a highly scaffolded approach to oral reading. Every introduction of a text is preceded by a teacher reading the text either through a read-aloud or through echo or choral reading. Only then is the text released to the students for their own practice, but even this practice is supported through partner reading.

Concomitantly, with practices that strongly encourage scaffolding, Wide FORI led to a decrease in the use of round robin reading and an increase in students' active interaction with texts (Kuhn et al., 2006). These findings suggest that students in Wide FORI classrooms were actively reading in the reading block. The change in the time spent on round robin reading in Wide FORI is a clear benefit because, according to Ash, Kuhn, and Walpole (2009), round robin reading is ineffective both at increasing students' proficiency with text and improving their comprehension (see also Rasinski & Hoffman, 2003). In fact, students participating in round robin reading are often passive, spending time off-task, reading ahead, or rehearsing their reading rather than listening to the reader and reading along. Nor do students perceive the purpose of their reading to be comprehension. Further, the modeling provided by round robin reading is often weak. The process is interruptive in nature, and reading prosody is often choppy. Finally, the anxiety and emotional distress experienced by many readers when they are required to participate in round robin reading makes the reading an unpleasant experience at best.

In contrast, readers in a Wide FORI classroom progress from very scaffolded oral reading (i.e., shared reading with the teacher undertaking the initial reading), through echo reading, to partner reading and eventually independent reading. In this progression, students are given strong modeling from the teacher up front; these approaches have also been suggested to increase student engagement (Chomsky, 1978; Dowhower, 1989; Labbo & Teale, 1990; Samuels, 1979). Once engaged, students are also reminded through prereading instruction, discussion, and extension activities that comprehension is the end goal of the reading process. The scaffolding also prevents the students from becoming "glued to print" (Chall, 1996, p. 46), allowing them to use their cognitive attention to focus on active meaning making.

Extensive Oral Reading Enables Reading Growth

We should not underestimate the importance of spending significant amounts of time on extensive oral reading practice. Earlier research (cf. Anderson, Wilson, & Fielding, 1988; Heald-Taylor, 1996; Guthrie, 1982; Leinhardt et al., 1981) has suggested that a "book flood," or an increase in text exposure, may improve students' ability to construct meaning. To this, we would add that oral reading, rather than silent reading, while students are in the developmental stages of learning to read is important. Young children, at least until they are significantly along the developmental continuum of reading, seem to understand what they are reading better when reading aloud than when reading silently (Miller & Smith, 1985, 1990).

Importantly, the Wide FORI program encourages teachers to have students practice oral reading for approximately 20–40 minutes per day. We have found in our own studies that when teachers do not spend extensive time on oral reading practice, progress in fluency is limited. In one large study we carried out, we found that teachers tended to spend only 5–10 minutes on reading practice, which, not surprisingly, did not yield the desired progress in reading fluency (Kuhn & Schwanenflugel, 2007). Although we do think that, at some point, the need for oral reading practice can be replaced by silent reading practice (i.e., when students can read with relative fluency), the same 20–40 minutes per day rule for reading connected text should continue to apply throughout schooling. Our research has shown that students in Wide FORI classrooms are engaged in more oral reading of text (Kuhn et al., 2006) than those in regular classrooms. Further, in a 36-week school year, students in a Wide FORI classroom would read 72 more texts than their peers in classrooms that rely on a basal or literature anthology for their weekly reading story—a 200% increase in the minimum number of texts read compared with traditional classrooms!

Repetition Promotes Reading Growth

It is, by this point, well understood by reading researchers and reading teachers alike that, when it comes to reading development, practice does indeed make perfect. In Wide FORI, the texts used in the program are read multiple times during the week. If one examines the weekly lesson plan presented in Table 11.1 closely, one can see that Text 1 is read between two and four times, and Texts 2 and 3 are read generally between one and three times. The amount of repetition of each passage depends on whether the student chose to carry out the assigned additional read-aloud at home and the amount of optional practice that the teacher carries out. However, in no case is the amount of repetition on a given passage excessive. How can such limited practice work to enhance fluency? Much of our understanding of the role of repetition in the development of automaticity and fluency up to this point has seemed to emphasize that considerable repetitive practice is needed to gain proficiency. The Wide FORI program simply does not have this level of repetitive practice.

We take our inspiration from theories of automaticity as described by Logan (1997). According to Logan (1997), every time a student reads a text, a trace of it is laid down in memory. When the student repeats a reading of a text, he or she begins to build up a knowledge base of reading traces. These traces can be at the letter, word, phrase, and higher order levels. Every reading of the same text leaves a trace at each level of representation.

If repetition is so useful, why should more repetition not be better than less? The reason has to do with some current thinking regarding the way that automaticity builds up (Logan, 1997; Logan, Taylor, & Etherton, 1999). When a student first encounters and creates a representation during reading, his or her performance is slow and gradual, or algorithmic, in nature. But rather quickly—researchers suggest within even a few encounters—readers switch from these slow, algorithmic routines to retrieving these past traces from memory. As a result, readers no longer have the need to re-create decoding procedures anew each time they encounter a given word, but instead rely on retrieval (Rawson & Middleton, 2009). Retrieval is quicker than algorithmic processing, so a student who has switched to retrieval reads a passage faster than one who is still algorithmically processing it. This shift toward retrieval and away from algorithmic processing is what we now refer to as automaticity.

When considering the benefits of Wide FORI in comparison with other repeated reading programs, it is the case that adding a few repetitions to the initial encounter with the text gains us much more than adding a repetition to the 100th encounter. To maximize the gains made, it makes sense to optimize the number of repetitions. In other words, there is little point in persisting with the same passage when greater gains may be made by moving on to new ones. In this way, FORI essentially allows us to avoid the situation of diminishing returns and places our classroom energies on the type of practice that can give us the biggest benefit.

Challenging Texts Lead to Reading Growth

The Wide FORI approach provides texts that challenge many students by exposing them to both wide-ranging narratives and significantly greater numbers of expository texts than is typical. In our research, teachers used selections from either the basal reader series or the literature anthology being used as the primary language arts text (Text 1). For the texts used later in the week (Texts 2 and 3), teachers were given grade-level sets of books for their classroom library, one for each student in the room. The wide-reading texts for the second-grade classrooms were chosen on the basis of the Fountas and Pinnell (1999) guided reading levels J–M or N or some other similar leveling system, such as the ones provided by Scholastic or Rigby. It is important to note that sometimes even grade-level basal stories can be quite difficult for many students to read without support (Hiebert, 2009). This research extended earlier findings (Kuhn, 2005; Stahl et al., 2005) that more challenging texts can be used if students have modeling and multiple exposures to the text, and if they are provided with appropriate scaffolded practice with a teacher, parent, or peer.

We consider access to complex texts to be an important ingredient of an effective literacy program throughout the primary grades. We feel the level of complexity should be a factor in determining the texts to which students should be exposed for reading practice. If we think of complexity as a continuum, there will be texts that are too easy for certain students; however, at some point, the level of complexity will go beyond students' ability to comprehend reasonably, even with scaffolding.

At present, students are regularly directed toward what have been called "just right" texts (Cunningham et al., 2005; Stahl, Heubach, & Holcomb, 2005). We think that these "just right" texts have limitations as well as advantages. For example, Wolfe et al. (1998) found that, for adults, the use of texts that were somewhat more sophisticated than their current knowledge level was more effective in further developing that knowledge and vocabulary than were texts that were either too simplistic or too challenging. Assuming that the same pattern occurs for children learning to read, reading somewhat more complex texts could have an enormous impact on their broader reading skills.

Let us consider how this might work. Currently, there are a number of computational linguistic tools that can be used to quantify elements of text complexity beyond usual measures of readability formulas. For example, Coh-Metrix (Graesser, McNamara, Louwerse, & Cai, 2004) is a computational tool that produces a variety of measures of text complexity, among them, lexical difficulty, readability, cohesion, and syntactic complexity. Similarly, CPIDR (Brown, Snodgrass, Kemper, Herman, & Covington, 2008) is a computational tool that produces counts of idea units and a measure of complexity called propositional idea density (i.e., ratio of propositions to the number of words in the text). For the most part, these tools have been used to measure the complexity of texts for older, sophisticated readers, rather than the texts typically provided for young children. But we have used them here to compare texts varying along the Scholastic and Fountas and Pinell book-leveling continuums. The leveling systems used by publishers are designed around children's readability more than anything else, but our analysis has shown that they also distinguish books according to conceptual complexity.

To illustrate our point, we analyzed 16 books (shown in Table 11.2) that we had at our disposal and for which the Scholastic website provided grade and Fountas and Pinnell levels. Essentially, we compared eight second-grade books that were relatively easy (roughly, Scholastic Grade Level of 2.1–2.5) against eight somewhat more difficult books (roughly, Scholastic Grade Level 2.8–3.8). All the books were within Fountas and Pinnell levels J through N.

We input the first 150 words or so (to the nearest end of sentence) of each book in these Coh-Metrix and CPIDR tools to determine if there were other ways in which the books differ outside of standard readability. Indeed, there were several ways in which the easy and difficult texts differed. First, difficult books showed greater causal cohesion than simple books did. That is, a text is said to be cohesive in a causal way if event A in the story had not occurred, then, event B in the story would not have occurred. Let us take the first few sentences from one of our difficult texts, *Make Way for Ducklings* (McCloskey, 1941):

Table 11.2. Text Complexity Analysis of a 150-Word Segment of 16 Second-Grade Books

Easy	Hard
Big Max (Platt, 1965)	*Amber Brown Goes Fourth* (Danziger, 1995)
Days With Frog and Toad (Lobel, 1979)	*Dinosaurs Before Dark* (Osborne, 1992)
Frog and Toad Are Friends (Lobel, 1970)	*Lentil* (McCloskey, 1957)
Green Eggs and Ham (Seuss, 1960)	*Make Way for Ducklings* (McCloskey, 1941)
Henry and Mudge and the Best Day of All (Rylant, 1995)	*Matilda the Moocher* (Bluthenthal, 1997)
Hooray for the Golly Sisters! (Byars, 1990)	*Rudi's Pond* (Bunting, 1999)
Little Red Hen (Galdone, 1973)	*Sleeping Ugly* (Yolen, 1981)
Teach Us, Amelia Bedelia (Parish, 1977)	*Thunder Cake* (Polacco, 1990)

Mr. and Mrs. Mallard were looking for a place to live. But every time Mr. Mallard saw what looked like a nice place, Mrs. Mallard said it was no good. There were sure to be foxes in the woods or turtles in the water, and she was not going to raise a family where there might be foxes or turtles. (n.p.)

Note that in this case, Mrs. Mallard's reaction was the direct result of Mr. Mallard's choice. The underlying cause for the choice is provided right away. Having a clear, causal connection between events has been shown to assist story comprehension and recall (Trabasso & Sperry, 1985). Narratives, such as the books we chose for this analysis, are more likely to have causally related bits of text than, say, expository texts, but expository texts can have them, too.

Difficult books also showed greater idea overlap (i.e., argument overlap; Kintsch & van Dijk, 1978) than simple books did. Argument overlap refers to the extent to which sentences in the text share common nouns, linking pronouns, noun phrases, or word stems. If we consider the text excerpt above, among other things, we can see that *Mallard, Mr., Mrs., place, foxes,* and *turtles* are presented over and over (and indirectly with the pronouns *she* and *it*). Both high causal cohesion and argument overlap should enhance comprehensibility. What is important to consider, however, is that cognitively every time an argument or cohesive event is brought up within text (assuming that the student makes the connection), it is likely that the antecedent text is also implicitly referred to and implicitly rehearsed. This may have indirect effects on fluency on its own.

There were several ways in which more difficult texts were truly more difficult. The more difficult books were statistically significantly denser in term of ideas (i.e., more idea units per words in the text) than easy books were. They also had greater lexical diversity (i.e., greater type-token ratio or the number of unique words over the number of words in the text). In the long term, then, emphasis on more difficult books might provide students with greater vocabulary and introduction of more ideas for each minute spent reading. This, too, might have the effect of enhancing fluency over the long term.

Practice with difficult text may also assist in the development of fluency indirectly through its encouragement of expressive reading. Expressiveness is generally determined by reading prosody. Prosody is the music of language and captures changes in pitch, rhythm, stress, pause, and elision associated with certain words and phrases in oral communication. Prosody acoustically brackets key informational units such as phrases and assists in maintaining an utterance in working memory until a more complete semantic analysis can be carried out (Koriat, Greenberg, & Kreiner, 2002). Prosody is well designed to scaffold comprehension.

As students become fluent readers, they move from reading word by word in a staccato fashion to reading with expression or good intonation (Cowie, Douglas-Cowie, & Wichmann, 2002; Miller & Schwanenflugel, 2006, 2008; Schwanenflugel, Hamilton, Kuhn, Wisenbaker, & Stahl, 2004). Developing good reading prosody is related to the development of good fluency and comprehension (Miller & Schwanenflugel, 2006, 2008).

Complex texts may call on the cognitive functions of reading prosody more than simple texts do because they tax working memory. Benjamin and Schwanenflugel (2010) analyzed the prosody of children reading a difficult (i.e., above grade-level text) and a simple text and found that the complex text encouraged more prosodic readings in both second graders and adults. Further, Young and Bowers (1995) found that the parsing ability (which is somewhat related to prosody) in children actually increased as a function of text difficulty rather than decreased. Taken together, these findings provide converging support for the proposition that more complex texts might encourage more prosodic readings, enhancing their overall reading fluency.

Note that all of these aspects of text difficulty may have the effect of increasing students' fluency and comprehension. Cohesive texts scaffold comprehension while encouraging students to set up new ideas and vocabulary in memory. Moreover, having three rather than one of such texts each week will greatly expand students' linguistic and knowledge base. The implicit repetition and reference to new ideas and vocabulary through cohesion processes, as well as through actual repeated readings, may have the effect of automatizing multiple new concepts.

How Might Teachers Move Students Toward Silent Reading Using Wide FORI?

Eventually, students need to make the transition to silent reading, and a continued emphasis on oral reading beyond the appropriate developmental point may impede their progress. Simply put, students should reach a point where they will be able to read faster silently than orally (Coke, 1974). To aid this process, it may be possible that some of the oral reading practice in the Wide FORI approach might be carried over to silent reading practice, thereby helping to scaffold students as they make the transition from oral reading to silent reading. Recent research suggests that scaffolded silent reading (ScSR; Reutzel, Fawson, & Smith, 2008; Reutzel, Jones, Fawson, & Smith, 2008) creates equal fluency growth (with a slight advantage in expression) as Guided Repeated Oral Reading with Feedback (GROR), which is a procedure that is similar to paired repeated reading when undertaken with peers. "ScSR makes use of silent, wide reading of independent-level texts selected from varied genres; periodic teacher monitoring of and interaction with individual students; and accountability through completed book response assignments" (Reutzel, Fawson, et al., 2008, p. 39; see the discussion on ScSR in Chapter 8, this volume). An interesting finding in the ScSR research was that too much of either approach was viewed as monotonous by the students. Reutzel and his colleagues suggested that students might respond well to variations in the approaches to fluency development.

In addition to variation being linked to increased motivation to read (see also Schwanenflugel et al., 2009), other research suggests that the wide-reading element of the Wide FORI approach might be increased through more inclusion of silent reading. Silent reading takes approximately one third less time than does oral reading to complete a text, with no corresponding loss in comprehension (McCallum, Sharp, Bell, & George, 2004); so if the amount of time spent on silent reading is similar to the 20–40 minutes we recommend, silent reading could result in considerably more text being processed throughout the school year than oral reading. A focus on moving students to silent reading will permit them to encounter a greater variety of texts through the weeks.

Both oral and silent reading fluency may be increased through Wide FORI reading approaches. Greenwood, Tapia, Abbott, and Walton (2003) show that the use of scaffolded oral reading practices in the classroom, such as those practiced in Wide FORI, resulted in larger slopes in silent reading growth for second graders than for other second graders who were not exposed to such practices. Likewise, research that attempted to increase the silent reading fluency of students who struggle indicate that when these students are pushed to increase their silent reading rate through accelerated training, they experience both increased rate and comprehension in their silent reading (Snellings, van der Leij, de Jong, & Blok, 2009).

Teachers looking to increase the silent reading in their early reading classrooms might consider that recent research on ScSR, the efficacy of silent reading for meeting comprehension goals, and the promise of combining oral and silent reading practice may offer a rationale for adaptations of the wide-reading approach in practice.

How can Wide FORI be modified for additional silent reading practice? We think that the transition to silent reading should be experimented with for typical students in the second half to last quarter of second grade. By third grade, there needs to be an orderly transition from an emphasis on oral reading to silent reading practice. Indeed, we believe that, for most students, the need for Wide FORI can be reserved for the most difficult texts by the end of third grade. Table 11.3 presents what we think might be a good approach for intensifying the inclusion of silent reading practice within the structure of Wide FORI. Of course, this has yet to be tested empirically.

There are several features worth noting about the lesson plan presented in Table 11.3. The plan inherently assumes that the transition to silent reading will occur at different times for students at different fluency levels. The scaffolded instructional practices will continue to exist for students who need it. Yet all students end up reading the same complex, challenging texts, sharing in the same benefits for comprehension and linguistic growth.

Conclusions About Wide FORI and Silent Reading

In this chapter, we have provided an enhanced sense of the underlying theoretical viewpoint as to why we believe Wide FORI is an appropriate and effective means of enhancing students' reading fluency and comprehension. Good oral reading fluency is predictive of good silent reading fluency later. We have also described

Table 11.3. Wide FORI Transition Approach to Silent Reading

	Monday	Tuesday	Wednesday	Thursday	Friday
Wide-reading instruction lesson plan	Teacher introduces story. Students do prereading activity. Teacher reads Text 1 to class, class reads along silently (shared reading), then discusses story.	Students choral/echo/partner read Text 1 with teacher. Students partner read Text 1, with one partner reading orally, while the other reads along silently. Pairs complete graphic organizers or other comprehension activities that scaffold their comprehension.	Students reread Text 1 silently. Students do extension activities: writing in response to story, reading a similar story and making connections, etc. Teacher assesses students' oral reading on Text 1. Text 2 is introduced.	Students partner read Text 2 or read Text 2 silently. Teacher works with students who need additional scaffolding for Text 2, carrying out echo or choral reading. Struggling readers follow up with partner reading. Students do extension activities connecting Texts 1 and 2, or over Text 2 alone. Text 3 is introduced.	Students partner read Text 3 or read Text 2 silently. Teacher works with students who need additional scaffolding for Text 3, carrying out echo or choral reading. Struggling readers follow up with partner reading. Students do extension activities connecting Texts 1, 2, and 3 or over Text 3 alone. Students reflect on strategies learned and used and the connections among or between the stories across the week.
Home reading	Students take Text 1 and read to parents (or other) aloud or read silently.	Students read silently 15–30 minutes daily in self-chosen book.	Students take Text 2 home to read silently (with scaffolded guide).	Students take Text 3 home to read silently (with scaffolded guide).	Students read 15–30 minutes per day in a book of their choosing.

why an emphasis on complex texts may permit more than just the development of good oral reading fluency, a reading goal that, in itself, serves a partial bridge to comprehension. Wide reading permits students to have greater access to new worlds and new concepts with greater, and more optimal, comprehension, ultimately what reading is all about.

REFERENCES

Anderson, R.C., Wilson, P.T., & Fielding, L.G. (1988). Growth in reading and how children spend their time outside of school. *Reading Research Quarterly*, 23(3), 285–303. doi:10.1598/RRQ.23.3.2

Ash, G.E., Kuhn, M.R., & Walpole, S. (2009). Analyzing "inconsistencies" in practice: Teachers' continued use of round robin reading. *Reading & Writing Quarterly*, 25(1), 87–103. doi:10.1080/1573560802491257

Benjamin, R., & Schwanenflugel, P.J. (2010). *Text complexity and oral reading prosody in young readers. Reading Research Quarterly*, 45(4).

Brown, C., Snodgrass, T., Kemper, S.J., Herman, R., & Covington, M.A. (2008). Automatic measurement of propositional idea density from part-of-speech tagging. *Behavior Research Methods*, 40(2), 540–545.

Chall, J.S. (1996). *Stages of reading development* (2nd ed.). Fort Worth, TX: Harcourt Brace.

Chapman, J.W., & Tunmer, W.E. (2003). Reading difficulties, reading-related self-perceptions, and strategies for overcoming negative self-beliefs. *Reading and Writing Quarterly: Overcoming Learning Difficulties*, 19(1), 5–24.

Chomsky, C. (1978). When you still can't read in third grade after decoding, what? In S.J. Samuels (Ed.), *What research has to say about reading instruction* (pp. 13–30). Newark, DE: International Reading Association.

Coke, E.U. (1974). The effects of readability on oral and silent reading rates. *Journal of Educational Psychology*, 66(3), 406–409. doi:10.1037/h0036511

Cowie, R., Douglas-Cowie, E., & Wichmann, A. (2002). Prosodic characteristics of skilled reading: Fluency and expressiveness in 8–10-year-old readers. *Language and Speech*, 45(1), 47–82. doi:10.1177/00238309020450010301

Cunningham, J.W., Spadorcia, S.A., Erickson, K.A., Koppenhaver, D.A., Sturm, J.M., & Yoder, D.E. (2005). Investigating the instructional supportiveness of leveled texts. *Reading Research Quarterly*, 40(4), 410–427. doi:10.1598/RRQ.40.4.2

Dowhower, S.L. (1989). Repeated reading: Research into practice. *The Reading Teacher*, 42(7), 502–507.

Fountas, I.C., & Pinnell, G.S. (1999). *Matching books to readers: Using leveled books in guided reading, K–3*. Portsmouth, NH: Heinemann.

Fuchs, L.S., Fuchs, D., & Maxwell, L. (1988). The validity of informal reading comprehension measures. *Remedial and Special Education*, 9(2), 20–28. doi:10.1177/074193258800900206

Gambrell, L.B. (1984). How much time do children spend reading during teacher-directed reading instruction? In J.A. Niles & L.A. Harris (Eds.), *Changing perspectives on research in reading/language processing and instruction: 33rd yearbook of the National Reading Conference* (pp. 193–198). Rochester, NY: National Reading Conference.

Gathercole, S.E., & Baddeley, A.D. (1993). *Working memory and language*. New York: Psychology Press.

Graesser, A.C., McNamara, D.S., Louwerse, M.M., & Cai, Z. (2004). Coh-Metrix: Analysis of text on cohesion and language. *Behavior Research Methods*, 36(2), 193–202.

Greenwood, C.R., Tapia, Y., Abbott, M., & Walton, C. (2003). A building-based case study of evidence-based literacy practices: Implementation, reading behavior, and growth in reading fluency, K–4. *The Journal of*

Special Education, 37(2), 95–110. doi:10.1177/0 0224669030370020401

Guthrie, J.T. (1982). Research: The book flood. *Journal of Reading, 26*(3), 286–288.

Hardyck, C.D., & Petrinovich, L.F. (1969). Treatment of subvocal speech during reading. *Journal of Reading, 12*(5), 361–368, 419–422.

Heald-Taylor, B.G. (1996). Three paradigms for literature instruction in grades 3 to 6. *The Reading Teacher, 49*(6), 456–466.

Hiebert, E.H. (2009). The (mis)match between texts and students who depend on schools to become literate. In E.H. Hiebert & M. Sailors (Eds.), *Finding the right texts: What works for beginning and struggling readers* (pp. 1–20). New York: Guilford.

Holmes, B.C., & Allison, R.W. (1985). The effect of four modes of reading on children's comprehension. *Reading Research and Instruction, 25*(1), 9–20.

Juel, C., & Holmes, B. (1981). Oral and silent reading of sentences. *Reading Research Quarterly, 16*(4), 545–568. doi:10.2307/747315

Kintsch, W., & van Dijk, T.A. (1978). Toward a model of text comprehension and production. *Psychological Review, 85*(5), 363–394. doi:10.1037/0033-295X.85.5.363

Koriat, A., Greenberg, S.N., & Kreiner, H. (2002). The extraction of structure during reading: Evidence from reading prosody. *Memory & Cognition, 30*(2), 270–280.

Kuhn, M.R. (2005). A comparative study of small group fluency instruction. *Reading Psychology, 26*(2), 127–146. doi:10.1080/02702710590930492

Kuhn, M.R., & Schwanenflugel, P.J. (2007, May). *Time, engagement, and support: Lessons from a five-year fluency intervention.* Paper presented at the preconference institute #6 of the annual meeting of the International Reading Association, Toronto, ON, Canada.

Kuhn, M.R., Schwanenflugel, P.J., Morris, R.D., Morrow, L.M., Woo, D.G., Meisinger, E.B., et al. (2006). Teaching children to become fluent and automatic readers. *Journal of Literacy Research, 38*(4), 357–387. doi:10.1207/s15548430jlr3804_1

Kuhn, M.R., & Stahl, S.A. (2003). Fluency: A review of developmental and remedial practices. *Journal of Educational Psychology, 95*(1), 3–21.

Labbo, L.D., & Teale, W.H. (1990). Cross-age reading: A strategy for helping poor readers. *The Reading Teacher, 43*(6), 362–369.

Leinhardt, G., Zigmond, N., & Cooley, W.W. (1981). Reading instruction and its effects. *American Educational Research Journal, 18*(3), 343–361.

Logan, G.D. (1997). Automaticity and reading: Perspectives from the instance theory of automatization. *Reading & Writing Quarterly, 13*(2), 123–146. doi:10.1080/1057356970130203

Logan, G.D., Taylor, S.E., & Etherton, J.L. (1999). Attention and automaticity: Toward a theoretical integration. *Psychological Research, 62*(2/3), 165–181. doi:10.1007/s004260050049

McCallum, R.S., Sharp, S., Bell, S.M., & George, T. (2004). Silent versus oral reading comprehension and efficiency. *Psychology in the Schools, 41*(2), 241–246. doi:10.1002/pits.10152

Meisinger, E.B., Schwanenflugel, P.J., Bradley, B.A., & Stahl, S.A. (2004). Interaction quality during partner reading. *Journal of Literacy Research, 36*(2), 111–140. doi:10.1207/s15548430jlr3602_1

Miller, J., & Schwanenflugel, P.J. (2006). Prosody of syntactically complex sentences in the oral reading of young children. *Journal of Educational Psychology, 98*(4), 839–853. doi:10.1037/0022-0663.98.4.839

Miller, J., & Schwanenflugel, P.J. (2008). A longitudinal study of the development of reading prosody as a dimension of oral reading fluency in early elementary school children. *Reading Research Quarterly, 43*(4), 336–354. doi:10.1598/RRQ.43.4.2

Miller, S.D., & Smith, D.E. (1985). Differences in literal and inferential comprehension after reading orally and silently. *Journal of Educational Psychology, 77*(3), 341–348. doi:10.1037/0022-0663.77.3.341

Miller, S.D., & Smith, D.E. (1990). Relations among oral reading, silent reading and listening comprehension of students at differing competency levels. *Reading Research and Instruction, 29*(2), 73–84.

Morrow, L.M., Kuhn, M.R., & Schwanenflugel, P.J. (2006). The family fluency program. *The Reading Teacher, 60*(4), 322–333. doi:10.1598/RT.60.4.2

Mullikin, C.N., Henk, W.H., & Fortner, B.H. (1992). Effects of story versus play genres on the comprehension of high, average, and low-achieving junior high readers. *Reading Psychology, 13*(4), 273–290.

Prior, S.M., & Welling, K.A. (2001). "Read in your head": A Vygotskian analysis of the transition from oral to silent reading. *Reading Psychology*, 22(1), 1–15. doi:10.1080/02702710151130172

Quirk, M., Schwanenflugel, P.J., & Webb, M. (2009). A short-term longitudinal study of the relationship between motivation to read and reading fluency skill in second grade. *Journal of Literacy Research*, 41(2), 196–227. doi:10.1080/10862960902908467

Rasinski, T.V., & Hoffman, J.V. (2003). Oral reading in the school literacy curriculum. *Reading Research Quarterly*, 38(4), 510–522. doi:10.1598/RRQ.38.4.5

Rasinski, T.V., Padak, N.D., Linek, W.L., & Sturtevant, E. (1994). Effects of fluency development on urban second-grade readers. *The Journal of Educational Research*, 87(3), 158–165.

Rawson, K.A., & Middleton, E.L. (2009). Memory-based processing as a mechanism of automaticity in text comprehension. *Journal of Experimental Psychology: Learning, Memory, and Cognition*, 35(2), 353–370. doi:10.1037/a0014733

Reutzel, D.R., Fawson, P.C., & Smith, J.A. (2008). Reconsidering silent sustained reading: An exploratory study of scaffolded silent reading. *The Journal of Educational Research*, 102(1), 37–50. doi:10.3200/JOER.102.1.37-50

Reutzel, D.R., Jones, C.D., Fawson, P.C., & Smith, J.A. (2008). Scaffolded silent reading: A complement to guided repeated oral reading that works! *The Reading Teacher*, 62(3), 194–207. doi:10.1598/RT.62.3.2

Samuels, S.J. (1979). The method of repeated readings. *The Reading Teacher*, 32(4), 403–408.

Schwanenflugel, P.J., Hamilton, A.M., Kuhn, M.R., Wisenbaker, J.M., & Stahl, S.A. (2004). Becoming a fluent reader: Reading skill and prosodic features in the oral reading of young readers. *Journal of Educational Psychology*, 96(1), 119–129. doi:10.1037/0022-0663.96.1.119

Schwanenflugel, P.J., Kuhn, M.R., Morris, R.D., Morrow, L.M., Meisinger, E.B., Woo, D.G., et al. (2009). Insights into fluency instruction: Short- and long-term effects of two reading programs. *Literacy Research and Instruction*, 48(4), 318–336. doi:10.1080/19388070802422415

Snellings, P., van der Leij, A., de Jong, P.F., & Blok, H. (2009). Enhancing the reading fluency and comprehension of children with reading disabilities in an orthographically transparent language. *Journal of Learning Disabilities*, 42(4), 291–305. doi:10.1177/0022219408331038

Stahl, S.A., Heubach, K.M., & Holcomb, A. (2005). Fluency-oriented reading instruction. *Journal of Literacy Research*, 37(1), 25–60. doi:10.1207/s15548430jlr3701_2

Trabasso, T., & Sperry, L.L. (1985). Causal relatedness and importance of story events. *Journal of Memory and Language*, 24(5), 595–611. doi:10.1016/0749-596X(85)90048-8

Wolfe, M.B.W., Schreiner, M.E., Rehder, B., Laham, D., Foltz, P.W., Kintsch, W., et al. (1998). Learning from text: Matching readers and text by latent semantic analysis. *Discourse Processes*, 25(2/3), 309–336. doi:10.1080/01638539809545030

Young, A., & Bowers, P.G. (1995). Individual difference and text difficulty determinants of reading fluency and expressiveness. *Journal of Experimental Child Psychology*, 60(3), 428–454. doi:10.1006/jecp.1995.1048

LITERATURE CITED

McCloskey, R. (1941). *Make Way for Ducklings*. New York: Viking.

CHAPTER 12

The Impact of Professional Development on Students' Opportunity to Read

Devon Brenner

Mississippi State University

Elfrieda H. Hiebert

University of California, Berkeley

For seven weeks, third-grade teachers and literacy coaches in Reading First schools met for hour-long peer-coaching study team meetings to work through a set of professional development modules called Eyes on Text (Brenner, Hiebert, Riley, Tompkins, & Holland, 2008). During these meetings, teachers reflected on the logs they were keeping that recorded the time students read during reading instruction. Literacy coaches led discussions of teaching practices for increasing opportunity to read such as partner reading and repeated reading and, together, teachers and coaches evaluated the core reading program and one another's lesson plans for opportunity to read.

This study examines the impact of these Eyes on Text modules on reading instruction. Their effects were measured by documenting the amount that students read before and after the professional development. Before discussing the results of the study, we provide a rationale for investing in seven weeks of professional development focused on increasing opportunity to read. Following this, we discuss the research base on effective professional development for teachers, particularly the peer-coaching study team model.

Background for the Study

Opportunity to Read

Amidst the attention paid to ensuring that all of the skills and strategies involved in reading are taught, a basic premise of learning to read that frequently slips under the radar is that students need to regularly and frequently participate in the act of reading to become good at it. Students benefit from lessons where particular features and strategies of literacy are explicitly taught but, at the same time, proficient reading requires that students spend time reading and learning from text. Guthrie, Schafer, and Huang (2001) have coined the term *opportunity to read* (OtR)

Revisiting Silent Reading: New Directions for Teachers and Researchers, edited by Elfrieda H. Hiebert and D. Ray Reutzel. © 2010 by the International Reading Association.

to describe the occasions in classrooms when students read connected texts for extended periods of time. Three areas of scholarship provide the rationale for our emphasis of OtR and the design of our project: (1) the relationship between OtR and reading proficiency, (2) the effects of OtR on specific dimensions of reading, and (3) salient aspects for designing effective OtR.

The Relationship Between OtR and Reading Proficiency. Evidence is compelling that OtR is associated with literacy performance. Foorman et al. (2006), for example, used hierarchical linear modeling to examine the relationship between various instructional practices and impact on reading achievement for 1,285 first graders. Time allocated to reading was the only variable that significantly explained gains on any of the posttest measures, including word reading, decoding, and passage comprehension. Other time factors, such as time spent on word, alphabetic instruction, and phonemic awareness instruction, did not independently contribute to growth in reading achievement.

In a large-scale experiment, Block, Cleveland, and Reed (2006) compared the addition of 20 minutes of core program instruction, workbook instruction, or reading trade books to the standard 70-minute reading block in second-, third-, fourth-, and sixth-grade classrooms. Simply increasing basal instruction and workbook practice did not increase achievement; however, providing students with an additional 20 minutes of reading trade book literature supported vocabulary, comprehension, and fluency development.

Wu and Samuels (2004) conducted a quasi-experimental study to examine the impact of adding independent reading to existing reading instruction. The study was conducted in both third- and fifth-grade classrooms. In some classrooms, students read for an additional 15 minutes daily, while in other classrooms, the length of additional daily reading was 40 minutes. The students who read for 40 minutes had significantly better reading achievement, particularly in reading comprehension, than the students who read for 15 minutes. Guthrie et al. (2001) found that students who scored proficient and advanced on the National Assessment of Educational Progress (NAEP) read twice as many words during school than students who scored below basic. These and other studies (e.g., Kuhn & Schwanenflugel, 2009; Taylor, Frye, & Maruyama, 1990) suggest that student achievement in reading is related to OtR. It may be especially important for low-achieving students, such as those in Reading First classrooms, to receive increased OtR during the school day. Low-achieving students tend not to read at home (Cunningham & Stanovich, 1998). They may have limited access to texts, little support for reading, and little incentive to practice at home a skill they have struggled with during the school day.

The Effects of OtR on Specific Dimensions of Reading. Considerable evidence has amassed that the ability to read with fluency—with appropriate rate and expression—is highly related to comprehension (Daane, Campbell, Grigg, Goodman, & Oranje, 2005; Fuchs, Fuchs, Hosp, & Jenkins, 2001; National

Institute of Child Health and Human Development [NICHD], 2000). Fluent readers have developed automaticity with a critical number of words in a text, and that automaticity frees up attention resources, supporting meaningful reading (LaBerge & Samuels, 1974). OtR supports the development of reading fluency. Research by Kuhn and colleagues (e.g., Kuhn et al., 2006; Kuhn & Schwanenflugel, 2009) has shown that by increasing the amount of text read (i.e., providing several texts rather than a single basal passage for a week's instruction and practice), students' fluency can be enhanced. Just seven additional minutes of reading distinguished the classrooms of students whose fluency levels rose from those where fluency levels were stagnant, regardless of whether or not their teachers participated in a fluency intervention (Kuhn & Schwanenflugel, 2009). Kuhn et al. (2006) conclude that "increasing the amount of time children spend reading challenging connected text with the proper scaffolds will lead to improvements in word reading efficiency and reading comprehension" (p. 382).

OtR also supports comprehension through its effects on vocabulary acquisition. The vocabulary of written texts is more sophisticated than that of oral language (Hayes, Wolfer, & Wolfe, 1996), and students who read more are exposed to more words (Critchley, 1998). Explicit vocabulary instruction on particular words is effective and may be essential for teaching specific words students need for content area instruction or reading a particular text; however, Stahl and Fairbanks (1986) demonstrate that students can learn only about 8 to 10 words a week, or 400 words a year, through direct, explicit word instruction. The gap between this amount and the tens of thousands of unique words in textbooks can be addressed through incidental learning of vocabulary (Herman, Anderson, Pearson, & Nagy, 1987). Herman et al. (1987) estimate that, with a modicum of daily reading (i.e., approximately 15 minutes), students can acquire the meanings of up to 75 words weekly or approximately 3,000 words a year. As the National Reading Panel (NRP; NICHD, 2000) concludes, both direct instruction and incidental learning are needed if students' vocabularies are to grow. Students who know more words are more likely to recognize and read words in new texts, supporting comprehension and increasing the likelihood of future reading (Cunningham & Stanovich, 1998).

Increased OtR may also support comprehension, in that wide reading supports the development of background knowledge. Wide reading builds knowledge of the world in ways that other media do not (Cunningham & Stanovich, 1998). Successful reading of a text about a topic such as spiders or medieval castles supports future readings of other texts about the topic (Reutzel & Hollingsworth, 1991). Time spent reading may also help readers to internalize understanding of text structures (Richgels, McGee, Lomax, & Sheard, 1987). Readers familiar with the ways in which narratives and expository texts are organized can use those resources to mentally organize the texts they read, supporting comprehension.

Salient Aspects for Designing Effective OtR. OtR, then, supports reading achievement by building fluency, vocabulary, and background knowledge. However, OtR is not only a function of the provision of time for reading but also the use that students make of the time they are given to read. Engaged reading—extended reading in which students actively work to make meaning of the text, apply strategies, learn content, or become involved in the plot—supports reading growth in ways that simply running your eyes over the page does not (Guthrie, 2004; Guthrie et al., 2001). Multiple factors in the classroom and environment can influence students' engagement, but three aspects of text seem to be especially salient to the quality and quantity of OtR: difficulty, genre, and format.

Text difficulty affects reading engagement in complex ways. Students may be bored or disinterested in texts that they perceive as too easy. Students seem to derive a small benefit from reading slightly challenging texts rather than texts that are easy (Miller & Meece, 1999). In general, however, the greater concern is with texts that are too difficult to read. Readers are unlikely to engage in sustained reading of texts that they find too challenging to read (Allington, 2001; Gambrell, Wilson, & Gantt, 1981). Struggling readers, in particular, are frequently asked to read texts with vocabulary far beyond that with which they are proficient (Hiebert, 2009).

Scaffolding may support struggling readers in reading texts that are too difficult for independent reading. Scaffolding can include instructional procedures such as choral reading, repeated reading, and following along as someone else reads aloud. We call these forms of reading *assisted reading*, because the reader receives assistance during reading. Kuhn and Stahl (2003) propose that assisted reading gives students access to more challenging text, provides models of fluent reading, and allows struggling students multiple exposures to difficult words that they would not encounter by reading text alone. Although assisted reading may provide support that allows students to engage with more difficult texts and even build fluency (NICHD, 2000), unassisted reading of readable texts may do more for building reading comprehension. During unassisted reading, students are responsible for using all of the processes of reading to comprehend, such as making connections or reading ahead to figure out unknown words—strategies students may not apply when they are engaging in assisted reading (Frey, Fisher, & Berkin, 2008). In general, then, teachers must find a balance between providing readers with texts they can read without assistance and challenging texts that may require assistance.

Genre of text also affects reading engagement. In many primary-grade classrooms, students read narrative texts almost exclusively (Duke, 2000; Symons, MacLatchy-Gaudet, Stone, & Reynolds, 2001). A balance between informational and narrative texts, however, is important for building reading proficiency. Duke and Bennett-Armistead (2003) argue that students benefit from the inclusion of informational text in the classroom, because such texts pervade daily life (e.g., newspapers, Internet, user manuals), allow for exploration of interests, and answer questions students have about the world around them. Informational text also provides support for struggling readers, in that it often defines and repeats new vocabulary in ways that narrative text often does not (Hiebert, 2010). Although teachers often assume that young and beginning readers prefer narrative texts, this assumption is likely to be inaccurate. Cervetti, Bravo, Hiebert, Pearson, and Jaynes (2009) found that third and fourth graders, including struggling readers, equally preferred informational and narrative texts.

The format of text refers to whether the text is a selection in the core program basal, a leveled text that accompanied the core program, or another format, such as a trade book or a multimedia text. Although the core program provides a common text for reading instruction, many passages may be too difficult for some readers and too easy for others, and it is often used to the exclusion of other texts. Leveled readers can be used to match students with readable texts for guided reading and for independent reading practice (Fountas & Pinnell, 1999), which can foster greater engagement. Trade books have been shown to improve achievement and motivation when they are part of classroom instruction (Morrow, 1992).

The Eyes on Text professional development aimed to provide teachers with strategies to increase OtR during the school day. The professional development involved a set of instructional modules that provided a rationale and strategies for increasing OtR and also addressed aspects of reading engagement by encouraging teachers to select readable text, to incorporate a variety of genres of text (especially informational text), and to examine their ratio of assisted versus unassisted reading.

Eyes on Text Professional Development

Bringing about change in teaching practices is no easy task. Anders, Hoffman, and Duffy (2000) reviewed research on professional development and inservice teacher learning and concluded that professional development that focuses on teacher knowledge, teacher thinking, and decision making can bring about changes in teaching practice, but "intensive levels of support, with sustained and concentrated effort, are critical for success" (p. 730). Traditionally, much professional development has followed an ineffective model of delivering information to teachers, who are then expected to apply it in the classroom. In recent decades, however, professional development has been based on deepening understandings of teacher cognition as both situated and social (Putnam & Borko, 2000).

Theories of situated cognition (Cobb & Bowers, 1999; Greeno, 1997) emphasize that learning is influenced by the physical and social contexts in which learning takes place. That is, where and how learning occurs affects what is learned. Effective professional development includes authentic activities—activities situated in problems of real classroom practice. An example of effective professional development might involve analyzing student data and conducting an action research study around an intervention designed to address data-driven problems (National Staff Development Council, 2001).

Theories of social cogitation emphasize the social nature of learning (Resnick, 1991; Soltis, 1981) and suggest that what we know and how we act are influenced by our social interactions. As we interact with others, we acquire their ways of thinking, acting, and perceiving. Effective professional development allows time for teacher interaction by organizing teachers into learning communities and supporting collaboration, often with a more knowledgeable peer or expert (National Staff Development Council, 2001).

Current models of professional development based on an understanding of teacher learning as situated and social are different from the lectures and information delivery of previous decades. Anders et al.'s (2000) review of inservice learning for literacy teachers found that effective programs of professional development that change teacher practice include the following:

- Coaching or monitoring that provides support and feedback as practices are brought into the classroom
- Time, support, and tools for teachers to engage in reflection
- Opportunities for dialogue and discussion about teaching and teaching practices
- Voluntary participation or choice
- Collaboration between teachers and teacher educators or researchers

Peer Coaching. One model for professional development consistent with these characteristics is peer coaching. Showers and Joyce (Joyce & Showers, 1980; Showers, 1984; Showers & Joyce, 1996) developed the peer coaching model. Based on their understanding of teacher learning, they undertook a meta-analysis of research comparing the efficacy of a variety of professional development programs. They found that a few teachers changed their practices when presented with knowledge, demonstrations, or opportunities to practice with feedback. Many more teachers, however, changed their teaching practices when professional development involved coaching support.

Peer coaching takes place when teachers meet regularly to collaborate on issues of practice. During peer coaching, teachers discuss classroom practice and help one another solve problems and implement reform (Denton, 2003). Peer coaching can include study groups, collaborative planning of lessons and curriculum, observation and discussion of classroom practice, and problem solving about difficult teaching situations (Swafford, 2000).

Peer Coaching and Reading First. Reading First is a reform effort initiated by Part B of the No Child Left Behind 2002 reauthorization of the Elementary and Secondary Education Act. Reading First legislation aimed at improving reading achievement in grades K–3 by increasing the use of scientifically based reading research (SBRR) to guide instruction provided in high-poverty, low-performing classrooms. Mechanisms to bring about this goal included mandating that schools spend at least 90 minutes per day on reading instruction and requiring schools to use SBRR programs (with a focus in most states on commercially available core reading programs).

Reading First also placed a premium on professional development. The Reading First legislation mandated that 20% of all funding be spent on professional development for classroom teachers (U.S. Department of Education, 2001). The content of that professional development was also specified—the essential components of reading instruction identified in the NRP report (NICHD, 2000), comprising phonemic awareness, phonics, vocabulary development, reading fluency, and comprehension strategies. The perspective that the U.S. Department of Education promoted with respect to the kind of professional development that should be provided in Reading First schools was described in a document entitled *Guidance for the Reading First Program* (U.S. Department of Education, 2002), which stated that professional development should "be an ongoing, continuous activity, and not consist of 'one-shot' workshops or lectures" (p. 26) and it should include "coaches and other teachers of reading who provide feedback as instructional strategies are put into practice" (p. 26).

To be successful in receiving Reading First funding, a state department of education needed to show how it was going to provide coaching and feedback in professional development. In the particular state that was the focus of this study, teachers were required to attend workshops and to complete online modules about teaching phonemic awareness, phonics, fluency, comprehension, and vocabulary. In addition, teachers were required to meet twice weekly in peer coaching study team (PCST) meetings at their local school sites. PCST meetings were to include activities such as analyzing student data to make instructional decisions, modeling of teaching lessons and follow-up discussions, collaborative planning, discussion of classroom observations, and teacher reflection on classroom instruction (National Center for Reading First Technical Assistance, 2005; Theodore, 2008). PCSTs were led by literacy coaches who were classroom teachers given additional responsibility to guide the implementation of Reading First at the building level and support change in practice (Learning Point Associates, 2004). PCST meetings became the site for the Eyes on Text professional development.

A Study of Professional Development and OtR

This study began in the fourth year of Reading First implementation. Prior to this time, no professional development had focused on OtR during reading instruction. After three years of Reading First implementation, students had limited OtR, about 18 minutes per day. Concerned about these initial observations, the Reading First leaders at the state's department of education invited our team to develop and lead the Eyes on Text professional development. They hoped that it would both increase OtR during reading instruction and boost reading achievement. This study examines the impact of that professional development.

Methods

At the time of this study, the state had 65 Reading First schools from 32 school districts. Thirty-three schools were in the fourth year of implementation, and the remainder were in the second year of implementation. The population of students in these schools was 84% African American and 15% Caucasian, and 87% were eligible to receive free or reduced-cost lunch. All of the districts used one of six core reading programs as the center of the Reading First effort, 82% for 90 minutes per day, the other 18% for either 105, 110, or 120 minutes per day.

Although all of the schools participated in the Eyes on Text professional development modules, only one school from each of the 32 districts was randomly selected for this study. In each school, two third-grade classrooms were randomly selected. In each classroom, six students were selected for observation. Student distribution was as follows: two low achieving, two average, and two high achieving, one male and one female at each achievement level. Achievement levels were based on students' scores on the oral reading fluency (ORF) subtest of the Dynamic Indicators of Basic Early Literacy Skills (DIBELS; Good & Kaminski, 2002). Students for whom we had both preintervention and postintervention observations were included in data analysis, which resulted in 591 pairs of observations in 64 classrooms in 32 schools.

Classrooms were observed twice, on two days of the week, before and after the professional development. Investigators observed in each class on the same day during the Reading First block. The first half of the reading block was spent observing Teacher 1 and the second half was spent with Teacher 2, with the order being reversed on the second observation. Observations were conducted using a modification of an observation instrument created by Fisher and Hiebert (1990). During the recording, each student was observed for 20 seconds. Students who kept their eyes on text (i.e., appeared to be reading) for more than half of those 20 seconds were coded as reading. The contexts of reading were also coded, including whether reading was assisted or unassisted, the format (e.g., basal, leveled reader, multimedia) of the text read, and the genre of the text. Observers had 10 seconds to record the information before moving on to the next student. Once the recording cycle began, all behaviors were coded regardless of classroom activities until the end of the reading instructional period. A full round of observations was completed every three minutes.

Observers included literacy professors, graduate assistants, and regional literacy coordinators. After testing the observation instrument in a third-grade classroom in a non–Reading First school, regional literacy coordinators were trained using videotapes and classroom simulations. To further ensure impartiality, coordinators did not observe in their own regions.

To obtain feedback from the teachers on the effectiveness of the modules, teachers and literacy coaches completed a survey in February 2007. The survey was anonymous and used a Likert scale, along with a space for teacher comments for each statement. The survey was administered to third-grade teachers in all 65 Reading First schools, and 214 surveys were returned, a 30% return rate.

Data were analyzed by comparing the observations of time spent reading, the contexts of reading, and assessments before and after the professional development. Initial screening of observation data indicated that the results were nonparametric in nature. While the number of minutes of OtR ranged from 0 to 42, the mode for total minutes of reading was 0, and a large percentage of students, both before and after the intervention, read fewer then 10 minutes. Because of this, the Wilcoxon test, a nonparametric measure, was used to determine whether a significant change in OtR had occurred after the implementation of the Eyes on Text modules. Assessment data were compared using a paired samples t test.

The Intervention

During a daylong workshop in early October, a member of our research team presented the Eyes on Text modules to literacy coaches from all of the state's Reading First schools. Literacy coaches were required to return to their schools and present each of the Eyes on Text modules during PCST meetings over the following 10 weeks and document their implementation in PCST agendas and minutes that were submitted as requirements of Reading First. Coaches worked through each module during the workshop, had time to answer questions and consider translating the modules into the PCST context in their district, and were given copies of all handouts, slides, and materials to share with teachers. Each module included a short presentation or hands-on activity focused on a particular aspect of reading volume and fluency instruction, described as follows:

- Module 1: The importance of eyes on the page—This module summarized research on OtR and the relationship between OtR and fluency, vocabulary, and comprehension. During this module, teachers were also given forms and procedures for keeping reading logs that would be discussed at each of the subsequent PCST meetings. Teachers were asked to use the log to record an estimate of the number of minutes and number of pages a high-achieving, middle-achieving, and low-achieving student read each day of the week, as a way to reflect on the volume of reading they were providing their students.

- Module 2: Reading-rich and reading-poor instruction—This module presented definitions of what our team calls reading-rich and reading-poor instruction. Reading-rich instruction provides an opportunity for students to engage in substantial amounts of reading connected text, such as independent reading, paired reading, or rereading a passage to identify facts and opinions. Reading-poor instruction involves little or no OtR. Examples of reading-poor instructional practices include round robin reading, sorting words, and answering worksheet questions. This module asked teachers to brainstorm lists of both reading-rich and reading-poor instructional practices and asked teachers to estimate the amount of reaching-rich instruction recommended in a sample weekly lesson plan printed in the teachers' edition of a core reading program.

- Module 3: Selecting texts for OtR—This module presented a rationale and some tools for matching students with readable texts, including ways to use Lexile measures (Schnick & Knickelbine, 2000) to evaluate text difficulty.

Teachers were given an opportunity to look up the Lexile readability level of texts in their core programs and compare those with students' current Lexile scores. The module also provided a rationale for increasing the ratio of informational text students read during reading instruction. Teachers were asked to develop a list of sources of informational and readable texts to supplement the core reading program (e.g., leveled texts, trade books, textbooks from lower grades, multimedia texts). Finally, teachers were shown how to find informational texts at various Lexile levels using an online database.

- Module 4: Independent reading with accountability—Unless students are engaged during and accountable after independent reading, they may not actually read (Griffith & Rasinski, 2004). This module explained the importance of holding students accountable for demonstrating comprehension or engagement after independent reading and presented a variety of prompts (e.g., summarize, make a connection, identify the most important word or phrase, tell who would like this text and why) and procedures (e.g., discuss with a neighbor, write in a journal, random selection of five students sharing with the whole class, draw) for demonstrating reading comprehension. Teachers were also asked to reflect on and revise procedures for independent reading in their classrooms.

- Module 5: Partner reading—Partner reading provides more time with eyes on text than other contexts of reading, such as turn-taking or round robin reading, but still provides an audience and some support for solving reading problems. This module provided a rationale for partner reading and some examples of partner-reading procedures. This module asked teachers to set up pairs for reading partners on the basis of current student assessments. Teachers were encouraged to consider pairing students of like achievement provided with appropriately leveled texts.

- Module 6: Repeated reading—Repeated reading provides targeted reading practice and scaffolds the reading of difficult texts (Rasinski, 1989). This module presented procedures for various forms of repeated reading (e.g., echo reading, Readers Theatre) and for targeted repeated reading of 100-word passages for fluency practice. The module recommended that teachers select passages for repeated reading practice that contain substantial numbers of high-frequency words, words for which struggling students need to develop automaticity (Hiebert, 2002), and asked teachers to locate appropriate repeated reading passages from selections in their core reading programs.

- Module 7: Putting it all together—During this final module, teachers and literacy coaches collaborated to critique one another's lesson plans, including identifying reading-rich and reading-poor activities, estimating minutes of reading over a week, and identifying teaching practices discussed in previous modules.

Results

Reading in Third-Grade Classrooms Prior to the Eyes on Text Modules

Before the Eyes on Text professional development sessions, students spent an average of 9.32 minutes reading ($SD = 8.45$) during our observations of one half of the reading instructional period. We found no significant differences between observations conducted during the first half or the second half of the reading instructional block. This finding leads to the extrapolation that students spent on average 18.6 minutes with eyes on text during the 90- to 120-minute reading instructional period in third-grade Reading First classrooms. The modal number of minutes of OtR was 0. One fifth of the students, 20%, did not read during observations. The majority of students, 61%, read for fewer than 10 minutes during our observations. Half of the time they read, third graders engaged in assisted reading ($X = 4.61$ minutes, $SD = 6.42$), typically following along as someone else read aloud. Third graders engaged in unassisted reading the other half of the time ($X = 4.79$ minutes, $SD = 6.38$). (See Brenner, Hiebert, & Tompkins, 2009, for additional analysis of the first round of observations.)

The most common format of text was a basal passage, accounting for 52.69% of time spent reading ($X = 4.92$ minutes, $SD = 6.44$), followed by leveled texts at 20.82% ($X = 1.94$, $SD = 4.57$), and trade books at 9.76% ($X = 0.91$, $SD = 2.95$). The sources for the remaining reading included computer-based texts, content area textbooks, teacher-made texts, and peers' compositions. Third graders read more narratives than any other kind of text, accounting for 71.46% of the time spent reading ($X = 6.66$, $SD = 7.56$). Expository text accounted for 22.75% of reading ($X = 2.12$, $SD = 4.79$).

Compliance With Professional Development

Two measures indicate that literacy coaches led the professional development sessions during PCST meetings. First, schools were required to submit their PCST agendas and minutes to the state's department of education. All schools included all of the Eyes on Text modules on their agendas and in their minutes. Second, when teachers completed the follow-up survey, they indicated that they had spent time on the modules. On a scale of 1 (*strongly disagree*) to 5 (*strongly agree*) teachers strongly agreed that their literacy coach had led the modules during PCST meetings ($X = 4.59$, $SD = 0.87$) and agreed that they had done the Eyes on Text activities ($X = 4.43$, $SD = 0.78$).

The survey also indicates that teachers believed the modules to be beneficial. Items on the usefulness of the models attained an average of 4.22 ($SD = 0.87$) and 4.24 ($SD = 0.98$) that the project was a good use of their time. Teachers also agreed that the professional development would help them with teaching and planning ($X = 4.18$, $SD = 0.91$) and reported that they planned to use the presented materials in their classrooms ($X = 4.5$, $SD = 0.69$).

Students' OtR After the Professional Development

Literacy coaches completed the implementation of the Eyes on Text modules just before the winter break. We returned to classrooms for the postintervention round of data collection in February of the following year. At this time, students' mean total volume of OtR was 14.04 minutes (SD = 11.12), mean assisted reading was 5.81 minutes (SD = 6.33), and unassisted reading was 8.3 minutes (SD = 9.12). OtR for formats of text were 7.63 for basal texts (SD = 9.27), 2.85 for leveled readers (SD = 5.52), and 1.88 for trade books (SD = 5.04). Students read narrative texts an average of 9.77 minutes (SD = 8.84), expository texts for 1.68 minutes (SD = 3.90), and poetry for 0.38 minutes (SD = 2.04).

The amount of time students spent reading in third-grade classrooms increased by 50.64%, from 9.32 minutes per half of instructional period to 14.04 minutes (see Table 12.1). This was a significant change in time spent reading (z = 8.55, p = 0.00) that resulted in nearly 10 minutes per day of additional reading. While 20% of students did not read at all during observations before the intervention, only 15% of students did not read after the intervention. A smaller proportion of students, 43% instead of 61%, read for fewer than 10 minutes. The volume of time increased by 20.65%, a significant increase (z = 3.87, p = 0.00). The amount of time spent in unassisted reading increased by 59.29%, also a significant increase (z = 9.02, p = 0.00).

Significant increases occurred in the reading of all text formats, including reading the selection from the basal (4.92 to 7.63 minutes, z = 5.69, p = 0.00), leveled texts (1.94 to 2.85 minutes, z = 3.33, p = 0.00), and time spent reading trade books (0.91 to 1.88 minutes, z = 4.43, p = 0.00). Overall, the proportion of time spent reading each of these formats remained nearly the same (see Table 12.2). Students continued to spend the majority of their reading time on selections from the core reading program (53–54% of total reading time) before and after the treatment and also continued to spend a significant amount of time reading leveled texts (21% to 20% of reading time.)

There were also significant increases in the amount of time students spent reading narrative texts but not in the time spent reading expository text. The volume of narrative text increased from 6.66 minutes to 9.77 minutes (z = 5.55, p = 0.00). Time spent reading expository texts decreased, though not significantly so, from 2.12 minutes to 1.68 minutes (z = 0.25, p = 0.14). Overall, the proportion of time with narrative text increased by 2%, and the proportion of time reading expository text decreased by about half.

Table 12.1. Time Spent Reading: Pretreatment and Posttreatment

	Pretreatment	Posttreatment
Minutes of reading	9.32	14.04
Minutes of assisted reading	4.61 (49%)	5.81 (41%)
Minutes of unassisted reading	4.79 (51%)	8.30 (59%)

Table 12.2. Time Spent Reading Particular Text Formats and Genres

Observed Reading Sources	Pretreatment Percentage of Total Reading	Posttreatment Percentage of Total Reading
Basal anthology	53	54
Leveled text	21	20
Trade books	10	13
Narrative	68	70
Expository	23	12
Poetry	2	3

Changes in Student Achievement

Paired t tests comparing observed students' scores on the DIBELS ORF, Peabody Picture Vocabulary (PPVT), and Woodcock–Johnson tests from the beginning and end of the year indicate mixed achievement results. Mean scores on the ORF rose from 74 words per minute (SD = 42.84) to 106 (32.33), a significant difference: $t(331)$ = 14.37, p = 0.00. However, mean scores on the PPVT decreased from 92 (SD = 46.02) to 90 (14.44), as did scores on the Woodcock–Johnson, which decreased slightly, from 99 (SD = 12.07) to 98 (SD = 13.01). These decreases were not significant: $t(322)$ = 0.64, p = 0.53 for PPVT scores, $t(321)$ = 1.01, p = 0.27 for Woodcock–Johnson.

All Reading First schools participated in the professional development. For the entire population of Reading First students, achievement results were also mixed. Table 12.3 compares the proportion of students at proficient on four assessments for the cohort of third graders at the end of second grade (prior to the intervention) and the end of third grade (after the intervention). The ratio of students achieving proficient increased on two measures (PPVT and DIBELS ORF), stayed the same on one measure (Woodcock–Johnson), and decreased on the state's curriculum test, the MCT.

Table 12.4 provides a summary of the percentages of students who were at different risk designations according to their DIBELS ORF performances. In the year prior to the project, 3% of the cohort of third graders had moved from low-risk to medium-risk designations as a result of their DIBELS performances. By contrast,

Table 12.3. Percentages of Students Designated Proficient on Assessments

Year	PPVT	DIBELS ORF	Woodcock–Johnson	MCT
End of second grade (2006)	28%	42%	58%	81%
End of third grade (2007)	33%	45%	58%	77%

Table 12.4. Percentages of Students Designated in Various Risk Categories on DIBELS

Cohort	Percentage at High Risk	Percentage at Medium Risk	Percentage at Low Risk
Prior Third-Grade Cohort (05–06)			
Beginning of year	27	33	41
End of year	25	37	38
Target Third-Grade Cohort (06–07)			
Beginning of year	25	34	41
End of year	20	35	45

the percentage of students within the target cohort who were at low risk increased by 4%, and the percentage of high-risk students decreased by 5% (rather than the 2% in the year prior to the project).

Conclusions About Professional Development and Recommendations

Observations indicate that teachers made more time for students to have eyes on text during reading instruction after they participated in the Eyes on Text modules during PCST meetings. Students spent about 18% of reading instruction engaged in reading before the professional development, compared with 30% after. Some literacy coordinators reported that they had observed students reading novels at the end of the year, a practice not seen at the beginning of Reading First.

The Eyes on Text professional development was a fairly low-cost and easy to implement professional development. In design, it was based on some, but not all, of the features of successful professional development defined by Anders et al. (2000) and outlined in the National Staff Development Council (2001) standards. Teachers did not volunteer to participate, nor did they have choice about the content of professional development for these seven weeks. However, the modules were sustained, lasting for seven weeks, and were provided as part of ongoing professional development focusing on multiple aspects of literacy instruction. The sessions also took advantage of the coaching model of the PCST meetings, using the established format for regular teacher discussion and reflecting the social nature of teacher learning. The modules were intended to support the growth of situated knowledge by being based on authentic problems of real practice. Teachers kept logs of the volume of reading in their classrooms, referred to student assessments, and worked to analyze and adapt their core reading programs by collaboratively planning and critiquing lessons.

Unfortunately, however, achievement did not make a significant increase following the professional development. The relationship among professional development, teaching practice, and student learning is complex (Elmore, 1995; Taylor, Pearson, Peterson, & Rodriguez, 2003). Even when teaching practices are changed by professional development, there is no straightforward linear progression to having an impact on student achievement and it may take a great deal of time to see a resultant change in student achievement. For example, in their work with schools in urban settings, the Advanced Reading Development Demonstration Project (2008) saw a 20% change in students' standardized test scores after five years in schools where teachers had participated in intensive professional development. These changes were greater than those in schools where comparable professional development had not occurred but the longevity of the effects on the reading instruction in these schools is uncertain, as district policies change and the researchers are no longer there to lend support (Raphael, 2009). In the case of the present study, the Eyes on Text professional development was not the only teacher professional development or reform effort taking place in Reading First schools. Teachers continued to be required to implement the core reading program and to attend workshops and other PCST meetings that focused on other components of literacy instruction.

It may also be that 10 additional minutes of reading per day is not a sufficient change in reading volume that can meaningfully influence student achievement, especially for struggling readers such as those in many of the state's Reading First classrooms. Although there is some evidence that seven additional minutes of reading has a beneficial impact on both word recognition and comprehension (Kuhn & Schwanenflugel, 2009), it may matter whether those additional minutes replace some other beneficial form of instruction, or whether the reading volume gained during observations was offset by time reading lost during some other time of the school day we did not observe.

In addition, the increase in reading that led to improved achievement in the Kuhn and Schwanenflugel (2009) study was assisted reading, not the unassisted reading that comprised the greater portion of the additional reading in which students in this study engaged. The issue of assisted and unassisted reading has been one of the most contentious of those raised by the findings of the NRP (NICHD, 2000). Often, the discussion around this topic has been polemic, rather than data driven. Recent data on the performances of students in oral and silent reading contexts are now available to better understand issues with assisted and unassisted reading.

One source of evidence comes from a study conducted by Trainin, Wilson, Hiebert, Erickson, and Laughridge (2007). They found that it is the students in the bottom quartile whose performances differ substantially in an unassisted context relative to an assisted one. Low-performing students may fail to read when the text is too hard and when the reading context lacks sufficient guidance. The data in Table 12.4 indicate that more than half of the students in the present sample remained at medium to high risk as measured by their oral reading rates at the end of third grade. Many of the students in our study fell into the group that Trainin et al. (2007) describe as engaging in ineffective behaviors when reading silently without assistance.

When the text and task are carefully scaffolded, students can use unassisted reading contexts more productively (Reutzel, Fawson, & Smith, 2008). It is likely, however, that the scaffolding that is necessary—especially when the majority of students in a classroom begin with poor silent reading behaviors—was not developed sufficiently in our professional development. Although the Eyes on Text modules included one session on selecting readable texts and one session on postreading accountability, these sessions likely did not provide sufficient guidance to change teachers' practices in ways that provide enough support for low-achieving students.

Our resources for observations were not extensive, and we do not have data to allow us to draw conclusions about whether students were reading readable texts or whether they were held accountable for demonstrating comprehension after reading. As the length of time students were expected to spend with eyes on text increased, it may be that substantial numbers of students did not have sufficient stamina for sustaining reading because of a lack of skills and perceived lack of autonomy and proficiency in the task.

The timing of the state test may also have affected measures of student achievement. Our post-intervention round of observations was collected in February, about eight school weeks after the end of the professional development. However, by late March or early April, most teachers reported changing their instructional focus from the core program to preparing for the state test, administered in May. Even though teachers were incorporating more time with eyes on text in February, the few weeks between the end of Eyes on Text in December and the start of testing season in March may not have provided enough reading practice to noticeably change student achievement.

It may also be that the requirements of Reading First prevented teachers from devoting sufficient time to OtR to affect students' reading achievement. Reading First mandated at least 90 minutes of reading instruction per day. Following national Reading First and state guidelines, all of the schools in our study had selected one of six leading core reading programs to guide instruction, and teachers were required to implement the core program with fidelity. However, our analysis of these core programs indicates that when teachers closely follow the recommended lesson plans in the teachers' editions, students will be given only a limited OtR. The volume of reading suggested in the lesson plans in these six core programs amounts to an average of 15 minutes per day (Brenner & Hiebert, 2010). The constraints of core programs may make it difficult to increase volume of reading to the point where achievement increases.

In addition, the relative ratio of time spent reading informational texts actually decreased in relation to narrative texts. Teachers increased the amount of time students spent reading both trade books and core program texts, including leveled texts and the basal anthology. Although the ratio of informational texts in reading programs is on the rise, narratives still comprise most of texts available for reading instruction in most core programs (Moss & Newton, 2002; Yopp & Yopp, 2006). Teachers may not have had access to sufficient, readable informational texts to increase their use.

Teachers increased the volume of OtR in the weeks following the professional development. However, the 10 additional minutes of reading per day were not associated with a rise in reading achievement. This study raises more questions about the impact of OtR and professional development than it answers. Many more studies of this approach, including studies using statistical methods such as hierarchical linear modeling, are necessary to answer these questions about the length of OtR needed to improve reading practice and the impact of this sort of professional development on students' reading achievement.

QUESTIONS FOR PROFESSIONAL DEVELOPMENT

1. How much time do low-, middle-, and high-achieving students in your classroom spend reading on a typical day? How many pages a day do they read?

2. How could you adjust your routines to increase opportunity to read during reading instruction and throughout the school day?

3. Where might you find sources of accessible, easy-to-read texts that you could pair with the selections in your reading program? Are there leveled texts you are not currently using? Trade books? Older textbooks?

4. Versions of the modules used in this study are available online (see Brenner et al., 2008). Who might be interested in working through these modules with you?

REFERENCES

Advanced Reading Development Demonstration Project. (2008). Partnerships for improving literacy in urban schools. *The Reading Teacher*, 61(8), 674–680. doi:10.1598/RT.61.8.11

Allington, R.L. (2001). *What really matters for struggling readers: Designing research-based programs.* New York: Longman.

Anders, P.L., Hoffman, J.V., & Duffy, G.G. (2000). Teaching teachers to teach reading: Paradigm shifts, persistent problems, and challenges. In M.L. Kamil, P.B. Mosenthal, P.D. Pearson, & R. Barr (Eds.), *Handbook of reading research* (Vol. 3, pp. 719–742). Mahwah, NJ: Erlbaum.

Block, C.C., Cleveland, M.D., & Reed, K.M. (2006). When twenty minutes of literacy instruction is added to the day: Which learning environments increase students' overall achievement, vocabulary, comprehension, fluency, and affective development? In *Scholastic classroom books compendium of research* (pp. 18–36). New York: Scholastic.

Brenner, D., & Hiebert, E.H. (2010). If I follow the teachers' editions, isn't that enough? Analyzing reading volume in six core reading programs. *The Elementary School Journal*, 110(3), 347–363.

Brenner, D., Hiebert, E.H., Riley, M., Tompkins, R., & Holland, J. (2008). *Resources for the Eyes on Text Professional Development Modules.*

Retrieved June 22, 2010, from www2.msstate.edu/%7Edevon/

Brenner, D., Hiebert, E.H., & Tompkins, R. (2009). How much and what are third graders reading? Reading in core programs. In E.H. Hiebert (Ed.), *Reading more, reading better* (pp. 118–140). New York: Guilford.

Cervetti, G.N., Bravo, M.A., Hiebert, E.H., Pearson, P.D., & Jaynes, C.A. (2009). Text genre and science content: Ease of reading, comprehension, and reader preference. *Reading Psychology, 30*(6), 487–511.

Cobb, P., & Bowers, J. (1999). Cognitive and situated learning perspectives in theory and practice. *Educational Researcher, 28*(2), 4–15.

Critchley, M.P. (1998). Reading to learn: Pedagogical implications of vocabulary research. *The Language Teacher, 22*(12), 15–19.

Cunningham, A.E., & Stanovich, K.E. (1998). What reading does for the mind. *American Educator, 22*(1/2), 8–15.

Daane, M.C., Campbell, J.R., Grigg, W.S., Goodman, M.J., & Oranje, A. (2005). *Fourth-grade students reading aloud: NAEP 2002 special study of oral reading* (NCES 2006-469). Washington, DC: National Center for Education Statistics, Institute of Education Sciences, U.S. Department of Education.

Denton, D.R. (2003). *Reading First: Lessons from successful state reading initiatives.* Atlanta, GA: Southern Regional Education Board. Retrieved April 28, 2010, from publications.sreb.org/2003/03H01_Reading_First.pdf

Duke, N.K. (2000). 3.6 minutes per day: The scarcity of informational texts in first grade. *Reading Research Quarterly, 35*(2), 202–224. doi:10.1598/RRQ.35.2.1

Duke, N.K., & Bennett-Armistead, V.S. (2003). *Reading and writing informational text in the primary grades: Research-based practices.* New York: Scholastic.

Elmore, R.F. (1995). Structural reform and educational practice. *Educational Researcher, 24*(9), 23–26.

Fisher, C.W., & Hiebert, E.H. (1990). Characteristics of tasks in two approaches to literacy instruction. *The Elementary School Journal, 91*(1), 3–18. doi:10.1086/461634

Foorman, B.R., Schatschneider, C., Eakin, M.N., Fletcher, J.M., Moats, L.C., & Francis, D.J. (2006). The impact of instructional practices in grades 1 and 2 on reading and spelling achievement in high poverty schools.

Contemporary Educational Psychology, 31(1), 1–29. doi:10.1016/j.cedpsych.2004.11.003

Fountas, I.C., & Pinnell, G.S. (1999). *Matching books to readers: Using leveled books in guided reading, K–3.* Portsmouth, NH: Heinemann.

Frey, N., Fisher, D., & Berkin, A. (2008). *Good habits, great readers: Building the literacy community.* Upper Saddle River, NJ: Prentice Hall.

Fuchs, L.S., Fuchs, D., Hosp, M.K., & Jenkins, J.R. (2001). Oral reading fluency as an indicator of reading competence: A theoretical, empirical, and historical analysis. *Scientific Studies of Reading, 5*(3), 239–256. doi:10.1207/S1532799XSSR0503_3

Gambrell, L.B., Wilson, R.M., & Gantt, W.N. (1981). Classroom observations of task-attending behaviors of good and poor readers. *The Journal of Educational Research, 74*(6), 400–404.

Good, R.H., & Kaminski, R.A. (Eds.). (2002). *DIBELS: Dynamic Indicators of Basic Early Literacy Skills* (6th ed.). Longmont, CO: Sopris West.

Greeno, J.G. (1997). On claims that answer the wrong questions. *Educational Researcher, 26*(1), 5–17.

Griffith, L.W., & Rasinski, T.V. (2004). A focus on fluency: How one teacher incorporated fluency with her reading curriculum. *The Reading Teacher, 58*(2), 126–137. doi:10.1598/RT.58.2.1

Guthrie, J.T. (2004). Teaching for literacy engagement. *Journal of Literacy Research, 36*(1), 1–29. doi:10.1207/s15548430jlr3601_2

Guthrie, J.T., Schafer, W.D., & Huang, C. (2001). Benefits of opportunity to read and balanced instruction on the NAEP. *The Journal of Educational Research, 94*(3), 145–162. doi:10.1080/00220670109599912

Hayes, D.P., Wolfer, L.T., & Wolfe, M.F. (1996). Schoolbook simplification and its relation to the decline in SAT-verbal scores. *American Educational Research Journal, 33*(2), 489–508.

Herman, P.A., Anderson, R.C., Pearson, P.D., & Nagy, W.E. (1987). Incidental acquisition of word meaning from expositions with varied text features. *Reading Research Quarterly, 22*(3), 263–284. doi:10.2307/747968

Hiebert, E.H. (2002). Standards, assessments, and text difficulty. In A.E. Farstrup & S.J. Samuels (Eds.), *What research has to say about reading instruction* (pp. 337–369). Newark, DE: International Reading Association.

Hiebert, E.H. (2009). The (mis)match between texts and students who depend on schools to become literate. In E.H. Hiebert & M. Sailors (Eds.), *Finding the right texts: What works for beginning and struggling readers* (pp. 1–20). New York: Guilford.

Hiebert, E.H. (2010). Understanding the word-level features of texts for students who depend on schools to become literate. In M.G. McKeown & L. Kucan (Eds.), *Bringing reading research to life* (pp. 207–231). New York: Guilford.

Joyce, B., & Showers, B. (1980). Improving in-service training: The messages of research. *Educational Leadership, 37*(5), 379–385.

Kuhn, M.R., & Schwanenflugel, P.J. (2009). Time, engagement, and support: Lessons from a 4-year fluency intervention. In E.H. Hiebert (Ed.), *Reading more, reading better* (pp. 141–160). New York: Guilford.

Kuhn, M.R., Schwanenflugel, P.J., Morris, R.D., Morrow, L.M., Woo, D.G., Meisinger, E.B., et al. (2006). Teaching children to become fluent and automatic readers. *Journal of Literacy Research, 38*(4), 357–387. doi:10.1207/s15548430jlr3804_1

Kuhn, M.R., & Stahl, S.A. (2003). Fluency: A review of developmental and remedial practices. *Journal of Educational Psychology, 95*(1), 3–21. doi:10.1037/0022-0663.95.1.3

LaBerge, D., & Samuels, S.J. (1974). Toward a theory of automatic information processing in reading. *Cognitive Psychology, 6*(2), 293–323. doi:10.1016/0010-0285(74)90015-2

Learning Point Associates. (2004). *Reading First coaching: A guide for coaches and Reading First leaders.* Naperville, IL: Author. Retrieved September 22, 2009, from www.learningpt.org/pdfs/literacy/coachesguide.pdf

Miller, S.D., & Meece, J.L. (1999). Third graders' motivational preferences for reading and writing tasks. *The Elementary School Journal, 100*(1), 19–35. doi:10.1086/461941

Morrow, L.M. (1992). The impact of a literature-based program on literacy achievement, use of literature, and attitudes of children from minority backgrounds. *Reading Research Quarterly, 27*(3), 251–275. doi:10.2307/747794

Moss, B., & Newton, E. (2002). An examination of the informational text genre in basal readers. *Reading Psychology, 23*(1), 1–13. doi:10.1080/027027102317345376

National Center for Reading First Technical Assistance. (2005). *Leading for reading success: An introductory guide for Reading First coaches.* Washington, DC: Author. Retrieved September 22, 2009, from www2.ed.gov/programs/readingfirst/support/coaches.pdf

National Institute of Child Health and Human Development. (2000). *Report of the National Reading Panel. Teaching children to read: An evidence-based assessment of the scientific research literature on reading and its implications for reading instruction* (NIH Publication No. 00-4769). Washington, DC: U.S. Government Printing Office.

National Staff Development Council. (2001). *NSDC's standards for staff development* (Rev. ed.). Dallas, TX: Author. Retrieved September 22, 2009, from www.nsdc.org/standards/index.cfm

Putnam, R.T., & Borko, H. (2000). What do new views of knowledge and thinking have to say about research on teacher learning? In B. Moon, J. Butcher, & E. Bird (Eds.), *Leading professional development in education* (pp. 11–29). New York: RoutledgeFalmer.

Raphael, T.E. (2009, December). *Defying gravity: Whole school literacy reform in urban schools.* Oscar S. Causey address at the 59th annual meeting of the National Reading Conference, Albuquerque, NM.

Rasinski, T.V. (1989). Fluency for everyone: Incorporating fluency instruction in the classroom. *The Reading Teacher, 42*(9), 690–693.

Resnick, L.B. (1991). Shared cognition: Thinking as social practice. In L.B. Resnick, J.M. Levine, & S.D. Teasley (Eds.), *Perspectives on socially shared cognition* (pp. 1–20). Washington, DC: American Psychological Association.

Reutzel, D.R., Fawson, P.C., & Smith, J.A. (2008). Reconsidering silent sustained reading: An exploratory study of scaffolded silent reading. *The Journal of Educational Research, 102*(1), 37–50. doi:10.3200/JOER.102.1.37-50

Reutzel, D.R., & Hollingsworth, P.M. (1991). Reading time in school: Effect on fourth graders' performance on a criterion-referenced comprehension test. *The Journal of Educational Research, 84*(3), 170–176.

Richgels, D.J., McGee, L.M., Lomax, R.G., & Sheard, C. (1987). Awareness of four text structures: Effects on recall of expository text. *Reading Research Quarterly, 22*(2), 177–196. doi:10.2307/747664

Schnick, T., & Knickelbine, M.J. (2000). *The Lexile framework: An introduction for educators.* Durham, NC: MetaMetrics.

Showers, B. (1984). *Peer coaching: A strategy for facilitating transfer of training.* Eugene, OR: Center for Educational Policy and Management.

Showers, B., & Joyce, B. (1996). The evolution of peer coaching. *Educational Leadership, 53*(6), 12–16.

Soltis, J.F. (1981). Education and the concept of knowledge. In J.F. Soltis (Ed.), *Philosophy and education: 80th yearbook of the National Society for the Study of Education* (pp. 95–113). Chicago: University of Chicago Press.

Stahl, S.A., & Fairbanks, M.M. (1986). The effects of vocabulary instruction: A model-based meta-analysis. *Review of Educational Research, 56*(1), 72–110.

Swafford, J. (2000). Teachers supporting teachers through peer coaching. In B. Moon, J. Butcher, & E. Bird (Eds.), *Leading professional development in education* (pp. 107–115). New York: RoutledgeFalmer.

Symons, S., MacLatchy-Gaudet, H., Stone, T.D., & Reynolds, P.L. (2001). Strategy instruction for elementary students searching informational text. *Scientific Studies of Reading, 5*(1), 1–33. doi:10.1207/S1532799XSSR0501_1

Taylor, B.M., Frye, B.J., & Maruyama, G.M. (1990). Time spent reading and reading growth. *American Educational Research Journal, 27*(2), 351–362.

Taylor, B.M., Pearson, P.D., Peterson, D.S., & Rodriguez, M.C. (2003). Reading growth in high-poverty classrooms: The influence of teacher practices that encourage cognitive engagement in literacy learning. *The Elementary School Journal, 104*(1), 3–28. doi:10.1086/499740

Theodore, K. (2008, July). Leading for reading success: Reading First coaches. Presentation at the fifth annual National Reading First Conference, Nashville, TN. Retrieved September 22, 2009, from www2.ed.gov/programs/readingfirst/2008conferences/rfcoaches.pdf

Trainin, G., Wilson, K.M., Hiebert, E., Erickson, J., & Laughridge, V. (2007, April). *An examination of silent reading rates and comprehension: Tasks, proficiency levels, and length of text.* Poster presented at the annual meeting of the American Educational Research Association, Chicago, IL.

U.S. Department of Education. (2001). *No Child Left Behind Part B, Subpart 1—Reading First.* Retrieved May 19, 2010, from www2.ed.gov/policy/elsec/leg/esea02/pg4.html

U.S. Department of Education. (2002). *Guidance for the Reading First program.* Washington, DC: Office of Elementary and Secondary Education, U.S. Department of Education. Retrieved April 28, 2010, from www2.ed.gov/programs/readingfirst/guidance.pdf

Wu, Y., & Samuels, S.J. (2004, May). *How the amount of time spent on independent reading affects reading achievement: A response to the National Reading Panel.* Paper presented at the 49th annual convention of the International Reading Association, Reno, NV.

Yopp, R.H., & Yopp, H.K. (2006). Informational texts as read-alouds at school and home. *Journal of Literacy Research, 38*(1), 37–51. doi:10.1207/s15548430jlr3801_2

Silent Reading: Different Contexts, Different Readers

CHAPTER 13

Silent Reading and Online Reading Comprehension

Jacquelynn A. Malloy

George Mason University, Virginia

Jill M. Castek

University of California, Berkeley

Donald J. Leu

University of Connecticut

S trategic and efficient reading comprehension is the uncontested aim of all reading, whether it occurs silently or orally, and whether the material being read is offline or online. Although we know of the myriad processes that must occur in the mind of a reader to make sense of text while reading silently, we are just now coming to understand the nature of these processes while reading silently online. Because of the influx of new technologies, today's readers navigate a multitude of texts that require the development of new literacies to use them (Coiro, Knobel, Lankshear, & Leu, 2008). Recent research shows that reading online involves a complex set of decision-making and problem-solving skills (Leu, O'Byrne, Zawilinski, McVerry, & Everett-Cacopardo, 2009) and that readers essentially create their own texts as they locate resources, evaluate them critically, synthesize ideas across sites, and communicate about them (Leu et al., 2008). These decisions are made as readers react either strategically or with a trial-and-error response to text as they read silently online. Educators are coming to find that online comprehension strategies, developed through instruction and experience, can lead to effective and efficient comprehension of information accessed through digital formats.

Given emerging research that online reading comprehension requires skills and strategies that are complex, some of which are unique to the online context (Coiro, 2007), a central question is, How do we build into the literacy curriculum opportunities for students to acquire the requisite skills and strategies for online reading comprehension? Further, what classroom reading activities encourage students to read a broad range of texts both online and offline?

This chapter discusses how the Internet is shaping the way we read, write, and communicate and how it is transforming the way educators teach literacy in

Revisiting Silent Reading: New Directions for Teachers and Researchers, edited by Elfrieda H. Hiebert and D. Ray Reutzel. © 2010 by the International Reading Association.

today's schools. Changes to the literacy landscape are framed in a perspective of new literacies of online reading comprehension (Leu, O'Byrne, et al., 2009). We introduce findings from a three-year research initiative that sought to develop an instructional model that supports students in acquiring the skills and strategies essential for online reading comprehension. We discuss how communities of readers are transformed when reading shifts from page to screen. Included are practical suggestions for ways educators can integrate the types of sustained reading and writing experiences that will increasingly define literacy in the 21st century. Recommendations for the development of literacy standards, assessments, and school policies are also addressed.

The Changing Literacy Landscape

The Internet is an increasingly important source of information and is central to all aspects of daily life (International Reading Association, 2009; International Society for Technology in Education, Partnership for 21st Century Skills, & State Educational Technology Directors Association, 2007; National Council of Teachers of English, 2007; National Telecommunications and Information Administration & Economics and Statistics Administration, 2002). Its widespread use is fundamentally redefining what it means to be literate in the 21st century (Roberts, Foehr, & Rideout, 2005). However, instruction in our literacy classrooms is slow to respond. The RAND Reading Study Group (2002) summarizes its concerns, stating that "accessing the Internet makes large demands on individuals' literacy skills; in some cases, this new technology requires readers to have novel literacy skills, and little is known about how to analyze or teach those skills" (p. 4). Research is beginning to emerge about the contexts and conditions that facilitate learning these novel skills and strategies and how to create those contexts within classrooms (see Castek, 2008).

The New Literacies of Online Reading Comprehension

Online reading comprehension instruction is informed by theoretical work in new literacies (Coiro et al., 2008; Cope & Kalantzis, 2000; Gee, 2003; Kress, 1999; Lankshear & Knobel, 2006; Leu, O'Byrne, et al., 2009; The New London Group, 2000; Street, 1998). New literacies theory suggests that the nature of literacy is rapidly changing and transforming, as new information and communication technologies emerge.

Within this broader context of new literacies theory, a more specific theory of online reading comprehension has also emerged (Castek & Carter, 2006; Coiro, 2003; Henry, 2007; Leu, Kinzer, Coiro, & Cammack, 2004; Leu, O'Byrne, et al., 2009). This theory frames online reading comprehension as a process of problem-based inquiry, with the major skill sets clustering in the following areas:

(a) developing questions, (b) locating information, (c) evaluating information, (d) synthesizing information, and (e) communicating information. During this process, additional online and traditional offline reading comprehension skills are required, often in complex and interrelated ways.

Providing Time in School for Students to Read Offline and Online Is Critical

According to some researchers, middle school and high school students spend more time reading teacher-made handouts or textbook passages (Orange & Horowitz, 1999; Weinstein, 2002) than real-world materials (Wade & Moje, 2000). For these reasons, it is important for elementary, middle, and high school students to develop skills for critically reading and thoughtfully communicating about texts by engaging with them in a sustained manner and being driven by authentic purposes.

Primary sources and real-world materials are prevalent and plentiful online, making the Internet the ideal context for reading materials on numerous topics that meet readers' interests. Providing purposeful opportunities for students to read online encourages them to interpret, analyze, and engage with multiple forms of text and exchange perspectives with those inside and outside the classroom.

Comprehension Processes Common to Reading Offline and Online

There is much that must occur internally while one reads. Some of these are skills, such as decoding and word recognition, that become automated in skilled readers and therefore come to require relatively little cognitive effort. However, and depending on the skill of the reader and the complexity or novelty of the text, there are cognitive strategies that must be explicitly taught by educators and practiced by students in order for them to become useful to attaining high levels of successful and efficient reading comprehension. Many of the strategies that are important to deriving meaning from print text are also important to comprehending online text, such as questioning, predicting, and making inferences. However, important differences in online text comprehension exist (Coiro, 2003; Leu et al., 2007). Examining these differences has led to research efforts aimed at better understanding what is required for online reading comprehension (Leu, Reinking, et al., 2005).

Strategic Offline Reading

Because narrative text is linear and must be read from beginning to end without skipping paragraphs or pages to make sense, online and offline (i.e., print) narrative reading can be assumed to be somewhat similar. Although the online format introduces interactive options for reading narrative text, the Internet has become a compelling resource for reading and communicating about expository text. The purposes for reading, use of background knowledge, and relevant cognitive strategies to support comprehension lend themselves to different strategic behaviors in online versus offline formats.

First, offline expository texts are written in a page to page and front to back configuration, but they do not have to be read in a linear fashion. Authors organize printed information in a variety of ways, depending on their goals and preferences, and they use various text structures to indicate how the information is presented (e.g., table of contents, headings and subheadings, indexes). In addition, authors can support readers in understanding the text by providing glossaries or visual aids such as diagrams, charts, pictures, or photographs. However, the texts, headings, and written or visual supplements are unchangeable and given in a fixed order.

The reader, depending upon his or her individual goals, then reads all or part of the text provided to gain a general understanding of the topic or to answer specific questions. For example, the reader who wishes to learn more about an interesting but novel topic might choose an appealing informational text and leaf through its pages to observe the pictures, photographs and captions, and chapter headings. Deciding that the book is indeed a good introduction to the topic, the reader may begin with the first section, where the author most likely has made an attempt at hooking the reader on the significance of the topic and providing a road map of the sections that follow. The reader may then choose to skim or carefully read other sections according to personal interests or to simply fill in gaps in understanding. The reader is constructing a model of the factual and conceptual knowledge provided by the text, scanning at times to find quick answers to questions, or reading more deeply where aspects of the passage are particularly interesting. However, no matter how comprehensive or cursory the author's presentation, the information remains fixed in its content and structure.

Strategic Online Reading

Although we know a great deal about what strategic offline readers do to actively construct meaning from text, our knowledge of skills and strategies for online reading is just emerging (Coiro, 2007; Coiro & Dobler, 2007; Eagleton & Dobler, 2007). It is our view that online reading differs from offline reading in that it requires multiple levels of decision making (Landow, 1994; Reinking, 1992, 1998). The vastness of the information available online requires that readers develop skill in narrowing and discriminating the field to address the particular purpose for reading as well as developing strategies for evaluating the accuracy and usefulness of the information found.

Even when investigating the same topic, a text that is read by two readers may be markedly different because of the decisions each reader makes when locating websites and navigating webpages. Although the purposes for reading, such as developing a general understanding of a topic or searching for information to answer a particular question, might be similar online and offline, the additional process of self-directed text construction (Coiro & Dobler, 2007) leads readers to assemble an individualized set of texts to read depending on the choices they make while navigating through the online environment. Reading online involves a user-defined compilation of information from a vast, open-ended, and dynamic array.

Websites and their webpages have text structures, such as headings or tabs, that mirror a table of contents in print text, but they often include links that lead to other areas of information. These intertextual links may lead readers away from one webpage and onto others or expand the scope of the information provided; however, they may also lead the reader to become "lost in the tree" of the online hierarchy. Savvy online readers have developed useful strategies for navigating through the layers of the Internet to find information efficiently and to evaluate and synthesize what they find. While maintaining a clear purpose for reading, and with an understanding of how the online environment is structured and organized, readers can develop the necessary skills and strategies for compiling an appropriate information set to solve problems, answer questions, and synthesize and communicate information from online sources.

Findings From the Teaching Internet Comprehension to Adolescents Project

The Teaching Internet Comprehension to Adolescents project (TICA; Leu, Reinking, et al., 2005) used verbal protocols with think-alouds to gather information about the reasoning that occurred as a group of 53 seventh-grade students gathered information online to solve problems posed by researchers and conducted personally generated online searches. These 53 students were selected from a sampling frame of more than 1,100 students from two regions of the United States on the basis of their reported frequency and diversity of Internet use using an online survey and a sampling of their online skill set assessed through a series of open-ended questions.

Students' online reading actions were recorded using a screen capture program called Camtasia (www.techsmith.com/camtasia). An audio recording of their verbal think-aloud was also collected. In the third session, students were asked to reflect on their particular skills and strategies while reading online. Data from Camtasia recordings, transcripts of verbal protocols, and follow-up stimulated recall interviews were coded and analyzed to search for patterns across skilled students' online reading actions, verbal reports, and stimulated recall of online strategy use. Common patterns of online skill and strategy use were then categorized into larger skill sets (e.g., generating search terms, navigating websites, evaluating information critically, communicating with online audiences) and used to inform an evolving taxonomy of Internet skills. The findings of this exploratory research provided a foundation to developing this taxonomy and supported further research into instructional models for teaching online reading comprehension. Information regarding the identification of these students, the nature of the tasks they completed, and the taxonomy can be found at www.newliteracies .uconn.edu/iesproject/.

What We Learned From Verbal Protocols With Skilled Online Readers

Developing Questions. In the TICA research, we presented our 53 focal students with three online tasks: two involved researcher-designed problem sets and the third was a student-generated online search. When these students were interviewed about the types of questions they had in mind when beginning an online search, they reported that they approach tasks differentially for teacher-designed and personal searches. Their responses indicated that when they do have a question in mind, it is nearly always because they are investigating a teacher-selected question As one student stated when asked if she has a specific question in mind when beginning an online search, "When I'm searching on the Internet and it's an assignment that's directed at a question…I would actually type in a question, like 'how do penguins take care of their young?'"

Depending on whether the task was open (i.e., allowing a choice of topic or research focus) or closed (i.e., posing a question for which there is one correct answer), students were observed to search and to read differentially online. (For a discussion of task types, please see Turner & Paris, 1995.) Closed tasks that require such specific information as "How do penguins take care of their young?" sometimes lead to the type of cursory reading that students display when asked to answer the questions at the end of a social studies chapter: Instead of carefully reading the information presented, the student frequently scans a passage to find the requested information and offers little in the way of critical engagement with the text. However, when the question was of interest to the student, as when our focal students were asked to conduct a search about a personally relevant topic, the student often demonstrated thoughtful search strategies and careful reading of both the results pages and the websites chosen.

When searching online for their own personal interests, students reported beginning with a search of the general topic, as indicated in the following exchange:

Researcher: What if it was something that you were just interested in on your own?

Student: I usually take a topic approach 'cause I usually, like, if I wanted to find like spiders, I'd type in spiders.

Although teacher-designed projects often prompt students to search with a specific question in mind, the students we interviewed rarely reported doing so on their own. Their home Web-surfing habits were frequently reported as occurring when they were "just bored" and that they enter names of people, bands, sports teams, or interesting words or phrases they have encountered that day and "click around." This form of "schema diving" was widely reported by our focal students as a recreational form of online browsing and as a form of reading for pleasure.

Locating Information. The strategic importance of developing suitable questions before beginning an online search for information is revealed in students' strategies for determining keywords and phrases for locating appropriate information to answer their questions. For example, online readers may attempt to find websites using a less effective "dotcom" strategy, whereby they enter the topic as a URL (i.e., uniform resource locator, or Web address) into the address bar of a Web browser. For example, a student attempting to locate information about spiders might enter "www.spiders.com" into the address bar, which would lead to a website for a consulting firm rather than a site about arachnids.

Effective searches were more likely to occur when students were familiar with how search engines work and how to turn their questions into keywords or phrases, which most often employs a topic and a focus word. The topic allowed the search engine to find results that lead to general websites, whereas the focus word allowed the user to narrow the number of results, or hits, to a more manageable and useable number. For example, a student who was interested in determining which spiders are the most poisonous might enter the word *spider* into a search bar and receive 19,200,000 entries on the results page. However, a search for *spiders poisonous* would narrow the results to 3,670,000 entries, while reordering the keywords as *poisonous spiders* would further narrow the results to 860,000 entries. Effective and efficient searches require both a clear conception of what is sought and an understanding of how search engines order the search results.

Once a results page was provided by the search engine, the truly strategic reading began. Although some students expressed a belief that their carefully chosen search terms listed the most appropriate website first, others read the descriptions underneath the entries carefully. In a search to discover who invented algebra, the following student used the results descriptions to narrow down potential websites to answer her question:

Student: OK. Well, I went to Ask.com, and then I typed in "who invented algebra" and um now I'm just looking to figure out which one I think's the best. Hmm. I'm thinking that I'll go to this one.

Researcher: Why are you thinking you like that one?

Student: Um, it says they invented algebra. I just wanna look at it and see what it says. [reads from site] And right here it says they have hmm...in the algebra...Hmm...I'm gonna go back.

Researcher: Now tell me what you're thinking about.

Student: Um, I'm looking for another site 'cause that one didn't really have the information I wanted. I'm going to click on this link, because it actually has what I actually typed in there. I'll click on this one, because it says "who founded algebra."

A less effective strategy for choosing likely websites for information is called the "click and look" strategy, in which the reader proceeds systematically through the search engine results in a first-to-last listwise search. This trial-and-error approach often results in spending unnecessary time in waiting for website to load and then scanning the page to determine its usability in addressing the question at hand.

TICA researchers (Coiro, Malloy, & Rogers, 2006) identified the following three search-and-locate tactics as evincing a higher degree of strategic thinking:

1. Description reading—Action based on specific reading of search results (e.g., identifying boldfaced words from keyword input, related words)

2. Touring results page—Action based on scrolling through results page prior to close reading or change of keywords (e.g., taking a virtual text walk)

3. URL reading—Action based on specific reading of URLs (e.g., identifying certain elements of URLs, such as the top-level domains of .com, .edu, .gov)

Strategic online readers often exhibit knowledge of the particular text structures offered on webpages that can help them to locate information. Our students were familiar with how to navigate tabs, headings, and links and would frequently remark on pictures, images, or videos. One strategy that we noticed savvy readers using is a text walk, or tour, of the webpage from top to bottom and side to side, moving the cursor over headings and features to preview drop-down menus and other information that would appear when "mousing over." Students reported that they used these text walks to determine the usability of a page and to assess its organizational structure. If more specific information was desired, the text structures offered could be used to narrow down where the information might be. If students were looking for general information about a topic, they might begin to read the text on this page, or if more specific information was required, they might click through to other layers of the site on the basis of their assessment of the menu options and links. Rarely did students open a webpage and begin reading the text from top to bottom. If students were reading for a specific answer to a question, they would often scan the text quickly, looking for keywords and phrases that would lead them to the desired information. However, when reading for more generalized or open-ended understandings, students read more carefully, often using the cursor to follow the line of the text as they read.

Evaluating Information. The students who participated in our research were less sophisticated about determining the reliability of websites. In the first of our verbal protocol activities, they were asked to judge the reliability of a website titled *Help Save the Endangered Pacific Northwest Tree Octopus From Extinction!* (zapatopi.net/treeoctopus/), a hoax site that provides information about an allegedly endangered species of octopus that live in pine trees in the Pacific temperate rainforest. Prior to being given this task, our students were asked to tell the researcher what they knew about the octopus. Every student described a clear awareness of the creature as being a sea dweller. However, as the site is convincingly presented and provides photographs of an octopus in a pine tree, nearly every student in our sample judged the site to be somewhat or very reliable and the information to be true—often scratching their heads at the wonder of it all. The face validity of a website is a powerful and misleading feature for most students, and they would justify their judgment of reliability by stating that the site provided a great deal of good scientific information, pictures, and intact links, as demonstrated by the following posttask interview:

Student: Yeah. Um, number three. The reasons for my answer [to the prompt "Why I think the site is reliable"] is that they have a lot of other links [types this] and that they also have pictures that you can see. [types this] Alright.

Researcher: OK. Now what if I told you that this was a bogus site?

Student: I don't know. [laughs]

Researcher: Did you see enough that you believe that it's true? Because you had some questions as you worked.

Student: Um, I don't know, 'cause it would seem real, because it was talking about where they live and how they move.

Researcher: Right!

Student: And all the extra information in here.

Researcher: Mm hmm—it's a very good-looking site, isn't it?

Student: Yes. [laughs]

Before and after the "Tree Octopus" task, students were asked to define what they thought the word *reliability* meant in relation to Internet sites. The terms that emerged most frequently included *accurate*, *truthful*, and *trustworthy*. When students were asked how they would go about determining a website's reliability, the approach of comparing across sites was most frequently cited. Students also indicated that they check the webpage's source or author, ask a teacher or parent, refer to a book, or just use common sense. However, in the case of the Pacific Northwest Tree Octopus, students' common sense did not prevail.

The ability to effectively evaluate the accuracy, usefulness, and potential biases of online resources is a clear area of need for all online users, including the students we selected for our study. The critical reading skills that we incorporate in our instruction for print text sources, such as recognizing bias and stance, are entirely applicable in online settings. However, because of the accessibility of the online environment for authors with various purposes and knowledge bases, educators need to provide explicit and scaffolded instruction for evaluating the accuracy, biases, and usability of online sources. To this end, resources to support teachers in delivering instruction aimed toward the development of critical evaluation of online texts are becoming available (see Coiro, 2009; Eagleton & Dobler, 2007).

It was surprising to many of our student participants that such clearly inaccurate information could be presented online in such a convincing manner. Truly, anyone can print anything on the Internet, and it is the reader's responsibility to determine the worth of the information. As a result of this awareness, our taxonomy skills and strategies for online reading comprehension instruction includes the following learning targets:

- Determining accuracy—Evaluating the extent to which information contains factual and updated details that can be verified by consulting alternative or primary sources
- Determining bias—Evaluating information in relation to the stance an author takes (i.e., the lenses, viewpoint, or agenda embedded within the information)
- Determining relevancy—Evaluating information in relation to its utility or relevancy to the question or problem (i.e., the information's level of importance to a particular reading purpose or stated information need)
- Determining site reliability—Evaluating the trustworthiness of a website on the basis of its publisher and author information

Synthesizing Information. Synthesis involves integrating separate pieces of information and using that information to come to a new understanding. Successful online reading comprehension requires the ability to synthesize efficiently (Jenkins, 2006). The Internet introduces challenges with synthesis, because vast amounts of information can be accessed and readers need to determine what is relevant and how much is needed to draw a conclusion. These resources can take a variety of forms and can range from highly related to highly disparate, depending on the choices that readers make (Castek, Zawilinski, McVerry, O'Byrne, & Leu, in press). Because very little is known about the processes readers use as they synthesize information online, the verbal protocols from highly skilled online readers were particularly helpful in pinpointing instances of synthesis and examining what is involved in synthesizing across online information sources. One such instance is illustrated in the following think-aloud:

Student: I'm going to Ask.com. I'm going to search for "yellow tang"...find "yellow tang." [pause] I'm going to back up and type in yellow tang.

Student: [After locating a website from a list of search results] Lipstick tangs belong in a large aquarium and generally do well with other large nonaggressive fishes. Lots of free space must be provided as well as algae on which they graze. The salinity of 1.023 is preferred.

Student: I have no clue what salinity is so I think I might just search it. [searches for the term *salinity* on Google and clicks on one of the resulting sites] And this one says it means to surface salinity.

[after going back to the original site] I guess it has to do with salt, dissolve salts. [searches on dictionary.com] Yes, it is. Salinity.

Student: [When wrapping up] I learned that salinity is the amount [pause] of salt found in water. I found that pretty interesting, because I had no idea what it is.

Communicating Information. Online readers do not just read, they communicate with others continuously as a means of processing what they are learning. In the process, they incorporate new opinions and consider new information that has come their way. Online reading and writing are so closely connected that it is not possible to separate them; we read online as authors and we write online as readers (Huffaker, 2004, 2005; McVerry, 2007; Zawilinski, 2009). Thus, the communication processes involved in using a range of online tools appear to be inextricably linked to aspects of online reading comprehension (Boyd & Ellison, 2008; Forte & Bruckman, 2006; Lewis & Fabos, 2005).

Vehicles for online communication include podcasts, blog postings, instant messages, e-mails, and videos. Shared-writing spaces such as wikis and Google docs and social networks such as Ning.com offer multiple platforms for online communication exchanges—and new forms are evolving and emerging daily. To examine the unique processes students use to communicate information, students were asked to research a topic and share the information they learned with another seventh-grade class. Options for communicating their information were offered and included posting to a class blog, composing to a class e-mail address, or communicating in real time with a member of the class using an instant messenger function—none of which were widely used in the participating schools. The following exchange follows a skilled online reader through the decisions she made in using a blog to communicate the results of her online research.

Student: I'm gonna go to the blog. Um, how do you post a comment?

Researcher: That's a good question. Can you figure that out or think out loud the decisions you're making on your own?

Student: Um, I'm wondering where it is. It's usually in the front, um, um, go to comments and see if that's post a comment. There we go. I'm gonna go to this.... Copy that. Whoops. I'm gonna paste it right here.

Researcher: Could you tell me about what you are going to do now?

Student: Um, I'm gonna log in and publish and see if that works, and I think I'm gonna post as anonymous and publish my comment. [checks the blog] Um, yep it's up there.

Cultivating Communities of Readers

New definitions of literacy in the 21st century position reading as more than a set of skills and strategies (Lankshear & Knobel, 2006) and literacy education as more than a means of promoting academic achievement (Hiebert, 1991). The RAND Reading Study Group (2002) drew attention to the importance of reading comprehension as a social activity and asserted that text, the activity, and the reader are all situated within a larger sociocultural context. The social context, in particular, influences how learners make sense of, interpret, and share understandings. Over a period of years, Guthrie and McCann (1996), Raphael, Florio-Ruane, and George (2001), and Daniels (2002), guided teachers' implementation of social reading activities such as book clubs, literature circles, cooperative book discussion groups, and idea circles. Without regard to the structure these reading activities take in an individual classroom, the purpose is the same—to create a community of readers who construct understandings together. Participation motivates students to read for a range of purposes, use knowledge gained from previous experiences to generate new understandings, and actively engage in meaningful social interactions around reading. These activities tangibly illustrate to students that sustained reading has a social purpose and is more than a solitary, self-fulfilling activity.

Integrating these social learning activities fulfills an important need, because many students, especially adolescents, are driven by social interaction. One such indication is the proliferation of teen activity on social networking sites (Lenhart, Smith, Macgill, & Arafeh, 2008). Many adolescents spend their time connecting with friends by texting on cell phones, instant messaging, and using websites such as Facebook, MySpace, and Twitter and are highly skilled in creating their own communities and establishing affinity groups within those networks to connect with others and exchange ideas.

Despite the proliferation of skilled Internet use among adolescents, the majority of students attend schools where they are required to "disconnect" (Selwyn, 2006) and rely solely on face-to-face communication as the primary means of sharing ideas. This paradox brings to mind several important questions for educators:

- What benefits to literacy and learning could be realized if students were encouraged to merge their powerful social networking skills to support their academic pursuits?

- In what ways could social networking skills and the strong desire students possess to develop vast social networks be used to have a positive impact on literacy learning and academic achievement?

- How can teachers cultivate online communities of readers who collaborate, problem solve, and negotiate multiple perspectives?

The answers to these questions may be more easily found if, as educators, we are willing to change our collective mind-set toward the use of the Internet in school. Although nearly 100% of all U.S. classrooms have one or more Internet-connected computers available for student use (Wells & Lewis, 2006), few teachers are knowledgeable about how to guide students' active participation in today's networked world. As a result, literacy educators play a vitally important role in paving the road for Internet integration in our teaching and learning practices in a manner that supports literacy growth and learning.

Despite this important call to action, many educators lack familiarity or preparation in teaching the skills and strategies required for online reading, writing, and collaboration. Even those who consider themselves experienced in this arena recognize that the online literacy landscape is complex and constantly changing. Perhaps a better way to navigate these changes is to become comfortable in learning them along with students. Leu (1996) reports that this sort of learning is frequently constructed through social interactions in classrooms, not only among students but also between teachers and students. In fact, encouraging students to take on a leadership role in sharing their online skills and strategies has proven to be a beneficial means of promoting acquisition of the new literacies of online reading comprehension (Castek, 2008). The findings from this study suggest that students learn online reading comprehension skills best from other students, within the context of challenging activities designed by the teacher. Increased levels of challenge appeared to prompt students to try multiple approaches to making sense of complex information and encouraged them to think deeply about solving problems. Such an environment encourages sharing and learning by teachers and students alike as new ways to engage with and communicate texts evolve.

A Fundamental Shift From Page to Screen

The Internet has become today's technology for literacy and learning, offering classrooms a wide range of reading options and providing new opportunities for social interaction and collaboration with others (Boling, Castek, Zawilinski, Barton, & Nierlich, 2008; Coiro, 2003; Zawilinski, 2009). By developing communities of readers online, networks extend far beyond classroom walls and include members of the worldwide online community (see Greenhow, Robelia, & Hughes, 2009). Providing opportunities to communicate and collaborate with their peers from other schools nationally and globally helps to broaden perspectives and exposes students to different ways to approach and solve problems. By creating an online learning network, students can collaborate, using forums such as e-mail, blogs, and wikis to create, invent, and showcase their work in ways that promote engagement and advance learning outcomes. These tools, when chosen thoughtfully and accompanied by explicit instruction in the new literacies of online reading comprehension, can become fertile ground for students acquiring the skills necessary to communicate and collaborate in a global marketplace.

Developing an Online Community of Readers in Your Classroom

In the following sections, we suggest ways to extend the practice of silent reading by creating a community of readers online through implementation of online book clubs, online pen pals, and collaborative online projects.

Online Book Clubs. Online book clubs celebrate great books by assembling a diverse audience to discuss and appreciate them. Participation has the potential to promote higher level thinking, communication skills, deeper understanding of text, and strong social reasons for reading, because it involves a process of constructing and sharing meanings gained with others. ePals Book Club (www.epals .com) promotes sharing ideas about books and invites students of all ages to simultaneously participate in book discussions. Students discuss their favorite books and authors, submit short stories and poetry, and share the books they love with others. Planet Book Talk (www.planetbookclub.com) makes it possible for students to read comments other students have posted about books, access book reviews written by students of all ages, and post their own book review. Online book clubs such as these illustrate how communities of readers are flourishing online.

Online Pen Pals. The ePals Global Community connects classrooms around the world by offering safe, teacher-monitored e-mail accounts. Teachers can easily prescreen students' accounts, making it possible to spot problems and encourage positive communication. Integrating e-mail exchanges into your classroom program is particularly powerful in providing authentic purposes for sharing ideas, using language, and developing literacy among students of all ages.

Charron (2007) conducted a four-month study of an online pen pal program. Thirteen thousand students in 12 elementary schools, 3 middle schools, and 2 high schools participated. The social nature of learning was evident in the engagement and enthusiasm students displayed as they corresponded with their online pen pals. Results indicated that the use of the Internet for e-mail exchanges positively affected students' written-language production. In addition, students reported increased motivation in sustained reading and composing. Exchanges promoted problem solving and supported critical thinking in written-language acquisition.

Collaborative Online Projects. ePals also offers easy-to-implement projects for classroom collaboration, such as Digital Storytelling, Black History, and Biodiversity. Participation in collaborative online projects such as these transforms school-based learning into events that are meaningful, authentic, and social. By supporting students' engagement in collaborative activities, educators capitalize on their interests and motivation to share their learning.

Participation in online social action projects provides opportunities for young people to transform the world around them and makes it possible for them to see themselves, their abilities, and their school activities in a different light. Not only does this give students the opportunity to effect change and gain valuable experience with the new forms of online communication that are quickly defining our world, but also it builds confidence that the skills they are learning have value beyond the classroom. The United Nations has organized a Cyberschoolbus Global Teaching and Learning Project (cyberschoolbus.un.org/) as a means of exposing students to issues of global concern. Social action projects such as Feeding Minds Fighting Hunger (www.feedingminds.org/) provide resources to learn about current international issues that plague our world. These projects seek solutions to problems such as world hunger and racial or ethnic discrimination and promote the advancement of universal human rights. Placing students in the role of problem solvers empowers them to find ways to use what they are learning in school to change the reality of the world around them, and perhaps their futures.

Despite our enthusiasm for integrating these online literacy activities throughout the school day, we recognize the barriers that currently exist that impede widespread implementation. Though some may stem from limited Internet access in schools or filters meant to ensure child safety, others may stem from U.S. policies or competing reform efforts. The section that follows discusses the reforms needed to support teachers as they forge new ground in preparing students for the reading experiences that will define their future.

Literacy Standards, Assessments, and School Policies

Research in the new literacies of online reading comprehension reveals an important concern for any society based on egalitarian principles—U.S. public policies in reading may actually serve to increase achievement gaps, not close them (Leu, McVerry, et al., 2009). The problem stems from the fact that none of the current state reading assessments measure any of the novel skills required for successful online reading comprehension. The following observations have not changed since they were first observed several years ago (Leu, Ataya, & Coiro, 2002):

- Not a single state in the United States measures students' ability to read search engine results during state reading assessments.

- Not a single state in the United States measures students' ability to critically evaluate online information to determine its reliability.

- No state writing assessment in the United States measures students' ability to compose effective e-mail messages.

- Few, if any, states in the United States permit all students to use a word processor on the state writing assessment.

These state reading assessments and public policies resulting from No Child Left Behind legislation are actually helping the rich get richer and the poor get poorer. How does this happen? Students in the poorest school districts in the United States have the least amount of Internet access at home (Cooper, 2004). Unfortunately, the poorest schools are also under the greatest pressure to raise scores on tests that have nothing to do with online reading comprehension (Henry, 2007). As a result, there is little incentive to teach the new literacies of online reading comprehension because they are not tested. Thus, students in the poorest schools become doubly disadvantaged: They have less access to the Internet at home, and schools do not always prepare them for the new literacies of online reading comprehension at school.

Now, consider students in the most privileged schools. Cooper (2004) indicates that most students from advantaged communities have broadband Internet connections at home. As a result, teachers feel greater freedom to integrate the Internet into their curriculum and support their students with its use (Henry, 2007); it is easy to assign homework requiring Internet use when one knows that students have Internet access at home. Lazarus and Wainer (2005), for example, found that 63% of students from households earning more than $75,000 annually reported that they used the Internet at school, compared with only 36% of students from households earning less than $15,000 annually. Thus, students in richer districts become doubly privileged: They have greater access to the Internet at home, and they use it more often at school.

It is the cruelest irony of No Child Left Behind that students who need to be prepared the most at school for an online age of information are precisely those who are being prepared the least. This public policy failure has important consequences for education, because the Internet is now a central source of information and learning is dependent on the ability to read and comprehend complex information at high levels (Alexander & Jetton, 2000; Bransford, Brown, & Cocking, 2000).

Conclusion and Future Research Recommendations for Online Reading Comprehension

In this chapter, we have examined the changing literacy landscape and reviewed what we know about the skills and strategies of online reading comprehension as they are distinguished from offline formats. We have also addressed how communities of readers are transformed when reading shifts from page to screen and suggested ways to help students develop the literacy skills essential for online reading comprehension.

We recognize that most of the silent reading instruction and practice in classrooms is designed to enhance offline reading competency; however, we suggest that informed instruction and engaging practice in the silent reading of online formats are of critical importance as well. In terms of future research, there are several areas where advancements in the area of online silent reading would lead to improved instruction in the classroom.

First, there is a need for the continued development of curriculum and instruction that would guide teachers at the late elementary and middle/high school levels to specifically address silent online reading comprehension with their students. A well-developed pedagogy for integrating online and offline reading and communication skills would enhance the synergistic properties inherent in addressing these two formats concurrently. For example, reading for bias and accuracy is just as important in print text as it is on the webpage. The processes for determining these qualities may require different skills; however, the need to read critically in all contexts is paramount. The nature of reading informational text, whether online or offline, requires a conditional knowledge of both skimming and careful reading skills, and although the decisions made regarding the text may lead to different actions between the two formats, these are skills that efficient and strategic readers require.

Further, future research may uncover more about how the structure and organization of various digital formats affects how readers process and understand what they read. Does the reader process information differently according to the visual layout of the page, wiki, or blog, or through the layering of texts that are accessed only through tabs and hyperlinks? More important, how do we learn to adapt to the continually changing formats that present themselves as contexts for learning? Are there transferable sets of skills or knowledge that can be transported from existing digital formats to newer ones?

Finally, are there aspects of online reading that support the growth of offline reading skills for struggling readers, English Learners, or the aliterate? If so, how can we incorporate these aspects into our increasingly inclusive classrooms? Likewise, are there motivational elements of online reading that can be useful for these groups of students?

As we grapple to understand the constantly changing textual landscape that develops in a digital climate, researchers and educators must embrace a formatively inquisitive stance toward investigating the skills and strategies required of our citizens of tomorrow. With little time to breathe between innovations, we must come to understand the nature of the skills required to adapt to newer and newer literacies and create instruction that addresses the requisite comprehension skills and strategies. Using a formative method in a variety of classrooms to systematically design the most promising instructional strategies may lead us more quickly to the classroom instruction we need to develop. The success of our students in navigating the 21st-century landscape hangs in the balance.

QUESTIONS FOR
PROFESSIONAL DEVELOPMENT

1. How can we support teachers in expanding options for purposeful reading both online and offline? Think of ways that you can provide relevant and authentic tasks for questioning, locating, evaluating, synthesizing, and communicating information using online and offline formats, perhaps by incorporating some of the suggestions provided in this chapter.

2. How do we support students as they participate in online reading communities? Preparing our students for a tech-savvy world requires that they become accustomed to the venues for accessing, and methods of sharing, information online. Learning to approach these tasks with thoughtful strategies, a critical eye, and appropriate interactions requires targeted instruction and sufficient time for mastery. Think of ways that you can structure your instructional time and classroom activities to provide these experiences.

REFERENCES

Alexander, P.A., & Jetton, T.L. (2000). Learning from text: A multidimensional and developmental perspective. In M.L. Kamil, P.B. Mosenthal, P.D. Pearson, & R. Barr (Eds.), *Handbook of reading research* (Vol. 3, pp. 285–310). Mahwah, NJ: Erlbaum.

Boling, E., Castek, J., Zawilinski, L., Barton, K., & Nierlich, T. (2008). Collaborative literacy: Blogs and Internet projects. *The Reading Teacher, 61*(6), 504–506. doi:10.1598/RT.61.6.10

Boyd, D.M., & Ellison, N.B. (2008). Social network sites: Definition, history, and scholarship. *Journal of Computer-Mediated Communication, 13*(1), 210–230. doi:10.1111/j.1083-6101.2007.00393.x

Bransford, J.D., Brown, A.L., & Cocking, R.R. (Eds.). (2000). *How people learn: Brain, mind, experience, and school* (Rev. ed.). Washington, DC: National Academy Press.

Castek, J.M. (2008). *How do 4th and 5th grade students acquire the new literacies of online reading comprehension? Exploring the contexts that facilitate learning.* Unpublished doctoral dissertation, University of Connecticut, Storrs.

Castek, J.M., & Carter, A. (2006, April). *Adapting reciprocal teaching to the Internet using telecollaborative projects.* Poster presented at the annual meeting of the American Educational Research Association, San Francisco.

Castek, J.M., Zawilinski, L., McVerry, J.G., O'Byrne, W.I., & Leu, D.J. (in press). The new literacies of online reading comprehension: New opportunities and challenges for students with learning difficulties. In C. Wyatt-Smith, J. Elkins, & S. Gunn (Eds.), *Multiple perspectives on difficulties in learning literacy and numeracy.* New York: Springer.

Charron, N.N. (2007). "I learned that there's a state called Victoria and he has six blue-tongued lizards!" *The Reading Teacher, 60*(8), 762–769. doi:10.1598/RT.60.8.6

Coiro, J. (2003). Reading comprehension on the Internet: Expanding our understanding of reading comprehension to encompass new literacies. *The Reading Teacher, 56*(5), 458–464.

Coiro, J. (2007). *Exploring changes to reading comprehension on the Internet: Paradoxes and possibilities for diverse adolescent readers.* Unpublished doctoral dissertation, University of Connecticut, Storrs.

Coiro, J. (2009). *Instructional strategies for critically evaluating online information.* Retrieved September 17, 2009, from www.lite.iwarp.com/CoiroCritEval.html

Coiro, J., & Dobler, E. (2007). Exploring the online reading comprehension strategies used by sixth-grade skilled readers to search for and locate information on the Internet. *Reading Research Quarterly, 42*(2), 214–257. doi:10.1598/RRQ.42.2.2

Coiro, J., Knobel, M., Lankshear, C., & Leu, D.J. (2008). Central issues in new literacies and new literacies research. In J. Coiro, M. Knobel, C. Lankshear, & D.J. Leu (Eds.), *Handbook of research on new literacies* (pp. 25–32). Mahwah, NJ: Erlbaum.

Coiro, J., Malloy, J., & Rogers, A. (2006). *Patterns of effective strategy use among adolescent online readers.* Poster presented at the annual meeting of the American Education Research Association, San Francisco.

Cooper, M. (2004). *Expanding the digital divide and falling behind on broadband: Why a telecommunications policy of neglect is not benign.* Washington, DC: Consumer Federation of America and Consumers Union. Retrieved April 17, 2007, from www.consumerfed.org/pdfs/digitaldivide.pdf

Cope, B., & Kalantzis, M. (2000). Multiliteracies: The beginnings of an idea. In B. Cope & M. Kalantzis (Eds.), *Multiliteracies: Literacy learning and the design of social futures* (pp. 3–8). New York: Routledge.

Daniels, H. (2002). *Literature circles: Voice and choice in book clubs and reading groups* (2nd ed.). Portland, ME: Stenhouse.

Eagleton, M.B., & Dobler, E. (2007). *Reading the Web: Strategies for Internet inquiry.* New York: Guilford.

Forte, A., & Bruckman, A. (2006). From Wikipedia to the classroom: Exploring online publication and learning. In S.A. Barab, K.E. Hay, & D.T. Hickey (Eds.), *Proceedings of the 7th international conference of the learning sciences* (Vol. 2, pp. 182–188). Mahwah, NJ: Erlbaum.

Gee, J.P. (2003). *What video games have to teach us about learning and literacy.* New York: Palgrave Macmillan.

Greenhow, C., Robelia, B., & Hughes, J.E. (2009). Web 2.0 and classroom research: What path should we take *now*? *Educational*

Researcher, 38(4), 246–259. doi:10.3102/0013189X09336671

Guthrie, J.T., & McCann, A.D. (1996). Idea circles: Peer collaborations for conceptual learning. In L.B. Gambrell & J.F. Almasi (Eds.), *Lively discussions! Fostering engaged reading* (pp. 87–105). Newark, DE: International Reading Association.

Henry, L.A. (2007). *Exploring new literacies pedagogy and online reading comprehension among middle school students and teachers: Issues of social equity or social exclusion?* Unpublished doctoral dissertation, University of Connecticut, Storrs.

Hiebert, E.H. (Ed.). (1991). *Literacy for a diverse society: Perspectives, practices, and policies.* New York: Teachers College Press.

Huffaker, D. (2004). Spinning yarns around the digital fire: Storytelling and dialogue among youth on the Internet. *Information Technology in Childhood Education Annual*, 63–75.

Huffaker, D. (2005). The educated blogger: Using weblogs to promote literacy in the classroom. *AACE Journal, 13*(2), 91–98.

International Reading Association. (2009). *New literacies and 21st-century technologies: A position statement of the International Reading Association.* Newark, DE: Author. Retrieved April 29, 2010, from www.reading.org/Libraries/Position _Statements_and_Resolutions/ps1067 _NewLiteracies21stCentury.sflb.ashx

International Society for Technology in Education, Partnership for 21st Century Skills, & State Educational Technology Directors Association. (2007). *Maximizing the impact: The pivotal role of technology in a 21st century education system.* Retrieved April 29, 2010, from www.setda.org/c/document_library/get_file ?folderId=191&name=P21Book_complete.pdf

Jenkins, H. (with Purushotma, R., Weigel, M., Clinton, K., & Robison, A.J.). (2006). *Confronting the challenges of participatory culture: Media education for the 21st century.* Cambridge, MA: MIT Press.

Kress, G. (1999). Design and transformation: New theories of meaning. In B. Cope & M. Kalantzis (Eds.), *Multiliteracies: Literacy learning and the design of social futures* (pp. 153–161). New York: Routledge.

Landow, G.P. (1994). What's a critic to do? Critical theory in the age of hypertext. In G.P. Landow (Ed.), *Hyper/text/theory* (pp. 1–48). Baltimore: Johns Hopkins University Press.

Lankshear, C., & Knobel, M. (2006). *New literacies: Everyday practices and classroom learning* (2nd ed.). New York: Open University Press.

Lazarus, W., & Wainer, A. (with Lipper, L.). (2005). *Measuring digital opportunity for America's children: Where we stand and where we go from here.* Santa Monica, CA: The Children's Partnership. Retrieved April 29, 2010, from www.childrenspartnership.org/ AM/Template.cfm?Section=Home&section =Technology1&template=/CM/ContentDisplay .cfm&ContentFileID=1238

Lenhart, A., Smith, A., Macgill, A.R., & Arafeh, S. (2008). *Writing, technology and teens.* Washington, DC: Pew Research Center. Retrieved September 16, 2009, from pew research.org/pubs/808/writing-technology -and-teens

Leu, D.J., Jr. (1996). Sarah's secret: Social aspects of literacy and learning in a digital information age. *The Reading Teacher, 50*(2), 162–165.

Leu, D.J., Jr., Ataya, R., & Coiro, J. (2002, December). *Assessing assessment strategies among the 50 states: Evaluating the literacies of our past or the literacies of our future?* Paper presented at the 52nd annual meeting of the National Reading Conference, Miami, FL.

Leu, D.J., Coiro, J., Castek, J., Hartman, D.K., Henry, L.A., & Reinking, D. (2008). Research on instruction and assessment in the new literacies of online reading comprehension. In C.C. Block & S.R. Parris (Eds.), *Comprehension instruction: Research-based best practices* (2nd ed., pp. 321–346). New York: Guilford.

Leu, D.J., Jr., Kinzer, C.K., Coiro, J.L., & Cammack, D.W. (2004). Toward a theory of new literacies emerging from the Internet and other information and communication technologies. In R.B. Ruddell & N.J. Unrau (Eds.), *Theoretical models and processes of reading* (5th ed., pp. 1570–1613). Newark, DE: International Reading Association.

Leu, D.J., McVerry, J.G., O'Byrne, W.I., Zawilinski, L., Castek, J., & Hartman, D.K. (2009). The new literacies of online reading comprehension and the irony of No Child Left Behind: Students who require our assistance the most actually receive it the least. In L.M. Morrow, R. Rueda, & D. Lapp (Eds.), *Handbook of research on literacy and diversity* (pp. 173–194). New York: Guilford.

Leu, D.J., O'Byrne, W.I., Zawilinski, L., McVerry, J.G., & Everett-Cacopardo, H. (2009).

Comments on Greenhow, Robelia, and Hughes: Expanding the new literacies conversation. *Educational Researcher, 38*(4), 264–269. doi:10.3102/0013189X09336676

Leu, D.J., Reinking, D., et al. (2005). *Teaching Internet comprehension to adolescents: Developing Internet comprehension strategies among poor, adolescent students at risk to become dropouts.* Retrieved April 29, 2010, from www.new literacies.uconn.edu/iesproject/index.html

Leu, D.J., Zawilinski, L., Castek, J., Banerjee, M., Housand, B.C., Liu, Y., et al. (2007). What is new about the new literacies of online reading comprehension? In L.S. Rush, A.J. Eakle, & A. Berger (Eds.), *Secondary school literacy: What research reveals for classroom practice* (pp. 37–68). Urbana, IL: National Council of Teachers of English.

Lewis, C., & Fabos, B. (2005). Instant messaging, literacies, and social identities. *Reading Research Quarterly, 40*(4), 470–501. doi:10.1598/RRQ.40.4.5

McVerry, J.G. (2007). Forums and functions of threaded discussions. *New England Reading Association Journal, 43*(1), 79–85.

National Council of Teachers of English. (2007). *21st-century literacies: A policy research brief.* Urbana, IL: Author. Retrieved April 29, 2010, from www.ncte.org/library/NCTEFiles/Resources/Positions/Chron1107ResearchBrief.pdf

National Telecommunications and Information Administration & Economics and Statistics Administration. (2002). *A nation online: How Americans are expanding their use of the Internet.* Washington, DC: U.S. Department of Commerce.

The New London Group. (2000). A pedagogy of multiliteracies: Designing social futures. In B. Cope & M. Kalantzis (Eds.), *Multiliteracies: Literacy learning and the design of social futures* (pp. 9–37). New York: Routledge.

Orange, C., & Horowitz, R. (1999). An academic standoff: Literacy task preferences of African American and Mexican American male adolescents versus teacher-expected preferences. *Journal of Adolescent & Adult Literacy, 43*(1), 28–39.

RAND Reading Study Group. (2002). *Reading for understanding: Toward an R&D program in reading comprehension.* Santa Monica, CA: RAND.

Raphael, T.E., Florio-Ruane, S., & George, M. (2001). Book club plus: A conceptual framework to organize literacy instruction. *Language Arts, 79*(2), 159–168.

Reinking, D. (1992). Differences between electronic and printed texts: An agenda for research. *Journal of Educational Multimedia and Hypermedia, 1*(1), 11–24.

Reinking, D. (1998). Introduction: Synthesizing technological transformations of literacy in a post-typographic world. In D. Reinking, M.C. McKenna, L.D. Labbo, & R.D. Kieffer (Eds.), *Handbook of literacy and technology: Transformations in a post-typographic world* (pp. x–xxxii). Mahwah, NJ: Erlbaum.

Roberts, D.F., Foehr, U.G., & Rideout, V. (2005). Generation M: Media in the lives of 8–18 year-olds. Washington, DC: The Henry J. Kaiser Family Foundation. Retrieved April 29, 2010, from www.kff.org/entmedia/upload/Generation-M-Media-in-the-Lives-of-8-18-Year-olds-Report.pdf

Selwyn, N. (2006). Exploring the 'digital disconnect' between net-savvy students and their schools. *Learning, Media and Technology, 31*(1), 5–17. doi:10.1080/17439880500515416

Street, B. (1998). New literacies in theory and practice: What are the implications for language in education? *Linguistics and Education, 10*(1), 1–24. doi:10.1016/S0898-5898(99)80103-X

Turner, J., & Paris, S.G. (1995). How literacy tasks influence children's motivation for literacy. *The Reading Teacher, 48*(8), 662–673.

Wade, S.E., & Moje, E.B. (2000). The role of text in classroom learning. In M.L. Kamil, P.B. Mosenthal, P.D. Pearson, & R. Barr (Eds.), *Handbook of reading research* (Vol. 3, pp. 609–627). Mahwah, NJ: Erlbaum.

Weinstein, S. (2002). The writing on the wall: Attending to self-motivated student literacies. *English Education, 35*(1), 21–45.

Wells, J., & Lewis, L. (2006). *Internet access in U.S. public schools and classrooms: 1994–2005* (NCES 2007-020). Washington, DC: National Center for Education Statistics, Institute of Education Sciences, U.S. Department of Education.

Zawilinski, L. (2009). HOT blogging: A framework for blogging to promote higher order thinking. *The Reading Teacher, 62*(8), 650–661. doi:10.1598/RT.62.8.3

CHAPTER 14

Productive Sustained Reading in a Bilingual Class

Jo Worthy
The University of Texas at Austin

Nancy Roser
The University of Texas at Austin

Marcus folds his lanky frame over an orange plastic chair, his face two inches from a book whose pages he has not turned since the beginning of free-reading time in Mr. Graves's fifth-grade classroom. Sprawled on opposite ends of the couch, Sam and Sergio are each engrossed in their own copies of the latest book in the Percy Jackson & the Olympians series by Rick Riordan. Marta has just settled into reading the book she brought from home when Cinthia interrupts her to show off her new cell phone. A music and history buff, Mr. Graves has been has been reading a bestseller about Woodstock during the sustained reading time. As Roger returns to his seat from his second trip to the bathroom, Misty goes to the bookshelf to trade the novel she has been flipping through for another book. She runs her finger slowly along the shelf of class novel sets, tattered discards from the public library, basal readers, chapter books, and outdated information books Mr. Graves has collected from used book stores and garage sales. Gerry shows Melissa a drawing from the science fiction book he checked out from the library, and they both gasp and laugh. Noticing the noise and activity level increasing, Mr. Graves scans the room and admonishes students to get back to their reading.

Like many language arts teachers, Mr. Graves knows the importance of providing opportunities for his students to read in school. There is wide agreement among literacy researchers that time spent reading is essential for growth in literacy and academics. Time spent reading is related to growth in vocabulary, language learning, reading fluency and comprehension, confidence, general intelligence, and general knowledge (Anderson, Wilson, & Fielding, 1988; Elley & Mangubhai, 1983; Stanovich, 1986; Taylor, Frye, & Maruyama, 1990). Insufficient opportunities to read have been explained by obstacles such as limited access to reading materials and limited opportunities in school (Ivey & Broaddus, 2001; Worthy, Moorman, & Turner, 1999). Goals for sustained reading time include promoting enjoyment and motivation and improving reading skill. Although some

Revisiting Silent Reading: New Directions for Teachers and Researchers, edited by Elfrieda H. Hiebert and D. Ray Reutzel. © 2010 by the International Reading Association.

teachers find success with the practice, many tell us the designated time is frequently wasted because, as shown in the opening scenario, many students do not use it productively. One key, according to Guthrie (2004), is engagement. Engaged readers, "look, behave, feel, and interact very differently than disengaged readers" (p. 1).

In Mr. Graves's classroom, Sergio and Sam appear to be what Guthrie (2004) would call "engaged readers" set among peers who are less engaged in a text environment that is perhaps less than engaging. Guthrie's description includes other aspects of the school and home literacy lives of engaged readers. If Sergio and Sam fit the mold for engaged readers, they are active and strategic as they read and write both for enjoyment and in school subjects. They are involved in class discussions and make good use of teacher guidance. They talk to their friends about the books they read and follow intriguing ideas through other sources. For instance, when they read the Percy Jackson series with its hero-descendents of Greek gods, students might become curious about Greek mythology and check for books on gods and titans in the school library, or seek information on the Internet. They always have books and other texts handy to read during free time at school, and they read at home for enjoyment and information.

Other students in Mr. Graves's classroom appear to be disengaged during independent reading time. "Disengaged readers" as described by Guthrie (2004) are passive learners and thinkers. Easily distracted, their involvement with and comprehension of text are minimal, and this stance affects their learning and progress in all academic areas. In discussions of texts during reading and other content areas, disengaged readers are usually silent and uninvolved. They may read only what is assigned and rarely at home. According to Guthrie (2004), "the crisis of our schools today is that too many children are disengaged from literacy. Their disaffection and retreat leads to mediocre reading comprehension, which prevents them from gaining subject matter and world knowledge" (p. 2) and starts a vicious cycle: Less proficient at and less satisfied by reading, they read less.

It makes sense that for most students to put real effort into schoolwork and thus make academic progress, their classroom instruction and materials must be engaging (Guthrie, 2004). What does this mean for sustained reading time? How can this time be made more productive for all students, including students of poverty and those who are learning English while trying to maintain their first language?

We turned to research to address these questions in our work with a teacher, Monica Reyes (pseudonym), whose fifth-grade bilingual class was being monitored because of low scores on the previous year's state achievement tests. The students were first generation U.S. citizens, or the children of recent immigrants from Mexico, who were in various stages of language and literacy learning in Spanish and English. Together with Monica, we transformed the sustained reading portion of their language arts curriculum by adding teacher conferences and peer sharing and by adding books to the classroom through a book flood (Elley, 2000; Neuman, 1999) targeted to the academic and language needs, interests, and experiences of the students.

Opportunity to Read

When the National Reading Panel (NRP; National Institute of Child Health and Human Development, 2000) report did not find sufficient evidence to conclude that reading independently is effective in improving student achievement, there was an outcry from literacy researchers and educators (Allington, 2002; Coles, 2000). One controversy associated with the finding was that varied implementations of sustained reading, including Accelerated Reader, reading at home, and reading in classrooms, were grouped together in the meta-analysis, an indication that informed self-selected reading was not necessarily the variable under scrutiny. Another issue was that the NRP members considered only experimental and quasi-experimental studies; thus, nuanced descriptions of interventions and findings were absent. Further, only studies in which there was no teacher supervision were included. To be sure, there is no one accepted approach to sustained reading, and the most common nomenclature, sustained silent reading, typically implies minimal teacher guidance. However, research has suggested some key factors that are important in implementations of sustained reading (e.g., teacher guidance, social interaction, book access).

Teacher Guidance

Teacher guidance is frequently the missing piece in implementations of sustained reading. In its earliest manifestations, teachers offered students little guidance. Most teachers understood they were to read their own books so as to model enjoyment rather than interact with students (Campbell, 1989), advice Mr. Graves (in the opening vignette) chose to follow. Although modeling is important, the teacher's guidance is essential to ensure that students are reading instructionally appropriate books, reading strategically, and understanding what they are reading (Kelley & Clausen-Grace, 2006; Reutzel, Jones, Fawson, & Smith, 2008). Getting to know students, their interests, academic needs, and experiences is especially important for challenged readers and those who have difficulty choosing books (Clements, 2002; Fisher & Ivey, 2006).

Social Interaction

Avid readers share what they are reading with their friends and read what their friends recommend (Carlsen & Sherrill, 1988). Similarly, talking with peers about reading improves students' reading attitudes and may influence and stretch their choices (Adler, Rougle, Kaiser, & Caughlan, 2004). Students value their peers' recommendations (Edmunds & Bauserman, 2006; Kelley & Clausen-Grace, 2006). Adolescents in voluntary after-school book clubs valued the "real" discussions that took place, contrasting that talk with "boring," teacher-directed classroom book discussions (Alvermann, Young, Green, & Wisenbaker, 1999).

Book Access

Children read more when books are accessible in their homes, schools, and classrooms (Chambliss & McKillop, 2000; Morrow, 1991; Neuman & Celano, 2001). However, students from economically impoverished homes have far less access to print in their communities than do students from middle- and high-income homes (Feitelson & Goldstein, 1986; Neuman & Celano, 2001). Students who live in poverty, then, may be more dependent on schools for reading materials. However, libraries in such schools often have limited text resources for students (Constantino, 2005, 2008; Worthy et al., 1999).

An intervention called "book flood" has shown promise in improving achievement and attitudes toward reading for students in high-poverty communities and for second-language learners in developing countries. Book floods infuse large numbers of books into a classroom or school, and teachers are given professional development in effective ways to use the books, including read-alouds, partner reading, and drama (Elley, 2000; Neuman, 1999). Elley's review of studies conducted in developing countries found that book floods showed consistent positive effects on language, literacy, and learning.

Neuman (1999) conducted a large-scale book flood study paired with professional development in child care centers serving low-income neighborhoods in Philadelphia, Pennsylvania, USA, and examined the effects on the literacy attitudes, motivation, and skills of the students. Qualitative and statistical analyses of early literacy measures showed that students in the intervention centers made greater gains in early literacy measures than did students in comparison centers, and the gains were still evident eight months after the end of the study. Both Neuman (1999) and Elley (2000) stress that, although providing access to books is essential, instruction and engagement are also key determinants of students' reading progress in book flood studies.

Classroom Libraries and Students' Preferences

Even when classroom libraries contain sufficient numbers of books, the books may be too difficult, not relevant, or otherwise inappropriate for students and, as illustrated in the opening scenario, books may sit on shelves collecting dust, with only a small proportion used by students (Martinez, Roser, Worthy, Strecker, & Gough, 1997). Thus, classroom library materials should be chosen carefully. For any group of students, age-appropriate magazines, high-quality picture books, information texts, and poetry should be included in a classroom library. Students' experiences, cultural backgrounds, and interests should be represented as well as books that positively depict many cultural and ethnic groups. Instructionally appropriate texts—those that provide a balance of support and challenge—are essential to a classroom collection (Donovan, Smolkin, & Lomax, 2000). Teachers of bilingual students and English learners need to consider accessibility and familiarity of text content and language, authenticity and relevancy of the cultural content, quality and accessibility of illustrations, and accessibility of vocabulary and textual organization (Vardell, Hadaway, & Young, 2006).

In interviews with adult avid readers, Carlsen and Sherrill (1988) found that access to materials of their own choosing, including popular materials, was an important factor in reading motivation. Students also like to choose their own materials and, like adults, their tastes are varied and individual (Edmunds & Bauserman, 2006; Ivey & Broaddus, 2001; Worthy et al., 1999). Like adults, students revel in visually rich and current information texts, novels and popular culture texts, including series books, graphic novels, comics, and magazines (McGill-Franzen & Botzakis, 2009). Books in which the first language is represented positively are also important resources for bilingual students (Martínez-Roldán & López-Robertson, 1999).

With upper elementary and older students, who may already be apathetic toward reading (McKenna, Kear, & Ellsworth, 1995; Ryan & Patrick, 2001), schools have an important responsibility for providing access to reading materials that are appropriate, appealing, and relevant. Yet schools often do a poor job of providing materials students like to read, and students whose families are poor are doubly disadvantaged because they have few opportunities to supplement what is available in schools (Worthy et al., 1999). In a study of book access in Los Angeles, California, USA, Constantino (2008) reports that although many school libraries contained popular books, there were rarely enough to go around. As one student said, "I know I won't ever get a Star Wars book. My class comes to the library too late in the day, and someone else has it. It's the only thing I really want to read, and it ain't there" (p. 61). Another student reported, "I wanted a Harry Potter book, but I did not get it all year" (p. 61).

The Story of the "Flood"

Intrigued by Elley's (2000) and Neuman's (1999) studies of ready access, we wondered how students' reading choices, habits, and proficiencies would be affected if books they wanted to read were within easy reach. We flooded a fifth-grade bilingual classroom in a school serving a low-income community with books that were carefully selected in consideration of students' interests, personal preferences, languages, instructional needs, and background experiences. Our intent was to make interesting and relevant books as accessible to these students as they would be to students from more privileged backgrounds. We also worked with the classroom teacher to plan a sustained reading intervention that included teacher conferences and peer sharing. Using ethnographic data gathering and analysis methods, we examined the combined effects of the book flood and its accompanying instructional supports on the reading habits, attitudes, purposes, and achievement of the students.

The School

Chavez Elementary School (pseudonym) is located on the edge of a large city in the southwest, in a neighborhood filled mostly with tiny wood-frame houses. Most residents are of Mexican heritage, and billboards and other neighborhood signs surrounding the school are in both English and Spanish. There are no bookstores within an eight-mile radius. There is at least one bilingual classroom at each grade level from prekindergarten to fifth grade. More than 90% of the students in the school qualify for free or reduced-cost lunch.

The Teacher and Her Students

Monica Reyes, the child of Mexican immigrants who are now naturalized citizens, was in her second full year of teaching during the year of the book flood. She had taught fifth grade the previous year at the same school. We knew Monica because she was a graduate of the teacher preparation program at our university and Chavez, her school, was where we ran a literacy-tutoring program and taught many of our field-based teacher preparation classes.

Monica's classroom was large, colorful, and filled with student work and book posters. At any given time, there were approximately 18 students in her classroom. Because of movement into and out of the classroom, only 15 participants had a yearlong record to examine. Almost half of her students were born in Mexico; the others were born in the United States to parents who had recently emigrated from Mexico, and all spoke Spanish in their homes. The students were bilingual and biliterate to various degrees. Although the major focus of instruction was English, in accordance with district transitional bilingual education guidelines for fifth grade, Monica used Spanish as a support for students as needed, and students chose when to use English, Spanish, or a combination of the two languages.

Learning About the Students

Reading Interests. Because we wanted to provide books of specific appeal, we started the year by interviewing each student. We asked about reading choices and interests, influences, purposes, attitudes, and habits in and out of school. Of the 15 students, 10 reported reading for approximately 30 minutes per day outside of school, which was a homework requirement. Three students said they sometimes read more than the required time.

As we had anticipated, students had limited access to books outside of school; their personal libraries ranged from a low of 1 book to a high of 25, with students averaging about 6 books of their own. Most of the books students owned had been provided by Reading Is Fundamental (RIF), a nonprofit organization that provides three books per year to students in low-income communities. Some students mentioned purchasing books at grocery or convenience stores. Two of the students had been to a bookstore. Eight reported visiting the public library when they were younger; two had been in the past two years.

During these interviews, we also tried to learn what books or materials each student was interested in reading, so we could plan the book flood to match those interests. Surprisingly, only two students named specific book titles or authors beyond those recently read aloud by the teacher. A few students named topics or subjects they would be interested in reading about, but none had read books on those topics.

To gain a complete picture of students' preferences, we prepared a box with about 50 books representing a variety of genres, formats, content, and readability levels, including popular magazines, comic books, and other materials not typically found in schools, and asked students to look through the box with us and indicate which texts appealed to them and why. The box generated great excitement among the students, and most asked to borrow one or more books, which gave us some early insights into students' preferences. The most popular materials were scary stories, bilingual picture books with Latino characters, magazines, comic books, and books Monica had previously introduced to the class (e.g., those by Marc Brown and Kevin Henkes). Information books, particularly those focusing on animals and science, piqued interest as well.

Reading Achievement. The focus of our inquiry was how the book flood and supported sustained reading time may influence students' reading attitudes, habits, and purposes, as well as reading achievement. At the beginning of the school year, we assisted Monica in administering an individual reading assessment required by the school. The average reading level on the English version was early second grade, with scores ranging from mid-first- to fifth-grade levels. In Spanish, students' reading levels ranged from third grade to middle school, with an average of fourth-grade level. On the previous year's state standardized achievement test administered in English, the students' scores had been dismal. Only three of Monica's fifth graders had earned a passing score as fourth graders (of the 11 who had been Chavez students). Fewer than half of her prior fifth graders had passed the test. Thus, she felt particularly intense pressure from the school principal who frequently raised concerns for students' test scores, urging all of us to keep scores uppermost as we worked with the class. We knew the principal well from our history of working in the school, and we talked with her openly and often. Although she professed to trust that the book flood procedures were instructionally sound, she keenly felt the accountability pressures and frequently stopped by the classroom to observe.

Initiating the Flood

Observing the Classroom. We entered the classroom three weeks after the beginning of school to give the students and Monica time to establish routines without disruption. We spent the following four weeks observing instruction and book use. For the first week, we observed in the classroom all day to get a sense of when and how books were used. For the following two weeks, we targeted our observations, observing during all reading and language arts instruction and occasionally during other content areas, but mostly during free reading time when students were given 20 to 30 minutes to read books of their choice.

Choosing Books. After the initial interviews, we worked with Monica to identify reading materials to use in the book flood. Beginning in the second month of school, we added, in three phases (i.e., October, January, April), approximately 180 books to the classroom collection. The three-phase book flood allowed us to add books on the basis of our observations of students' interests and preferences. Choosing the materials was important and complex, because students had a wide variety of interests as well as a range of proficiency levels in English and Spanish literacy. We carefully selected books to include a range of genres, formats, and topics on the basis of research into students' interests (gathered through observations and interviews), the fifth-grade curriculum, Monica's specific plans and preferences, and our own and experts' knowledge of children's literature. We also included culturally relevant books as well as books that introduced less familiar cultural groups.

Typically, students in upper elementary and middle school classrooms are expected to read grade-level materials, with a focus on novels. Indeed, Monica's classroom had a number of class sets with such highly regarded novels as *My Side of the Mountain* and *Julie of the Wolves* both by Jean Craighead George. In our flood, though, we provided books that might not usually be in a middle grade classroom library—those which students specifically requested, as well as those we thought could contribute to students' developing English and Spanish literacies. There were pattern books (e.g., *Fortunately* by Remy Charlip), easy readers (e.g., *In a Dark, Dark Room and Other Scary Stories* by Alvin Schwartz), transitional chapter readers (e.g., *Fox Outfoxed* by James Marshall), and easy information books. Each phase of the flood included a good portion of bilingual picture books by and about Latina/os, including *Pepita Talks Twice/Pepita Habla Dos Veces* by Ofelia Dumas Lachtman and *Friends From the Other Side/Amigos del Otro Lado* by Gloria Anzaldúa. We also included books that were not available in the school library, such as the newest book in a favorite series (e.g., Harry Potter by J.K. Rowling and Captain Underpants by Dav Pilkey), comic books, cartoons, and books on such student-preferred topics as medicine and crime detection. There were also biographies, science fiction, and challenging fantasy. Comic books, cartoon collections, joke books, and magazines were included in the flood and available for students to keep at their desks, read during free times, and check out but not read during the instructional reading time.

For each phase, we brought approximately 60 different titles and introduced them one by one, reading the title and author and providing short but compelling descriptions. Books were then displayed on tables with all titles showing, and students were given 30 minutes to browse through them. They could read individually or in pairs, and they could try out as many books as they wanted. At the end of the browsing time, the books were placed on a counter near the classroom library in tubs labeled by category (e.g., jokes and comics, novels, fiction picture books, and information picture books).

Providing Sustained Reading Time. Each day during a 30-minute sustained reading time before lunch, students read silently the books they had chosen. Students were guided to choose books on their instructional level (i.e., providing an appropriate degree of success and challenge). Students were asked to have their books at their desks before the start of this time rather than to spend any of the reading time choosing books. Immediately after the reading time, Monica provided a five-minute sharing time for students to hold up and talk about their books to the class. Students kept a brief log of books they read, recording the pages they read each day along with a one-sentence reaction, prediction, or other response. If a book was abandoned, we noted it in the student's log and remembered to gently query the action.

We alternated our time in Monica's classroom, such that one of us was typically there during sustained reading time to take field notes or, as Monica did, to confer individually with students. Conferences were recorded on individual student forms developed for the study but designed for regular classroom use. We began each conference by observing the student for 30 seconds or so to note the apparent level of engagement. We recorded this information, along with the date, book title, and book's approximate difficulty level on the student's form. This was followed by a whispered book conversation, in which, from our pulled-up chair, we asked the students, as Anderson (2000) does with his writing conferences, "How's it going?" That question opened to talk about the book, reasons for reading it, and a review of the book. We ended each conference by asking the student to read a short excerpt of about 100 words from the book and tell us about it so far. Our notes included a running-record type list of sample reading errors, a holistic description of fluency and comprehension, and our approximate determination of whether the book was on the student's independent, instruction, or frustration level. We then asked the student to rate the book as "easy," "about right," or "difficult" and also included this in the notes. If the book was not instructionally appropriate or if the student was clearly not enjoying it, we suggested other books on the basis of what we knew about the student and the available books. Although the conversations were time-consuming at first, after several weeks, students began to anticipate the routine and volunteer the information they knew we would ask. The conferences typically lasted between 4 and 6 minutes.

We also accompanied students to the library, lunch, and recess (at least once weekly for each activity) and frequently asked students to describe the books they had in their possession (on or in their desks or in backpacks). We kept written records of whatever we heard and observed about book choices and book talk.

Looking Closely at Data

The data we examined were initial interviews and informal talks with students as well as field notes and conference forms. Using open coding, we first read through the data in chronological order, writing phrasal summaries and reactions. We then wrote analytic memos in an attempt to uncover what was happening in the classroom with respect to the book flood and sustained reading time. We did not seek to infer cause but to interpret and identify general categories that described how students used and reacted to the books and instruction provided. In addition to the data, our own perspectives and experiences combined with existing theory and research helped to shape the categories.

What We Learned

Before the Flood

Before the book flood, our observations indicated that Monica's instruction included many activities that have been shown to have positive influences on reading, such as (a) daily read-alouds from chapter books, (b) daily opportunities for students to read in self-selected books, (c) use of trade books to introduce units of study in content areas, and (d) occasional informal assessments of students' reading. Monica was a dramatic reader who encouraged students to share their thoughts and experiences when she read aloud. Most students listened intently to read-alouds and engaged in discussions of books.

In contrast, the designated free reading looked very much like the description of Mr. Graves's classroom from the opening scenario. Although two students, Esperanza and Leila (all student names are pseudonyms), consistently read during the sustained reading time, and a handful of other students occasionally found books that captured their interests, the most common student behaviors we saw were flipping pages, rifling through desks, surreptitiously talking to classmates, and going to the bathroom or for water. Most students changed books frequently; books seemed to be started without clear purpose and were rarely finished. In short, there appeared to be few engaged readers in Monica's classroom.

The classroom materials available to students offered limited choices. There were many books, but few were taken up by students. The school provided two class sets of grade-level basal readers in both English and Spanish (with accompanying small paperbacks); there were some novels in Spanish, but most were too difficult for the majority of students. Monica had built her classroom collection through yard sales, the libraries of retiring teachers, and used bookstores. Too few were in Spanish or contained culturally relevant content. Thus, although Monica clearly had some knowledge about effective reading instruction, her classroom did not contain the variety of books she believed necessary to engage her students in reading.

After the Flood

During an academic year in which students were given the daily opportunity to read interesting, varied, high-quality, self-selected books with teacher guidance and peer sharing, data analysis showed many positive changes in students' reading attitudes and habits. Further, although it is not possible to claim causation, students' reading achievement vastly improved. Most important to the school principal was that while only 27% of the students in this class had passed the state's achievement test as fourth graders and slightly less than 50% of Monica's students the previous year had passed the fifth-grade test, all but one student in the current class passed the test at the end of the study year, and that student came within one point of a passing score.

Our major interest was how the responses of students to the combination of the book flood and sustained reading implementation can inform instructional practice. In analyzing the field notes, interviews, and book conferences, we found three themes that described students' responses. First, the value students placed on books and reading increased and stayed elevated throughout the year. Second, students discovered that reading served personal as well as academic purposes. Third, many students were proactive in seeking and finding book sources beyond those provided in the classroom.

Elevated Value of Reading and Books. Monica's fifth graders were introduced to an abundance of interesting texts and were consistently asked about their reading by new adults in the classroom. In such an environment, it would be only natural to observe a surge in interest or at least feigned interest in reading and books. Students knew why we were there, and they were eager to oblige our interests by sharing their reading. Thus, there was an initial giddiness around reading, as students vied for the opportunity to show and tell us they were reading, but the value of reading and books stayed high through the year. By midyear, the class came to be seen by themselves and by others in the school as readers. Students who "fooled around" during self-selected reading were subject to irritated stares by students who wanted to read. Talk about books became commonplace.

We began to see physical manifestations of this classroom community's valuing of reading as well. Once-bare desktops gradually became book repositories. As the year progressed, the stacks grew until nearly every student in the room had as many as 10 books conspicuously placed on his or her desk—books he or she was currently reading or was "saving to read later." Students' book stacks included a range of difficulty levels and types, and most included several books in Spanish. Each stack included at least one book that had been read aloud in class or recommended by peers or teachers. Just as avid readers maintain a teetering book stack on their bedside tables or next to a favorite chair, these student-constructed book stacks appeared to be a public way for the students to reveal something about themselves as literate beings and their valuing of reading.

As with some coffee table volumes, some texts in the stacks seemed to serve as status symbols. They were clearly too difficult for students to read on their own, but students seemed to want to be viewed as readers of those texts. Andrés, for example, borrowed a copy of Shakespeare's *Romeo and Juliet* from his teenage sister, which he took every opportunity to show adults. Other high-status books included the Harry Potter volumes and thick information books. According to one researcher's notes,

> Emilio has been carrying around Harry Potter all day (he talked the teacher next door into lending it to him). He even took it to lunch, taking every possible opportunity to show it off (accidentally dropping it on the floor, striking up a conversation with whomever happens to walk by). He showed me where he was in the book, and I asked him what was happening so far. He had no idea, but he's so proud of holding that book.

As Monica pronounced the final word in a read-aloud, 18 hands shot up before she could ask the question "Who wants to read it now?" Every book read aloud was quickly appropriated by a student but, in addition, students developed a keen sense of who might like the book they were reading. During sharing time, they suggested books to others; they wrote reviews and placed them on sticky notes inside the books in the classroom collection.

Academic and Personal Motivations for Reading. In beginning-of-year interviews with students, only 3 of the 15 reported they voluntarily spent their own time reading. Those interviews, along with our classroom observations, suggested that most students saw reading as something to be done for assignments (sometimes), mostly in school, and mostly because it was required. During early free-reading observations, students were eager to talk about the books they were reading, but they seemed to be parroting ideas they thought we wanted to hear or that they had heard Monica mention as reasons to read. For example, when asked the question, "Why are you reading this book?" the students' early responses focused on improving reading, explaining, for example: "I want to be a better reader" or "I want to pass the [achievement test] this year." At the outset, we seldom heard expression of a personal interest in a topic, plot, or character.

As the year went on, we observed students reading for a variety of purposes. For example, although fifth grade is usually a time when the focus is on learning information through reading rather than building basic literacy skills, there were many students in the class who were just beginning to feel comfortable reading in English. Easy books are rarely available in middle and upper elementary classes, and often students do not feel comfortable reading them in front of their peers. Through read-alouds and enthusiastic introductions of specially selected easy readers (e.g., those with punch, humor, or "attitude") from the book flood, students came to see there was no shame in choosing and reading easy books (McGill-Franzen, 1993).

Rubén, who had moved back and forth to Mexico several times during his elementary years and was uncomfortable speaking English, at first refused to try books in English. After reading several books designed for beginners with Monica or with us, he began collecting them in his desk and reading them on his own.

Along with more difficult materials in Spanish, Rubén kept easy readers under his desk, neatly stacked in a file box for several months. His conference forms and reading logs showed he read those books regularly, with steady improvement in his English reading and oral proficiency. Even students who were relatively proficient in both languages frequently alternated challenging books with easier ones, the latter providing practice for fluency and reading "for fun."

Students expressed different purposes for reading books written in Spanish and bilingual books as well: Some used bilingual books to check their understanding of English. Isabel was reading the Spanish translation of *My Name Is María Isabel* by Alma Flor Ada, which Monica had previously read aloud in English, "because I want to hear the words in Spanish." Berta's father had made it clear that his children were expected to continue with their Spanish while learning English. This value carried over to Berta's reading choices, as she typically alternated between reading books in English and Spanish. David, who was concerned about his eroding Spanish literacy skill, was determined to read one book a week in Spanish "so I won't forget." The increased availability of Spanish books made such pledges easier to keep. Esperanza, having read the Harry Potter books in English, wanted to reread the series in Spanish, to "see how they tell the story different." In reading the first book of the series, she discovered that "it's longer in Spanish. They use more words to describe things."

Our original intention was for students to read independently and silently for the majority of the reading time and then to have a separate time for sharing. However, we had not fully considered how students' "ways of being" (i.e., social and cultural dimensions that affect literacy learning) were different from our intentions (Compton-Lilly, 2008, p. 668). Berta and Isabel set a precedent for partner reading and sharing when they checked out *Charlotte's Web* by E.B. White from the library to read together after Monica finished reading it aloud. Berta, a fluent English reader and speaker, helped Isabel with her English while they both relived an emotional classroom moment—the day Charlotte died. As Isabel pointed to a paragraph in the book, Berta said, "Mrs. Reyes cried right here," and began reading it aloud. The talk was clearly about what they were reading, and they were clearly constructing shared meanings and interpretation. As long as the time and conversations were productive, paired reading became an option for sustained reading. Students also chose the language in which they spoke during book discussions, which aids both in learning English and maintaining Spanish (Hubbard & Shorey, 2003).

Although there were books that appealed to the majority of students, the fifth graders were becoming increasingly discriminating in their tastes. Each had unique, individual interests, which they expressed through the books they displayed in their desktop stacks and in conversations. Most students' stacks revealed a preference for a particular topic or genre. Alicia had several how-to books for making crafts and doing magic tricks; Leila's taste ran to realistic fiction in English and Spanish; Maricela read science books written in Spanish, with a focus on human biology and natural phenomena; Isabel's stack consisted primarily of bilingual picture books and Golden books of Disney fairy tales; Roberto collected books by Dav Pilkey.

Learning to Fish: Students Finding Their Own Sources for Books

The variety and quantity of books in the flood impressed and excited students, but it was not long before there were not enough books in the room to satisfy the growing purposes and burgeoning interests of the fifth graders. After having books handed to them on silver platters, students began to seek other sources of access to satisfying books. Thus, the book flood became a catalyst for extending the number and reach of the books in the classroom. The book flood had included the first book in a series by Dav Pilkey. Roberto, Yolanda, and Julio discovered the rest of that series and other popular series in the reading specialist's office and asked to borrow the books for the classroom.

When Monica brought books by her favorite authors from the library, they multiplied as students discovered other books by those authors. During the read-aloud of Pam Muñoz Ryan's *Esperanza Rising*, the students, having many questions about the book's events, decided to send the author an e-mail. When Ryan responded with a personal e-mail and postcards for each student, a delegation of boys went to the library to ask for her other books. Soon, Ryan's other novels and picture books were being passed around the room. By the middle of the year, students had extended their searches for books to a variety of previously undiscovered or underused sources outside the classroom. They uncovered treasure troves of reading materials in the library, including a basket of donated Sports Illustrated for Kids magazines (complete with trading cards) tucked behind a couch. Students began using the library more frequently and finding gems. They borrowed books from friends and relatives, and some used their school snack money to buy books from the school book cart, which offered books for a dollar or less.

Some students used their resources collectively, offering to share, trade, and pool their means for gaining access to more books. They also were fulfilling one another's book wishes, suggesting titles, pointing out sections in the library, and lending personal copies. Books from RIF, meant to be "owned," traveled through the room once each student had completed his or her turn reading. Students' words and actions demonstrated the developing classroom belief that books are to be read and shared.

Conclusions About Sustained Reading in Bilingual Classrooms

Through the ready access to books that were relevant to their lives and a "reading culture" that included time to read, book talk, and value of literacy, students' reading interests were strengthened, awakened, and extended. The once apathetic readers in Monica's class had come to "own literacy and relate to literate behavior in ways that affirm their worth as individuals and their identity within a cultural community" (McGill-Franzen, Lanford, & Adams, 2002, p. 461).

Few classrooms have the luxury of a flood of reading materials or additional adult helpers. However, this research suggests implications for sustained reading that hold promise for supporting the development and nurturance of engaged readers. Attending to students' personal preferences and purposes was essential. Although interest and preference surveys can provide valuable information for building classroom libraries, it is also essential to gather information from individuals about their personal histories and experiences, purposes for reading, interests, and social influences and to help them find materials that resonate with them. When instructional funds are scarce, that money can be used to buy new and popular books that are difficult to check out from the library while using the school and public library for staples. To stretch classroom libraries further, teams of teachers within and across grade levels can rotate classroom collections, so there is always something new for students to read.

Carving out and preserving time in the day for sustained reading not only provided time for reading for the students in Monica's classroom but also demonstrated the value of reading to them. If the time was ever shortened because of an assembly, students requested and usually were granted makeup time. Components of the reading time that appeared to be important influences for students' valuing of reading were teacher book introductions, teacher interest in what students were reading, peer sharing, and partner reading. As teachers and researchers, we learned it was important to let go of some control during the reading time; when we did this, students read, shared, and supported one another's literacy development in dynamic, fruitful ways.

QUESTIONS FOR PROFESSIONAL DEVELOPMENT

1. Compare the sustained reading time described in Mr. Graves's and Monica's classrooms with that in your own classroom or what you have seen in other classrooms.

2. How do you or how would you incorporate sustained reading into your literacy curriculum? What other aspects of literacy instruction would you include to ensure that students make progress in all aspects of reading?

3. The students in Monica's classroom were in various stages of becoming biliterate in English and Spanish; thus, the classroom library included a large portion of books focused on helping them improve English and Spanish literacies. Considering the students you teach (and remembering that you will consider individual preferences as you get to know your students), what kinds of materials will you need in your classroom library?

4. The authors provided some suggestions for building classroom libraries when funds are scarce. What are some other inexpensive ways teachers, especially those new to the profession, can gather interesting and relevant materials for their classrooms?

REFERENCES

Adler, M., Rougle, E., Kaiser, E., & Caughlan, S. (2004). Closing the gap between concept and practice: Toward more dialogic discussion in the language arts classroom. *Journal of Adolescent & Adult Literacy, 47*(4), 312–322.

Allington, R.L. (Ed.). (2002). *Big brother and the national reading curriculum: How ideology trumped evidence.* Portsmouth, NH: Heinemann.

Alvermann, D.E., Young, J.P., Green, C., & Wisenbaker, J.M. (1999). Adolescents' perceptions and negotiations of literacy practices in after-school read and talk clubs. *American Educational Research Journal, 36*(2), 221–264.

Anderson, C. (2000). *How's it going? A practical guide to conferring with student writers.* Portsmouth, NH: Heinemann.

Anderson, R.C., Wilson, P.T., & Fielding, L.G. (1988). Growth in reading and how children spend their time outside of school. *Reading Research Quarterly, 23*(3), 285–303. doi:10.1598/RRQ.23.3.2

Campbell, R. (1989). The teacher as a role model during sustained silent reading (SSR). *Reading, 23*(3), 179–183.

Carlsen, G.R., & Sherrill, A. (1988). *Voices of readers: How we come to love books.* Urbana, IL: National Council of Teachers of English.

Chambliss, M.J., & McKillop, A.M. (2000). Creating a print- and technology-rich classroom library to entice children to read. In L. Baker, M.J. Dreher, & J.T. Guthrie (Eds.), *Engaging young readers: Promoting achievement and motivation* (pp. 94–118). New York: Guilford.

Clements, R. (2002). Perfect match. *Pen, 134,* 2–7.

Coles, G. (2000). *Misreading reading: The bad science that hurts children.* Portsmouth, NH: Heinemann.

Compton-Lilly, C. (2008). Teaching struggling readers: Capitalizing on diversity for effective learning. *The Reading Teacher, 61*(8), 668–672.

Constantino, R. (2005). Print environments between high and low socioeconomic status (SES) communities. *Teacher Librarian, 32*(3), 22–25.

Constantino, R. (2008). It's not rocket science: Students know what is good for them: The efficacy of a quality school library. *Knowledge Quest, 36*(4), 60–63.

Donovan, C.A., Smolkin, L.B., & Lomax, R.G. (2000). Beyond the independent-level text: Considering the reader–text match in first graders' self-selections during recreational reading. *Reading Psychology, 21*(4), 309–333. doi:10.1080/027027100750061949

Edmunds, K.M., & Bauserman, K.L. (2006). What teachers can learn about reading motivation through conversations with children. *The Reading Teacher, 59*(5), 414–424. doi:10.1598/RT.59.5.1

Elley, W.B. (2000). The potential of book floods for raising literacy levels. *International Review of Education, 46*(3/4), 233–255. doi:10.1023/A:1004086618679

Elley, W.B., & Mangubhai, F. (1983). The impact of reading on second language learning. *Reading Research Quarterly, 19*(1), 53–67. doi:10.2307/747337

Feitelson, D., & Goldstein, Z. (1986). Patterns of book ownership and reading to young children in Israeli school-oriented and nonschool-oriented families. *The Reading Teacher, 39*(9), 924–930.

Fisher, D., & Ivey, G. (2006). Evaluating the interventions for struggling adolescent readers. *Journal of Adolescent & Adult Literacy, 50*(3), 180–189. doi:10.1598/JAAL.50.3.2

Guthrie, J.T. (2004). Teaching for literacy engagement. *Journal of Literacy Research, 36*(1), 1–29. doi:10.1207/s15548430jlr3601_2

Hubbard, R.S., & Shorey, V. (2003). Worlds beneath the words: Writing workshop with second language learners. *Language Arts, 81*(1), 52–61.

Ivey, G., & Broaddus, K. (2001). "Just plain reading": A survey of what makes students want to read in middle school classrooms. *Reading Research Quarterly, 36*(4), 350–377.

Kelley, M., & Clausen-Grace, N. (2006). R⁵: The sustained silent reading makeover that transformed readers. *The Reading Teacher, 60*(2), 148–156. doi:10.1598/RT.60.2.5

Martinez, M.G., Roser, N.L., Worthy, J., Strecker, S., & Gough, P. (1997). Classroom libraries and children's book selections: Redefining "access" in self-selected reading. In C.K. Kinzer, K.A. Hinchman, & D.J. Leu, Jr. (Eds.), *Inquiries in literacy theory and practice: 46th yearbook of the National Reading Conference* (pp. 265–272). Chicago: National Reading Conference.

Martínez-Roldán, C.M., & López-Robertson, J.M. (1999). Initiating literature circles in a first-grade bilingual classroom. *The Reading Teacher, 53*(4), 270–281.

McGill-Franzen, A. (1993). "I could read the words!" Selecting good books for inexperienced readers. *The Reading Teacher, 46*(5), 424–426.

McGill-Franzen, A., & Botzakis, S. (2009). Series books, graphic novels, comics, and magazines: Unauthorized texts, authorized literacy practices. In E.H. Hiebert (Ed.), *Reading more, reading better* (pp. 101–117). New York: Guilford.

McGill-Franzen, A., Lanford, C., & Adams, E. (2002). Learning to be literate: A comparison of five urban early childhood programs. *Journal of Educational Psychology, 94*(3), 443–464. doi:10.1037/0022-0663.94.3.443

McKenna, M.C., Kear, D.J., & Ellsworth, R.A. (1995). Children's attitudes toward reading: A national survey. *Reading Research Quarterly, 30*(4), 934–956. doi:10.2307/748205

Morrow, L.M. (1991). Promoting voluntary reading. In J. Flood, J.M. Jensen, D. Lapp, & J.R. Squire (Eds.), *Handbook of research on teaching the English language arts* (pp. 681–690). New York: Macmillan.

National Institute of Child Health and Human Development. (2000). *Report of the National Reading Panel. Teaching children to read: An evidence-based assessment of the scientific research literature on reading and its implications for reading instruction* (NIH Publication No. 00-4769). Washington, DC: U.S. Government Printing Office.

Neuman, S.B. (1999). Books make a difference: A study of access to literacy. *Reading Research Quarterly, 34*(3), 286–311. doi:10.1598/RRQ.34.3.3

Neuman, S.B., & Celano, D. (2001). Access to print in low-income and middle-income communities: An ecological study of four neighborhoods. *Reading Research Quarterly, 36*(1), 8–26. doi:10.1598/RRQ.36.1.1

Reutzel, D.R., Jones, C.D., Fawson, P.C., & Smith, J.A. (2008). Scaffolded silent reading: A complement to guided repeated oral reading that works! *The Reading Teacher, 62*(3), 194–207. doi:10.1598/RT.62.3.2

Ryan, A.M., & Patrick, H. (2001). The classroom social environment and changes in adolescents' motivation and engagement during middle school. *American Educational Research Journal, 38*(2), 437–460. doi:10.3102/00028312038002437

Stanovich, K.E. (1986). Matthew effects in reading: Some consequences of individual differences in the acquisition of literacy. *Reading Research Quarterly, 21*(4), 360–407. doi:10.1598/RRQ.21.4.1

Taylor, B.M., Frye, B.J., & Maruyama, G.M. (1990). Time spent reading and reading growth. *American Educational Research Journal, 27*(2), 351–362.

Vardell, S.M., Hadaway, N.L., & Young, T.A. (2006). Matching books and readers: Selecting literature for English learners. *The Reading Teacher, 59*(8), 734–741. doi:10.1598/RT.59.8.1

Worthy, J., Moorman, M., & Turner, M. (1999). What Johnny likes to read is hard to find in school. *Reading Research Quarterly, 34*(1), 12–27. doi:10.1598/RRQ.34.1.2

Assessing English Learners' Silent Reading Ability: Problems, Perils, and Promising Directions

Gary J. Ockey
Kanda University of International Studies, Japan

D. Ray Reutzel
Utah State University

The number of English Learners (ELs) in U.S. schools has increased dramatically over the last several decades (Montero & Kuhn, 2009). ELs struggle to attain high levels of literacy in U.S. schools for a variety of reasons. Failure to attain high levels of literacy often results in high dropout rates, unemployment or underemployment, and poverty for ELs (Kindler, 2002; National Center for Education Statistics, 2004). As a result of these factors, an increased focus on understanding and assessing the literacy development of ELs is urgently needed.

The report of the National Literacy Panel on Language-Minority Children and Youth (August & Shanahan, 2006) represents one of the first comprehensive efforts in the United States to collect and synthesize the findings of research focused on how second-language learners become readers and writers of English. One of the unfortunate outcomes, depending on one's point of view, found within the pages of this report was the persistent and general admission that the empirical research base in relation to developing ELs' literacy in English is fragile in terms of both quality and quantity. A more positive view on this lack of an empirical research base would be that there is plenty of room for more research on how to effectively develop ELs' English print literacy.

Complicating Factors in Assessing ELs' Silent Reading

Research suggests that ELs' reading ability depends to some extent on their general language proficiency (Brisbois, 1995; Taillefer, 1996; Yamashita, 2002). ELs with limited lexical, grammatical, textual, sociolinguistic, or other language abilities, normally brought to a silent reading task by primary or native language speakers

Revisiting Silent Reading: New Directions for Teachers and Researchers, edited by Elfrieda H. Hiebert and D. Ray Reutzel. © 2010 by the International Reading Association.

(L1s), may use additional or somewhat different cognitive and metacognitive processes. For instance, beginning L1 readers are generally faced with the task of decoding words that are already a part of their active vocabulary, while ELs more frequently encounter words they do not know. Proctor, Carlo, August, and Snow (2005) indicate that ELs often have smaller oral English vocabularies, which have been shown repeatedly to negatively affect reading comprehension.

To further complicate the matter, EL (as well as L1) beginning readers' general English language abilities are vastly different, ranging from completely proficient to absolute beginner. On one end of the continuum are students who are proficient English speakers when they begin to read. These students, like L1 beginning readers, have typically acquired English through oral interaction and, consequently, bring a great deal of English language proficiency to the task of silent reading. At the other end of the continuum are ELs who have no general English ability. In fact, many of these students begin communicating orally and reading English simultaneously. It is unlikely that the reading acquisition processes of students toward this end of the continuum are the same as those of L1s (or ELs) who learn to read after having acquired a fair amount of English language ability through oral communication. In addition, some ELs are literate in their primary language while others are not, and research suggests that some L1 reading strategies may transfer to the second language, especially for students who are somewhat proficient in English (Brisbois, 1995; Taillefer, 1996; Yamashita, 2002). Recent longitudinal research results, however, seem to suggest that L1s and ELs are more alike than different when acquiring English print literacy in the beginning stages (Fitzgerald, Amendum, & Guthrie, 2008). However, in later grades where reading comprehension, academic language, and content texts dominate literacy instruction, ELs tend to struggle (August & Shanahan, 2006).

Sorting out the reasons why many ELs struggle to attain print literacy levels comparable to their native speaking peers (L1s) is a persistent problem in literacy assessment (Garcia & DeNicolo, 2009). Questions about accurately assessing ELs' literacy attainment levels often involve several interrelated issues. First, for many ELs the presumed transfer of print literacy in the primary language to print literacy in English is not always reliable, because print literacy levels are often also low or nonexistent in the ELs' primary language. Second, literacy achievement tests are seldom norm referenced to a predominantly EL population (Butler & Stevens, 2001). Low levels of English print literacy can also result when tests of English print literacy are given to ELs who have low oral English skills (Butler & Stevens, 2001; Helman, 2009). Finally, sorting out learning disabilities from first- and second-language learning issues when testing ELs' print literacy in English is an even thornier issue (August & Shanahan, 2006). As a consequence, issues associated with assessing silent reading among ELs will likely be compounded and confounded by these factors in addition to known difficulties associated with assessing silent reading in the L1 population.

ELs face other challenges to their development of English print literacy. Many ELs live below the poverty level and, as a consequence, have access to few books of interest or books written in their native language available in their homes or in school and classroom libraries. In addition, many books available to ELs in classrooms are too difficult for the majority of students to read (see Chapter 14, this volume). Martínez-Roldán and López-Robertson (1999) found that Latina/o students enjoyed books in which they saw people like themselves and in which their native language, Spanish, was represented. On the other hand, Mohr (2003) found that 84% of first-grade students, including Latina/o and African American students preferred English information books to a vast array of culturally relevant picture books they could have selected to keep. Au (2009) found that Hawaiian and Southeast Asian students neither knew how to find books in libraries nor how to choose books from those accessible to them. Perhaps one of the most encouraging findings from recent research on ELs' silent reading habits suggests that when ELs access interesting, culturally relevant, and appropriately challenging books and then have the opportunity to read daily in school with accountability, attitudes and reading habits are positively affected as well as end-of-year achievement test results (see Chapter 14, this volume).

A search for information about how to effectively assess ELs' English literacy acquisition results in a pronounced lack of empirical research evidence. It also is clear from this search that more federal investment in research that investigates the reliability, validity, and fairness of standards-based and norm-referenced literacy achievement assessments is clearly needed (Garcia & DeNicolo, 2009). Given the dearth of information about how to effectively assess ELs' English literacy acquisition, it should come as no surprise that a review of research on how to specifically measure ELs' silent reading performance would turn up a similar paucity of research evidence. Consequently, we rely not only on research addressing the assessment of silent reading among ELs but also on L1s as we discuss the potential problems, perils, and promises related to the assessment of ELs' silent reading processes.

What We Know About ELs' Silent Reading

For many years, silent reading was assumed to be one of the most effective practices for promoting ELs' English print literacy (Freeman & Freeman, 2008). This assumption was based largely on the work of Elley and Mangubhai (1983). These researchers reported a book flood project in which Fijian students read high-interest storybooks written in a second language. Volume reading of books in the second language led to reading growth rates twice that of students who did not read such books. This finding was interpreted into the widespread practice of engaging ELs in high-volume, independent, silent reading of English print materials as a means to increase their reading acquisition as the previous research had promised (Elley, 2000; Freeman & Freeman, 2008; Herrell & Jordan, 2004; Pilgreen, 2000). This presumption of independent, silent reading as effective practice held sway among teachers of ELs until the release of the National Reading Panel's (NRP; National Institute of Child Health and Human Development [NICHD], 2000) report, detailing the results of a research review and analysis. The NRP found the existing body of evidence for independent, silent reading practice among L1s to be lacking in quality and quantity as well as failing to converge on a consistent finding that practice of this type yielded better reading achievement or motivation despite vehement claims to the contrary (Allington, 2002; Krashen, 2002). As a result, independent, silent reading as found in programs like sustained silent reading (SSR) or Drop Everything and Read was abruptly halted in many classrooms across the United States. The sudden cessation of independent, silent reading practice also blunted current and future efforts to seriously understand how one could assess the effectiveness of independent, silent reading on L1 or EL reading acquisition and motivation.

Independent, silent reading, although now making a comeback in many classrooms with recent research reports showing some convergence on the conditions to support effective silent reading practice (Kelley & Clausen-Grace, 2006; Kamil, 2008; Reutzel, Jones, Fawson, & Smith, 2008), remains elusive in terms of measurement for at least three reasons. First, measurement of the effectiveness of independent, silent reading practice on ELs' (and L1s') literacy acquisition or motivation remains elusive because silent reading practice is a cognitive activity not fully amenable to behavioral observation alone. Even though students' external reading behaviors, such as lip movement or vocalizations, may appear to be appropriate or inappropriate (see Chapter 4, this volume), there is no assurance that the necessary cognitive processes in reading are being employed by the student as he or she sits semiquietly in the corner with book in hand. Gaining a window into the silent, private cognitive processes of readers has long vexed those who would assess students' silent reading performance. Past attempts at measuring ELs' (and L1s') silent reading have centered almost exclusively on one of four assessment approaches or their variants: (1) asking students to read aloud brief portions of that which they have read silently; (2) having students complete self-reports of perceived reading ability and motivation, such as interest surveys, motivation surveys, or inventories before or after silent reading; (3) asking students probed and free recall questions about what they have read; and (4) asking students to retell what they have read silently. Recent variants of these approaches include use of computer technology and test accommodations aimed at increasing their validity.

A Survey of Assessment Problems and Perils With ELs' Silent Reading

Using Brief Oral Reading Events to Assess SSR

In the first of these typical assessment paradigms, students are asked to read aloud a short excerpt from their silent reading. Typically, the aim of the assessment is to establish that oral reading accuracy rates are sufficiently high, 95% or above, so that students are reading at their independent level, because little or no help or scaffolding with word-reading accuracy is available when reading silently (Stahl & Heubach, 2006).

A typical silent reading assessment may require a student to read aloud for one minute or less. This approach for measuring ELs' silent reading is inherently unsatisfactory because the task is not authentic; one cannot assume that a short, oral reading of a lengthy text is likely to be representative of students' accuracy or reading rate when engaged in lengthy periods of silent text reading. Although admittedly similar in cognitive demands, reading aloud and silently are different tasks. Because of these differences, one must question the authenticity of measuring the efficacy of silent reading with oral reading (see Chapter 9, this volume). Authenticity requires that to the extent possible, the characteristics of the test task (oral reading) must match the characteristics of the target language-use situation (SSR). The match between the tasks is crucial because it is an important determiner of the extent to which the test results can validly predict what test takers can do in the target language-use situation (Bachman & Palmer, 1996).

When silent reading ability is assessed by having students read aloud, the actual ability to read silently is confounded with oral abilities such as pronunciation and other verbal skills unnecessary for reading comprehension (Alderson, 2000). For instance, an EL may comprehend the text and read it accurately, but because of inaccurate or inarticulate pronunciation, an examiner may assume a lack of reading accuracy and assign the student an invalid score. Moreover, because ELs may have greater difficulty in articulating English words clearly than do L1s, they may demonstrate slower oral reading rates and, consequently, receive lower scores than their L1 silent reading ability counterparts. This is especially true in the earliest stages of English-language acquisition before the EL acquires English phonemic awareness and subsequently develops the ability to orally articulate unfamiliar phonemes in English.

Furthermore, a failure to read aloud accurately does not necessarily imply a lack of reading comprehension during silent reading. Occasional miscues, or deviations from what is written on the page when reading aloud, occur among even very skilled readers (Wallace, 1992). Goodman and Gollasch (1980) contend that miscues may be important for a reader's pursuit of understanding a text. For instance, some miscues may be used to reduce redundancy in text without changing the intended meaning. Miscues, when they are not driven by cognitive and metacognitive processes, have been generally viewed as reading errors in reading aloud assessments when, in fact, these miscues or deviations may be the product of lucid text comprehension in fluent readers (Goodman & Goodman, 1994).

Assessing ELs' silent reading with one-minute oral reading probes may also be problematic, because ELs may not be able to maintain the same reading rate for 15 minutes that they can sustain for a single minute. Some scholars refer to this phenomenon as reading stamina. Much like running, one's rate for running the quarter mile is quicker than one's rate for completing a marathon. As with runners, reading stamina relates to readers' ability to read longer texts while gradually increasing their rate. Because we do not know much about how reading stamina functions when students read silently, it is likely that the continued prevalent use of one-minute oral reading assessments used to calibrate current oral reading rate norms fail to accurately estimate students' silent reading rates when reading for sustained periods of time in longer connected texts.

Students' reading stamina can be influenced by a variety of potential factors to include the amount of time and the length of text students are asked to read. Whether students struggle with word decoding or comprehension, which both make silent reading more effortful, the amount of effort required increases with the amount of time and the length of text to be read resulting in decreased reading stamina. Effortful word calling or a failure to understand what is read may be well tolerated in brief, one-minute oral reading assessment situations, but reading silently for longer periods of time is likely to lead ELs to disengagement from reading. Once disengaged, these readers often pretend to read silently or out of boredom engage in off-task behaviors, such as disrupting other students and wandering around the room. Thus, students who are assessed with short, oral reading assessments are motivated to perform at levels they might not otherwise choose to perform to please a teacher or to avoid appearing incompetent. Students who are placed in brief, oral reading testing situations experience different motivations to read than when they read independently and silently in books. One such example is the practice of teacher–student conferencing, in which students read aloud for one minute a small portion of the text they have been reading silently to assess the effectiveness of independent, silent reading practice. When reading silently for extended periods of time, those motivating conditions typically associated with the brief, oral reading testing situation alongside a teacher are not present.

The inauthentic use of brief, oral reading assessments to estimate ELs' silent reading accuracy, rate, or comprehension likely leads to erroneous conclusions about students' true silent reading rate or reading stamina. In addition, the inauthentic use of brief, oral reading assessments to estimate silent reading imposes on readers a different set of motivational conditions leading to different levels of engagement, or reading stamina, than what is associated typically with independent, silent reading.

Using Self-Report to Assess Silent Reading Ability and Motivation

Another approach for measuring ELs' (and L1s') silent reading is to have these students complete self-assessments of their perceived reading ability or an interest or motivation survey instrument prior to or after reading. Self-assessments typically ask students to indicate what they can read and understand. For example, DIALANG (Alderson & Huhta, 2005), a Computer Based Testing (CBT) system designed to assess second-language reading ability (as well as other second-language skills), contains a reading self-assessment (DIALANG is discussed in more detail later in this chapter). DIALANG uses "can-do" statements to obtain students' perceptions of their EL reading abilities. For instance, an example can-do statement from Level A1, a low level, is "I can understand very short, simple texts, putting together familiar names, words and basic phrases, by, for example, re-reading parts of the text." An example of a can-do statement from Level C1, a high-level ability, states, "I can understand in detail a wide range of long, complex texts of different types provided I can re-read difficult sections." Although self-assessment of EL reading abilities has been shown to correlate highly (0.7) with objective tests of the same abilities (Ross, 1998), it is not clear that either the objective tests or the self-assessments are valid indicators of ELs' second-language reading abilities. Personality, mood, and other factors may all contribute to students' perceptions of second-language reading ability. Hiebert, Wilson, and Trainin (see Chapter 9, this volume) also note that self-reports of silent reading rates are problematic, because students may "fudge" the results when noting how many words they actually read during a timed reading, and they could make inadvertent mistakes during silent reading, such as skipping words, lines, or sections, resulting in skewed silent reading rate reporting.

The relationship between student motivation to read and reading stamina or engagement has been established for more than a decade (Guthrie & Wigfield, 1997). As with many correlations, however, we do not know if sustained reading generates interest and motivation for reading, interest and motivation generate sustained reading, or a third variable is the cause of both. To determine causality, there is a need for empirical studies that untangle the cause and effect of this relationship.

Using Probed and Free Recall to Assess Silent Reading

Using probed and free recall to evaluate silent reading comprehension presents yet another set of problems and perils when assessing ELs. In probed recall assessments of reading comprehension, students are asked questions about what was read silently. In free recall assessments of reading comprehension, the students are asked to give an oral retelling of what was read silently. A large number of task types have been used as probed and free recall assessments of silent reading comprehension.

Although the focus here is on ELs, probed and free recall, with few differences, are also used to assess L1s' silent reading abilities. One of the first probed recall tasks used to assess silent reading ability was the multiple-choice (MC) test developed by Kelly (1915). Kelly's silent reading test, the first published multiple-choice test for any purpose, used short stems (typically one or two sentences) along with a few possible answer choices, one or more of which were correct, and one or more of which were incorrect, to assess a students' silent reading ability (Barnwell, 1996). This MC format (with minor variations) has continued to be used for this purpose (as well as many other purposes) for nearly a century. Kelly's purpose in designing the MC format was to make large-scale testing more practical; the format made it possible for nonassessment experts to reliably and quickly score large numbers of tests. MC tests continue to be used widely as formats for assessing silent reading ability, because they remain practical, now even more so than when they were developed by Kelly, because of the ability of computers to process and score such tests quickly and economically.

Over the past few decades, however, there has been mounting criticism of MC tests. Critics argue that they do not produce valid measures of reading ability, because the task is not authentic. Most readers do not interrogate themselves with questions during or after silent reading nor does comprehension of a text involve looking at answer choices after reading and attempting to identify the one which most associates information in the passage to information in a question stem. Moreover, many test takers do not follow their typical silent reading processes when taking MC tests, as is evinced by the reams of readily available published study guides designed to help students pass MC tests. These materials recommend such test-taking strategies as reading questions first and then scanning the text for answers. Given the lack of correspondence between students' typical silent reading cognitive processes and those employed when trying to achieve a high score on a MC test, it is highly unlikely that a score obtained from this probed recall assessment task type is a valid indicator of students' silent reading ability.

Other probed recall tasks that require students to respond to questions for assessing reading comprehension suffer similar shortcomings as the MC format. Alderson (2000) discusses a number of tasks designed to assess what readers comprehend. In matching tasks, students are given two lists and asked to match items on one with related items on the other. For instance, short passages might be matched with possible titles for the passages. Ordering tasks require students to place words, sentences, or paragraphs in an appropriate order. Some tasks designed to assess reading require students to use the additional skill of writing and therefore have limited validity as tests of silent reading ability. Short-answer tests require students to write responses to questions related to a text, and summary tests require students to read a text and then write a summary of its main points. Such tasks have been shown to assess writing ability as well as reading comprehension (Imao, 2008).

Using Oral Story Retellings to Assess Silent Reading

Story oral retelling, or free recall, is another popular task used for assessing ELs' silent reading ability, especially among young language learners. After a recorded story is played or read by a test administer, students are expected to orally retell the story, usually in as much detail as possible. As with brief oral reading events, inaccurate or inarticulate oral pronunciation may decrease the validity of the assessment. Moreover, effective completion of free recall tasks relies heavily on memory for text. Students may be able to comprehend what they have read but may forget to include some details when retelling the story. On the other hand, some students may be able to recite a text in detail without comprehending its meaning. Students who anticipate the requirement of producing a free recall or retelling a text following silent reading may employ strategies that are not typically employed during SSR. It follows, then, that the priming effect of knowing that a free recall is required after reading a text may not yield tests scores that are valid indicators of students' authentic silent reading processes or products.

Using Technology to Aid in Assessing Silent Reading

The rather recent advent of CBT has affected the way silent reading ability is assessed. Early researchers believed that CBT had the potential to greatly increase the validity of assessment tasks (Green, 1983). CBT technology has made it possible to better control how assessment tasks are delivered to students and the processes needed to complete them. For instance, an experimental task used in DIALANG (Alderson & Huhta, 2005) is mapping and flowcharting. After test takers read a text and click on "continue," they select words from a list to drag into a map or a flowchart. Test takers can return to the text but cannot see both the text and the map or flowchart simultaneously. To some extent, the computer controls the strategies and processes the test taker uses to complete this task, because test takers are unable to see both the passage and the map or flowchart at the same time. Unfortunately, CBT-delivered tasks such as this one may be worse than their paper-and-pencil equivalents. Prohibiting test takers from viewing both the text and the flowchart simultaneously may further alter the processes a student might employ when reading silently. The CBT version of this test task may require more dependence on memory and less on comprehension and recognition abilities thought to be more closely tied to typical silent reading processes (Ockey, 2009). Lack of access to or familiarity with computers can also limit the validity of CBT assessment scores for ELs (Choi, Kim, & Boo, 2003; Sawaki, 2001; Taylor, Kirsch, Jamieson, & Eignor, 1999). For instance, test takers who are not familiar with computers may fail to answer an item or even an entire section correctly, because they do not understand how to effectively and efficiently use the computer to complete the task. CBT continues to develop and may help to limit the challenges associated with making silent reading tests more valid, but, to date, they have had limited effectiveness in achieving this objective.

In a more recent look at the use of computers in silent reading assessment, Hiebert et al. (Chapter 9, this volume) conducted mode studies (i.e., studies that investigate the conditions of assessment administration) of the linkage between oral and silent reading rates and comprehension as measured by computer-administered testing and paper-and-pencil testing. Results indicated silent reading rates were faster than oral reading rates, and no differences were found between the testing conditions of paper-and-pencil versus computer-administered rate and comprehension tests. They also found that reading comprehension was not compromised by allowing students in fourth grade to read silently with accountability a comprehension test for the students in the top three quartiles of reading achievement. However, for those students scoring in the bottom quartile of reading achievement, oral reading with feedback was recommended.

Using Testing Accommodations to Aid in Assessing Silent Reading

With the aim of increasing the validity of assessment tasks for ELs, some researchers and practitioners have turned to the use of accommodations, analogous to ones used by students with disabilities. In fact, a number of laws aimed at ensuring the inclusion of ELs in high-stakes assessments require the use of accommodations when assessing this population of students (Koenig & Bachman, 2004). Testing accommodations for ELs refer to changes in the testing process that help students demonstrate their actual abilities on the construct of interest despite their limited language proficiency—without providing them an unfair advantage over other students. The aim of such accommodations is to help students best demonstrate their actual reading abilities on reading tests (Afflerbach, 2007). A number of accommodations have been used when assessing the silent reading ability of ELs, including bilingual instructions and questions, linguistic modification, test preparation, extra time, oral instructions, and a glossary of key terms or bilingual dictionaries.

Two of the more popular and appealing accommodations are bilingual and linguistic modifications. Bilingual accommodations provide ELs with the instructions and test questions in both English and the first language of each student who takes the test. Studies designed to assess this accommodation have compared the silent reading test scores (usually MC probed recall) of ELs given the accommodation and ELs not given the accommodation. Although such studies have used large samples to maximize their power, the general finding has been a failure to find a difference between the scores of ELs who received instructions and comprehension questions in both English and their first language and those who received them only in English (Anderson, Liu, Swierzbin, Thurlow, & Bielinksi, 2000).

Another accommodation, which has received a great deal of attention for improving the validity of assessments for ELs, is linguistic modification or simplification. This accommodation has been used in reading assessments to limit the effects of assessment language on student test performance. Questions designed to assess students' reading comprehension are linguistically simplified, so the language in them does not create an additional challenge for the students. For instance, passive voice is changed to active, conditionals are replaced with separate phrases, and relative clauses are removed (Abedi & Lord, 2001). However, despite the attractiveness of this accommodation, little evidence has been garnered that suggests that it increases the validity of the silent reading scores of ELs (Francis, Rivera, Lesaux, Kieffer, & Rivera, 2006).

Research on the effects of other accommodations to assess the abilities of ELs has similarly failed to indicate that they effectively improve the validity of the assessments. A meta-analysis conducted by Francis et al. (2006) indicated that of seven of the more common accommodations used, only English-language dictionaries and glossaries were shown to significantly influence ELs' scores, and the effect size for this accommodation was very small. Thus, although the use of accommodations for assessing the reading abilities of ELs is popular and appealing and current laws even require the approach, so far, they have had limited effectiveness in increasing the validity of ELs' scores on reading assessments.

Summing Up Problems and Perils in Assessing ELs' Silent Reading

It is clear that free and probed recall silent reading assessments such as retelling what was read or asking probing questions about what was understood are lacking. MC, matching, summary writing, story retell, and other similar task types all require skills not necessary for comprehending a text read silently and often change the typical processes students use while reading silently. Consequently, these methods introduce construct irrelevant variance into the silent reading scores that they yield and, hence, the obtained scores may not be considered representative indicators of students' silent reading ability. Future developments of CBT and testing accommodations may play a positive role in improving these approaches, but, to date, neither has been shown to markedly increase the validity of silent reading assessment scores.

The logic associated with question answering and retelling is that if students have read the text and comprehended it, they will be able to give back what the text was about or answer questions about it. Although this logic is both appealing and popular, it fails to shed light on the actual cognitive processing of L1s or ELs while reading silently. In silent reading, retelling or answering questions focuses on the "product" of the reading, not the process. Furthermore, retelling or question answering falls short of adequately measuring current conceptualizations of reading comprehension, such as those described in the theoretical work of Kintsch's (2004) construction-integration (CI) theory. To gain access to the unseen cognitive processes associated with silent reading, one must be able to pierce the curtain obstructing the view of students' silent reading processes and link these to product measures of silent reading. What might such assessments entail in the future?

Promising Directions for Silent Reading Assessment of ELs

The use of high-speed, infrared, eye-movement photography has long represented the hopes of those who would measure cognitive processing during silent reading (see Chapter 2, this volume). Eye movements known as saccades and fixations are photographed using high-speed, infrared tracking of the pupil of the eye as it moves along a line of print. The mapping of saccades and fixations onto the line of the print by the use of computer software programs allow measurement of silent reading processes, because past basic research has shown clearly that the effectiveness and efficiency of eye movements (i.e., saccades and fixations) along a line of print are driven by cognitive processing factors (Rayner & Pollastek, 1989). Saccades, or short, jerking jumps of the eyes over print, indicate that the eyes are actively taking in print stimuli to be processed in the mind. Fixations, or points in the line of print where the eyes stop for a moment, are indicators that the eyes have taken in a chunk of printed language for processing in the mind and those visual stimuli are currently being processed.

The complexity of the eye-movement equipment programming, the need to bring students into a laboratory environment, and the cost of the necessary cameras and computer hardware were in the past prohibitive. Emerging technologies such as fMRIs, MRIs, and optical scanning that could be used to effectively link brain processing during silent reading suffer from the same problems as those associated with past generations of eye-movement photography—complex operations, cost, and nonportability.

However, contemporary eye-movement photography systems such as those produced by *Reading Plus* have become much less complex to operate, are highly portable, and are far less expensive. When using older eye-movement systems, students had to place their chins on stands and hold their heads very still for the cameras to operate properly. In next generation eye-movement photography systems, students wore helmets with pencil-sized cameras or had to remain confined to a small range of head movements while viewing text on a television screen, and their eyes were tracked with a fixed pan tilt camera. Today's eye-movement photography allows a student to wear a lightweight set of clear plastic goggles (much like safety glass goggles) to read a text held in their hands. Nevertheless, even with these advances current eye-movement photography has not advanced to the point of allowing researchers to measure reading of self-selected books. Instead, students must read texts that the eye-movement photography equipment developers have preselected and calibrated for assessment purposes. Although less ecologically valid than measuring students' silent reading eye movements of self-selected texts, the newer generation eye-movement photography equipment does allow for tracking eye movements during reading and, consequently, the cognitive processes ELs (and L1s) might be employing while reading silently.

Another interesting measure associated with eye movements is the duration of gaze, or how long the eyes take to make the short, jerky jump over a segment of print, usually a single word (Just & Carpenter, 1987). The duration of gaze measure has been hypothesized to be a measurement of how difficult a word is to process for either decoding or comprehension reasons. Some words are more difficult to decode because of length or structure. Other words take longer to process, because the meaning of the word is unfamiliar or difficult to retrieve from memory. Thus, the duration of gaze measurement may hold some promise in determining not only if one is processing or can process a word, but also how quickly and easily a word's visual, phonological, and lexical elements can be accessed. Also eye-movement photography may at some point provide an in-process means for determining which word meanings or vocabulary within a text obstruct reading fluency and comprehension. Eye-movement photography may also provide a window into silent reading rates, both those in short text excerpts and those used in longer readings of connected text. Eye-movement photography could also one day provide insights on differing levels of students' silent reading stamina and how reading stamina as measured by efficient and effective eye movements may be associated with later reading acquisition and motivation.

The work of Hiebert et al. (Chapter 9, this volume) provides another promising avenue for assessing ELs' silent reading rates and comprehension. Assuming that reading comprehension tests could be devised for and norm referenced to an EL population, using the computer-based silent reading and comprehension testing format described by these researchers could provide classroom teachers with an effective and efficient process for measuring ELs' silent reading rates and comprehension in the future.

Another variable that obstructs, or in some ways at least obfuscates, the measurement of ELs' (and L1s') reading acquisition and engagement during silent reading is the invisible social context in which silent reading is often practiced—isolation or independence. Downing and Leong (1982) observe that most of our reading is done for our own private purposes and not in overtly observable social contexts. Going off and silently reading alone was presumed to be best practice for many years for ELs to acquire English reading facility and motivation (Freeman & Freeman, 2008; Krashen, 2002). In fact, in typically implemented SSR programs, asking students to talk about, discuss, or report in any way on their reading was seen as undesirable, having some of the alleged effects of the much-maligned written or oral book reports.

Going off alone to read impedes the beneficial human interactions around text that have been shown repeatedly to facilitate reading comprehension and motivate students to engage in sustained reading of texts (NICHD, 2000; Stahl, 2004). However, insofar as measuring ELs (and L1s') silent reading, the independence factor removes from view the overtly observable interactions around text that might provide a glimpse into students' comprehension processes and motivation. Even if such social exchanges were to be standard classroom practice during silent reading, this approach to measurement of silent reading suffers from the "product not process" measurement issues previously discussed in this chapter. However, it is clear that the private nature of independent reading provides yet one more obstruction to a clear view of silent reading processes and how these operate to influence reading achievement and motivation.

Advances in silent reading comprehension assessment are also beginning to emerge out of a general dissatisfaction expressed with the current comprehension assessment tools and processes (Paris & Stahl, 2005). One such example is Duke's (n.d.) Concepts of Comprehension Assessment (COCA). The COCA is designed to measure four contributors to reading comprehension: comprehension strategy use, vocabulary strategy use and knowledge, knowledge of informational text features, and comprehension of graphics in the context of text. The COCA was designed for use by classroom teachers, reading specialists, and paraprofessionals to inform their comprehension instruction and decision making, and it can be used by researchers to evaluate students' silent or oral reading comprehension. The COCA represents new thinking about how to measure the multidimensional nature of reading comprehension that is aligned with current theories such as Kintsch's (2004) CI theory (Duke, 2005).

Conclusions About Assessing ELs' Silent Reading

There are many obstacles impeding the measurement of ELs' (and L1s') English print literacy acquisition and motivation during silent reading. Findings of the National Literacy Panel on Language-Minority Children and Youth (August & Shanahan, 2006) present an EL literacy acquisition empirical research base that is weak in both quality and quantity. There is even less known about how to effectively assess ELs' English literacy acquisition during silent reading.

For many years, silent reading was assumed to be one of the most effective practices for promoting ELs' English print literacy (Freeman & Freeman, 2008). The NRP (NICHD, 2000) found the existing body of evidence for independent, silent reading practice to be lacking in quality and quantity as well as failing to converge on a consistent finding that independent, silent reading practice yielded better reading fluency, achievement, or motivation results. The sudden cessation of independent, silent reading practice in classrooms also brought to a standstill attempts to understand how to assess independent, silent reading. Although independent, silent reading is now making a comeback in many classrooms, effective assessment of silent reading processes and products remains elusive. Silent reading is a cognitive activity not easily accessed through behavioral observations. The invisible social context in which silent reading is often practiced, quiet isolation, greatly frustrates and complicates researchers' attempts to assess silent reading processes. Past attempts at measuring ELs' silent reading process and products have centered almost exclusively on one of several less than satisfactory assessment approaches discussed in this chapter.

New technologies such as high-speed infrared eye-movement photography and brain function measures such as MRIs and fMRIs promise to provide new and exciting insights on the processes used in silent reading. This will be especially true when eye-movement photography can be directly linked to measures of cognitive processing, such as those now available through fMRI and other time-elapsed brain functioning measures. As researchers gain access to the otherwise hidden operations of silent reading processes, they will then be able to fashion increasingly sensitive, valid, authentic, and responsive silent reading assessment tools, protocols, and procedures. Although the current status of silent reading process and product assessment is frustratingly inadequate (Paris & Stahl, 2005), technological advances in measuring human information processing and newer multidimensional comprehension assessment tools hold out considerable promise for reading researchers to come to better understand and assess the silent reading of ELs.

QUESTIONS FOR
PROFESSIONAL DEVELOPMENT

1. How are ELs different from L1s?
2. Describe the four methods discussed for assessing ELs' silent reading.
3. What are the problems and perils of each of these four methods?
4. How might these methods be adapted to limit these problems?
5. What is infrared rapid eye movement technology and what promises does it hold for assessing ELs' silent reading?

REFERENCES

Abedi, J., & Lord, C. (2001). The language factor in mathematics tests. *Applied Measurement in Education, 14*(3), 219–234. doi:10.1207/S15324818AME1403_2

Afflerbach, P. (2007). *Understanding and using reading assessment, K–12.* Newark, DE: International Reading Association.

Alderson, J.C. (2000). *Assessing reading.* New York: Cambridge University Press.

Alderson, J.C., & Huhta, A. (2005). The development of a suite of computer-based diagnostic tests based on the Common European Framework. *Language Testing, 22*(3), 301–320. doi:10.1191/0265532205lt310oa

Allington, R.L. (Ed.). (2002). *Big brother and the national reading curriculum: How ideology trumped evidence.* Portsmouth, NH: Heinemann.

Anderson, M., Liu, K., Swierzbin, B., Thurlow, M., & Bielinski, J. (2000). *Bilingual accommodations for limited English proficient students on statewide reading tests: Phase 2* (Minnesota Rep. No. 31). Minneapolis, MN: National Center on Educational Outcomes, University of Minnesota. Retrieved April 29, 2010, from www.cehd.umn.edu/NCEO/OnlinePubs/archive/AssessmentSeries/MnReport31.html

Au, K.H. (2009). Culturally responsive instruction: Application to multiethnic, multilingual classrooms. In L. Helman (Ed.), *Literacy development with English learners: Research-based instruction in grades K–6* (pp. 18–39). New York: Guilford.

August, D., & Shanahan, T. (Eds.). (2006). *Developing literacy in second-language learners: Report of the National Literacy Panel on Language-Minority Children and Youth.* Mahwah, NJ: Erlbaum.

Bachman, L.F., & Palmer, A.S. (1996). *Language testing in practice.* New York: Oxford University Press.

Barnwell, D.P. (1996). *A history of foreign language testing in the United States: From its beginnings to the present.* Tempe, AZ: Bilingual.

Brisbois, J.E. (1995). Connections between first- and second-language reading. *Journal of Reading Behavior, 27*(4), 565–584.

Butler, F.A., & Stevens, R. (2001). Standardized assessment of the content knowledge of English language learners K–12: Current trends and old dilemmas. *Language Testing, 18*(4), 409–427.

Choi, I., Kim, K.S., & Boo, J. (2003). Comparability of a paper-based language test and a computer-based language test. *Language Testing, 20*(3), 295–320. doi:10.1191/0265532203lt258oa

Downing, J.A., & Leong, C.K. (1982). *Psychology of reading.* New York: Macmillan.

Duke, N.K. (2005). Comprehension of what for what: Comprehension as a nonunitary construct. In S.G. Paris & S.A. Stahl (Eds.), *Children's reading comprehension and assessment* (pp. 93–104). Mahwah, NJ: Erlbaum.

Duke, N.K. (n.d.). *Informational comprehension assessment in the primary grades: Concepts of Comprehension Assessment (COCA).* East Lansing, MI: Literacy Achievement Research Center. Retrieved April 29, 2010, from www.msularc.org/html/project_COCA_materials.html

Elley, W.B. (2000). The potential of book floods for raising literacy levels. *International*

Review of Education, 46(3/4), 233–255. doi:10.1023/A:1004086618679

Elley, W.B., & Mangubhai, F. (1983). The impact of reading on second language learning. Reading Research Quarterly, 19(1), 53–67. doi:10.2307/747337

Fitzgerald, J., Amendum, S.J., & Guthrie, K.M. (2008). Young Latino students' English-reading growth in all-English classrooms. Journal of Literacy Research, 40(1), 59–94. doi:10.1080/10862960802070459

Francis, D.J., Rivera, M., Lesaux, N., Kieffer, M., & Rivera, H. (2006). Practical guidelines for the education of English language learners: Research-based recommendations for the use of accommodations in large-scale assessments. Portsmouth, NH: Center on Instruction, RMC Research Corporation. Retrieved September 9, 2009, from www.centeroninstruction.org/files/ELL3-Assessments.pdf

Freeman, Y.S., & Freeman, D.E. (2008). Academic language for English language learners and struggling readers: How to help students succeed across content areas. Portsmouth, NH: Heinemann.

García, G.E., & DeNicolo, C.P. (2009). Making informed decisions about the language and literacy assessment of English language learners. In L. Helman (Ed.), Literacy development with English learners: Research-based instruction in grades K–6 (pp. 64–86). New York: Guilford.

Goodman, K.S., & Gollasch, F.V. (1980). Word omissions: Deliberate and non-deliberate. Reading Research Quarterly, 16(1), 6–31. doi:10.2307/747347

Goodman, Y.M., & Goodman, K.S. (1994). To err is human: Learning about language processes by analyzing miscues. In R.B. Ruddell, M.R. Ruddell, & H. Singer (Eds.), Theoretical models and processes of reading (4th ed., pp. 104–123). Newark, DE: International Reading Association.

Green, B.F. (1983). The promise of tailored tests. In H. Wainer & S. Messick (Eds.), Principals of modern psychological measurement (pp. 69–80). Hillsdale, NJ: Erlbaum.

Guthrie, J.T., & Wigfield, A. (1997). Reading engagement: Motivating readers through integrated instruction. Newark, DE: International Reading Association.

Helman, L. (Ed.). (2009). Literacy development with English learners: Research-based instruction in grades K–6. New York: Guilford.

Herrell, A., & Jordan, M. (2004). Fifty strategies for teaching English language learners (2nd ed.). Upper Saddle River, NJ: Prentice Hall.

Imao, Y. (2008). Investigating the effects of reading and writing on summaries written by L2 writers. Unpublished doctoral dissertation, University of California, Los Angeles.

Just, M.A., & Carpenter, P.A. (1987). The psychology of reading and language comprehension. Boston: Allyn & Bacon.

Kamil, M.L. (2008). How to get recreational reading to increase reading achievement. In Y. Kim et al. (Eds.), 57th yearbook of the National Reading Conference (pp. 31–40). Oak Creek, WI: National Reading Conference.

Kelley, M., & Clausen-Grace, N. (2006). R⁵: The sustained silent reading makeover that transformed readers. The Reading Teacher, 60(2), 148–156. doi:10.1598/RT.60.2.5

Kelly, F.J. (1915). The Kansas silent reading test. Topeka: Kansas State Printing Plant.

Kindler, A.L. (2002). Survey of the states' limited English proficient students and available educational programs and services: 2000–2001 summary report. Washington, DC: National Clearinghouse for English Language Acquisition & Language Instruction Educational Programs.

Kintsch, W. (2004). The construction–integration model of text comprehension and its implications for instruction. In R.B. Ruddell & N.J. Unrau (Eds.), Theoretical models and processes of reading (5th ed., pp. 1270–1328). Newark, DE: International Reading Association.

Koenig, J.A., & Bachman, L.F. (Eds.). (2004). Keeping score for all: The effects of inclusion and accommodation policies on large-scale educational assessments. Washington, DC: National Academies Press.

Krashen, S. (2002). More smoke and mirrors: A critique of the National Reading Panel report on fluency. In R.L. Allington (Ed.), Big brother and the national reading curriculum: How ideology trumped evidence (pp. 112–124). Portsmouth, NH: Heinemann.

Martínez-Roldán, C.M., & López-Robertson, J.M. (1999). Initiating literature circles in a first-grade bilingual classroom. The Reading Teacher, 53(4), 270–281.

Mohr, K.A.J. (2003). Children's choices: A comparison of book preferences between Hispanic and non-Hispanic first-graders. Reading Psychology, 24(2), 163–176. doi:10.1080/02702710308231

Montero, M.K., & Kuhn, M.R. (2009). English language learners and fluency development: More than speed and accuracy. In L. Helman (Ed.), *Literacy development with English learners: Research-based instruction in grades K–6* (pp. 156–177). New York: Guilford.

National Center for Education Statistics. (2004). *The condition of education 2004* (NCES 2004-077). Washington, DC: U.S. Department of Education. Retrieved April 29, 2010, from nces.ed.gov/pubs2004/2004077.pdf

National Institute of Child Health and Human Development. (2000). *Report of the National Reading Panel. Teaching children to read: An evidence-based assessment of the scientific research literature on reading and its implications for reading instruction* (NIH Publication No. 00-4769). Washington, DC: U.S. Government Printing Office.

Ockey, G.J. (2009). Developments and challenges in the use of computer-based testing for assessing second language ability. *The Modern Language Journal, 93*(Special Focus Issue), 836–847. doi:10.1111/j.1540-4781.2009.00976.x

Paris, S.G., & Stahl, S.A. (Eds.). (2005). *Children's reading comprehension and assessment.* Mahwah, NJ: Erlbaum.

Pilgreen, J.L. (2000). *The SSR handbook: How to organize and manage a sustained silent reading program.* Portsmouth, NH: Boynton/Cook.

Proctor, C.P., Carlo, M., August, D., & Snow, C. (2005). Native Spanish-speaking children reading in English: Toward a model of comprehension. *Journal of Educational Psychology, 97*(2), 246–256. doi:10.1037/0022-0663.97.2.246

Rayner, K., & Pollatsek, A. (1989). *The psychology of reading.* Hillsdale, NJ: Erlbaum.

Reutzel, D.R., Jones, C.D., Fawson, P.C., & Smith, J.A. (2008). Scaffolded silent reading: A complement to guided repeated oral reading that works! *The Reading Teacher, 62*(3), 194–207. doi:10.1598/RT.62.3.2

Ross, S. (1998). Self-assessment in second language testing: A meta-analysis and analysis of experiential factors. *Language Testing, 15*(1), 1–20.

Sawaki, Y. (2001). Comparability of conventional and computerized tests of reading in a second language. *Language Learning & Technology, 5*(2), 38–59. Retrieved February 12, 2008, from llt.msu.edu/vol5num2/sawaki/default.html

Stahl, S.A. (2004). What do we know about fluency? Findings of the National Reading Panel. In P. McCardle & V. Chhabra (Eds.), *The voice of evidence in reading research* (pp. 187–211). Baltimore: Paul H. Brookes.

Stahl, S.A., & Heubach, K. (2006). Fluency-oriented reading instruction. In K.A.D. Stahl & M.C. McKenna (Eds.), *Reading research at work: Foundations of effective practice* (pp. 177–204). New York: Guilford.

Taillefer, G.F. (1996). L2 reading ability: Further insight into the short-circuit hypothesis. *The Modern Language Journal, 80*(4), 461–477.

Taylor, C., Kirsch, I., Jamieson, J., & Eignor, D. (1999). Examining the relationship between computer familiarity and performance on computer-based language tasks. *Language Learning, 49*(2), 219–274. doi:10.1111/0023-8333.00088

Wallace, C. (1992). *Reading.* New York: Oxford University Press.

Yamashita, J. (2002). Mutual compensation between L1 reading ability and L2 language proficiency in L2 reading comprehension. *Journal of Research in Reading, 25*(1), 81–95. doi:10.1111/1467-9817.00160

Independent Silent Reading for Struggling Readers: Pitfalls and Potential

Angela Hairrell

The University of Texas at Austin

Meaghan Edmonds

The University of Texas at Austin

Sharon Vaughn

The University of Texas at Austin

Deborah Simmons

Texas A&M University

M rs. Long's sixth-grade classroom is quiet while students settle in for their daily 30 minutes of Drop Everything And Read (DEAR) time. Students are at their desks with books or other reading materials. Mrs. Long is at her desk with the latest bestseller. All seems well. On closer inspection, one student is randomly turning a book's pages, pausing for no more than a couple of seconds on any single page. One student stares blankly at the same page for 10 minutes, while another sleeps with her head strategically hidden behind a book. Another student composes a text message between the pages of a book. Many of the successful readers are reading; however, several students with reading difficulties are occupied with nonreading activities.

In this chapter, we assert that students with reading difficulties need extended opportunities to read silently and to engage with others in a structured discourse about their reading. However, traditional procedures that provide time for reading without adequate preparation and scaffolds are unlikely to be associated with the benefits struggling readers require (Reutzel, Jones, Fawson, & Smith, 2008; Shanahan, 2004). In this chapter, we propose that struggling readers benefit optimally from silent reading when provided adequate preparation, instructional support during reading, and extended time for expression (oral and written) with teacher feedback about their reading.

Students struggle with extended periods of silent reading for a variety of reasons. Among these reasons are difficulty reading complex words, understanding

Revisiting Silent Reading: New Directions for Teachers and Researchers, edited by Elfrieda H. Hiebert and D. Ray Reutzel. © 2010 by the International Reading Association.

critical vocabulary, or maintaining focus. Often, students with reading difficulties have inadequate opportunity to build their independent, silent reading skills. For students who struggle with reading, the challenges that extended periods of unmonitored, silent reading present can be overwhelming and lead to unproductive reading.

The process of devoting time within the school day for independent, silent reading has many labels, including sustained silent reading (SSR), DEAR (Clay, 1991), Sustained QUIet Reading Time (Benedict, 1982), and Uninterrupted Sustained Silent Reading (Hunt, 1970). In this chapter, we refer to the periods of time in the school day designated to independent, silent reading as SSR. SSR is designed to provide students with time to practice reading, on the premise that practice makes perfect and that students reap benefits from ongoing exposure to text. Although there are variations of SSR, common characteristics include (a) a block of time devoted to silent reading, (b) students' self-selection of reading materials, (c) an adult who models silent reading, and (d) limited accountability (Pilgreen, 2000; Yoon, 2002). SSR has widespread use in classrooms at all grade levels. It is also encouraged through the use of popular computer-based reading comprehension programs such as Accelerated Reader (AR; Renaissance Learning, n.d.), which is used by more than 63,000 schools, according to the company's website. AR has an additional component, Accelerated Reader Best Classroom Practices, which provides guidelines for the implementation of independent reading. A recent report by the What Works Clearinghouse (2008) identifies two studies that met the evidence standards and concludes that AR had no discernible effects on reading fluency, mixed effects on comprehension, and potentially positive effects on general reading ability. Though SSR is a widely implemented practice and intuitively right-headed, the benefits for the range of readers in classrooms remain equivocal.

Benefits of SSR

That extended periods of silent reading benefit students may seem like common sense (Garan & DeVoogd, 2008): The more one reads, the more one learns and wants to read and learn. If practice makes perfect, then more time reading should lead to improved reading achievement. Cunningham and Stanovich (1998b) hold that reading much and reading often is beneficial, regardless of the ability of the student.

Although it may seem logical that SSR would have a positive impact on student achievement, the research is not so clear. Two published reviews of SSR (National Institute of Child Health and Human Development [NICHD], 2000; Sadoski, 1984) failed to find conclusive evidence of the positive effects of SSR on reading achievement. The National Reading Panel (NRP; NICHD, 2000) reviewed 14 studies and concluded that more research was needed to determine whether SSR is an effective component of a reading program, if the goal is to improve reading achievement. A primary conclusion was that the majority of the studies were based on methodologically weak designs. However, there has been much criticism of these conclusions (Allington, 2002; Krashen, 2005). Among the criticisms is that the NRP review excluded many studies, including correlational studies. Krashen argues that the NRP findings misrepresented the existing literature. In addition, Pilgreen (2000) reviewed 32 studies, reporting that SSR treatment groups did as well or better than control groups in all but two cases. Therefore, it seems reasonable that SSR is an integral component of reading instruction and practice. However, it is essential to better understand the components and conditions of SSR that lead to effective outcomes. This understanding would require more rigorous studies of the effects of independent reading on reading achievement, fluency, engagement, and motivation. In particular, we think it is important to understand the effects of SSR on students who struggle with reading.

Although experimental and quasi-experimental studies on SSR are sparse, numerous correlational studies have documented improvements in reading outcomes. Time spent reading meaningful connected text has been linked to increases in vocabulary knowledge (Cunningham & Stanovich, 1998a; Graves & Watts-Taffe, 2002; Nagy, 2005), background knowledge (Marzano, 2004), fluency and word recognition (Adams, 1990; Cunningham & Stanovich, 1998a), motivation (Yoon, 2002), and overall reading and listening comprehension (Taylor, Frye, & Maruyama, 1990).

In the edited volume *Teaching and Learning Vocabulary: Bringing Research to Practice*, Nagy (2005) argues for the importance of wide reading—not just for vocabulary learning, but for reading comprehension. Cunningham and Stanovich (1998a) measured the print exposure of 98 fifth-grade students. Using the title recognition test (TRT) and the author recognition test (ART), the researchers found that both the TRT and the ART accounted for a significant portion of the variance, even after adjusting for third-grade reading scores. In a second study, they found that individual differences in exposure to print in first grade predicted reading comprehension even after the 11th grade. Both studies suggested that students who read widely are more likely to demonstrate improved comprehension.

Focusing on academic vocabulary, Marzano (2004) proposes that vocabulary knowledge and background knowledge are closely tied. He advocated an SSR program to indirectly build background knowledge. In a recent analysis of reading comprehension outcomes, Cromley and Azevedo (2007) found that vocabulary knowledge and background knowledge were most predictive of reading comprehension outcomes in ninth-grade students. Though indirect, the logic chain suggests that wide reading fosters background knowledge, which in turn facilitates reading comprehension.

An increase in student motivation is one frequently reported benefit of SSR. Yoon (2002) conducted a meta-analysis of SSR and student attitudes toward reading and identified seven studies published in a 30-year span, which resulted in a small overall effect size of 0.12. When disaggregated by age, findings from the meta-analysis indicate that SSR was more effective at influencing the attitude of younger students (i.e., third grade and below, Effect Size [ES] = 0.32) than older students (i.e., fourth grade and above, ES = 0.06). Length of treatment (i.e., less than six months versus more than six months) did not significantly account for variation in the effects. Chua's (2008) survey of students participating in an SSR program found that over the course of one year, students reported that they enjoyed reading more and read more during school. However, students did not report a change in the amount of time engaged in reading outside of school.

Taylor et al. (1990) conducted a study with 195 fifth- and sixth-grade students. Over 17 weeks, students recorded the time and number of pages they read. Students averaged 15.8 minutes of reading during their 50-minute reading period and 15.0 minutes of reading at home. In their analysis, the researchers found that the minutes of reading in class contributed significantly to reading comprehension but that reading at home was not a significant predictor.

Challenges of SSR

SSR may be most appropriate for average- and high-ability readers who enjoy reading, but SSR may be challenging for students with reading difficulties (Walker, 2000). Even for better readers, SSR may present challenges such as inadequate access to high-interest materials and insufficient methods for students to demonstrate their engagement with and understanding of texts. In addition, the absence of any preteaching and follow-up instruction can be an obstacle, especially when students confront unfamiliar genres and concepts. Students who have limited experience reading silently may need time to "ramp up" to reading for extended periods of time. Although the age of the reader is considered in the amount of time set aside for SSR, students may be unable to remain engaged for the entire silent reading period.

Determining the appropriate role of the teacher during SSR is a research goal of considerable merit. Most SSR approaches suggest that the teacher model silent reading by reading with the students. Consequently, while teachers read, they do not monitor the activities of the students, thus, students are not held accountable for their progress. We think that it would be valuable to determine whether a more active teacher role during SSR would positively influence outcomes for students— particularly students with reading difficulties. This more active role might include working with a group of struggling readers to preselect common text, previewing the text and preteaching keywords, and providing opportunities after reading to respond to the reading orally and through writing.

Another challenge students face is selecting text at an appropriate level. Most SSR programs identify self-selection of text as an essential feature to instill motivation and enjoyment of reading. Yet students often choose reading materials on the basis of what their peers are reading and not on their own abilities. The result is that students select books that are too easy or too difficult. Without teacher monitoring of student work during silent reading time, there is no feedback loop to assist students in making appropriate choices.

Research on SSR and Struggling Readers

The research on SSR with students with reading difficulties is scarce. Studies examining silent reading and struggling students in a variety of settings (e.g., elementary classroom, remedial reading class, resource room) were conducted decades ago, showing mixed results for the relationship between time spent reading silently and reading comprehension outcomes (Clark, 1975; Clark & Spath, 1979; Haynes & Jenkins, 1986; Leinhardt, Zigmond, & Cooley, 1981; Stallings, 1980). More recent studies with populations of struggling readers in SSR programs show limited impact from SSR. Davis (1988) randomly assigned eighth graders to a teacher-directed group or to SSR, concluding that SSR was more appropriate for high- and medium-ability readers than for low-ability readers.

In a quasi-experimental study of SSR (Melton, 1993), 12 third- and fourth-grade students with learning disabilities were compared with a control group. SSR in this condition contained several modifications. First, the reading of students was monitored and recorded, and times were scheduled for students to talk to their classmates about what they were reading. No difference was found between the word-reading scores of the two groups. However, a statistically significant difference was found between groups on reading words in context and reading comprehension where the SSR condition outperformed the control condition.

Methe and Hintze (2003) manipulated teacher modeling during SSR in a third-grade classroom with 14 students—making up the entire third-grade population of the school district. Using a multiple-baseline design, Methe and Hintze observed a higher percentage of on-task behavior using SSR when the teacher modeled reading than when the teacher completed paperwork at her desk.

Wu and Samuels (2004) reported several interesting findings regarding silent reading time and student outcomes. The study used a 2 × 2 × 2 design, with the groups representing time (15 minutes versus 40 minutes) × grade level (third grade versus fifth grade) × reading ability (above grade level versus below grade level). Wu and Samuels did not report a main effect for time, but they did report a significant interaction between reading ability and time spent reading. They interpreted their findings as suggesting that less time (e.g., 15 minutes) on SSR was needed to improve reading speed and comprehension. If the goal of SSR was to build vocabulary, more time was needed (e.g., 40 minutes).

A recent comparison of six methods of reading instruction was conducted in four elementary schools and in one middle school across four districts, with a total sample of 660 students (Block, Parris, Reed, Whiteley, & Cleveland, 2009). The conditions were workbook practice, individualized schema-based learning, situated practice, conceptual learning, transactional learning, and basal readers. Common characteristics of the three most successful approaches were the student selection of books for guided independent reading, the reading of more than seven pages of text, and 15–20 minutes of teacher-monitored SSR. During these reading times, teachers provided personalized scaffolds, expository reading choices, and time to read a teacher-selected book for 5 of the 20 minutes of the SSR period. Analyses were conducted on the basis of reading ability. The key finding from this study was that students participating in teacher-monitored SSR significantly outperformed students in the other conditions on a measure of reading comprehension, regardless of reading ability.

In a survey conducted by Nagy, Campenni, and Shaw (2000) of 96 teachers in 32 school districts on the use of silent reading in seventh-grade classrooms, low-achieving readers were often excluded from this practice. Bryan, Fawson, and Reutzel (2003) report that when students were held accountable and teachers monitored student reading during SSR, even disengaged students remained on task.

Obstacles Struggling Readers Face During SSR

In this chapter, we examine four obstacles that struggling readers may face during SSR: text selection, reading comprehension, accountability, and attention and motivation. Anderson's (2009) observational study of four dyslexic students highlighted the challenges of SSR for students with reading difficulties. The primary challenges were the lack of time spent reading and the text that students selected. Students in this study selected their own reading material. When checking students' ability to read the text, Anderson found that error rates for three of the four students were much higher (16–30%) than recommended for adequate comprehension (5%). In addition, one student selected his text on the basis of what his friends were reading but was unable to read it independently. Another challenge Anderson identified was off-task behavior. One student spent 82% of the SSR time not reading. Asking students to do something they find difficult for an extended period of time may not be best practice (Reutzel & Cooter, 2005). Anderson's observations are similar to those of other researchers: Students with disabilities were distracted, so they scanned the text or avoided the task (Bryan et al., 2003; Fisher, 2004; Lee-Daniels & Murray, 2000).

For struggling readers, the SSR process can pose many obstacles, one of which being text selection. As reported in the Anderson (2009) study, only one of the four students selected text that he or she could read independently. Often, when students select texts for reasons other than readability, the inability to decode or understand the majority of the words leads to breakdowns in comprehension. Therefore, it is essential that students receive guidance on how to make appropriate reading choices.

Reading comprehension is another obstacle for students with reading difficulties. Many students have difficulty reading for understanding, and this problem is amplified when students choose text that is too difficult. The lack of accountability in SSR can create many problems for struggling readers. For all students, including those who scan the text, turn pages, or spend a large portion of the time off-task, there is no record of what was or was not accomplished and little motivation to change. This lack of task engagement leads to unproductive reading. In SSR, students do not interact with the teacher and other students, which may hinder the development of struggling and reluctant readers who need interaction and collaboration in relation to text (Guthrie & Wigfield, 2000).

The problems of text difficulty and reading comprehension are exacerbated by the lack of accountability and monitoring in SSR. Because the teacher is also reading during SSR, students do not have instructional support when breakdowns in reading occur. The goal of SSR will likely not be met if the challenges of the text exceed the students' levels of motivation and interest.

Staying focused on the reading task is another obstacle for many struggling readers. It may be beneficial to scaffold the length of reading time each day for SSR, gradually progressing to longer periods (Sindelar, Espin, Smith, & Harriman, 1990; Stallings, 1980). Although many students are able to focus and maintain on-task reading for short periods of SSR, long periods of time cause breakdowns in attention and on-task behavior. A study by Fisher (2004) shows that less than 40% of high school students actually read during SSR time. Anderson (2009) labels these students as uninterested readers and uninterested dissemblers. However, Bryan et al. (2003) found that teacher monitoring of student progress through brief conferences increased engagement, even with the students who were most disengaged.

The Next Generation of SSR

Modifications to SSR typically involve providing more structure to the silent reading through higher levels of teacher interaction and peer interaction. Among the new types of SSR are Read, Relax, Reflect, Respond, and Rap (R^5; Kelley & Clausen-Grace, 2006); scaffolded silent reading (ScSR; Reutzel, Jones, et al., 2008), Independent Reading (IR; Calkins, 1997; Fountas & Pinnell, 2001); and supported independent reading (SIR; Reis, Eckert, McCoach, Jacobs, & Coyne, 2008).

In the R^5 (Kelley & Clausen-Grace, 2006) modification of SSR, teacher–student conferences are held, engagement is encouraged with the use of a reading log, students respond to the text they are reading, and the teacher reviews the strategies to be used. Although the authors reported no quantitative data, they did report descriptive outcomes such as students discussing their books in class, competing to be the first to read a new book, and asking for more R^5 time. The authors also observed disengaged readers becoming engaged readers.

ScSR (Reutzel, Jones, et al., 2008) is another modification to traditional SSR. ScSR was implemented in four third-grade classrooms with 72 students. Unlike traditional SSR, ScSR provides support, guidance, structure, accountability, and monitoring. In a comparison of ScSR to guided oral reading, the only statistically significant difference between the groups was on expression with one passage, favoring the ScSR condition.

During IR (Fountas & Pinnell, 2001), the teacher takes an active role in selecting text, modeling in conferences, and providing guidance and feedback. The five components of IR are (1) the teacher guides text selection, (2) students keep records of what and how much they read, (3) students reflect on what they read, (4) the teacher conducts minilessons and discussions with students, and (5) the teacher does not read at the same time as the students. Trudel (2007) describes the implementation of IR in her elementary classroom. Four changes she observed when implementing IR instead of SSR were more on-task behavior, more appropriate selection of reading materials, the creation of response documents (i.e., journals of what students read), and high-quality teacher–student discussions that focused on student needs and provided some instruction.

SIR was one component of the school enrichment model in a study by Reis et al. (2008). SIR requires students to read silently from self-selected literature for 10–25 minutes in Phase 1 and for 35–40 minutes in Phase 2. Implementation of SIR during Phase 3 varied by site. During this time, teachers coached students in conferences held two to three times weekly to select books slightly above their independent level. During these conferences, teachers also assisted struggling readers with decoding and inferring vocabulary. Students were required to log their daily progress in the number of minutes read. In addition, students responded to teacher-generated questions weekly. Findings included the treatment condition scoring significantly higher in fluency, with no differences in comprehension (as measured by the Iowa Tests of Basic Skills) or reading attitudes.

In a study of three teachers using instructional conversations during SSR, Parr and Maguiness (2005) report that most of the students valued the conversations and benefited by "getting into" the books. These conversations focused on helping students learn how to select or reject a book prior to reading. This strategy was especially effective with reluctant readers.

Instructional Practices to Support Struggling Readers During SSR

For many proficient and motivated readers, reading time is enjoyable. For many struggling readers, periods of SSR are filled with challenges and lack support structures necessary to read difficult words, understand the meanings of words and concepts, and monitor their understanding. The greatest challenge may be the oft-described distant role of the teacher in SSR (i.e., student self-selection of text, little accountability, little support for reading). We propose in Figure 16.1 steps for a teacher to take in SSR for students with reading difficulties. Although this role has not been tested empirically, it serves as an example of the ways in which teachers could become more actively engaged in supporting SSR for students with reading difficulties.

Step 1: Support Book Selection That Matches Students' Interests and Reading Levels

An initial step in supporting struggling readers during periods of SSR is to help them select text that is both interesting and near their independent reading level. This step may involve booklists or technology-based searches that enable students to achieve a better match with interest and reading level. Several websites are available that can assist teachers with this task (e.g., www.reading.org/Resources/

Figure 16.1. Steps to Support Silent Reading for Struggling Readers

Step 5: Wrap up the reading and stimulate future reading

Step 4: Scaffold SSR through progressively longer increments of reading, progress monitoring, and paired readings

Step 3: Preview the text and set a purpose for reading

Step 2: Identify challenging words and promote word consciousness

Step 1: Support book selection that matches students' interest and reading

Booklists.aspx, www.rif.org/parents/resources/books/default.mspx, www.ala.org/ala/mgrps/divs/yalsa/booklistsawards/bestbooksya/bbyahome.cfm). The teacher should also teach students strategies to identify appropriate text difficulty independently. For example, students could be taught to turn to a random page in the text and read a paragraph. If the student encounters more than five words that he or she cannot decode or does not know the meaning of, the text would be considered too difficult for silent reading time.

Step 2: Identify Challenging Words and Promote Word Consciousness

The next step to support struggling readers during silent reading is to identify challenging words in the text and to promote students' independent interest in words. For example, students can scan a page (prior to reading) to identify words they do not recognize and then create a vocabulary log of unfamiliar words. The teacher can then circulate during the SSR session to provide "just-in-time" support. From the vocabulary logs, teachers can identify a select number of words and follow up with extended instruction to the large group for high-priority words.

Step 3: Preview the Text and Set a Purpose for Reading

Previewing the text orients students to the task of reading, creates an opportunity for the teacher to provide necessary background knowledge, and helps students set a purpose for reading. Previewing the book title, chapter titles, major headings, and any visuals (e.g., illustrations, graphs) helps students set a purpose for reading and make predictions. In addition, the teacher can provide any background knowledge necessary for adequate reading comprehension. Although previewing is important, it should be kept relatively short—only about five minutes. For example, the teacher and student could preview a book by reading the title, skimming the chapter titles in the table of contents, and previewing any illustrations in the first chapter. The teacher could then guide the student in predicting what the chapter is about. If students are in the middle of a chapter book, the events of previous chapters can be reviewed.

Step 4: Scaffold SSR Through Progressively Longer Increments of Reading, Progress Monitoring, and Paired Readings

During SSR time, the teacher should be actively involved in monitoring and providing continued support to struggling readers. The teacher can scaffold the silent reading time in several ways. First, the time allotted for SSR should begin small and gradually increase as the ability, attention, and motivation of students increase. For example, only 5 minutes of silent reading may be initially appropriate for a struggling reader. This time could then be increased by 2 minutes every 3 to 4 weeks, until the student is reading independently for about 30 minutes.

A second way to scaffold struggling readers during silent reading time is to monitor their progress. This monitoring could include simply observing the students and ensuring they are using the time to read. The teacher should be available to assist students when they encounter unknown words or feel there is a breakdown in their understanding of the text. The opportunities for just-in-time minilessons on comprehension fix-up strategies and vocabulary words can be numerous.

Implementing paired readings (Fuchs & Fuchs, 2005) is another scaffold teachers can provide to struggling readers. Pairs help students decode difficult words, assist students when comprehension falters, and provide peer models of fluent reading.

Step 5: Wrap Up the Reading and Stimulate Future Reading

At the close of the SSR period, the teacher can support struggling readers by providing time for them to summarize their reading. One method is to focus this time on "fantastic events, fabulous finds, and fascinating vocabulary." Students can recount fantastic events by first returning to their initial purpose for reading and asking themselves, Did I figure out what I wanted? Did I accurately predict what happened? Teachers can have students write or orally provide a summary statement of what they read or learned. If students were reading a chapter book, these statements could be logged and used to review before the next reading session, providing a prompt to help students remember what they last read.

Students can also be encouraged to identify fabulous finds. A fabulous find is something the students learned or read that was unexpected or exciting. Students can identify fabulous finds by asking themselves, What did I learn that was surprising? Students can also be given the opportunity to share fascinating vocabulary, or vocabulary they found especially interesting. Fascinating vocabulary encourages word consciousness in students. By focusing on new words they are encountering, students build independent word-learning strategies. Figure 16.2 is a graphic organizer that can be used to record fantastic events, fabulous finds, and fascinating vocabulary from a chapter book, and Figure 16.3 provides a daily record for fantastic events, fabulous finds, and fascinating vocabulary.

Figure 16.2. Sample Chapter Book Organizer

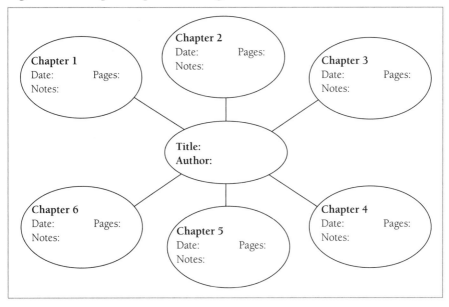

Figure 16.3. Sample SSR Daily Recording Sheet for Fantastic Events, Fabulous Finds, and Fascinating Vocabulary

Book title: Date: Pages read:	
Fantastic Events	
Fabulous Finds	
Fascinating Vocabulary	

Concluding Thoughts on Independent Silent Reading for Struggling Readers and Directions for Future Research

Some studies indicate the promise of SSR to build vocabulary, motivation, background knowledge, and reading comprehension. However, SSR can present unique challenges to students struggling with reading. Because a limited number of studies target struggling readers during silent reading, we drew from the literature on SSR with typical readers. Based on this knowledge and current best practices for students with reading difficulties, we provided suggestions regarding steps to scaffold SSR with struggling readers (see Figure 16.1). The lack of teacher support and involvement is one of the chief obstacles struggling readers face during SSR. Our model has teachers provide support at critical points of the silent reading process so that students can benefit from SSR time. Following the scaffolds in the model, the teacher provides support and instruction before, during, and after the reading time. The practices suggested in this model can be used for both narrative and informational text.

We suggest several future directions for research. First, few experimental studies have been conducted on SSR, and, more precisely, few target a population of struggling readers. Therefore, much is yet to be known empirically about the benefits and obstacles these students face. Research questions to be addressed include the following:

- What is the optimal amount of time for SSR with struggling readers? Does this optimal time depend on age, reading level, or a combination of both?
- How does SSR benefit wide reading and vocabulary, background knowledge, motivation, fluency, and reading comprehension for the range of struggling readers?
- How might selected modifications to SSR affect students' vocabulary, background knowledge, motivation, fluency, and reading comprehension?

QUESTIONS FOR PROFESSIONAL DEVELOPMENT

1. What obstacles have you observed struggling readers in your class encountering during SSR?
2. What support have you provided to struggling readers during SSR?
3. How could the model presented in this chapter help students overcome the obstacles you identified in Question 1?
4. How could you adapt the steps to support SSR for struggling readers, presented in Figure 16.1, to meet the needs of your students?

REFERENCES

Adams, M.J. (1990). *Beginning to read: Thinking and learning about print.* Cambridge, MA: MIT Press.

Allington, R.L. (Ed.). (2002). *Big brother and the national reading curriculum: How ideology trumped evidence.* Portsmouth, NH: Heinemann.

Anderson, R. (2009). Interested reader or uninterested dissembler? The identities constructed by upper primary aged dyslexic pupils during silent reading sessions. *Literacy, 43*(2), 83–90. doi:10.1111/j.1741-4369.2009.00523.x

Benedict, G. (1982). Making reading a habit for students. *Reading Improvement, 19*(1), 48–49.

Block, C.C., Parris, S.R., Reed, K.L., Whiteley, C.S., & Cleveland, M.D. (2009). Instructional approaches that significantly increase reading comprehension. *Journal of Educational Psychology, 101*(2), 262–281. doi:10.1037/a0014319

Bryan, G., Fawson, P.C., & Reutzel, D.R. (2003). Sustained silent reading: Exploring the value of literature discussion with three non-engaged readers. *Reading Research and Instruction, 43*(1), 47–73.

Calkins, L.M. (1997). Get real about reading. *Instructor, 106*(8), 37–41.

Chua, S.P. (2008). The effects of the sustained silent reading program on cultivating students' habits and attitudes in reading books for leisure. *The Clearing House, 81*(4), 180–184. doi:10.3200/TCHS.81.4.180-184

Clark, R.M. (1975, March/April). *A study of teacher behavior and attitudes in elementary schools with high and low pupil achievement.* Paper presented at the annual meeting of the American Educational Research Association, Washington, DC.

Clark, R.M., & Spath, G. (1979, April). *Exemplary schools—the statistical problems of identifying them, and the results of the study.* Paper presented at the annual meeting of the American Educational Research Association, San Francisco.

Clay, M.M. (1991). Introducing a new storybook to young readers. *The Reading Teacher, 45*(4), 264–273. doi:10.1598/RT.45.4.2

Cromley, J.G., & Azevedo, R. (2007). Testing and refining the direct and inferential mediation model of reading comprehension. *Journal of Educational Psychology, 99*(2), 311–325. doi:10.1037/0022-0663.99.2.311

Cunningham, A.E., & Stanovich, K.E. (1998a). The impact of print exposure on word recognition. In J.L. Metsala & L.C. Ehri (Eds.), *Word recognition in beginning literacy* (pp. 235–262). Mahwah, NJ: Erlbaum.

Cunningham, A.E., & Stanovich, K.E. (1998b). What reading does for the mind. *American Educator, 22*(1/2), 8–15.

Davis, Z.T. (1988). A comparison of the effectiveness of sustained silent reading and directed reading activity on students' reading achievement. *The High School Journal, 72*, 46–48.

Fisher, D. (2004). Setting the "opportunity to read" standard: Resuscitating the SSR program in an urban high school. *Journal of Adolescent & Adult Literacy, 48*(2), 138–150. doi:10.1598/JAAL.48.2.5

Fountas, I.C., & Pinnell, G.S. (2001). *Guiding readers and writers, grades 3–6: Teaching comprehension, genre, and content literacy.* Portsmouth, NH: Heinemann.

Fuchs, D., & Fuchs, L.S. (2005). Peer-assisted learning strategies: Promoting word recognition, fluency, and reading comprehension in young children. *The Journal of Special Education, 39*(1), 34–44. doi:10.1177/00224669050390010401

Garan, E.M., & DeVoogd, G. (2008). The benefits of sustained silent reading: Scientific research and common sense converge. *The Reading Teacher, 62*(4), 336–344. doi:10.1598/RT.62.4.6

Graves, M.F., & Watts-Taffe, S.M. (2002). The place of word consciousness in a research-based vocabulary program. In A.E. Farstrup & S.J. Samuels (Eds.), *What research has to say about reading instruction* (3rd ed., pp. 140–165). Newark, DE: International Reading Association.

Guthrie, J.T., & Wigfield, A. (2000). Engagement and motivation in reading. In M.L. Kamil, P.B. Mosenthal, P.D. Pearson, & R. Barr (Eds.), *Handbook of reading research* (Vol. 3, pp. 403–422). Mahwah, NJ: Erlbaum.

Haynes, M.C., & Jenkins, J.R. (1986). Reading instruction in special education resource rooms. *American Educational Research Journal, 23*(2), 161–190.

Hunt, L.C., Jr. (1970, May). *Updating the individual approach to reading: IPI or IRP?* Paper presented at the annual convention of the International Reading Association, Anaheim, CA.

Kelley, M., & Clausen-Grace, N. (2006). R^5: The sustained silent reading makeover that transformed readers. *The Reading Teacher, 60*(2), 148–156. doi:10.1598/RT.60.2.5

Krashen, S. (2005). Is in-school free reading good for children? Why the National Reading Panel Report is (still) wrong. *Phi Delta Kappan, 86*(6), 444–447.

Lee-Daniels, S.L., & Murray, B.A. (2000). DEAR me: What does it take to get children reading? *The Reading Teacher, 54*(2), 154–155.

Leinhardt, G., Zigmond, N., & Cooley, W.W. (1981). Reading instruction and its effects. *American Educational Research Journal, 18*(3), 343–361.

Marzano, R.J. (2004). *Building background knowledge for academic achievement: Research on what works in schools.* Alexandria, VA: Association for Supervision and Curriculum Development.

Melton, E.J. (1993). *SSR: Is it an effective practice for the learning disabled?* Scranton, PA: Marywood College. (ERIC Document Reproduction Service No. ED397569)

Methe, S.A., & Hintze, J.M. (2003). Evaluating teacher modeling as a strategy to increase student reading behavior. *School Psychology Review, 32*(4), 617–623.

Nagy, N.M., Campenni, C.E., & Shaw, J.N. (2000). *A survey of sustained silent reading practices in seventh-grade classrooms.* Newark, DE: International Reading Association.

Nagy, W. (2005). Why vocabulary instruction needs to be long-term and comprehensive. In E.H. Hiebert & M.L. Kamil (Eds.), *Teaching and learning vocabulary: Bringing research to practice* (pp. 27–44). Mahwah, NJ: Erlbaum.

National Institute of Child Health and Human Development. (2000). *Report of the National Reading Panel. Teaching children to read: An evidence-based assessment of the scientific research literature on reading and its implications for reading instruction* (NIH Publication No. 00-4769). Washington, DC: U.S. Government Printing Office.

Parr, J.M., & Maguiness, C. (2005). Removing the silent from SSR: Voluntary reading as social practice. *Journal of Adolescent & Adult Literacy, 49*(2), 98–107. doi:10.1598/JAAL.49.2.2

Pilgreen, J.L. (2000). *The SSR handbook: How to organize and manage a sustained silent reading program.* Portsmouth, NH: Boynton/Cook.

Reis, S.M., Eckert, R.D., McCoach, D.B., Jacobs, J.K., & Coyne, M. (2008). Using enrichment reading practices to increase reading fluency, comprehension, and attitudes. *The Journal of Educational Research, 101*(5), 299–315. doi:10.3200/JOER.101.5.299-315

Renaissance Learning. (n.d.). Accelerated Reader [Computer software]. Wisconsin Rapids, WI: Author. Retrieved September 29, 2009, from www.renlearn.com/ar/

Reutzel, D.R., & Cooter, R.B., Jr. (2005). *The essentials of teaching children to read: What every teacher needs to know.* Upper Saddle River, NJ: Merrill/Prentice Hall.

Reutzel, D.R., Jones, C.D., Fawson, P.C., & Smith, J.A. (2008). Scaffolded silent reading: A complement to guided repeated oral reading that works! *The Reading Teacher, 62*(3), 194–207. doi:10.1598/RT.62.3.2

Sadoski, M.C. (1984). SSR, accountability and effective reading instruction. *Reading Horizons, 24*(2), 119–123.

Shanahan, T. (2004). Critiques of the National Reading Panel Report: Their implications for research, policy, and practice. In P. McCardle & V. Chhabra (Eds.), *The voice of evidence in reading research* (pp. 235–265). Baltimore: Paul H. Brookes.

Sindelar, P.T., Espin, C.A., Smith, M.A., & Harriman, N.E. (1990). A comparison of more and less effective special education teachers in elementary-level programs. *Teacher Education and Special Education, 13*(1), 9–16. doi:10.1177/088840649001300102

Stallings, J. (1980). Allocated academic learning time revisited, or beyond time on task. *Educational Researcher, 9*(11), 11–16.

Taylor, B.M., Frye, B.J., & Maruyama, G.M. (1990). Time spent reading and reading growth. *American Educational Research Journal, 27*(2), 351–362.

Trudel, H. (2007). Making data-driven decisions: Silent reading. *The Reading Teacher, 61*(4), 308–315. doi:10.1598/RT.61.4.3

Walker, B.J. (2000). *Diagnostic teaching of reading: Techniques for instruction and assessment* (4th ed.). Upper Saddle River, NJ: Prentice Hall.

What Works Clearinghouse. (2008). *WWC intervention report: Accelerated Reader.* Washington, DC: Institute of Education Sciences, U.S. Department of Education. Retrieved April 29, 2010, from ies.ed.gov/ncee/wwc/pdf/wwc_accelreader_101408.pdf

Wu, Y., & Samuels, S.J. (2004, May). *How the amount of time spent in independent reading affects reading achievement: A response to the National Reading Panel.* Paper presented at the 49th annual convention of the International Reading Association, Reno, NV.

Yoon, J. (2002). Three decades of sustained silent reading: A meta-analytic review of the effects of SSR on attitude toward reading. *Reading Improvement, 39*(4), 186–195.

Revisiting Silent Reading in 2020 and Beyond

Elfrieda H. Hiebert
University of California, Berkeley

D. Ray Reutzel
Utah State University

As the title of this book indicates, our interest lies in addressing how the current knowledge base about silent reading practice can provide a foundation for future instruction and research. Based on what we know in 2010, we might ask the question, What changes in reading instruction and practice need to be made now to positively influence students' literacy proficiencies in a decade? We have chosen the year 2020 not only because it directs us into the future but also because it is the year that President Obama (Dillon, 2010) has targeted as the point when the majority of high school graduates should have the literacy skills that successfully prepare them for college and a later career.

This goal is ambitious but even if modest movement is made toward achieving it, increased attention needs to be directed toward the use of effective silent reading in classrooms. In the digital–global world of the 21st century, accessing, organizing, creating, sharing, and using knowledge are critical commodities. The acquisition and use of knowledge require that students and employees develop the ability to read silently with skill and stamina in a variety of texts for a variety of purposes, as these texts are presented to the reader using a variety of traditional and digital media. For the necessary shift from oral repeated reading with feedback to effective silent reading to occur, literacy educators need to be reflective and strategic going forward. If the researchers who revisit the topic of silent reading in 2020 are to see movement toward greater literacy capacity among elementary students and high school graduates, literacy educators will need to recognize the unique contributions and roles of both oral and silent reading in developing proficient, lifelong readers.

In this conclusion, we summarize and synthesize content from chapters in this volume to describe, first, the role of oral reading in balanced and thoughtful reading instruction and, second, silent reading practices. We close with descriptions of three sources for effective silent reading practices that are offered in this book: (1) instructional techniques and practices, (2) teacher support, and (3) digital contexts.

Revisiting Silent Reading: New Directions for Teachers and Researchers, edited by Elfrieda H. Hiebert and D. Ray Reutzel. © 2010 by the International Reading Association.

Clarifying the Role of Oral Reading

In the decade since the publication of the National Reading Panel report (NRP; National Institute of Child Health and Human Development [NICHD], 2000), reading practice has been largely confined to repeated, oral reading. Allington and McGill-Franzen (see Chapter 3) discuss the consequences of an overemphasis on oral reading, especially when much of it occurs as round robin reading. An overemphasis on either oral or silent reading at particular points in time is not a unique phenomenon (see Chapter 1 by Pearson & Goodin). When viewed from the perspective of the digital age in which the selection, evaluation, and interpretation of information is paramount, however, an overemphasis on oral reading seems particularly out of sync with the needs of individuals who are prepared to participate fully in the communities and marketplace of the 21st century.

We hasten to emphasize that the near-singular attention given to repeated, oral reading practice with feedback has reflected an underlying misinterpretation of the findings of research related to the role and use of silent reading in classrooms. That is, the near-exclusive emphasis on oral reading seen in many of today's classrooms resulted from several inappropriate practice conditions associated with or embedded within past silent reading and self-selected reading practice routines.

An appropriate response to the observed overemphasis on oral reading practice in the past decade in classrooms is not to overreact by moving in the opposite direction and eliminating oral reading in favor of silent reading. Oral and silent are not competing forms of reading. Rather, they are complementary forms of reading that reflect students' developmental growth as readers. When reading educators revisit the topic of silent reading in a decade or two, we would expect to see particular kinds of oral and silent reading practices used in classrooms in developmentally responsive ways (e.g., oral, repeated reading with younger, less proficient readers and silent, wide reading with older, more proficient readers). It is clear that most adults read silently whereas younger readers initially enjoy reading aloud to show off their new and emerging abilities as readers.

Among several important roles that oral reading can play in the initial and later stages of reading instruction is the teacher's use of oral reading to model fluent reading and guide younger readers toward increasingly fluent oral reading. By reading aloud to younger students, teachers make an otherwise mysterious, largely invisible process more concrete and accessible. Oral reading also provides a means whereby teachers can assess and monitor students' silent reading and give them timely feedback. A well-balanced reading program offers students numerous opportunities for reading, both oral and silent. As students evidence the ability to remain involved with reading for long periods of time (i.e., stamina) and increase their reading fluency, oral reading skills can be scaffolded through gradual release by knowledgeable teachers who help students move successfully into silent reading. In the study by Reutzel, Fawson, and Smith (2008), third-grade students' silent reading was carefully scaffolded by their teachers to ensure an effective silent reading experience (see Chapter 8 by Reutzel, Jones, & Newman).

Similarly, we would hope that upper primary and middle-grade students and beyond are not spending sizable chunks of their school days in oral round robin reading or listening to their teachers read aloud portions of a textbook. Although these uses of oral reading are typically aimed at compensating for some students' struggles in reading, such practices tend to constrain individual students' reading practice time in ways that undermine long-term reading progress. If a sufficient number of students in a class cannot read a textbook, teachers would do well to access alternative texts that struggling students can read. Neither teacher read-alouds nor oral round robin reading of textbooks is likely to lift middle school and high school students' reading achievement in preparation for college or a career.

Oral reading is also considered by many classroom teachers to be an essential part of monitoring student progress for the purpose of designing effective instruction and interventions to increase student reading fluency and achievement. Oral reading provides teachers with a window for understanding struggling students' knowledge and use of underlying systems of written language (Goodman, 1969). Classroom teachers have for decades kept running records of their students' oral reading (Clay, 1985). However, in the past decade, assessment of oral reading has been largely based on curriculum-based measurement models (CBM; Deno, 1985, 2003).

For oral reading, a CBM assessment consists of one-minute samples of students' rate and accuracy in reading a passage. For silent reading, the task involves reading a text in which words have been systematically deleted and several choices given for the deleted word. This latter design is intended to establish students' rate of reading with comprehension. For classroom teachers faced with many students and limited time, CBM assessments are an efficient way of gathering information on students' oral and silent reading.

Unfortunately, the data drawn from the CBM assessments have been used in inappropriate ways, such as designating students to different risk status levels—benchmarked, strategic, or intensive. Sadly, these one-minute CBM assessments have led to an overemphasis on reading speed at the expense of developing expression and comprehension with both native English speakers and English learners (see Chapter 15 by Ockey & Reutzel). Unless English learners are members of classrooms such as the ones that Worthy and Roser (see Chapter 14) describe, the potential benefits of well-intended mandates and policies will not have the desired outcomes.

To perform well on such assessments, teachers may have students spend an excessive amount of instructional time in reading short paragraphs and texts to increase reading speed. This leads inevitably to students who lack reading stamina because they are used to practicing their reading in "sprint-like" fashion for short periods. Of course, oral reading norms obtained from these one-minute samples are likely also to overestimate real sustained reading speeds orally or silently, because long-distance runners as compared with sprinters pace themselves differently (see Chapter 9 by Hiebert, Wilson, & Trainin). As Hairrell, Edmonds, Vaughn, and Simmons (see Chapter 16) caution, emphasizing sprinting over long-distance reading can have particularly devastating consequences on the reading development of those students who have reading disabilities.

Even more disappointing is the fact that these quick CBM assessments have also displaced more intensive and comprehensive examinations of struggling readers' oral reading miscues and behaviors. We argue that high-quality reading assessment should not be dismissed or displaced because of inappropriate applications of CBM and overuses of oral reading fluency measures during the past decade. Whether the displaced assessment was an informal reading inventory with leveled texts or a running record taken while students read "everyday" texts in the classroom, sampling students' oral reading for insight into their linguistic knowledge and their use (or lack) of monitoring and fix-up strategies was part of the assessment repertoire for many past generations of teachers (Pikulski & Shanahan, 1982).

Oral reading plays yet another role in classroom reading instruction. It is the means through which literary favorites and classics can be enjoyed through teacher read-alouds. Digital texts have increased student access to performances by great story readers such as Jim Dale reading the Harry Potter books. For creating community, offering a setting for expression, and offering a stage for performing and entertaining, oral reading is central (Rasinski & Griffith, 2008). Opportunities for students to select portions of texts or poems to read aloud or to participate in Readers Theatre contribute to the development of a classroom literacy community that is vibrant and alive (Wolf, 2004). Teacher read-alouds allow students to experience language and vocabulary they may not yet be able to process on their own.

Some research has shown that oral reading fluency correlates well with specific forms of silent reading comprehension (Schatschneider, Torgesen, Buck, & Powell-Smith, 2004). Although oral reading serves several critical functions as described previously, it is erroneous to assume that oral reading proficiency equals silent reading proficiency. There are significant differences between the two processes (see Chapter 1 by Pearson & Goodin). These differences are especially pronounced when students read texts presented in digital formats. Sifting through information, deciding what is credible, and choosing how to communicate one's response to information are not typically oral reading processes (see Chapter 13 by Malloy, Castek, & Leu).

Clarifying the Role of Silent Reading

For almost 40 years prior to the NRP report (NICHD, 2000), teacher educators and staff development specialists routinely recommended independent, silent reading practices such as those promoted by Hunt (1970) under the aegis of sustained silent reading (SSR). When using these models of silent reading, teachers were advised to allow students to read silently for extensive periods of time, regardless of their grade level or their proficiency levels. Even though evidence supporting the use of spending large chunks of class time on students' self-selected reading was anything but convincing, whole-language proponents in the mid-1980s began advocating for independent, silent reading practice to replace core reading instruction programs and oral reading (Hagerty, 1999). In readers' workshop that extended SSR practices to classroom instruction, students—even first graders—were encouraged to choose their own books, often without much teacher guidance or assistance. Reading instruction consisted of brief, randomly sequenced or incidental whole-class minilessons and, in rare cases, individual teacher–student conferences.

Recommendations such as these ignored research on silent reading practices that existed at that time. As Manning, Lewis, and Lewis (see Chapter 7) point out, several projects in the 1980s pointed to the need for adapting silent reading practices to increase greater student accountability and monitoring by teachers in book selection and purpose setting (Anderson, Wilson, & Fielding, 1988; Manning & Manning, 1984). However, as Stahl (1999) observed, these recommendations were often ignored in whole-language classrooms. Many teachers did not hold conferences with students during independent, silent reading, opting to read independently and silently themselves, thereby believing themselves to be a model of engaged silent reading.

After nearly 40 years of continuously recommending independent, silent reading, the NRP report (NICHD, 2000) cast a shadow of doubt on the practices associated with it, such as SSR. In a meta-analytic review of the research on SSR within classroom settings, the NRP members were able to identify 10 SSR studies that met their criteria of rigorous research. In five of those studies, researchers found effects that favored SSR. However, the effect sizes were relatively small. Subsequent analyses of the 10 studies (e.g., Lewis, 2002; Reutzel et al., 2008; Wu & Samuels, 2004) pointed out limitations in their design and execution. For example, the studies as a group did not report precisely how much time was spent in reading. The die was cast, however, when NRP members (e.g., Shanahan, 2006) strongly suggested—independent of the report—that evidence for time spent on independent, silent reading in classrooms compared with other reading approaches, such as guided, repeated, and oral reading with feedback, was not as effective.

Rather than constructively addressing the misinterpretations of the NRP's (NICHD, 2000) concerns, advocates of independent, silent reading sharply criticized the conclusions drawn by the NRP (e.g., Coles, 2000; Krashen, 2001, 2005). Since that time, several research groups (most represented by chapters in this volume) have reconsidered what it takes to get and keep students' eyes on the page during silent reading. From this sustained research, we describe three features of independent, silent reading practice that require attention to improve the silent reading performance of elementary and secondary students in the future.

Instructional Techniques and Practices

Although current research on independent, silent reading is not as extensive, or the findings as robust, as those surrounding phonemic awareness and alphabetics, there is an emerging research base that indicates that there are specific elements of classroom reading programs that can support the development of proficient silent reading habits.

To understand how these elements can be influenced by teachers and instruction, one needs to understand what distinguishes silent reading from oral reading. Moving from vocalization or subvocalization to "silent reading" is perhaps one of the hardest aspects of reading there is to "teach" (see Chapter 4 by Wright, Sherman, & Jones). For most students, this happens gradually with ample opportunities to read. There are also developmental and social factors that likely influence movement toward effective and sustained silent reading. However, if students do not have frequent opportunities to read, there may well be residual subvocalization behaviors that often characterize the silent reading habits of struggling readers. Wright, Sherman, and Jones indicate that teachers need to do more than assign texts for students to read "silently" and tell them to stop whisper reading.

Samuels, Hiebert, and Rasinski (see Chapter 2) note that some students may require carefully designed instructional programs to remediate or develop the eye movements that characterize proficient reading. Such programs have yet to be validated by sustained and carefully designed research studies that address how to efficiently train eye movements and the subsequent effects of doing so on students' reading automaticity and comprehension. In particular, the success of eye-movement training programs designed to support efficiency in silent reading as discussed in Chapter 2 needs to be disentangled from the eyes-on-the-text phenomenon conflated with current models of eye-movement training.

Proficient silent reading also requires that individuals be able to independently manage their attention. Unlike oral reading where there is a definite task (and a monitor in the form of an adult or a recording device), silent reading requires that readers choose to remain involved in reading, manage their time well, and take steps to correct or "fix up" failing comprehension when necessary. For example, students might struggle with the decision to keep their eyes on the text instead of skimming or scanning the text or acting like they are reading. As the findings described by Hiebert, Wilson, and Trainin (see Chapter 9) suggest, perseverance or reading stamina appears to be a considerable challenge for less proficient readers (see also Lee-Daniels & Murray, 2000). When reading silently, students must make internal choices they do not have to make during oral reading. The work of Swan, Coddington, and Guthrie (see Chapter 6) underscores how critical these internal choices to engage in silent reading are in the long run for students.

Of these reader behaviors that are unique to silent reading—managing one's time, choosing to remain engaged in reading a text, and monitoring and fixing up faulty comprehension—only the topic of monitoring strategies has received much focus (Pearson & Dole, 1987). Monitoring strategies become particularly critical when readers' purposes are vague or ill defined and when background knowledge is limited—circumstances that are often a part of silent reading for less proficient readers (McKeown, Beck, & Blake, 2009). As is often the case, published programs have overdone the number of strategies that are taught and practiced as part of lessons (Block & Duffy, 2008; Dewitz, Jones, & Leahy, 2009). Furthermore, past instruction has not aided students in knowing under what conditions particular strategies are useful or imperative and under what conditions they are not.

Although the work is still limited in scope, we are beginning to get a sense that the stamina of readers can be supported by effective independent, silent reading practice conditions put into place by well-informed and vigilant classroom teachers. Reutzel, Jones, and Newman (see Chapter 8) illustrate several scaffolds that are needed to increase the perseverance of students' silent reading during allocated independent reading time. Kelley and Clausen-Grace (see Chapter 10) illustrate a particularly critical aspect of instructional support for perseverance in independent reading. In their study, teachers monitored the degree to which students stuck with their books during allocated silent reading time. Students were not allowed to flit back and forth during independent reading period, glancing at a book and then going for another and then another, and so forth. The work of White and Kim (see Chapter 5) also argues for providing student programs that support after-school and summer reading. They also emphasize the need to provide silent reading scaffolds that support engagement with books and the development of reading stamina. What is clear from this group of studies is that Hunt's (1970) suggestion that the same silent reading program be implemented across different developmental and proficiency levels misrepresented the complexity of reading, texts, classrooms, and instruction. Although the simplistic message that all students should read silently in self-selected books may have been a point of departure, there is much that we have learned in the interim about the kinds of scaffolds that can ensure that students increase their capacity and interest in silent reading.

Teacher Support

Change of any kind takes time and information. Fundamental changes in silent reading practices in classrooms can be expected to require substantial amounts of support for the teachers who will be asked to make them. As the teachers' questions that provided the basis for Hiebert, Wilson, and Trainin's (see Chapter 9) development of comprehension-based silent reading rate illustrate, teachers ask many important questions. Often, these are questions for which researchers have few solid answers. Conversations between researchers and teachers are urgently needed on issues associated with independent, silent reading—so that the questions that teachers ask are addressed by future research and so that the questions that researchers pursue in relation to independent, silent reading are relevant to the real world of classrooms.

In the research described in this volume, the amount of teacher support and scaffolding required to sustain silent reading practice among students in classroom settings was extensive (White & Kim, Chapter 5; Reutzel, Jones, & Newman, Chapter 8; Kelley & Clausen-Grace, Chapter 10). Brenner and Hiebert (see Chapter 12) describe a series of modules designed to provide teachers with specific professional development on how to help students keep their eyes on the page during silent reading. Even with access to these modules and on-site coaching from peers, the teachers described in the study nevertheless required a great deal of continuous support to make even small changes in relation to supporting effective independent, silent reading practices in their own classrooms.

Digital Contexts

In the digital–global world of the 21st century, proficient silent reading is essential to meet the challenge of ensuring that more high school graduates are ready for the increasing demands of college and career-related literacy tasks. As Malloy, Castek, and Leu (see Chapter 13) explain, literacy proficiencies in traditional print contexts do not extend seamlessly to those practiced in digital contexts. Effective silent reading in online contexts requires that students adopt a problem-solving stance, where an initial task involves searching for and selecting from available information and a second involves evaluating whether the accessed information is valid and valuable to read. The text that is the focus of these tasks is almost always informational in nature, whereas much of past conventional print-based reading instruction has focused heavily on traditional print versions of narrative texts.

Informational and narrative texts differ in structure, conceptual density, and physical features such as diagrams, photo inserts, headings and subheadings, and a table of contents (Duke & Bennett-Armistead, 2003). Readers often skim sections of an informational text but closely read and reread those sections that provide the precise content they are seeking. By contrast, narrative texts are typically written to be read from beginning to end with a relatively uniform amount of focused attention.

Despite the fact that digital contexts have made the demands for processing informational texts more critical, there is evidence that opportunities for content area learning in elementary schools have decreased rather than increased. In a recent survey, elementary teachers reported devoting around an hour of time weekly to science instruction (Dorph et al., 2007). This amount of time was half that reported in a survey conducted in 2000 (Fulp, 2002). If students have not had adequate experiences with informational text, they are in considerable jeopardy when faced with the additional requirements needed to be successful in negotiating literacy tasks in digital contexts.

The digital age offers considerable opportunities for learners. For educators to ensure that students have the skills that allow them to take advantage of these opportunities, massive restructuring of the literacy curriculum needs to happen. Support for strong silent reading comprehension is fundamental to this restructuring, but it is not simply a matter of increasing silent reading practice with the texts and processes that have dominated the curriculum. This restructuring requires significant changes in the texts and contexts of instruction as well.

Final Thoughts

If we are to be successful in promoting efficacious silent reading over the next decade, educators need to be more strategic and thoughtful. Unexamined assumptions associated with past independent, silent reading practices have led to results that in the long run have not supported students in becoming more proficient independent, silent readers. Further, pitting oral reading versus silent reading has not supported students in transferring oral reading skills to silent reading.

As evident in the data reported by Schwanenflugel, Kuhn, and Ash (see Chapter 11), oral and silent reading both have critical roles in the development of proficient reading. The costs of failing to view oral and silent reading as having complementary rather than competing functions in the development of proficient literacy are high for the futures of our students. Teachers and researchers need to work together to solve conundrums around how best to support all readers through appropriate uses of both oral and silent reading at different points in students' literacy development.

REFERENCES

Anderson, R.C., Wilson, P.T., & Fielding, L.G. (1988). Growth in reading and how children spend their time outside of school. *Reading Research Quarterly, 23*(3), 285–303. doi:10.1598/RRQ.23.3.2

Block, C.C., & Duffy, G.G. (2008). Research on teaching comprehension: Where we've been and where we're going. In C.C. Block & S.R. Parris (Eds.), *Comprehension instruction: Research-based best practices* (2nd ed., pp. 19–37). New York: Guilford.

Clay, M.M. (1985). *The early detection of reading difficulties* (3rd ed.). Portsmouth, NH: Heinemann.

Coles, G. (2000). *Misreading reading: The bad science that hurts children.* Portsmouth, NH: Heinemann.

Deno, S.L. (1985). Curriculum-based measurement: The emerging alternative. *Exceptional Children, 52*(3), 219–232.

Deno, S.L. (2003). Developments in curriculum-based measurement. *The Journal of Special Education, 37*(3), 184–192. doi:10.1177/00224 669030370030801

Dewitz, P., Jones, J., & Leahy, S. (2009). Comprehension strategy instruction in core reading programs. *Reading Research Quarterly, 44*(2), 102–126. doi:10.1598/RRQ.44.2.1

Dillon, S. (2010, March 13). Obama calls for major change in education law. *The New York Times.* Retrieved May 10, 2010, from www.nytimes.com/2010/03/14/education/14child.html

Dorph, R., Goldstein, D., Lee, S., Lepori, K., Schneider, S., & Venkatesan, S. (2007). *The status of science education in the Bay Area.* Berkeley, CA: Lawrence Hall of Science, UC-Berkeley.

Duke, N.K., & Bennett-Armistead, V.S. (2003). *Reading & writing informational text in the primary grades: Research-based practices.* New York: Scholastic.

Fulp, S.L. (2002). *Status of elementary school science teaching.* Chapel Hill, NC: Horizon Research.

Goodman, K.S. (1969). Analysis of oral reading miscues: Applied psycholinguistics. *Reading Research Quarterly, 5*(1), 9–30. doi:10.2307/747158

Hagerty, P.J. (1999). *Readers' workshop: Real reading.* New York: Scholastic.

Hunt, L.C. (1970). The effect of self-selection, interest, and motivation upon independent, instructional, and frustration levels. *The Reading Teacher, 24*(2), 146–151.

Krashen, S. (2001). More smoke and mirrors: A critique of the National Reading Panel report on fluency. *Phi Delta Kappan, 83*(2), 119–123.

Krashen, S. (2005). A special section on reading research—Is in-school free reading good for children? Why the National Reading Panel Report is (still) wrong. *Phi Delta Kappan, 86*(6), 444–447.

Lee-Daniels, S.L., & Murray, B.A. (2000). DEAR me: What does it take to get children reading? *The Reading Teacher, 54*(2), 154–155.

Lewis, M. (2002). *Read more—read better? A meta-analysis of the literature on the relationship between exposure to reading and reading achievement.* Unpublished doctoral dissertation, University of Minnesota.

Manning, G.L., & Manning, M. (1984). What models of recreational reading make a difference? *Reading World, 23*(4), 375–380.

McKeown, M.G., Beck, I.L., & Blake, R.G.K. (2009). Rethinking reading comprehension instruction: A comparison of instruction for strategies and content approaches. *Reading Research Quarterly, 44*(3), 218–253. doi:10.1598/RRQ.44.3.1

National Institute of Child Health and Human Development. (2000). *Report of the National Reading Panel. Teaching children to read: An evidence-based assessment of the scientific research literature on reading and its implications for reading instruction* (NIH Publication No. 00-4769). Washington, DC: U.S. Government Printing Office.

Pearson, P.D., & Dole, J.A. (1987). Explicit comprehension instruction: A review of research and a new conceptualization of instruction. *The Elementary School Journal, 88*(2), 151–165. doi:10.1086/461530

Pikulski, J.J., & Shanahan, T. (1982). Informal reading inventories: A critical analysis. In J.J. Pikulski & T. Shanahan (Eds.), *Approaches to the informal evaluation of reading* (pp. 94–116). Newark, DE: International Reading Association.

Rasinski, T., & Griffith, L. (2008). *Building fluency through practice and performance grade 3.* Huntington Beach, CA: Shell Education.

Reutzel, D.R., Fawson, P.C., & Smith, J.A. (2008). Reconsidering silent sustained reading: An exploratory study of scaffolded silent reading. *The Journal of Educational Research, 102*(1), 37–50. doi:10.3200/JOER.102.1.37-50

Schatschneider, C., Torgesen, J.K., Buck, J., & Powell-Smith, K. (2004). *A multivariate study of factors that contribute to individual differences in performance on the Florida Comprehensive Reading Assessment Test* (Tech. Rep. No. 5). Tallahassee: Florida Center for Reading Research.

Shanahan, T. (2006, June/July). Does he really think kids shouldn't read? *Reading Today, 23*(6), 12.

Stahl, S.A. (1999). Why innovations come and go (and mostly go): The case of whole language. *Educational Researcher, 28*(8), 13–22.

Wolf, S.A. (2004). *Interpreting literature with children.* Mahwah, NJ: Erlbaum.

Wu, Y., & Samuels, S.J. (2004, May). *How the amount of time spent on independent reading affects reading achievement.* Paper presented at the annual meeting of the International Reading Association, Reno, NV.

Gough, P.B., 31, 32, 244
Graesser, A.C., 190
Graves, M.F., 68, 163, 277
Gray, L., 60
Gray, W.S., 12, 13, 14
Greathouse, S., 67, 69, 71, 83, 85
Green, B.F., 266
Green, C., 243
Green, H.R.H., 116
Greenberg, S.N., 191
Greene, A., 41
Greenhow, C., 233
Greenleaf, C.L., 133, 134
Greeno, J.G., 202
Greenwood, C.R., 193
Griffith, L.W., 155, 164, 207, 293
Griffith-Ross, D.A., 51
Grigg, W.S., 68, 154, 156, 199
Grolnick, W.S., 102, 105
Gross, A., 47
Guryan, J., 88
Guthrie, J.T., 16, 48, 76, 95, 96, 97, 98,
    99, 100, 101, 102, 103, 107, 108, 135,
    157, 169, 173, 187, 198, 199, 201, 232,
    242, 264, 280
Guthrie, K.M., 259

H
Hadaway, N.L., 245
Hagerty, P.J., 294
Hall, G.S., 10
Hamilton, A.M., 191
Hamm, D.N., 12
Hancock, D.R., 103
Hardyck, C.D., 58, 182
Hargis, C.H., 49, 169
Harriman, N.E., 281
Harris, A.J., 60
Harris, T.L., 58
Hart, B., 68
Hasbrouck, J.E., 153, 154, 157
Hayes, D.P., 200
Haynes, M.C., 279
Heald-Taylor, B.G., 187
Hebb, D.O., 30

Hedrick, W.B., 173
Helman, L., 259
Henk, W.H., 181
Henry, L.A., 222, 235, 236
Hepler, S.I., 129
Herman, P.A., 16, 163, 200
Herman, R., 190
Herrell, A., 260
Heubach, K.M., 137, 182, 189, 261
Heyns, B., 67, 69, 71, 72, 74, 75
Hickman, J., 129
Hicks, T., 46
Hidi, S., 173
Hiebert, E.H., 57, 63, 87, 129, 145, 151,
    158, 159, 163, 164, 169, 189, 198,
    201, 202, 205, 207, 208, 212, 213,
    232, 266
Higgins, D., 132
Higgins, K.J., 118
Hilden, K., 46
Hintze, J.M., 279
Hoa, L.W., 96, 101
Hochberg, J., 26
Hodges, R.E., 58
Hoffman, J.V., 13, 17, 187, 202, 203, 211
Holcomb, A., 182, 189
Holland, J., 198
Hollingsworth, P.M., 200
Holmes, B.C., 13, 16, 181, 182
Holton, B.A., 14
Hopkins, K.D., 116
Horowitz, R., 223
Horst, M., 46, 47
Hosp, M.K., 153, 155, 199
Hsiao, S., 67
Huang, C., 198, 199, 201
Hubbard, R.S., 253
Huey, E.B., 11, 13, 24, 57
Huffaker, D., 231
Hughes, J.E., 233
Huhta, A., 263, 266
Humenick, N.M., 48, 76, 101
Hunt, L.C., Jr., 13, 14, 113, 131, 132, 133,
    134, 135, 276, 293, 296

McMahon, S.I., 17
McNamara, D.S., 155, 190
McNaughton, S., 67
McQuillan, J., 74
McRae, A., 95, 96, 100, 107, 108
McVerry, J.G., 221, 222, 230, 231, 235
Mead, C.D., 11
Meece, J.L., 95, 102, 201
Meisinger, E.B., 184
Meister, C., 77
Melton, E.J., 120, 279
Menon, S., 164
Methe, S.A., 279
Metsala, J.L., 169
Meyers, R., 114
Michie, J.S., 14
Middleton, E.L., 188
Miller, D.C., 113
Miller, J., 191
Miller, S.D., 95, 102, 181, 187, 201
Minton, M.J., 116
Mish, F.C., 58
Mohr, K.A.J., 260
Moje, E.B., 15, 223
Monaghan, E.J., 6, 7, 8, 10
Montero, M.K., 258
Moody, S.W., 47
Moore, D.W., 135
Moore, J.C., 113
Moore, S.A., 132
Moorman, M., 134, 241, 244, 245
Moran, J., 164
Morrison, D., 97, 98, 100, 102
Morrow, L.M., 74, 76, 182, 202, 244
Mosenthal, P., 57–58
Moss, B., 214
Mueller, F.L., 133, 134
Mullikin, C.N., 181
Murray, B.A., 135, 280, 295

N
Nagy, N.M., 280
Nagy, W.E., 16, 163, 200, 277
National Center for Education Statistics, 258

National Center for Reading First
   Technical Assistance, 204
National Council of Teachers of English,
   222
National Education Association, 53
National Institute of Child Health and
   Human Development, xi, 18, 57, 75,
   78, 114, 129, 140, 151, 168, 199–200,
   201, 212, 243, 260, 270, 271, 276, 291,
   293, 294
National Research Council, 101
National School Boards Association, 107
National Staff Development Council, 202,
   203, 211
National Telecommunications and
   Information Administration
   & Economics and Statistics
   Administration, 222
Neuman, S.B., 15, 73, 242, 244, 245
The New London Group, 222
Newman, T., 134, 135, 146
Newton, E., 214
Nichols, A., 68, 71
Nichols, W.D., 103
Nicholson, S., 15
Nierlich, T., 233
Nye, B., 67, 69, 71, 83, 85

O
O'Byrne, W.I., 221, 222, 230
Ockey, G.J., 266
O'Connell, A.A., 71
Office of the Inspector General, 46
Ohlhausen, M.M., 176
Olen, S., 117
Oliver, M.E., 115, 125
Olson, D.R., 5
Olson, L.S., 67, 69, 70, 71–72, 73, 74, 75
Olson, W.C., 13
Orange, C., 223
Oranje, A., 154, 199
Ortiz, A., 29
Osborn, J., 18, 131
Otto, H.J., 53

Note. Page numbers followed by *f* and *t* indicate figures and tables, respectively.

content, relevance of, 106
content concepts, mastery goals based on, 102–103
context and comprehension-based silent reading rate: digital compared to paper, 156–157, 161*f*, 165; technology and, 266; vocabulary and, 163
continuum of readers, 171*f*
control over learning and engaged silent reading, 103–105
convergence insufficiency, 40–41
CORI, 99, 100
cornea, 27
CPIDR tool, 190
curriculum-based measurement: assessments of, 156; maze technique and, 157; oral reading norms and, 153; uses of, 292–293
Cyberschoolbus Global Teaching and Learning Project, 234

D

DEAR, 129, 130, 261, 275
decision making and online reading, 224–225
decoding: scaffolded oral reading practice and, 181; self-teaching hypothesis and, 52; switching attention between comprehension and, 36–37, 39
dedication to reading, 99–101, 101*f*
developmental stages of speech manifestations during silent reading: assessment and, 61–62; instruction and, 63; research on, 64; struggling readers and, 60–61; subvocal speech, 58; vocal speech, 59–60
DIALANG, 263–264, 266
DIBELS assessment system, 46, 142
digital contexts: comprehension-based silent reading rate in, 156–157, 161*f*, 163, 165, 266; opportunities in, 297; struggling readers and, 164
disengaged readers, 242, 263
Drop Everything And Read, 129, 130, 261, 275

Durham, North Carolina, silent summer reading program, 86–87
Dynamic Indicators of Basic Early Literacy Skills assessment system, 46, 142

E

Early Childhood Longitudinal Study, Kindergarten Class of 1998–1999 (ECLS-K), 68, 71
echo reading, 183–184
effect size in studies of sustained silent reading, 120–121
efficiency of reading, 60–61
ELs. *See* English Learners
Elson, William, 13
Emerson, Ralph Waldo, 10
engaged readers: description of, 242; encouragement of success and, 107–108; genre of text and, 201–202; instructional practices for, 101–102; interesting texts and, 106–107; mastery goals based on content concepts and, 102–103; momentary reading engagement compared to, 178–179; reading achievement and, 97–102, 101*f*; research on, 108; social collaboration and, 107
engaged silent reading: choice, control, and, 103–105; content, task relevance and, 106; dedication to reading and, 99–101, 101*f*; description of, 96–97, 108, 201; time on task and, 133–134
English Learners: brief oral reading events assessment and, 261–263; complicating factors in assessment of silent reading of, 258–260, 268, 271; description of, 258; eye-movement photography and, 268–270; oral story retelling assessment and, 265–266; probed and free recall assessment and, 264–265; promising directions for assessment of, 268–271; self-assessment and, 263–264; silent reading of, 260–261; technology to

aid in assessment of, 266; testing accommodations for assessment of, 267–268

ePals Book Club, 234

ePals Global Community, 234

ethnicity, amount of school reading, and achievement, 101*f*

evaluation of online information, 228–230

expansion period in U.S., 9–12

expository texts: offline, 223–224; online, 224–225

expressive reading, 191

eye movements: brain and, 27; cognitive processing and, 25; deficits in, 40–41; development of, 33*t*; discovery of, 26; early study of, 24; English Learners and, 268–270; essential role of in reading, 41–42; fixation pauses, 33–38, 36*f*; forward saccades, 39–40; perceptions of, 24–25; regressions and rereading, 38–39; types of, 26

eye physiology: abnormalities of, 40–41; cognitive psychology and, 30–33; human eye, 27*f*; overview of, 27–30

Eyes on Text professional development modules: changes in student achievement, 210–211, 210*t*, 211*t*, 212–214; compliance with, 208; conclusions and recommendations, 211–214; description of, 198, 202; interventions, 206–207; methodology, 204–206; reading in classrooms after, 209, 209*t*, 210*t*; reading in classrooms prior to, 208

F

fabulous finds, identifying and sharing, 284–285, 285*f*

fake readers, 169, 170*t*, 174

fall reading achievement and summer reading, 74

family support for reading and literacy, 73, 76–77

"faucet theory," 73

feedback, repeated oral readings with, xi–xii, 291

Feeding Minds Fighting Hunger, 234–235

"fiction problem" in public libraries, 9–10

fingerpointing to words, 38

fixations (eye movement), 26, 33–38, 36*f*, 268–269

fluency, 36–37, 200

fluency-oriented reading classrooms, 181

Fluency-Oriented Reading Instruction (FORI), 182. *See also* Wide Fluency-Oriented Reading Instruction

format of text and engaged reading, 202

forms: Parent Survey, 177*f*; Silent Reading Assessment, 62*f*; Tracking Form for Individual Student Reading Conferences, 141*f*

forward saccades, 26, 33, 39–40

fourth-grade slump, 95–96

fovea of eye, 28–29, 34, 37

free recall assessment, 265–266, 268

G

gaze duration, 33, 269

Gedike, Friedrich, 11

gender and education in colonial America, 7–8

genre of text and reading engagement, 201–202

genre wheel, 137–138, 138*f*

grade-level core reading programs, 46–47

Gray, William S., 13

grit, 99

GROR, 140, 142, 144–145, 192

Guided Repeated Oral Reading with Feedback, 140, 142, 144–145, 192

H

Handbook of Reading Research, 57–58, 155

Heyns, B., 67, 69, 72

high school classrooms, oral reading in, 48–49

home, reading at, 176–178, 278

Huey, E.B., 11, 13, 24
Hunt, Lyman, 13

I
iconic memory, 30
idea overlap, 191
independent reading. *See* silent reading; sustained silent reading
Independent Reading, 281–282
individualized reading approach, 13–14
individually guided education plans, 17
informational texts in classrooms, 201–202, 213–214
inner speech, 58, 59
instruction in silent reading behaviors, 63
instructional focus, shift in, in fourth grade, 95
instructional practices: for engaged silent reading, 101–105, 294–296; for struggling readers, 282–285, 283*f*
interactions around text: importance of, 134–136; R⁵ programs and, 172–173, 175
Interest and Wide Reading Inventory, 174
interests, learning for book floods, 246–247
Internet: access to, 235–236; literacy skills and, 222; navigating, 225; search-and-locate tactics for, 228; use of in classrooms, 232–233. *See also* online reading comprehension
intrinsic motivation to read, 96. *See also* engaged silent reading
IR, 281–282

J
Jefferson, Thomas, 7
"just right" texts, 189

L
lesson planning process, 49
letters: number of in focus on fovea, 28–29; span of apprehension, 29–30, 34
leveling systems, 190, 202
lexical diversity of books, 191
libraries in schools, funding for, 14. *See also* classroom libraries; public libraries

Library of Congress, 7
linguistic modification or simplification of assessments, 267
lip movement during silent reading, 59, 60–61, 63
literacy: culture of, 108; family support for, 73, 76–77; Obama goal for, 290; as social force, 9–10; World Wars and, 12
literature-based reading movement, 17
locating information online, 227–228
look–say approach, 13, 16

M
Make Way for Ducklings (McCloskey), 190–191
Mann, Horace, 10, 11
mastery goals based on content concepts, 102–103
Mather, Cotton, 6
Matthew effect, 16, 18, 51
maze technique, 157
MC tests, 264–265, 268
McDade, J.E., 13
McGuffey, William Holmes, *Eclectic Reader*, 8
measurement of effects of silent reading, 260–261
memory buffer, visual, 30, 31, 33–34
MetaMetrics, 86
miscues when reading aloud, 262
modeling of silent reading by teachers, 135–136, 278
monitoring aspects: of R⁵ programs, 174; of silent reading, 295–296
motivation to read: book floods and, 252–253; choice of reading materials and, 133, 245; decline in, 95; intrinsic, 96; oral reading and, 49–50; R⁵ programs and, 173–174; sustained silent reading and, 277–278. *See also* engaged silent reading
Multi-dimensional Fluency Scale, 142
multiple-choice tests, 264–265, 268
mumble reading, 59

N

National Literacy Panel on Language Minority Children and Youth, 258

National Reading Panel report: conclusions of, 18, 75, 129, 151; controversy over, 243, 276–277, 294; impact of, xi, 168–169, 260–261, 291; oral reading fluency and, 57

new literacies theory, 222–223

Newbery, John, 7

No Child Left Behind (NCLB) policies: grade-level texts and, 46–47; impact of, 122–123; online reading comprehension and, 235–236

NRP report. *See* National Reading Panel report

O

ocular–motor eye movements. *See* eye movements

Olson, Willard, 13

online reading comprehension: communicating information, 231; communities of readers, cultivation and development of, 231–235; conclusions and recommendations, 236–237; developing questions, 226–227; effective searches for information, 227–228; evaluating information, 228–230; literacy standards, assessments, and school policies, 235–236; locating information, 227–228; new literacies of, 222–223; overview of, 221–222; processes common to offline reading comprehension, 223; strategic online reading, 224–225; synthesizing information, 230–231; Teaching Internet Comprehension to Adolescents project, 225–231

open tasks, 226

opportunity to read: benefits of, 241; definition of, 198–199; designing effective, 200–202; effects of on specific dimensions of reading, 199–200; offline and online, 223–225; relationship between reading proficiency and, 199. *See also* book floods; Eyes on Text professional development modules

optic nerve, 27

oral reading: benefits of, 181–182; changing practice of, 50–53; debate over, 11; in high school classrooms, 48–49; motivation to read and, 49–50; as performance-based situation, 154–155; preferences for, 10; in primary-grade classrooms, 45–47, 50–51; reading growth and, 187–188; in remedial and special education classrooms, 47–48; role of, 291–293; as social practice, 4–6; speed of compared to silent reading, 35; as traditional practice, 53–54. *See also* round robin reading; Wide Fluency-Oriented Reading Instruction

oral reading rate: comprehension and, 154; norms for, 153, 154*t*

oral story retellings, 265–266, 268

OtR. *See* opportunity to read

out-of-school reading, 52, 52*t*, 176–178, 278

P

paper-and-pencil contexts, comprehension-based silent reading rate in, 156–157, 161*f*, 163, 266

parafovea of eye, 28, 34, 37

parent involvement and R^4 programs, 177–178, 177*f*

parent scaffolding, 77–78

parent support for reading and literacy, 73, 76–77

Parent Survey form, 177*f*

Parker, Francis, 11

partner reading, 184, 207, 253

peer coaching, 203–204

peer interactions about text, 135

pen pals, online, 234

peripheral area of visual field, 28, 34, 37

phonics approach, 16

Planet Book Talk, 234
pointing to words, 38
pretty books, 7, 8
previewing text, 283–284
primary-grade classrooms, oral reading in, 45–47, 50–51
probed and free recall assessment, 264–265, 268
processes and instruction in silent reading, 57–58
professional development: conclusions and recommendations, 211–214; Eyes on Text, 198, 202; models of, 202–203; peer coaching model, 203–204; Reading First and, 203–204; results of study of, 208–211, 209t, 210t, 211t; study of, 204–207
prosody, 191–192
Prussian education techniques, 10–11
public libraries: development of, 9–10; SES and, 73–74; social reform and, 12
punctuation, history of, 4–5
purpose for reading, setting, 283–284

R
R^4 (Read, Relax, Reflect and Respond) programs, 176–178
R^5 (Read, Relax, Reflect, Respond, and Rap) programs: classroom environment, 175; description of, 169, 170–171, 281; monitoring and accountability, 174; motivation and, 173–174; Rap phase of, 172–173, 175; Read and Relax phase of, 171–172; Reflect and Respond phase of, 172; scaffolding book selection, 175–176
rate of reading, 35, 151–152. *See also* comprehension-based silent reading rate
read-alouds, 293
readers: communities of, 231–235; continuum of, 171f; disengaged, 242, 263; fake, 169, 174; types of, and their behaviors, 170t. *See also* engaged readers; struggling readers

reading achievement: amount of school reading and, 101f; book floods and, 247, 251; of bottom quartile of students at three grade levels, 50t; engaged silent reading and, 97–102, 101f; reasons for differences due to SES, 72–75; socioeconomic differences in, 68; summer learning in development of SES differences in, 69–72, 70f; summer silent reading programs and, 75–85; sustained silent reading and, 115–120
reading comprehension. *See* comprehension; online reading comprehension
Reading First programs, 46, 203–204, 213
reading growth: challenging texts and, 189–192, 190t; oral reading and, 187–188; repetition and, 188–189; scaffolded oral reading practice and, 193
Reading Is Fundamental, 246
reading logs, 172
reading pedagogy: ancient and medieval practices, 6; in colonial America, 6–8; in contemporary America, 15–17; early research on, 11–12; in expansion period, 10–12; modern debate on, 17–19; research on, 12–13; silent reading and, 19–20; in twentieth century, 13–14. *See also* instructional practices
reading proficiency and opportunity to read, 199
reading stamina, 155–156, 164, 262–263, 296
reading-rich and reading-poor instruction, 206
Reformation ideal, 5–6
regressions (eye movement), 26, 38–39
reliability of websites, evaluation of, 228–230
religious influences: on oral reading, 4–5; on public libraries, 9; on reading

pedagogy, 6, 7; Reformation ideal and, 5–6

remedial classrooms, oral reading in, 47–48

repeated readings: with feedback, xi–xii, 291; opportunity to read and, 207; in Wide FORI, 185

repetition and reading growth, 188–189

rereadings (eye movement), 26, 38–39

research and educational practices, 52–53

response to text, 175

retention in grade, 53

retina, 27, 28

rod cells, 28, 29, 36, 39

round robin reading: history of, 8, 13; problems with, 35, 163; teacher response to errors during, 50–51; Wide FORI and, 186–187

Ryan, Pam Muñoz, 254

S

saccades, 26, 34, 38, 268–269

Saxe, J.G., "The Blind Men and the Elephant," 25

SBRR, 203

scaffolded oral reading practice: description of, 181; reading growth and, 193; in Wide FORI, 186–187

scaffolded silent reading: book selection strategy lessons, 138, 139f; classroom libraries for, 137, 137f; daily practice time, 139–140; description of, 136–140, 281; effectiveness of, 140, 142–145; fluency growth and, 192; genre wheel for, 137–138, 138f; guided oral reading compared to, 19; importance of, 213, 296–297; recommendations for, 145–147; struggling readers and, 201; teacher–student conferences, 140, 141f; in Wide FORI, 185

scaffolded silent summer reading program: description of, 67, 76; experimental findings, 83–85, 83t, 85t; experimental methodology, 79–81; logic model for, 78–79, 78f, 88; stages of, 81–83

scaffolding sustained silent reading, 284

school libraries, funding for, 14. *See also* classroom libraries; public libraries

scientifically based reading research, 203

ScSR. *See* scaffolded silent reading

search-and-locate tactics for Internet, 228

secular texts, reading of, 9–10

selective attention, 30–31

self-efficacy for silent reading, 97, 98

self-teaching hypothesis, 52

SES. *See* socioeconomic status

Shared Books programs, 118

sharing: through book response projects, 140; vocabulary, 285, 285f

silent reading: advantages of, 11–12; balanced approach to, 20; as cultural practice, 3, 19–20; in digital contexts, 297; as pedagogical practice, 19–20; research on, 15–17; role of, 293–294; speed of compared to oral reading, 35; teacher support for, 296–297; transition to, 192, 193, 194t; Wide FORI and, 192–193; word spacing, punctuation, and, 4–5. *See also* engaged silent reading; scaffolded silent reading; scaffolded silent summer reading program; sustained silent reading

Silent Reading Assessment Form, 62f

silent reading rate, 153, 154t

SIR, 281, 282

situated cognition, theories of, 202

Smith, N.B., *American Reading Instruction*, 57

social cogitation, theories of, 202–203

social collaboration: communities of readers, 231–233; engaged silent reading and, 107, 134–136, 172–173; R^4 programs and, 176–177; R^5 programs and, 175

social context of reading, 270

social interaction and sustained silent reading, 243

socioeconomic status: achievement gaps and, 67–68; book access and, 244;